Vietnam and the South China Sea

Studies of the escalating tensions and competing claims in the South China Sea overwhelmingly focus on China and its increasingly assertive approach, while the position of the other claimants is overlooked. This book focuses on the attitude of Vietnam towards the South China Sea dispute. It examines the position from a historical perspective, shows how Vietnam's position is affected by its wish to maintain good relations with China on a range of issues, and outlines how Vietnam has occasionally made overtures to both the United States and Japan in order to bolster its position, and considered the possibility, so far resisted, of taking China to formal arbitration under the auspices of the United Nations Convention on the Law of the Sea. The book concludes by assessing the future prospects for Vietnam's position in the dispute.

Do Thanh Hai is a Senior Fellow at the Institute for East Sea Studies, Diplomatic Academy of Vietnam. He has a PhD from the Australian National University, where he was a Prime Minister's Australian Asia Endeavour Awardee.

Routledge Security in Asia Pacific Series

Series Editors

Leszek Buszynski

Strategic and Defence Studies Centre, the Australian National University

and

William Tow

Australian National University

Security issues have become more prominent in the Asia Pacific region because of the presence of global players, rising great powers, and confident middle powers, which intersect in complicated ways. This series puts forward important new work on key security issues in the region. It embraces the roles of the major actors, their defense policies and postures and their security interaction over the key issues of the region. It includes coverage of the United States, China, Japan, Russia, the Koreas, as well as the middle powers of ASEAN and South Asia. It also covers issues relating to environmental and economic security as well as transnational actors and regional groupings.

For a full list of titles in this series, please visit https://www.routledge.com/Routledge-Security-in-Asia-Pacific-Series/book-series/SE899

26 India's Ocean
The story of India's bid for regional leadership
David Brewster

27 Defence Planning and Uncertainty
Preparing for the next Asia-Pacific war
Stephan Frühling

28 The South China Sea Maritime Dispute
Political, legal, and regional perspectives
Edited by Leszek Buszynski and Christopher B. Roberts

29 South Asia's Nuclear Security
Bhumitra Chakma

30 The New US Strategy towards Asia
Adapting to the American pivot
Edited by William T. Tow and Douglas Stuart

31 Vietnam and the South China Sea
Politics, Security and Legality
Do Thanh Hai

Vietnam and the South China Sea

Politics, Security and Legality

Do Thanh Hai

Routledge
Taylor & Francis Group
LONDON AND NEW YORK

First published 2017 by Routledge

2 Park Square, Milton Park, Abingdon, Oxfordshire OX14 4RN
52 Vanderbilt Avenue, New York, NY 10017

Routledge is an imprint of the Taylor & Francis Group, an informa business

First issued in paperback 2019

British Library Cataloguing in Publication Data
A catalogue record for this book is available from the British Library

Library of Congress Cataloging in Publication Data
A catalog record for this book has been requested

ISBN: 978-1-138-92997-5 (hbk)
ISBN: 978-0-367-18618-0 (pbk)

Typeset in Times New Roman
by Apex CoVantage, LLC

To Dad, Mum, and Trang

Contents

Figures

Acknowledgements

I would like to thank Leszek Buszynski for his inspirational supervision and mentorship. He encouraged and guided me through considerable confusion, frustration, and anxiety during my doctoral research and preparation for this book.

I am also intellectually indebted to many scholars who have inspired and supported me since my research idea took shape. Among them are Dang Dinh Quy, Christopher Roberts, Tran Truong Thuy, Carlyle A. Thayer, Nguyen Hong Thao, Nguyen Vu Tung, Tran Viet Thai, Nguyen Hung Son, Hoang Anh Tuan, and Nguyen Thi Lan Anh.

A note of thanks is due to Stephan Frühling, Benjamin Schreer, and Ron Huisken, who were my academic advisers at the Strategic and Defense Studies Centre at the Australian National University, for their valued assistance and critical feedback.

Many thanks go to Ha Anh Tuan, Le Hong Hiep, Kalman Robertson, Scott Bentley, Nguyen Binh Duong, and other friends for their willingness to offer a hand whenever I was in need.

I am very thankful to my parents, Do Hai Van and Ngo Thi Chuc, and my parents-in-law, Duong Van Ket and Nguyen Thi Dinh, for their unconditional love and support. I owe my deepest gratitude to my wife, Duong Thu Trang, for her dedication to and faith in me.

Last but not least, it is important to acknowledge that this study was made possible with the support of the Prime Minister's Australia Asia Endeavour Award, as provided by the Australian government.

Abbreviations

ADMM	ASEAN Defence Ministers' Meeting
AMM	ASEAN Foreign Ministers' Meeting
APT	ASEAN Plus Three
ARF	ASEAN Regional Forum
ASEAN	Association of the Southeast Asian Nations
BP	British Petroleum
CBM	Confidence building measure
CCP	Chinese Communist Party
CLCS	United Nations Commission on the Limits of the Continental Shelf
COC	Code of conduct
CPV	Communist Party of Vietnam
DOC	Declaration on the Conduct of Parties in the South China Sea
DRV	Democratic Republic of Vietnam
EAVG	East Asia Vision Group
EEZ	Exclusive Economic Zone
FDI	Foreign direct investment
GDP	Gross domestic product
GFC	Global financial crisis
ICJ	International Court of Justice
MOFA	Ministry of Foreign Affairs
n.m.	nautical mile(s)
PLA	Chinese People's Liberation Army
PRC	People's Republic of China
PRG	Provisional Revolutionary Government in South Vietnam
ROC	Republic of China
RVN	Republic of Vietnam
SARS	Severe acute respiratory syndrome
SEATO	Southeast Asia Treaty Organization
SOM	Senior official meeting
SRV	Socialist Republic of Vietnam
TAC	Treaty of Amity and Cooperation
UN	United Nations

UNCLOS	United Nations Convention on the Law of the Sea
UNESCO	United Nations Educational, Scientific and Cultural Organization
UNSC	United Nations Security Council
US	United States
VPA	Vietnamese People's Army

Introduction

This is a book about Vietnam's maritime posture under the shadow of a rising Chinese Dragon. It systematically traces continuity and changes in Vietnam's approach to the South China Sea – which is referred to as the East Sea (Bien Dong) in Vietnam – in the post–Cold War period. Vietnam's evolving maritime interests and claims are situated in the interplay of a global milieu and national politics that influence the foreign policy decision-making circle in Hanoi. But essentially, the book is all about Hanoi's strategic thinking and how it has been played out in Vietnam's attempts to defend its offshore interests, deny foreign control of the sea area critical to its national security, and shape strategic seascape beyond its shore. The study's major finding is that Beijing's maritime assertiveness made it difficult for Vietnam to maintain a traditional friendship with China. It is argued that concerns about China's attempts to control the South China Sea have driven Vietnam to increase its national strength and resilience and expand economic and security relations with other big powers.

The study focuses on Vietnam as a claimant in the South China Sea, one of the most contested areas in East Asia. Over the last decade, academic and public inquiry into the South China Sea disputes increased significantly as tensions in the South China Sea have flared up without any signs of abating. Enormous scholarly efforts had been made over the last five years to identify key determinants of these developments. However, much of the attention has been naturally focused on a rising China as the most powerful claimant in the dispute and the potential disrupter of the regional order. Other smaller claimants had been largely overlooked, or have been studied within the context of China's policy and big power politics. This imbalance in the literature has the potential of distorting the cycle of actions and reactions, which shaped the dynamics of the disputes. Against that backdrop, this book, which offers the view from a smaller claimant but a key rival to China, will be an important contribution that helps rebalance the current discourse.

Recent troubles in the South China Sea are no way just tempests in a teapot. The sea is rich in oil and fish. More importantly, it straddles principal maritime pathways that carry about 30 per cent of global trade and 50 per cent of global oil tanker shipments. Any conflicts to erupt there would lead to significant fallout on the global economy. Therefore, anxieties are not just about entitlements to maritime resources but also about rules, order, and secure access to this strategic body of water, which Robert Kaplan regarded as "the *throat* of the Western Pacific and Indian oceans" (emphasis added). It is fundamentally the question of Beijing's strategic intents, the nature of China's rise, and implications on the global maritime order. Will China rise peacefully? How will the United States and other powers responded to China's emergence as a global power? Clearly, rapid militarisation in China has sparked fears and disquiet across the Indo-Pacific region. Peace is still there but the sense of insecurity and uncertainty is prevalent. As Thucydides gives us some insight, the Peloponnesian War became inevitable because the rise of Athens set off an alarm in Sparta. John Mearsheimer, a distinguished professor at the University of Chicago, foretold a decade ago that China's rise would not be amicable. In this regard, the South China Sea is seen as a test case for China's long-heralded "peaceful development" and a barometer for power contests in the region.

Vietnam is arguably a major player in the balance of power in the South China Sea and Southeast Asia, not just because of its formidable military strength, but also its exceptional nationalism and strategic sturdiness. Geoff A. Dyer opines in *The Contest of the Century: The New Era of Competition with China* (2014), "Its combustible politics and deep-seated historical resentment make Vietnam the country one can most easily imagine fighting a war with China." Vietnamese collective identity originated from common ordeal and patriotic struggle against Chinese invaders. It is a nation of what Singaporean leader Lee Kuan Yew reckoned as "the Prussians of the Orient" who will in no way bow to greater powers. In ancient times, Vietnam, as a nation, survived Chinese domination for a thousand years and defeated dozens of major invasions from Chinese empires in the next millennium. In modern times, Vietnam has fought consecutive wars against four by far stronger powers, namely France, Japan, the United States, and China, to regain and preserve its independence.

Increased US-China rivalry in the South China Sea not only lifts Vietnam's strategic significance but also puts Vietnam in a difficult strategic quandary. Rising China has flexed its muscles to force other claimants to accept new rules in the South China Sea and beyond. As China's immediate neighbour, Vietnam is unsurprisingly the first to bear the brunt of the growth of Chinese power and runs the constant risk of being pulled into China's sphere of influence. Strategists in Washington seem to believe that the fate of the South China Sea is primarily hanging upon Hanoi, as Vietnam is Southeast Asia's principal contender to China in the area. If Vietnam acquiesces to China's claims, other Southeast Asian claimants would find it harder to resist China's control of the strategic maritime gateway. As a result, Washington is courting Hanoi to defend the existing maritime order, or the bedrock of the US global leadership. Fearful that Vietnam will be Finlandized by China, US officials and political elites have travelled to Hanoi more often. They are also considering arming Southeast Asia's David to help it resist Asia's growing Goliath. Whether it wanted to or not, Vietnam gradually got entangled in strategic competition between China and the United States. The case of Vietnam therefore presents an interesting case of a middle-sized power's response and adaptation to changes in China's foreign and security posture and shifts in regional power equation.

As for Vietnam, the South China Sea represents the country's greatest security challenge in the post–Cold War period. Over the last 25 years, Vietnam has settled most of its territorial and maritime disputes with its neighbours, demarcating land borders with China and Laos and delimiting a range of maritime boundaries with China, Indonesia, Malaysia, and Thailand. However, very little progress has been made regarding the sovereignty and maritime boundary disputes in the South China Sea proper. In this area, Vietnam has substantial sovereignty and maritime claims, wholly or partly in conflict with those of Brunei, the People's Republic of China (referred to as China in this research), the Philippines, Malaysia, Indonesia, and Taiwan, as discussed in Chapter 1. Vietnam lost control of the Paracels and a number of Spratly islets and reefs to China in two armed skirmishes in 1974 and 1988 respectively. These disputes are difficult to resolve due to a range factors, including complex history, intricate legal claims, high and multi-dimensional stakes for claimants and international users, and strong nationalism across the region.

China looms large as the principal dilemma for Vietnam in the South China Sea. On the one hand, China represents the greatest security challenge to Vietnam in three measures. First, China has the most extensive maritime ambition, claiming sovereignty over all island groups and approximately 60–80 per cent of the area. Second, China is the most powerful claimant, vastly superior to Vietnam in terms of economic and military power. Third, unlike other claimants, China usually acts in an assertive way. On the other hand, given its close proximity and size, China is important to every aspect of Vietnam's existence. Therefore, enduring friendship with China serves Vietnam's core national interests. On the whole, Vietnam's fundamental issue in the South China Sea is how it should deal with the conflict of interest with China in the sea given geographical closeness and large power disparity between them. What is Vietnam's endgame in the South China Sea? How has Vietnam defended its maritime interests in face of overwhelming odds from China in the future? What factors have shaped Vietnam's strategic posture? How has Vietnam responded to pushes and pulls by large rivalling powers? Is Vietnam destined to be a *pawn* in the global chessboard again?

Much has been written on Vietnam in the South China Sea but the answers to these questions are far from clear. Vietnam is generally portrayed as passive and reactive in the face of a rising China. There is also a widespread misperception that Vietnam is currently in a loss of strategic direction, and is wavering between China and the United States. China is considered as Hanoi's major strategic problem, while the United States is by no means a perfect solution. Vietnam's strategic policy has then been depicted as a "balancing act," "equidistance," a "careful dance," and "tightrope walking" between two great powers, without adequate explanations of these concepts. Interestingly, Vietnam's domestic politics have increasingly been presented as a contest between "pro-China" and "pro-America" factions. As veteran Vietnam watcher Carlyle A. Thayer commented, those overused labels are no guides to understand Vietnam's politics, as factional alignments in the political circle in Hanoi about the foreign policy are "more nuanced and complex."

The Western scholarship mostly approaches Vietnam and the South China Sea in the traditional logic of balance of power, which views Vietnam's behaviour as conditioned by systemic factors. In the face of China's rising assertiveness, Vietnam is supposed to follow a charted course of spinning out of China's orbit. Theoretically speaking, abandoning its minor territories to avoid the tip of the Chinese spearhead and to preserving basic sovereignty would be Vietnam's least bad option. However, it is generally assumed that Vietnam is in a course of colliding with China because the latter's rapid militarisation and heavy-handedness would stir up anti-Chinese nationalism in the former. The recent upticks in Hanoi-Washington security relations have been seen as the indications of an emerging alliance between Vietnam and the United States to counterbalance against China. Arguably, behind these views is an unspoken presupposition that Vietnam is dictated by a range of external push and pull factors, which are fundamentally actions and policies of great powers, particularly China and the United States.

Nonetheless, Hanoi often acts in a less straightforward manner, and its behaviour is rather contradicting. Though China acts assertively, Hanoi recurrently pledges and seeks ways to cultivate friendship and expand cooperation with Beijing. On the other hand, while acknowledging the US presence in the region as a stabilising factor, Hanoi is reluctant to quickly step up security cooperation with Washington. In spite of pervasive concerns about China's expansionism, Vietnamese officials repeatedly state that Vietnam will not join any military alliance, allow other countries to establish military bases in its territory, or seek relations with one country against the third party (implying China). Instead, Vietnam has participated in many multilateral arrangements and pursued a range of strategic and comprehensive partnerships with countries that it deems important to Vietnam's security and development. After all, Vietnam does not look as panic-ridden and alarmist as some Western scholars observed. There has not yet been any sign that Hanoi would seek military alliance with other greater powers, although China has appeared increasingly assertive and antagonistic.

As will be seen, this book is critical of simplistic ways of understanding Vietnam. It presents variants of perception of China in Hanoi and a range of strategic choices Vietnam has adopted to cope with a by far larger and more powerful neighbour. Throughout the course of the book, it becomes clearer that Hanoi exhibits greater activism and ingenuity in making use of systemic factors to achieve its own objectives, rather than being conditioned by the international system. If balance of power had dominated the Vietnamese's strategic calculations, Vietnam as an independent state would have ceased to exist a long time ago. The history of Vietnam-China interactions shows that power disparity does not equate to insecurity and disequilibrium, and superiority of power has not automatically transformed into domination for the stronger or subordination for the weak. For most of time over the last millennium, Vietnam lived at ease and in peace despite its imbalance of power with the northern Chinese empire without any source of countervailing power to balance against it. Though winning a succession of wars against Chinese invaders, Vietnamese strategists rarely attempted to go to all lengths to address its power asymmetry with China. Instead, they accepted China's supremacy and placed a premium on diplomacy to make peace with China and discourage any attempts to use force against Vietnam.

In Vietnamese strategic thinking, power is a comprehensive term, pervading all areas of military, politics, economy, legality, and morality. One's overwhelming army and superior firepower is no guarantee of triumph over its inferior adversary in battles or contests. Military force in relative terms matters as an important factor, but political, diplomatic, legal, and moral advantages also matter. There are always arts or stratagems to turn the enemy's strengths into its weaknesses. Ultimately, what really matters for Vietnamese strategic planners is how to use different sources of power effectively to diminish adversaries' morale, determination, or resolve. During their confrontations with stronger enemies, the Vietnamese has shown a high level of aptitude in bringing into full play "weapons of the weak" and using the power of persistence to frustrate its adversaries' attempts for quick victories.

How Vietnam confronted China during the *Haiyang Shiyou 981* oil rig crisis in mid-2014 is a case in point. While China was deploying the giant oil rig and an array of big vessels as a show of its superior power, the Vietnamese also sent its law enforcement vessels to the area to challenge China's actions. Though Vietnamese vessels suffered heavy damages due to Chinese vessels' deliberate ramming and firing of high-pressure water cannons, they stood firm and refused to leave the area. Vietnamese naval vessels were kept away from the oil rig area to avoid escalation. However, Vietnam's principal front was not at sea. Hanoi chose to counter China's powerful fleet from the side, not head-on, with an effective public relations campaign that caused significant political and diplomatic costs to Beijing. In an unprecedented move, Vietnam allowed international reporters on board their coast guard boats to witness how Chinese vessels manoeuvred. In the face of mounting political international criticism of its actions, China withdrew the oil rig before the date it intended. Without insight into Vietnam's strategic thinking, it is difficult to fully grasp the nature of the game between Vietnam and China in the South China Sea and the gist of Vietnam's strategy to cope with its powerful neighbour.

Another example is how Vietnam fought against the United States in the Second Indochina War, known as Vietnam War in the United States and the American War in Vietnam. The Vietnamese communists' overarching goal was not to defeat the American war machine in the battlefields but to beat the will of the United States to intervene in Vietnam and force it to withdraw from the country. In terms of firepower, North Vietnam and southern guerrilla forces never matched the United States and South Vietnam. Therefore, Hanoi launched diplomatic and political fronts, in addition to its military campaigns, to rally domestic and international support for its reunification cause, even inside the United States, and delegitimise and demoralise US military adventurism. Throughout its diplomatic and political campaigns, Hanoi also indicated that it could stand any cost to reunify the country. Overall, the Vietnamese communists lost more battlefields and suffered much higher casualties, but the American war apparatus lost its political battle right in Washington, DC. It was the power of persistence and resolve that created what D.R. SaiDesai called "the spectacle of a small nation, with far less sophisticated weaponry than its opponents and hardly any air power, immobilising the most advanced, militarily equipped nation" in his book *Vietnam: Past and Present* (1992).

In view of this discussion, it is rather misleading to assume that power prevails and small and medium-sized countries have no choice but to take the world as they find it. The study shows that Vietnam has not been submissive to and bound by harsh reality of realpolitik, but proactively attempts to take advantage of competition among great powers to advance its national interests. Accordingly, Vietnam's South China Sea policy has shaped by two principal contours. First, it is conditioned by strategic culture and learning process of the political elites in Vietnam in their experience with international relations, shifts in the global balance of power, and changes in the country's security environment. Second, the policy is documented as an evolving course of action with continuity and changes as the outcome of dynamic national politics with regard to defining national interests, assessing the country's security environment, and responding to threats and risks to its national security. In this light, this study will thoroughly examine Vietnam's South China Sea policy in terms of the interplay between Vietnam's relations with China and other claimants and its elitist politics on related issues. The policy outcomes can be seen as the result of the dynamics in the Vietnamese political system and the contest among major Vietnamese political elite groups on assessing, debating, and deciding on how to manage Vietnam-China relations and respond to regional politics over the South China Sea developments. As such, the study will trace the evolution of Vietnamese policy towards the South China Sea through the transition from a confrontational policy to a cooperative one, and the shifting strategies Hanoi adopted to cope with other claimants, especially a rising and assertive China.

The book in brief

The core chapters of the book, which provide empirical research, are arranged chronologically to present changes in Vietnam's approach to the South China Sea disputes through different periods of time after the Cold War. It concludes with a summary of evolution of Vietnam's South China Sea policy and reflections on how Vietnam has dealt with China and other powers to defend its interests.

Chapter 1 establishes a conceptual framework to guide analysis in the subsequent empirical chapters. It starts with a discussion of a Western-centric realist framework and develops a range of strategic choices for Vietnam's decision-making, which includes Vietnam's strategic culture and national politics. It also maps out the configuration of Vietnam's politics and contending strategies advocated by different camps within the Vietnamese leadership on how to deal with China. The politics of conservatism versus nationalist pragmatism serve as the backbone for analysis throughout the book.

Chapter 2 provides a history of Vietnam's maritime expansion as a background for its maritime position. The aim of the chapter is not only to understand the historical and legal bases of Vietnam's claims but also to explore the rationale behind Vietnam's persistent and determined efforts to pursue its claims. To this end, Hanoi's claims to sovereignty over the Paracels and Spratlys and to the maritime spaces will be analysed in the broader context of the country's territorial expansion, its struggle for independence and unification against foreign invaders, and nation building in peacetime.

Chapter 3 elaborates on Vietnam's shift from confrontation to conciliation between Vietnam and its neighbouring countries in the period 1991–1995. The shift occurred in the context of Vietnam's economic reform, foreign policy reorientation, and improved relationship with China and ASEAN countries. Under these circumstances, Vietnam and other claimants managed to initiate a wide range of bilateral mechanisms to negotiate land border and maritime boundary delimitations and manage the incidents at sea. Still, nationalist elites in the Vietnamese leadership were clearly anxious about China's assertive behaviour in some maritime areas it claimed and the slow progress in dispute settlement negotiations. Against that backdrop, they pushed for rapprochement with the US and admission to ASEAN to seek a more advantageous position vis-à-vis China in the South China Sea.

Chapter 4 analyses the further development of bilateral relationship with China and other ASEAN countries and discusses Vietnam's exercise of multilateral leverage to maintain the status quo in the South China Sea between 1995 and 2002. Many state-to-state and party-to-party mechanisms between Vietnam and China were put in place, which led to the successful completion of negotiations on land border demarcation and maritime limitation in the Gulf of Tonkin. In this period, though mainly relying on bilateral mechanisms to deal with most of incidents involving the South China Sea, Vietnam resorted to ASEAN as a political instrument. Aligning with ASEAN rules, Vietnam cooperated with other ASEAN countries to counter China in the Mischief Reef crisis and pressed China towards a code of conduct in the South China Sea. Eventually, the Declaration on the Conduct of Parties in the South China Sea (DOC) was signed in December 2002. Another positive development was the signature of the maritime delimitation and fishery cooperation agreements of the Gulf of Tonkin in 2000.

Chapter 5 documents Vietnam's experiment with DOC and efforts to broaden its strategic cooperation with major countries as a hedge against China. In this period, Hanoi carefully observed Beijing's charm offensive. The notable move on the side of Vietnam was that it decided to join the controversial China-Philippines initiative on Joint Marine Seismic Undertaking after initial protests. Concerns in Vietnam about China's ambition and aggressive actions in the South China Sea arose. Besides, it was clear that the DOC did not work out in the way Vietnam wanted. China had not been effectively tied by the high-profile political agreement and became increasingly assertive. As a result, some adjustments were made in Vietnam's foreign policy in general and its South China Sea policy in particular. As a result, Hanoi became more engaged with Washington strategically and tried to maintain a delicately balanced position between Washington and Beijing. However, Hanoi was careful enough to reassure Beijing that its relationship with Washington was not detrimental to its ties with Beijing.

Chapter 6 discusses a shift in Vietnam to a more nationalist stance on the South China Sea issue in the period 2009–2011. Vietnam was frustrated with China's newfound assertiveness and viewed its militarisation more in terms of a threat.

That led to a new package of measures that have been undertaken, including a naval power build-up and increased publicity of on-the-ground developments to mobilise national unity for the defence of the country's maritime interests. On the one hand, this set of measures increased the pressure on China. But on the other hand, it also put the Vietnamese leaders under the fire of increasing nationalism.

Chapter 7 discusses the international component of Vietnam's new strategy to the South China Sea disputes. In the face of China's assertiveness, Hanoi decided to bring the South China Sea issue to the ASEAN Regional Forum and other regional high-level meetings. The actions were discussed in the context that Vietnam has become more active and confident in multilateral forums such as the UNSC and ASEAN, and that Vietnam beefed up its security relations with the US, Russia, Japan, and India. Hanoi utilised these mechanisms to express its concerns over the South China Sea situation. However, it did not mean that Hanoi had shifted away from its strategic independence. Despite the war of words, Vietnam managed to compartmentalise South China Sea tensions and avoid the spillover effects on other areas of bilateral cooperation with China. Bilateral talks on the dispute were underway, resulting in the signing of the Agreement on Basic Principles Guiding the Settlement of Sea Issues between Hanoi and Beijing.

Chapter 8 is an account of Vietnam's handling of China's continued assertiveness and the increased rivalry between China and the United States. The Philippines' legal proceeding against China in January 2013 put pressure on Vietnam to follow the same track. However, Hanoi clearly intended to keep this open as a viable option to discourage China's drastic actions. China's deployment of the giant oil rig *Haiyang Shiyou 981* in the vicinity of the Paracels and its massive land reclamation in the Spratlys prompted Vietnam to further its hedging strategy. Hanoi continued its bilateral talks with Beijing with the hope to finally resolve the existing disputes. On the other hand, Vietnam increased security cooperation with other powers and took a more active role in multilateral arrangements to improve its stance vis-à-vis China. While maintaining its strategic autonomy, leaders in Hanoi finally forged a consensus on deep economic integration with the West as a way to avoid being further sucked into the China-dominated system.

In sum, the central thesis of the study is that the more China asserts itself and imposes its rules in the South China Sea, the more Vietnam veers away from the Chinese orbit.

1 Under the shadow of the Dragon

Introduction

Vietnam's South China Sea problem is essentially part of a larger problem about its relations with China, a much more powerful neighbour. The 1988 skirmish in the Spratlys signalled a shifting balance of power against Vietnam in the maritime domain, exposing its vulnerabilities to China's superior naval power as well as the limits of the alliance between Hanoi and Moscow. Without the Soviet Union's direct interventions, Vietnam was incapable of defending its offshore territories. Also, its military adventurism in Cambodia deprived Hanoi of necessary international support in the struggle against irredentist China. In the changing strategic environment, by the end of the 1980s leaders in Hanoi realised that confrontation with China did not best serve their national interest.

As Vietnam moved to restore its relations with China, the unresolved disputes in the South China Sea represented a different security dilemma to Vietnam. As events unfolded, China did not look like a status quo power. China's overwhelming naval power and revisionist agenda revealed through incessant assertiveness constitute the main threats to Vietnam's maritime security. On the other hand, as China was the most important remaining socialist country after the collapse of the Soviet Union, the communist leaders in Vietnam considered socialist solidarity with China as vital to the continuance of their rule. The interlocking and comprehensive character of the Vietnam-China relationship undoubtedly complicates Vietnam's handling of its existing disputes with China. Therefore, the proper point of departure for reading Vietnam's behaviour in the South China Sea is the spectrum of strategic choices and preferences in Vietnam about its relations with its powerful neighbour.

A range of strategic choices for a small and medium-sized state to cope with neighbouring big power

Appeasement

Classical realist Thucydides sees the world generally a harsh place where "the strong do what they can and the weak suffer what they must." The Melian Dialogue, as documented in Thucydides's *History of the Peloponnesian War*, is a popular example of the dilemma that a small state has to face in coping with a big power.[1] E. H. Carr later devises a strategic choice, called appeasement, for small states to avoid the fate of Milos after its refusal to accept the Athenian ultimatum. Calling for aligning foreign policy to reality, he proposes that states should adapt to the changed equilibriums of power by accommodating more powerful discontented adversaries to avoid destruction. The whole idea of Carr's appeasement policy is that states should adequately give in to the demands of the dictatorial powers to preserve peace rather than engage in unnecessary wars in which they "have nothing to gain and everything to lose."[2] Carr asserts that foreign policy making should be based on "the possession of military strength, or rather, on the ratio between the military strength of one's own country and that of others."[3] Statesmen must be aware that all policy options involve some strategic risk of war. As he argues, Carr is convinced that a farsighted policy maker must "balance the chances, and not pursue a policy which is likely to expose his country to war against equal or superior odds."[4] Therefore, "yielding to threats of force is a normal part of the process of peaceful change."[5]

Carr's preference for appeasement is based on the assumption that power is the mainstay of international order and morality is merely the product of power. Carr sees the world more in terms of conflict of interests between states that are not satisfied with the status quo and those that benefit from it.[6] In this vein, Carr considers the utopian view of common interest in peace, justice and international order as the vested interest of the latter, those who wish to maintain the status quo. On the other hand, rising powers, which see the status quo as unjust, tend to resort to force to alter the international order previously imposed on them. Carr states, "So the warmongering of the dissatisfied Powers was the 'natural, cynical reaction' to the sentimental and dishonest platitudinizing of the satisfied Powers on the common interest in peace."[7] He elaborates on the policy of appeasement as such:

> Those who profit most by (international) order can in the longer run only hope to maintain it by making *sufficient concessions* to make it tolerable to those who profit by it least.[8]

However, Carr's concept of making concessions to rising powers has two inherent weaknesses. First, it is almost impossible to decide how many concessions would be sufficient to satisfy an adversary. Despite its pragmatic nuance, appeasement is usually associated with fear and weakness. Second, Carr exaggerates the role of relative power and fails take into account the constraints imposed by the international system on states. In practical terms, the failure of British diplomacy vis-à-vis Nazi Germany in the late 1930s has made appeasement a dishonourable foreign policy option.

Bandwagoning versus balancing

Modern structural realists came up with more options, though they still saw the world through a dismal lens. Their central assumption is that a state's behaviour is primarily structured by the nature of the international system in which they interact with each other and the distribution of capabilities among them. They presuppose that in anarchy, which is the absence of a world government as the ultimate arbiter, all states, whether big or small, see survivability as the ultimate end.[9] In other words, anarchy is a self-help system in which states, as independent and self-serving actors, tend to compete with each other for superior power or greater security through alliances. In this environment, cooperation among states is possible, but short-lived as they act selfishly to defend their own interests.[10]

Though they may be left to their own devices to ensure security in the anarchical system, the outlook for small and medium-sized states is less dismal than Carr might argue. The competition among big powers for supremacy creates a balance of power among great states, which gives small and medium-sized states greater room for manoeuvre. In other words, it is less likely that a small state will be left helpless at the hands of a hostile larger power or a coalition of states. According to leading realist theorists, the offsetting system of rivalry among great powers forces small states to lean to one side.[11] As Stephen Walt points out, threats rather than power disparities shape alliance choice. As he argues, the level of threat posed to one state by another can be measured by four factors: aggregate strength, geographical proximity, offensive capabilities and offensive intent.[12] Walt suggests that when facing a major threat to its vital interests, a state has limited options: either balancing, that means "allying with others against prevailing threat," or bandwagoning, that is "aligning with the principal source of danger."[13]

Walt's understanding of balancing and bandwagoning has passive connotations because he assumes that weak states are rather helpless to external pressures. Specifically, Walt believes that the choice between balancing and bandwagoning is dependent on three factors: the degree of power disparity, the availability of allies, and the contextual condition of peace and war. Walt argues that the bigger the power gap, the more likely a state is to bandwagon with rather than balance against ascending power. States are also forced to give in to the greatest threat if balancing options are unavailable. Last but not least, balancing is more tempting in peacetime than in wartime. Based on these premises, Walt holds the conviction that balancing is by far the more usual option than bandwagoning.[14] However, his definition of "bandwagoning" is criticised for the fact that it is no different from "accommodation," "giving in to the threat" or "appeasement."[15] As a result, it is difficult to point out cases of bandwagoning as such in reality because the concept is narrowly defined.

In terms of foreign policy making, balancing and bandwagoning are strategies that small and medium-sized states can actively adopt to defend or advance their interest vis-à-vis bigger powers.[16] In this instance, balancing is defined in broader terms as the strategy used by a state to actively join with others through military alliances with the clearly defined purpose of preventing or deterring territorial expansion or military domination by a foreign power or coalition, or to contain a specific threat.[17] Balancing in this regard means augmenting a state's power through military alliances, if alliance choices are available, to purposefully redress the unfavourable balance of power with the predatory state. Internal arms build-up and mobilisation alone are not necessarily part of balancing, as these measures of a small and medium-sized state may not be sufficient to redress the imbalance of power with threatening great powers.

On the other hand, bandwagoning refers to the strategy where one weaker state decides to defer to or join the coalition led by threatening power with expectation of reciprocation with protection, respect for its autonomy and vital interests, or other political and economic benefits. In this sense, bandwagoning is different from appeasement in the way that the bandwagoning state may have its core interests preserved by agreeing to coordinate its external policies with the threatening power and accepting its leadership in certain areas. No doubt, bandwagoning is only possible if the preeminent power desperately needs friends and allies to preserve or advance its interests against other powers in the system. Randall L. Schweller argues that both balancing and bandwagoning as alliance choices can be motivated not only by fear (security) but also the appetite for opportunistic gains (profit).[18] Both options potentially carry political costs (ceding some measure of foreign policy and military autonomy to allies) and strategic risks (antagonising other powers).

However, balancing and bandwagoning by and large require the clear-cut perception of a significant and imminent threat, or an insatiable predator. Though Walt's definition of threat appears to be clear-cut and rigid, it fails to reflect the complexity of the post–Cold War world. In normal conditions of international relations, it is not an easy task to assess other states' aggressive intentions and the calculation of costs and benefits, for either balancing or bandwagoning, are usually complex. In case of uncertainty about the strategic intentions of big powers, small and medium-sized states have less incentive to choose one side at the expense of their relations with others.

Students of mainland Southeast Asian politics indicate that though Southeast Asian countries have concerns over China because of its sheer size, geographical proximity and history of Chinese domination, but they are far from considering China as an imminent threat.[19] As a result, there is still a debate as to which category is best to describe Southeast Asian states' responses to a rising China. David Kang argues that Asian countries are more likely to bandwagon with China than balance against it.[20] Robert Ross argues that Southeast Asian states differ in terms of strategies to deal with China, some deferring to China's growing power and others, especially those less exposed to China's military power, are prone to align with the United States to deter China.[21] Other scholars argue that each Southeast Asian country simultaneously adopts multiple strategies, ranging from engagement, enmeshment, indirect or low-intensity balancing, and hedging, to restrain great powers in East Asia.[22]

Hedging

Though expressed in different terms, Southeast Asian postures show a region-wide inclination to adopt a middle-way position between great powers to maximise economic gains and at the same time to reduce strategic risks. This practice of the Southeast Asian states could be termed as "hedging." Various scholars have used the term before in the context of Southeast Asia and China. According to Evelyn Goh, hedging is a strategy "aimed at avoiding (or planning for contingencies in) a situation in which states cannot decide upon more straightforward alternatives such as balancing, bandwagoning or neutrality."[23] She adds that small states do not want to lean to one side at the expense of their relationships with other powers. Denny Roy defines hedging as "keeping open more than one strategic option against the possibility of a future security threat."[24] In this regard, hedging can be seen as seeking insurance against a potential threat, or preparing options to cope with future uncertainties. However, hedging does not mean simply cultivating a middle position (or equidistance) between powers but also involves actively developing arrangements that could forestall great powers' propensity to use force to alter the status quo. As a matter of fact, Southeast Asian countries not only worked to broaden the range of choices vis-à-vis big powers but also attempted to shape rules and norms for regional politics.[25]

Fundamentally, hedging means having multiple options to cope with the potential threat emanating from a rising power. It can be multi-dimensional, including engagement with the rising power to induce its cooperation, and multilateralism and diversification of security partnerships to prevent its aggressive intents and attempts. In this connection, hedging is different from balancing (or direct balancing) that there are no commitments to the formation of military alliances to deter the rising power, though the option remains open. In operational terms, hedging is a multi-component strategy, composed of two sets of "mutually counteracting policies." The first component of hedging is "opportunity maximisation," which includes engagement with the larger power on bilateral and multilateral platforms to bind it into institutions and encourage it to play by commonly accepted norms and in a cooperative manner. Bilateral channels are clearly critical because they help reduce miscommunication and misunderstanding and serve as a safety valve to defuse tension if needed. In addition, a collaborative relationship with this preponderant power opens the door for settling disputes, which again reduces the likelihood for conflicts in the future, and brings economic benefits.[26] Expanded economic cooperation and increased interdependence with the ascending power would again serve as a constraint against its revisionist and aggressive attempts.

The second set of hedging elements includes risk-minimising measures or preemptive acts, which involves the creation of conditions and constraints on the dominant power's behaviour. They include a range of measures, including the promotion of multilateralism and international law, the greater involvement of external powers and other actors, which would limit the advantages of the ascending powers. In this regard, the smaller state would facilitate the presence of other big powers in the region and their involvement in regional affairs so as to offset the growing clout of the rising power.[27] In case of the South China Sea, the presence of the United States and other Western powers in the region and their participations in regional institutions were seen as a check on Chinese hegemony. In this regard, hedging is similar to "indirect balancing" or "soft balancing" which have been used in literature about international relations in Southeast Asia to indicate deepened political and security cooperation with foreign powers to resist pressure from China.[28] The central idea is that such cooperation would neither affect the third party nor pose any strategic threat to any country, but it would create other big powers' substantial interest or stake in the stability of this smaller state, enabling it to play one big power against another to avoid being bullied. In this sense, such enhanced relationships with other powers or organisations can be translated into leverage against the rising power. Also, hedging can been seen as a preparation for the possibility of direct balancing which involves closer strategic collaboration and coordination when the ascending power becomes more threatening.

In a snapshot, appeasement, bandwagoning, hedging and balancing are four pathways in a continuum of responses that one small and medium-sized state might adopt to cope with unsatisfied stronger powers. It is clear that international strategic setting, or the balance of power, is not the only factor that shapes the policy choice of states. The way states respond to similar structural-systemic changes varies from country to country. Ultimately, the policy of one state is the product of debates among its political elites. Their perceptions of threats and risks that come from relevant the dominant power also matter. For better or worse, each strategy involves some benefits, costs and risks that statesmen, who represent the states' interests, would have to calculate on their balance sheet. In this regard, as Schweller rightly points out, elites' preferences and perceptions, their consensus and disagreements matter.[29] Following this logic, the subsequent section will look into Vietnam internally to understand the political elite and relevant policy actors with their threat perception and policy preferences.

Shifting strategic goals and emerging cleavage among Vietnam's political elites: ideologue conservatives versus nationalist pragmatists

After the fall of Saigon in 1975, Vietnam as a unified country adopted an assertive foreign policy to seek greater territorial control and regional influence. The victories over foreign forces gave leaders in Hanoi an illusion about the invincibility of the Vietnamese People Army and the superiority of its socialist orientation. With the support of its ally, the Soviet Union, Vietnam defied China on all fronts, engaging in fights along the land border, expanding in the South China Sea, and taking military actions to oust the China-backed Khmer Rouge regime in Cambodia.[30] Much of Vietnam's post-war strategy was to carve out its own sphere of influence and challenge China's traditional domination in Southeast Asia. Vietnam's military campaigns in Cambodia also pitted it against ASEAN and the West, which viewed Vietnam as an extension of the Soviet Union in Southeast Asia.[31]

In the mid-1980s, leaders in Hanoi realised that prolonged hostility with its neighbouring countries, particularly China, was untenable. The foreign policy based on alliance with the Soviet Union and blunt use of force to assert its regional influence effectively undermined Vietnam's ability to defend its basic territorial integrity and communist rule. Despite its consolidated footing in Cambodia, Vietnam faced greater difficulties in the defence of its northern border and its position in the South China Sea. China's 1988 attack on the Spratlys indicated that Vietnam suffered greater maritime vulnerability in the face of China's rising naval power. At the same time, the Soviet Union signalled that it was unwilling to provide as much economic and military backup as Vietnam required. As the balance of power was shifting against Vietnam, Hanoi gradually lowered its strategic goal, seeking to maintain the status quo in its neighbourhood rather than imposing its will through coercive measures. Consequently, Vietnam placed a premium on breaking political isolation and preserving the country's basic sovereignty.

Though agreeing on that strategic reorientation, the Vietnamese leaders seemed unsure about the best way to achieve it. This situation prompted intense internal debate among national security actors in Hanoi about how to perceive the nature of the China problem and appropriate remedies, as Beijing consistently turned down Hanoi's proposal to resume bilateral talks.[32] After the border war in 1979, the Vietnamese political elites unanimously viewed China as the country's most imminent and dangerous enemy.[33] However, that consensus was cracked by the chain of revolutions in the socialist bloc in Eastern Europe and the Tiananmen Square incident in China in 1989. Since then, two major distinct schools of thought have emerged in the Vietnamese leadership: ideologically conservative leaders who prefer a policy of bandwagoning with China for the sake of defending the communist regime, and nationalist pragmatists who advocate a policy of reaching out beyond the communist bloc to hedge against China's territorial ambitions. At one end of the spectrum, the bandwagoning policy implies restraints on peripheral interests and deference to China's leadership position in return for a cordial relationship, preferably a socialist union with China. However, it does not equate to subordination of Vietnam's sovereignty and political autonomy to socialist solidarity with China. At the other end, the hedging policy placed emphasis on seeking rapprochement and greater cooperation with Western powers to restrain China's "great Han chauvinism." Except for the few extremists on the margins of the Vietnamese politics, the advocates of both schools agree on the dual goals of preserving the status quo in in their neighbourhood and perpetuating the communist rule in Vietnam.[34] However, they disagree on the best way to achieve it, especially how best to handle rising China.

The conservative segment of the Vietnamese leadership, mostly in the military and theoretical wing of the party, advocates bandwagoning with China because of their concerns about "peaceful evolution," code words for all alleged schemes by the Western countries and anti-communist forces to gradually change the regime in Vietnam. Labelled as "conservative ideologues," this political group fears that the wave of "velvet revolutions" that upturned communism in the Eastern Europe would sooner or later arrive in Vietnam. They allege that the US and Western democracies were behind these transformations and believed that China would have similar anxieties.[35] Therefore, though hostility still clouded the Vietnam-China relationship in the late 1980s, leading conservative leaders, particularly party chief Nguyen Van Linh and Minister of Defence Le Duc Anh, lobbied to revive traditional ideology-based alliance with China to defend socialism.[36] To this end, they were willing to cede Vietnam's influence over Cambodia and settle the Cambodian conflict in a way that promoted socialist solidarity and facilitated rapprochement between Hanoi and Beijing. However, China rejected this idea of reviving the old-type military alliance and preferred to be a comrade but not an ally.[37] Even then, the Vietnamese conservative elites still supported closer political and security ties with China rather than those with other partners. Perhaps, they assumed that their appeals to socialist internationalism and their deferential stance towards China as the leader of the socialist camp after the Cold War would be repaid with Chinese protection and cooperation in managing and resolving long-standing disputes between the two nations.

The conservative ideologues' bandwagoning approach is based on particular cultural and ideological premises. History shows that deference is deeply rooted in traditional relations between Vietnamese and Chinese dynasties, in which Vietnamese emperors symbolically recognised China's superiority through specific rituals in exchange for Chinese recognition of Vietnamese autonomy.[38] Almost all Vietnamese feudal rulers adopted the model of tributary relations with China, in which they accepted some symbolic reverence to the Chinese emperors to maintain their independence. David Marr summed up the typical dynastic relationship between Vietnam and China as follows:

> This reality (China's overwhelming size), together with sincere cultural admiration, led Vietnam's rulers to accept the tributary system. Providing China did not meddle in Vietnam's internal affairs . . . Vietnam monarchs were quite willing to declare themselves vassals of the Celestial Emperor. The subtlety of this relationship was evident from the way in which Vietnamese monarchs styled themselves "king" (vuong) when communicating with China's rulers, but "emperor" (hoang de) when addressing their own subjects or sending messages to other Southeast Asian rulers.[39]

Deference did not obligate Vietnam to send troops, resources and funds to assist China's military campaigns to conquer other territories, as was the case in Europe in the medieval era. It did not genuinely affect the way the Vietnamese rulers ran the nation except in a formalistic sense. The expenses for triennial material tributes in form of precious articles were considered as significantly smaller as compared to costs of wars. At the same time, deference could bring the real benefits to Vietnamese rulers in terms of formal recognition and the option to appeal to the support of the Chinese empire in times of need.[40] In the annals of Vietnam's imperial history, the courts requested the Chinese monarchs for assistance to suppress domestic uprisings on a number of circumstances. In the late nineteenth century, in the face of French takeover, the Vietnamese rulers called for help from Beijing, and the Chinese emperor did send troops to fight against the French forces in Lang Son, Vietnam's northern province.[41]

Likewise, deference did not involve the surrender of autonomy and sovereignty. During one thousand years of Chinese domination (221 BCE to 938 CE), the Vietnamese repeatedly rose up to fight for independence. Vietnam regained independence from the Chinese empire and was reborn in the name of Dai Co Viet (Great Viet) in 968. While agreeing to pay tribute annually, the Vietnamese determinedly resisted successive Chinese invasions, even though they were outnumbered in many battles. However, after most victories over the Chinese invading armies, the Vietnamese rulers took the conciliatory initiative by sending envoys to apologise for inconveniences caused by their victories and requesting honours and privileges (as form of recognition) from the Chinese emperors. The Vietnamese rulers attached importance to saving face of the Chinese rulers as a way to restore peace. This deferential yet defiant posture was found in generation after generation of Vietnamese rulers. They all believed that successive wars with China were unsustainable. It was manifest in the way Emperor Quang Trung (1753–1792) planned conciliation even before major battles with Chinese Qing invaders in December 1788. Quang Trung told his aides before going to war:

> Today, I am here in charge of the military campaign in person, fight or stand already planned. Within tens of days, the Qing invading armies will be destroyed. However, Qing is a big country, 10 times bigger than our country. Being defeated, the Chinese people will feel dishonoured and will find way to revenge. If the war drags on, it is unfortunate for our people, and I can't help let them suffer. Therefore, after my victories, we need to use pens and letters (diplomacy) in place for swords (wars).[42]

Quang Trung did exactly what he said. Although his army defeated the Qing's invaders, he took the first move to send emissaries to Beijing for reconciliation and ask for Chinese recognition of his rule.[43] This ingrained dynastic habit of deferring to China remains a factor in Vietnam's conduct of China affairs today. It was echoed in Defence Minister Le Duc Anh's explanation for the need to normalise Vietnam's relations with China in the early 1990s: "For the sake of our national interest, at the critical times, our ancestors used to actively establish relations with China, which caused *no harm to independence and sovereignty* but opportunities to struggle against their adverse impacts" (emphasis added).[44] When normal relations between Vietnam and China resumed in the 1990s, Secretary General Le Kha Phieu explained the rationale for Vietnam's prudent and deferential diplomacy with China: "We live adjacent to a big country; we cannot afford long-standing tensions with them because they are next door to us."[45]

Besides deep-rooted traditionalism, the party theoreticians and the military refer to their dogmatically rigid worldview of antagonism between socialist and capitalist camps to support engagement with China on the basis of shared ideology and political system. These ideological conservatives hold that "however expansionist it may be, China remains a socialist country," implying that China would cooperate with Vietnam to defend socialism and restrain its expansionist attempts.[46] As a result, they place a premium on binding and bonding with China through expanded multifaceted cooperation, especially in the area of ideology, in order to broaden the breadth of interest commonalities between the two countries without the precondition of settling historical differences. In the same vein, they attach importance to the exchange of experience between two communist parties in the fight against "peaceful evolution," regime maintenance and shared ideology to encourage China's cooperative attitude in other sectors, especially territorial disputes. To defend his push for normalisation with China in early 1990s, Minister of Defence Le Duc Anh told his aide:

> China is a big neighbour of Vietnam. If two countries are antagonistic with each other, not only do we fail to build our country, but we will also be exploited by the West. China and Vietnam has many similarities, particularly shared *adherence to communism*. Given complex international situation, we *need to proactively seek normal relations* with China.[47]

In the 1950s and 1960s, North Vietnam also jumped on the bandwagon with China to seek political and material support for its struggles for independence and reunification. At that time, North Vietnam and China were in an informal ideology-based alliance, often referred to "as close as lips and teeth," in which Vietnam received massive economic and military assistance from China to fight against France and the United States.[48] The relationship was not purely based on the idea of socialist internationalism but also on national interests. China helped North Vietnam largely because of its geopolitical aim to keep other powers distant from its border. Growing distrust between Vietnam and China led to the collapse of their comrades-in-arms relationship after Vietnam completed reunification in 1975.[49] However, Vietnamese ideologically conservative leaders, such as Nguyen Van Linh and Le Duc Anh, saw the relationship between Vietnam and China in the 1950s and 1960s as ideal and advocated the revival of this type of "alliance."[50]

Since normalisation in 1991, the ideologically conservative Vietnamese elites still pushed for bandwagoning with China. They advocated bonding with and binding China in a dense network of institutionalised party-to-party and state-to-state dialogues between the two countries' party and state officials at various levels to address the obstacles to the relations. These institutional ties serve two purposes. First, Hanoi made use of the annual meetings between high-level leaders of two communist parties to reassure Beijing of its non-aligned strategic posture, while at the same time communicating its primary concerns and securing high-level Chinese commitments to resolve territorial disputes in a peaceful and timely fashion. Second, these dialogues serve as mechanisms to foster a resolution of contentious issues. Normally, annual summit talks adopt guidelines and deadlines for lower-level official working groups to work out technical solutions to particular contentious issues.[51] Beijing is generally receptive to Vietnam's engagement efforts for two reasons. First, because both Vietnam and China are rare communist states that survived the Cold War, China has an interest in maintaining communist rule in Vietnam. Second, the Chinese officials see these institutionalised dialogues as a channel for influence over Vietnam's domestic politics and foreign affairs. Third, though having no desire to accept Vietnam as an ally, China has been interested in keeping Vietnam as a strategic buffer, forestalling penetration of other powers into its near abroad. In this regard, these different bilateral mechanisms are helpful to communicate Chinese concerns and desires to the Vietnamese leadership with the ultimate aim to keep Vietnam within its reach.

On the other end of the spectrum, nationalist minds in the foreign ministry and other government bureaucracies pursued a hedging approach because they were suspicious of Beijing's territorial ambitions and favoured a foreign policy firmly based on national interests. They hold the view that "in the immediate and foreseeable future, China is the *main source* of threats to our sovereignty and territorial integrity as well as our national security and development."[52] In their view, even when Vietnam and China normalised their relations, "the threat by China is *multi-dimensional, genuine, and present-day* and it is different from threats by other states, including the United States, which are somewhat predictive and precautionary in nature." Tran Quang Co, who served as deputy minister of foreign affairs of Vietnam and the closest aid to Foreign Minister Thach in the late 1980s and early 1990s, elaborated on the nature of the Chinese challenge as follows:

> In the immediate future, China is making every effort to materialize the goal of being a major power in Asia and the Pacific, which has the same footing with the United States and Japan. China's *first priority is to take control of the South China Sea*. China attached great importance to geostrategic aspect of the South China Sea because controlling the South China Sea means controlling Southeast Asia and the artery of trade between the Pacific and Indian Oceans, and owning an area rich in natural resources especially oil (South China Sea's hydrocarbon reserve is comparable to that of the Persian Gulf) that is indispensable for China to speed up development.[53]

To deal with the China problem, the nationalist faction in the Vietnamese leadership sees hedging as the most pragmatically viable option in the post–Cold War period. Deputy Foreign Minister Tran Quang Co argued: "in order to make China softer, Vietnam needs to show China that Vietnam has more and more *friends*." He added, "Otherwise, if we are dependent only on China and if China sees Vietnam weak and isolated, it will press against us."[54] When asked about China's attack on Vietnam's border in February 1979, Co answered:

> It is natural, in such a setting (neighbouring to China), we must foresee it. Our strategy should be to gain more friends and fewer enemies to grow strong. If we're strong, they (China) will respect us. The fewer friends we have, the more they bully us. It is exactly like kids on the street.[55]

There is still the question: how could "more friends" bring greater security for Vietnam vis-à-vis China?

The role of "friends" in Vietnam's national security needs further elaboration. In the process of resolving the Cambodian conflict in the second half of the 1980s, conservative leaders supported direct consultation between Vietnam and China as the best way to solve the problem. However, then Foreign Minister Nguyen Co Thach believed this formula put Vietnam in a disadvantageous position vis-à-vis China. Instead, he recommended that Vietnam should reach out beyond the socialist camp to find solutions to the Cambodian conflict. It was argued that the involvement of major Western powers and Southeast Asian states would constrain China and force Beijing to moderate its hard-line position and respect Hanoi's core interests. At that time Thach appeared as the most progressive leader in Hanoi and his idea of partnering with non-socialist powers was revolutionary in the heavily dogmatic politics of Vietnam in the late 1980s. Thach's pragmatic proposal was explicable as he was the first senior Vietnamese leader to openly reject the rigid worldview of "two camps" and to adopt a view of the world as economically interconnected and globalised. Thach stated that "global productive capacity is highly developed and the world is becoming an integrated market and we have the opportunity to make use of the world's production capacity, and we ought to do so."[56] Consequently, Thach pushed for new security thinking, enshrined in the Politburo Resolution of May 1988, which was to comprehensively empower Vietnam through a combination of "*strong* economy, *just enough* military might, and *expanded* international cooperation."[57]

Although Thach was dismissed from the Politburo in 1991 because of his anti-China stance, his security thinking laid the foundation for Vietnam's hedging policy in the post–Cold War period. Highest priority was given to economic development through integration with the global capitalist world. In foreign affairs, the armed forces were rolled back and diplomacy came to the forefront. The nationalist pragmatist leaders pushed for a foreign policy based on the national interest that was to multilateralise[58] and diversify (*da phuong hoa, da dang hoa*) its international relations regardless of ideological differences. The well-known motto of Vietnamese diplomacy is that "Vietnam wants to be a friend and a reliable partner with all countries in the international community."[59] Clearly, that "friend-to-all" approach to foreign relations was not only motivated by the need for economic development (to grow strong) but by the strategic need to expand the range of strategic choices and develop constraints on China's behaviour. A Vietnamese diplomat candidly explained how expanded international relations would benefit Vietnam in its relations with China:

> Sino-Vietnamese relations will be meshed within the much larger regional network of interlocking economic and political interests. It is an arrangement whereby anybody wanting to violate Vietnam's sovereignty would be violating the interests of other countries as well.[60]

Tran Quang Co presented a valuable account on the roles of different friends and partners in Vietnam's hedging strategy to constrain China in his report to the Politburo in 1993. The first in the list was the United States. Though also suspicious of the United States' attempts to foster regime change in Vietnam, Co believed that the United States had an interest in containing China and was the only power that is capable of constraining China strategically. The presence of the United States in the region therefore played an important role in checking Chinese aggressive behaviour. Co explains:

> The relationship with the United States is an important element of our policy to diversify and multilateralise foreign relations. Currently, the US is the only

> power that is able to act as a counterweight to and a check on Chinese power. Therefore, we need to persistently seek normal relations with US. It is necessary to *create direct interests of the US in Vietnam*, especially interest in the offshore oil and gas sector, so that the US could not ignore any destabilisations caused by assertive actions by China. An Asia watcher commented, "An oil rig of Mobil Oil (US) in the South China Sea is valued as much as the whole Seventh Fleet.[61]

He also viewed ASEAN countries as important diplomatic hedging partners, as ASEAN was the most vibrant regional organisation that all powers have to take into account in their Asia-Pacific policy. Co argued that ASEAN countries and Vietnam have shared interests in maintaining regional peace and security and neutralising challenges from both China and Japan. From this vantage point, fostering cooperation with Southeast Asian countries and joining ASEAN was a pathway to strengthening Vietnam's relative bargaining power vis-à-vis big powers.[62] Last but not least, as Co put it bluntly, other powers, especially Japan, Russia and the European Union, were also important in providing the benefits of economic development, creating a correlation of forces in favour of Vietnam in the region. They would also serve as a way to mobilise international public opinion to defend Vietnam's sovereignty and territorial integrity, by creating a web of political and economic interdependence to shield Vietnam from Chinese expansionism.[63] So, the whole idea of hedging is to actively expand cooperation with all big powers and ASEAN countries to broaden the base of shared and mutual interests among them as well as increase Vietnam's aggregate strength. If so, whenever China intends to encroach on Vietnam, it has to take into account the interests of other powers. Besides, increased cooperation with other big powers also leaves the door open for any upgrade to the strategic partnership in case China becomes a real military threat in the future.

However, most nationalist pragmatists had some reservations against balancing politics. When the Soviet Union was dissolved, nationalist pragmatist elites did not look for other sources of power to replace the Soviet Union as strategic patron but advocated a non-aligned strategic posture. A Vietnamese diplomat stated that a decade of hostility gave the Vietnamese political elite a valuable lesson that it was not wise to get deeply entangled in major power politics.[64] It was thought that one-sided relations do more harm than good, resulting in political isolation and economic difficulties.[65] More often, Vietnamese strategists referred to the United States' abandonment of its South Vietnamese ally when China attacked the Paracels in 1974 and the Soviet Union's strategic inaction when China moved into the Spratlys in 1988. In their view, Vietnam's security interests would now be best served by actively establishing friendly and cooperative relations with all major powers, but not to the extent of a military alliance since it would potentially trigger distrust and hostility from China. This non-aligned strategic policy (independence) no doubt turned Vietnam into a buffer zone for China, fending off any intrusion by China's strategic rivals. For Vietnam, this policy would not only avoid antagonism from China but also give Vietnam more opportunities to develop its economy, enhance its political bargaining power vis-à-vis all powers, create a balanced web of interwoven interests with other powers and partners in Vietnam and in the region, and also deter China's aggressive actions and mobilise public opinion and political support against it if necessary. In an important report to the Standing Committee of the Politburo in June 1993, Co argued:

> Our nation's painful experience over the last decades indicated that we need a policy of *balanced relations* with big powers *absolutely without* creating a misunderstanding that Vietnam has a scheme of colluding with one country against another. We need to bond our security and development interests to those of neighbours in the region to give our country a more favourable international stance.[66]

Collective leadership and choice between bandwagoning and hedging

In a snapshot, policy making in Vietnam rests within the communist party, which assumes monolithic control of political power. The two most important decision-making bodies within the CPV system are the Central Committee and the Politburo, which are elected by the National Party Congress held every five years. The CPV Central Committee, which selects the members of the powerful Politburo and the Secretariat and adopts the major guidelines in national building and defence, is composed of between 140 and 160 members from various party and state bureaucratic institutions at the central and provincial level. The Politburo, which meets weekly and has power to make important decisions requiring urgent action, is composed of between fourteen and seventeen members.[67] With these compositions, Vietnam's politics is by nature a collective leadership system, in which leaders make decisions on the basis of consensus.

Since the sixth Party Congress in December 1986, power is no longer concentrated in a single or a narrow group of political elites, but is diffused across the system due to the demise of Le Duan and other ageing revolutionary leaders. Without "strong men" or a paramount leader, the Vietnamese leadership has been fragmented into interest groups and patronage networks. Without institutionalised mechanisms to resolve differences, these groups constantly negotiate with each other on almost all policy areas.[68] David Elliot rightly points out, "Politics in this collective leadership system is perpetual renegotiation, which makes it difficult to achieve consistency on long-term objectives."[69] No doubt, in this system, consensus could be possible, but it is always delicate and temporary. In many cases, no decisions are made as deep divisions among leaders paralyse the whole system.

In the field of foreign affairs, the cleavage of opinion between the ideological conservatives and nationalist pragmatists signals constant competitions among different visions and policy choices. Given the struggle between two groups for domestic political power and for influence over policy making, Vietnam's foreign policy has oscillated between bandwagoning with and hedging against China. In case that one group becomes dominant or consensus is forged under certain external and internal pressures, the policy making and implementation would become more coherent and effective. If no consensus is reached, it is possible that no actions will be taken, or a dual track approach (with elements of both bandwagoning and balancing) would be implemented. As there is no arbitrator to decide which the best option is, policy outcomes are important in the struggle for offices. Policy failures and successes are likely to undermine or strengthen the position of one group vis-à-vis the other.

There are also two important developments that may strengthen the power base of the national pragmatists vis-à-vis that of the ideologues. First, the *Doi Moi* process, which prioritised economic reforms and integration into the world's economy, had broadened the range of actors that try to put their mark on the country's international relations, at the expense of traditional national security actors.[70] As *Doi Moi* unfolded and the Vietnamese economy expanded, the other dimensions of the South China Sea, notably maritime resources, maritime transport and safety navigation, natural disaster relief and prevention, and environmental protection, have become more salient. The day-to-day handling of South China Sea issues involves coordination of various portfolios such as Ministry of Trade and Industry (oil and gas exploration), Ministry of Agricultural and Rural Development (fishery issues), Ministry of Natural Resources and Environment, and provinces such as Da Nang (governing Hoang Sa) and Khanh Hoa (Truong Sa). Amid recent rising tensions in the South China Sea, the National Assembly of Vietnam has become more assertive in holding a number of hearings on the South China Sea developments.[71]

Moreover, public opinion has gained more influence thanks to the Internet and mass media. In the past, the party controlled all platforms of publication and easily manipulated public opinion. However, the rise of the Internet and cyber spaces makes it easier for members of the public to circulate their views and receive information. Over the last decade, some segments of society, especially retired officials, intellectuals, dissidents and overseas Vietnamese became critical of the government's policies and called for more transparency in decision-making. In this regard, foreign and security policy is no longer the exclusive realm of the state and the security apparatus that is free from public scrutiny. Though public opinion does not have a direct impact upon politics in Vietnam to the extent of that in liberal democracies, politicians in Hanoi have faced increased public scrutiny of their decisions.[72] This development also pushes the leaders to put policy making firmly on the ground of national interest. The broadened range of actors involved in foreign affairs is weakening the control of a small vanguard of conservative ideologues and the military over foreign policy.

Conclusion

The fundamental issue for Vietnam in the South China Sea is not just about how to settle and manage sovereignty and maritime disputes but also how to cope with China as a potential revisionist state. Theoretically speaking, Vietnam as the weaker part of the power equation has four options to deal with China as the stronger part: appeasement, bandwagoning, hedging and balancing. The period between 1975 and 1989 witnessed unified Vietnam's balancing attempts to form an alliance with the Soviet Union to challenge China's dominant position in Southeast Asia. Hanoi soon realised that such policy was too costly and unsustainable. Since the mid-1980s, Vietnam put priority on restoring peace and stability in their neighbourhood and preserving its basic sovereignty and territorial integrity at the expense of its influence over Indochina.

However, there has emerged a disagreement among the Vietnamese political elites on how to assess the international situation and the best pathway to achieve this primary objective. Conservative ideologues support bandwagoning with China for the sake of regime security, while nationalist pragmatists advocate rapprochement and expanded cooperation with other powers to modernise the nation and hedge against strategic uncertainties associated with irredentist China. These two preferences represent two ends of a spectrum of Vietnam's foreign policy in the *Doi Moi* period. Vietnam's political system, featured by atop collective leadership, offers a playground for competition of visions and policy initiatives behind closed doors.

Notes

1 R.B. Strassler, *The Landmark Thucydides: A Comprehensive Guide to the Peloponnesian War*, New York: Simon & Schuster, 1998, p.352.
2 E.H. Carr, *Britain: A Study of Foreign Policy from the Versailles Treaty to the Outbreak of War*, London and New York: Longmans Green, 1939, p.18.
3 Ibid., p.17.
4 Ibid.
5 E.H. Carr and M. Cox, *The Twenty Years' Crisis, 1919–1939: An Introduction to the Study of International Relations*, New York: Palgrave, 2001, p.199.
6 Ibid., pp. 75–8.
7 Ibid., p.77.
8 Ibid., p.152 (emphasis added).
9 K.N. Waltz, *Theory of International Politics*, Reading, MA: Addison-Wesley Pub. Co, 1979, p.126.
10 See ibid.
11 Ibid., pp. 102–28.
12 See S.M. Walt, *The Origins of Alliances*, Ithaca: Cornell University Press, 1987.
13 Ibid., p.110.
14 Ibid.
15 L.S. Randall, "Bandwagoning for Profit: Bringing the Revisionist State Back In," *International Security* 19, no. 1, 1994, pp. 72–107.
16 J.C. Liow, "Balancing, Bandwagoning, or Hedging? Strategic and Security Patterns in Malaysia's Relations with China: 1981–2002," In: Ho Khai Leong and Samuel C.Y. Ku (eds.), *China and Southeast Asia: Global Changes and Regional Challenges*, Singapore: Institute of Southeast Asia Studies, 2015, pp. 281–307.
17 L.S. Randall, "Unanswered Threats: A Neoclassical Realist Theory of Underbalancing," *International Security* 29, no. 2, 2004, p.166.
18 Randall, "Bandwagoning for Profit."
19 See D. Roy, "Southeast Asia and China: Balancing or Bandwagoning?," *Contemporary Southeast Asia* 27, no. 2, 2005, pp. 305–22.
20 D.C. Kang, "Getting Asia Wrong: The Need for New Analytical Frameworks," *International Security* 27, no. 4, 2003, pp. 57–85.

21 See R. S. Ross, “Balance of Power Politics and the Rise of China: Accommodation and Balancing in East Asia,” *Security Studies* 15, no. 3, 2006, pp. 355–95; L. Odgaard, “Deterrence and Co-Operation in the South China Sea,” *Contemporary Southeast Asia* 23, no. 2, 2001, pp. 292–306.
22 See D. Roy, “Southeast Asia and China: Balancing or Bandwagoning?,” pp. 305–22; E. Goh, “Great Powers and Hierarchical Order in Southeast Asia: Analyzing Regional Security Strategies,” *International Security* 32, no. 3, 2007/2008, pp. 113–57.
23 E. Goh, “Understanding ‘Hedging’ in Asia-Pacific Security,” *PacNet* 43, 2006.
24 D. Roy, “Southeast Asia and China: Balancing or Bandwagoning?,” p.306.
25 See Goh, “Great Powers and Hierarchical Order in Southeast Asia.”
26 K. Cheng-Chwee, “Rising Dragon, Crouching Tigers: Comparing the Foreign Policy Responses of Malaysia and Singapore toward a Re-Emerging China,” *Biblio Asia* 3, no. 4, 2008.
27 See K. Cheng-Chwee, “The Essence of Hedging: Malaysia and Singapore’s Response to a Rising China,” *Contemporary Southeast Asia* 30, no. 2, 2008, pp. 159–85.
28 See Goh, “Great Powers and Hierarchical Order in Southeast Asia”; K. Cheng-Chwee, “The Essence of Hedging: Malaysia and Singapore’s Response to a Rising China”; L. H. Hiep, “Vietnam’s Hedging Strategy against China since Normalisation,” *Contemporary Southeast Asia* 35, no.3, 2013, pp. 333–68.
29 Randall, “Unanswered Threats,” pp. 168–70.
30 S. C. Tucker, *Vietnam*, London: UCL Press, 1999, pp. 191–204.
31 C.A. Thayer, “Vietnam and ASEAN: A First Anniversary Assessment,” *Southeast Asian Affairs*, 1997, p.364.
32 T. Q. Co, *Hoi uc va Suy nghi*, unpublished manuscript, Chapter 4, p.31.
33 Ibid., Chapter 4. *Hoi uc va Suy nghi* (Memoir and Reflection) is a memoir by Tran Quang Co (1927–2015), who served as Vietnamese deputy minister of foreign affairs during the 1980s and early 1990s. The manuscript provides valuable insider’s view of intra-CPV debate about Vietnamese foreign affairs. The work is available online at: www.diendan.org/tai-lieu/ho-so/hoi-ky-tran-quang-co/hoiky-tqc-ch-1 (accessed 13 May 2015). The reliability of the work has been confirmed by authoritative Vietnamese sources.
34 Tran Xuan Bach, a Politburo member, advocated a multi-party political system in Vietnam. He was dismissed from the Politburo in a CPV plenum in March 1990. Bui Tin, once serving vice chief editor of the *Nhan Dan Daily (People’s Daily)*, the official paper of the Communist Party of Vietnam, left for exile in 1990 for dissatisfaction with the communist rule.
35 D.W.P. Elliot, *Changing Worlds: Vietnam’s Transition from Cold War to Globalisation*, New York: Oxford University Press, 2012, pp. 109–12.
36 Co, *Hoi uc va Suy nghi*, Chapter 12, pp. 84–95.
37 C.A. Thayer, “Sino-Vietnamese Relations: The Interplay of Ideology and National Interest,” *Asian Survey* 34, no. 6, 1994, p.523.
38 B. Womack, *China and Vietnam: The Politics of Asymmetry*, Cambridge, NY: Cambridge University Press, 2006, pp. 139–40.
39 D. G. Marr, “Sino-Vietnamese Relations,” *Australian Journal of Chinese Affairs*, no. 6, 1981, p.49.
40 D. R. SarDesai, *Vietnam: Past and Present*, Los Angeles, CA: Westview Press, 2005, pp. 19–31.
41 Ibid., p.42.
42 Quoted from T. V. Cuong, *Ngoai giao Viet Nam tu thuo dung nuoc den truoc Cach mang Thang Tam*, Hanoi: Hoc vien Quan he Quoc te, 2001, p.172.
43 L. V. Loi, *Ngoai giao Viet Nam*, Hanoi: Cong an Nhan dan, 2000, pp. 173–209.
44 V. V. Ninh, “Tuong Viet Nam ke chuyen binh thuong hoa quan he voi Trung Quoc,” *Vietnamnet*, 21 December 2011. Online. Available HTTP: <http://tuanvietnam.vietnamnet.

vn/2011–12–20-tuong-viet-nam-ke-chuyen-binh-thuong-hoa-quan-he-voi-trung-quoc> (accessed 24 October 2012).

45 Quoted from A.L. Vuving, "Changing Synthesis of Strategies: Vietnam's China Policy since 1990," paper presented at *Regenerations: New Leaders, New Visions in Southeast Asia*, New Haven, 11–12 November 2005.

46 Co, *Hoi uc va Suy nghi*, Chapter 4, pp. 31–2.

47 Ninh, "Tuong Viet Nam ke chuyen binh thuong hoa quan he voi Trung Quoc" (emphasis added).

48 T. Okabe, "Coping with China," In: James William Morley and Masashi Nishihara (eds.), *Vietnam Joins the World*, Armonk, NY: M.E. Sharpe, 1997, p.118.

49 Womack, *China and Vietnam*, pp. 162–85; C.A. Thayer, "Vietnamese Perspectives of the 'China Threat'," In: Herbert S. Yee and Ian C. Storey (eds.), *The China Threat: Perceptions, Myths and Reality*, New York: Routledge Curzon, 2002, pp. 270–92.

50 Thayer, "Vietnamese Perspectives of the 'China Threat'," p.275.

51 C.A. Thayer, "The Tyranny of Geography: Vietnamese Strategies to Constrain China in the South China Sea," paper presented at the *International Studies Association – 52nd Annual Convention*, Montreal, Canada, 16–19 March 2011.

52 Co, *Hoi uc va Suy nghi*, Chapter 21, p.134 (emphasis added).

53 Ibid. (emphasis added).

54 Ibid., Chapter 6, p.40 (emphasis added).

55 "Cuoc chien ngoai giao," *BBC Vietnamese*, 12 February 2009. Online. Available HTTP: <www.bbc.co.uk/vietnamese/lg/vietnam/2009/02/090220_tranquangco_tc2.shtml> (accessed 13 February 2015).

56 Quoted from S. Tomoda, "Detaching from Cambodia," In: James William Morley and Masashi Nishihara (eds.), *Vietnam Joins the World*, Armonk, NY: M.E. Sharpe, 1997, p.144.

57 N.V. Tung, "Vietnam's Security Challenges: Hanoi's New Approach to National Security and Implications to Defense and Foreign Policies," In: Eiichi Katahara (ed.), *Asia Pacific Countries' Security Outlook and Its Implications for the Defense Sector*, Tokyo: NIDS Joint Research Series No.5, 2010, p.108 (emphasis added).

58 "Da phuong hoa" is usually translated as "multilateralisation," but it does not mean participation in international organisations with multiple state members. "Da phuong hoa" means establishing relations with countries of different political systems without exclusion. A more accurate translation may be "multi-dimentionalisation."

59 The slogan has evolved from "them ban bot thu" ("gaining more friends, fewer enemies") in 1988 to "la ban voi tat ca cac nuoc" ("befriending every country") in 1991, and to "la ban, la doi tac tin cay" ("be a friend and reliable partner") in the 9th National Congress in 2001. See N.N. Duong, *Vietnamese Foreign Policy since Doi Moi: The Dialectic of Power and Identity*, PhD diss., School of Humanities and Social Sciences, University of New South Wales, Sydney, 2010.

60 Quoted from Thayer, "Sino-Vietnamese Relations," p.527.

61 Co, *Hoi uc va Suy nghi*, Chapter 21, pp. 136–8 (emphasis added).

62 Ibid., p.138.

63 Ibid., p.139.

64 Tomoda, "Detaching from Cambodia," p.138.

65 C.A. Thayer, "Vietnamese Foreign Policy: Multilateralism and the Threat of Peaceful Evolution," In: Carlyle A. Thayer and Ramses Amer (eds.), *Vietnamese Foreign Policy in Transition*, Singapore: Institute of Southeast Studies, 1999, p.8.

66 Co, *Hoi uc va Suy nghi*, Chapter 21, p.136 (emphasis added).

67 See C.A. Thayer, "Military Politics in Contemporary Vietnam: Political Engagement, Corporate Interests and Professionalism," In: M. Mietzner (ed.), *Military Politics in Contemporary Southeast Asia*, London: Routledge, 2011, pp. 65–86.

68 C.A. Thayer, "Political Legitimacy of Vietnam's One Party-State: Challenges and Responses," *Journal of Current Southeast Asian Affairs* 4, 2009, p.64; D. Koh, "The

Politics of a Divided Party and Parkinson's State in Vietnam," *Contemporary Southeast Asia* 23, no. 3, 2001, pp. 533–51.

69 Elliot, *Changing Worlds*, pp. 19–20.

70 J. Dosch, "Vietnam's ASEAN Membership Revisited: Golden Opportunity or Golden Cage?," *Contemporary Southeast Asia: A Journal of International and Strategic Affairs* 28, no. 2, 2006, pp. 234–58; C. Dixon, "State, Party and Political Change in Vietnam," In: Duncan McCargo (ed.), *Rethinking Vietnam*, London and New York: RoutledgeCurzon, 2004, pp. 15–26.

71 "Chinh phu bao cao tinh hinh Bien Dong truoc Quoc hoi," *Vnexpress*, 8 October 2014. Online. Available HTTP: <http://vnexpress.net/tin-tuc/thoi-su/chinh-phu-bao-cao-tinh-hinh-bien-dong-truoc-quoc-hoi-3090605.html> (accessed 8 November 2014); Bich Ngoc, "Quoc hoi hop kin ve Bien Dong: Hai long nhung . . ." *Bao Dat Viet*, 6 June 2015. Online. Available HTTP: <http://baodatviet.vn/chinh-tri-xa-hoi/tinh-hinh-bien-dong-van-de-bien-dong/quoc-hoi-hop-kin-ve-bien-dong-hai-long-nhung-3271501/> (accessed 3 July 2015).

72 In February 2011, 18 Vietnamese intellectuals and retired officials sent a letter to the Ministry of Foreign Affairs of Vietnam to request for information about Vietnam-China relations. In July and August 2011, Vietnamese intellectuals signed two open letters to the Vietnamese leadership to warn about China's threat and call for reforms to strengthen the nation. The letter is available online at http://boxitvn.blogspot.com.au/2011/08/thu-ngo-gui-cac-nha-lanh-ao-viet-nam-ve.html. In August 2012, 71 intellectuals renewed their call for reforms. In May 2014, amid tensions over China's Haiyang Shiyou oil rig 981, over 100 intellectuals also published their letter to the Vietnamese leadership, which described a "dangerous situation when the country's sovereignty is breached."

2 Vietnam's claims in the South China Sea

Introduction

Throughout the course of history, three major processes have shaped the political geography of Vietnam. Since the start of its civilisation, the Vietnamese continuously struggled to defend their fatherland from northern invaders. After gaining independence from the northern empire in the tenth century, the Vietnamese gradually marched southward. From their original villages in the Red River Delta, they overrode the Champa Kingdom and land in the rich Mekong River Delta and eventually reached the shore of the Gulf of Thailand by the mid-eighteenth century. A seventh-century conquest nearly tripled the length of the country and gave it the modern-day shape like a "starving sea horse."

As the country expanded southward, "oceanic Vietnam" had become increasingly important. The sea was always economically salient for coastal communities, providing cheap protein and a fast conduit for transportation. As described by French geographer Pierre Gourou, Vietnam is "the least coherent territory in the world" because rivers and mountain ranges divide it into diverse regional enclaves. As a result, the maritime corridor is also politically essential as a medium that encourages connectedness between the north and the south.[1] At a time when European warships were regularly present near the Vietnamese shore, the maritime theatre became the first line of defence for the mainland. Vietnam's extensive coastline, more than 3,000 km long, known as the "balcony of the Pacific," makes it more vulnerable to seaborne attack.[2] In addition, two major delta regions in the north and the south, both deeply penetrated by navigable waterways, deprive the country of hinterland and strategic depth. Since then, the sea has figured significantly in Vietnam's nation building and defence.

Discovery of the "Golden Sandbank"

The South China Sea, which is referred to as the East Sea (Bien Dong) in Vietnam, has long been the traditional fishing ground for Vietnamese fishermen. They were among the first discoverers of the two largest groups of uninhabited islands, banks, reefs and shoals – the Paracels and the Spratlys – in the middle of the South China Sea (see Figure 2.1).[3] For a long time the Vietnamese have

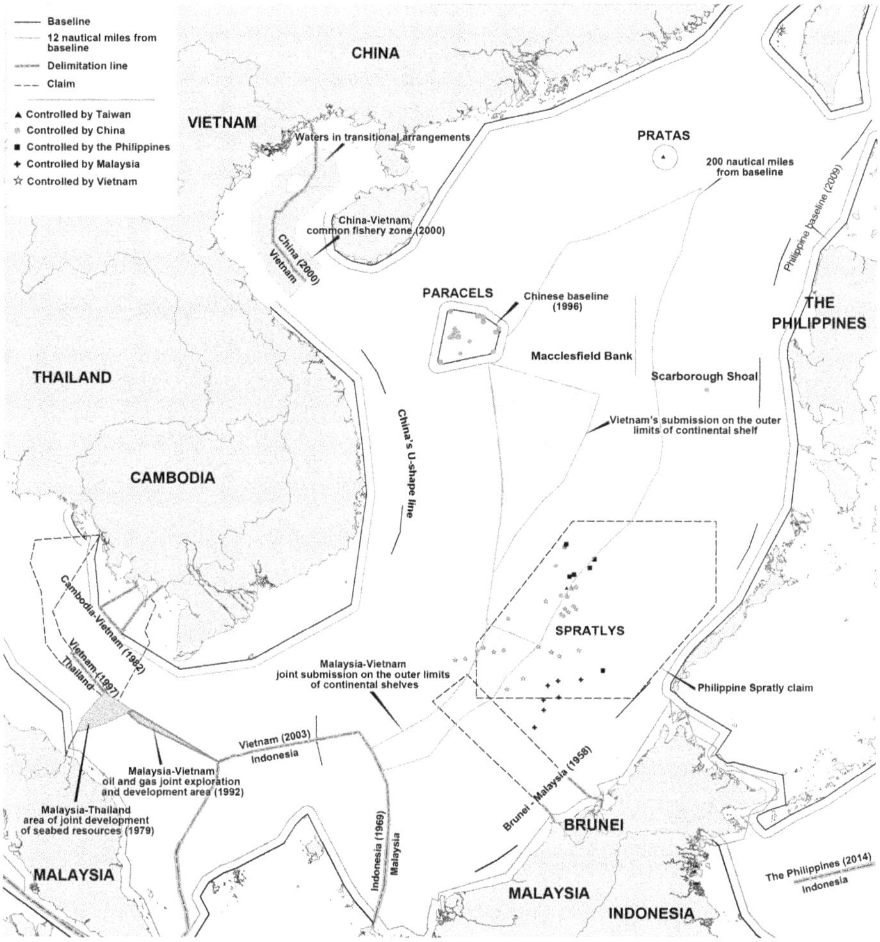

Figure 2.1 The claims in the South China Sea

Source: This map was prepared by the East Sea Institute of the Diplomatic Academy of Vietnam.

viewed these landmasses as integral units that are called "quan dao" (archipelagos) rather than separate insular formations. According to Vietnamese records, the Paracels, called the Hoang Sa Archipelago in Vietnam, are approximately 120 n.m. from Vietnam's Ly Son Island, 170 n.m. from Da Nang, and 156 n.m. from China's Hainan Island (see Figures 2.1 and 2.8). The archipelago consists of over thirty islets, sandbanks or reefs in an area of approximately 4,700 square n.m. of the ocean's surface.[4] The Spratlys, referred to as the Truong Sa Archipelago in Vietnam, are located about 250 n.m. east of Vietnam's Cam Ranh Bay, roughly 200 n.m. southeast of the Paracel Islands, approximately 540 n.m. from Hainan Province and 54 n.m. west of Palawan Island of the Philippines (see Figures 2.1 and 2.8).[5]

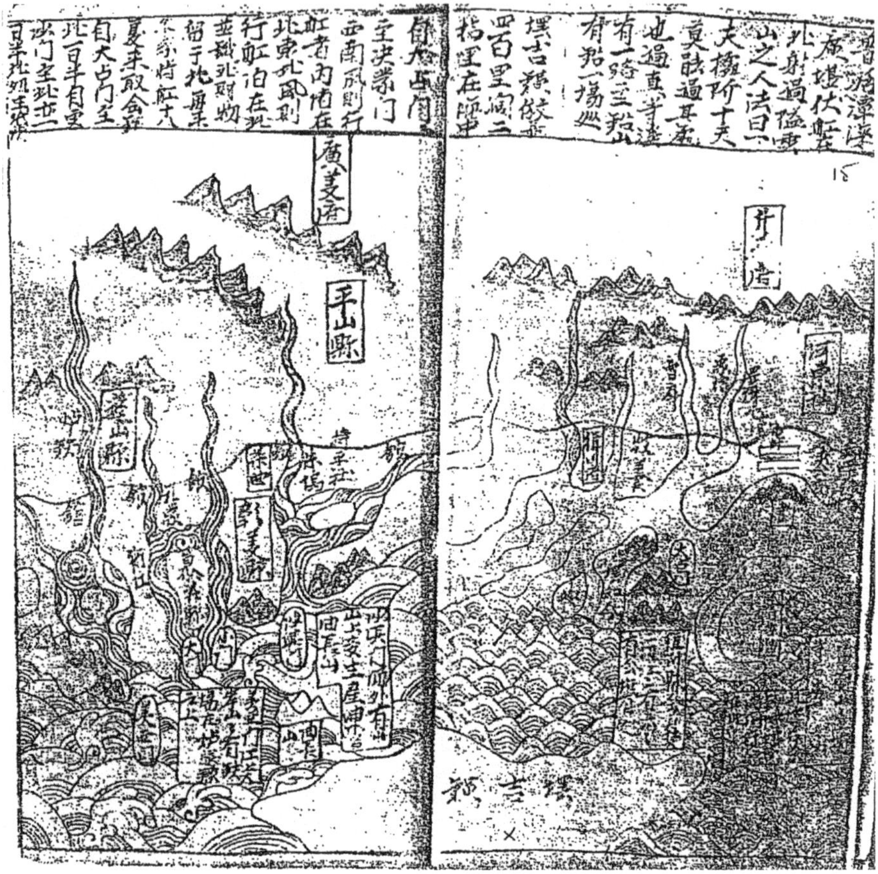

Figure 2.2 Toan tap Thien nam Chi lo do thu (Handbook of the South's Road Map), 1630–1635

"In the middle of the sea is a long golden sandbank, called Bai Cat Vang, with a length of 400 li and a width of 20 li, spanning in the middle of the sea from Dai Chiem to Sa Vinh Seaports. Foreign ships would be drifted and stranded on the bank if they travelled on the inner side (west) of the sandbank under the southwest wind or on the outer side under the northeast wind (east). Their sailors would starve to death and leave all their goods there."

Source: State Records Management and Archives Department of Vietnam

The inclusion of these offshore island groups into Vietnam's political geography was discernible in *Toan tap Thien nam Tu chi Lo do thu* (*Handbook of the South's Road Maps*) compiled by Do Ba (also known as Cong Dao) between 1630 and 1635. This is a collection of maps of the central part of Vietnam since the fifteenth century (see Figure 2.2). In the map of Quang Nghia Prefecture, it was noted that "in the middle of the sea, facing the coastline between the harbour of Dai Chiem[6] and the harbour of Sa Vinh[7] lies a long sandbank, called '*Bai Cat Vang*', which is

400 *ly*[8] long and 20 *ly* wide."[9] It is argued that, due to imprecision of geographic tools and methods, at the time the Vietnamese mistook the Paracel and Spratly archipelagos as a single group of islands, calling them wholly "*Bai Cat Vang*" (Golden Sandbank) or Hoang Sa[10] (a Sinicised name) or *Van ly Hoang Sa* (Tens of Thousands-*ly* Yellow Sand).[11] The Hoang Sa Islands were also found on *Giap Ngo binh nam do* (Map of the Pacified South in the Year of the Horse) drawn by Bui The Dat, a mandarin of the Nguyen court, in 1774.

Vietnam's most valuable historical reference in this regard is *Phu bien Tap luc* (*Miscellany Records on the Pacification of the Frontiers*) written by scholar Le Quy Don (1726–1784), who was appointed vice governor of Thuan Hoa in 1776. This work provides the most detailed description of the geographical location and natural conditions of the Hoang Sa Islands. Don describes in detail a wide range of the Hoang Sa fauna and flora, such as "sea swallows and their valuable nets," "elephant-ear conches," "mother of pearls, giant tortoises and variety of turtles and birds."[12] His narrative was the clearest and the most complete account of the Hoang Sa of this time.[13]

The Vietnamese were interested in these far-off, small islands primarily because of economic benefits. The Nguyen lords reportedly ordered the establishment of two maritime flotillas, called Hoang Sa and Bac Hai, to visit the islands regularly to collect goods, mainly jewellery, coins, guns and ammunition from shipwrecks.[14] The operation of the state-sponsored Hoang Sa and Bac Hai Flotillas was cited broadly as indications of the control that the Vietnamese state authorities had over the Paracel and Spratly Islands. So far, little reliable evidence has been found about the division of operating areas between the Hoang Sa and Bac Hai Flotillas. Some historians have argued that the Hoang Sa Flotilla might have operated in the area of Hoang Sa and the Bac Hai Flotilla further afield, including the Spratly area.[15]

Nguyen dynasty claimed the Paracels and Spratlys

The year of 1816 marked the first formal claim of the State of Vietnam over the Hoang Sa archipelago.[16] After Nguyen Anh (Gia Long) reunified the country in 1803 and declared himself emperor, he made an inventory of all the lands in the kingdom. The court's official historical records, especially *Dai Nam Thuc luc chinh bien* (*Annals of the Dai Nam Kingdom*) (see Figure 2.3), revealed that Emperor Gia Long paid special attention to the far offshore territories.[17] He ordered the resumption of the operation of the maritime flotillas and assigned four mandarins to be in charge of maritime exploitation. In 1816, the 15th year of the Gia Long reign, the emperor gave an order to the naval force and Hoang Sa Flotilla to sail to the so-called Hoang Sa archipelago to survey and map the islands and sea routes there.[18]

In 1833, the 14th year of the Minh Menh reign, Emperor Minh Menh ordered Bo Cong (the Ministry of Public Works) to erect a temple and a stele and plant trees on the islands as landmarks to help sea merchants and navigators avoid dangerous areas.[19] The order could not be fulfilled that year because of strong winds and rough sea. By 1835, Nguyen Van Nguyen and his subordinates had finished

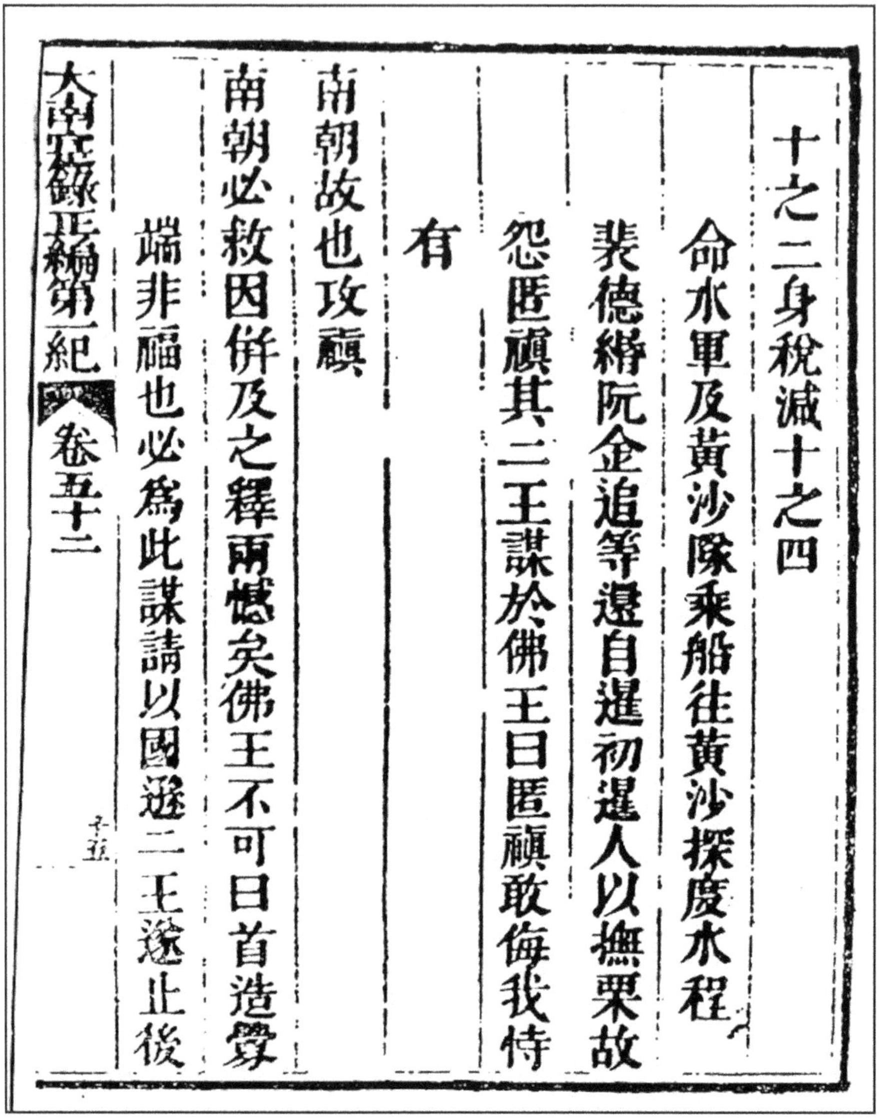
十之二身稅減十之四
命水軍及黃沙隊乘船往黃沙探度水程
裴德紳阮金追等還自暹初暹人以撫栗故
怨匿禛其二王謀於佛王曰匿禛敢侮我恃
有
南朝故也攻禛
南朝必救因併及之釋兩憾矣佛王不可曰首造釁
端非禛也必為此謀請以國遜二王遂止後
大南寔錄正編第二紀 卷五十二

Figure 2.3 A page about Hoang Sa Archipelago in Dai Nam Thuc luc Chinh bien (Chronicle of Greater Vietnam: main chapter), 1847

Volume 104

"In the eighth month, during the autumn, of the Quy Ty year, the 14th year of the Ming Menh Reign (1833) . . . His Majesty the Emperor told the Ministry of Public Works that: In the territorial waters of the Province of Quang Ngai, there is the Hoang Sa range. The water and the sky in that range cannot be distinguished from afar. Trading boats have recently become victims of its shoal. We shall prepare sampans, waiting until next year to go to the area for constructing temple, erecting stele, and planting many trees. Those trees will grow luxuriant in the future, thus serving as recognition remarks for people to avoid getting stranded in shoal. That shall benefit everyone forever."

Source: State Records Management and Archives Department of Vietnam

these assignments. Emperor Minh Menh then approved a proposal by Bo Cong to map the area and requested that Naval Commander Pham Huu Nhat lead a fleet to prepare large wooden posts to mark the places that had been inspected. Each wooden stele was engraved with following inscription:

> 17th year of the reign of Minh Menh by imperial order Commander of the Navy Pham Huu Nhat came to Hoang Sa for reconnaissance and to make topographical measurement and leaves this post as record of.[20]

The data gathered during these surveys was used to draw up the remarkable *Dai Nam Nhat thong Toan do* (*Detailed Complete Map of the Dai Nam*) which was completed about 1838 (see Figure 2.5). Although the locations of the archipelagos on the map were not as precise as those today, *Dai Nam Nhat thong Toan do* did mention close-to-shore islands and offshore islands of both Hoang Sa and Truong Sa by their names. It should be noted that imprecision was a problem, but that is common to all maps of that time. The map indicated that at this time, the Vietnamese had already realised the distinction between the Hoang Sa and Truong Sa archipelagos (see Figure 2.6).

Vietnamese historians draw on ample evidence of feudal state activities to prove Vietnam's actual administration of the Hoang Sa and Truong Sa Islands. In addition to the aforementioned sources, the Hanoi Han-Nom Institute holds dozens of official documents by the Nguyen court regarding activities in these areas.[21] Several historical and geographical books published in this period stated the same fact: that these offshore territories belonged to Quang Ngai Prefecture.[22] Besides, the Dang and Pham families in Ly Son Island off the central coast of Vietnam have preserved many official decrees by Emperor Minh Mang regarding the selection of personnel for the Hoang Sa Flotilla. The Vietnamese also referred to foreign historical maps and documents that recognised the Nguyen court's authority over the Hoang Sa and Truong Sa Islands.[23]

Drawing on these sources, the Vietnamese contended that Vietnam acquired the original title of sovereignty over the Paracels and Spratlys at least since the seventeenth century and consolidated it with the Nguyen dynasty's "systematic policy toward complete integration of the archipelago into the national community."[24] They clearly based their argument on state (imperial) authority and refuted China's argument based on the right of first discovery. In their view, Emperor Gia Long's proclamation in 1816 and a wide range of imperial decisions regarding the administration of the Hoang Sa and Truong Sa Islands represented the will of Vietnamese state authorities to act as sovereign. Also, the state-sponsored operations of the Hoang Sa and Bac Hai Flotillas, and a range of imperial measures to administer, defend and exploit the islands are presented as evidence of Vietnam's effective occupation in terms of regular presence and actual exercise of authority over these islands, even though the Vietnamese did not inhabit the islands on a permanent basis.[25] From the

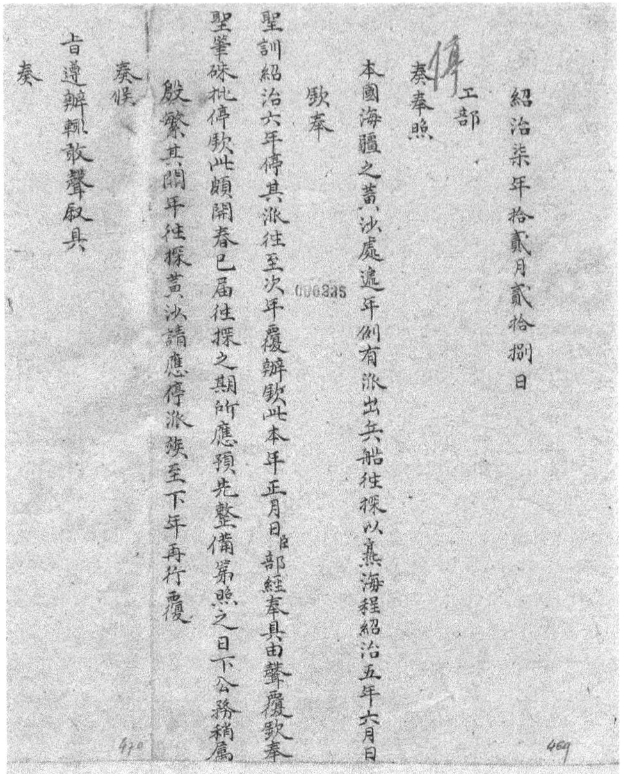
紹治柒年拾貳月貳拾捌日
工部
停
奏奉照
本國海疆之黃沙處遞年例有派出兵船往探以熟海程紹治五年六月日
欽奉
聖訓紹治六年停其派往至次年覆辦欽此本年正月日臣部經奉具由聲覆欽奉
聖筆硃批停欽此頃關春已屆往探之期所應預先整備第照之日下公務稍屬
殷繁其關年往探黃沙請應停派俟至下年再行覆
奏候
旨遵辦輒敢聲敘具
奏

Figure 2.4a, 2.4b A petition on Hoang Sa submitted to Emperor Thieu Tri, 1847

Date 28th December 1847,

7th Year off Thieu Tri's Reign

Reporter: Ministry of Public Works

Place of Archive: State Records Management and Archives Department of Vietnam

Reference: Volume 51, Sheet 235

The Ministry of Public Work would like to report as follows:

In accordance with the rules, Paracel Islands are part of our territory at sea, and imperial warships are sent annually to on a surveying mission to get used to the navigational routes. In June 1845, the 5th Year of Thieu Tri's Reign, following the order, the surveying mission to Paracels is to be postponed until next year when the request shall be submitted again and decided later. Please follow.

This year, the request was submitted again and was remarked by the King "to stop."

Now it is early spring, which is time to do the survey. We need to prepare everything in advance. However, considering that this is the very busy time of the year, we would like to request for a delay until next year, when the request shall be submitted again and decided later. Accordingly, we would like to report and request for an order for implementation.

Respectfully report,

Surveyed by Nguyen Huu Do

Drafted by Nguyen Truc

Read and approved by Nguyen Van Dien, Truong Quoc Dung, Nguyen Dinh Hung

Emperor's remark: Suspend.

Source: State Records Management and Archives Department of Vietnam

奏候
旨遵辦輒敢聲叙具
奏
臣阮有度奉攷
臣阮直奉草
臣阮文典臣張國用臣阮廷興奉閱

Figure 2.4a, 2.4b (Continued)

Vietnamese perspective, there was no reliable historical evidence that the Chinese state authority officially claimed, let alone occupied, the Paracels and Spratlys before 1909. Most Chinese maps published before 1909 depicted Hainan Island as the southernmost end of the Chinese empire.[26] The recent archaeological surveys of shipwrecks in the South China Sea found no evidence of Chinese participation in shipping to the Malay region before the eleventh century.[27]

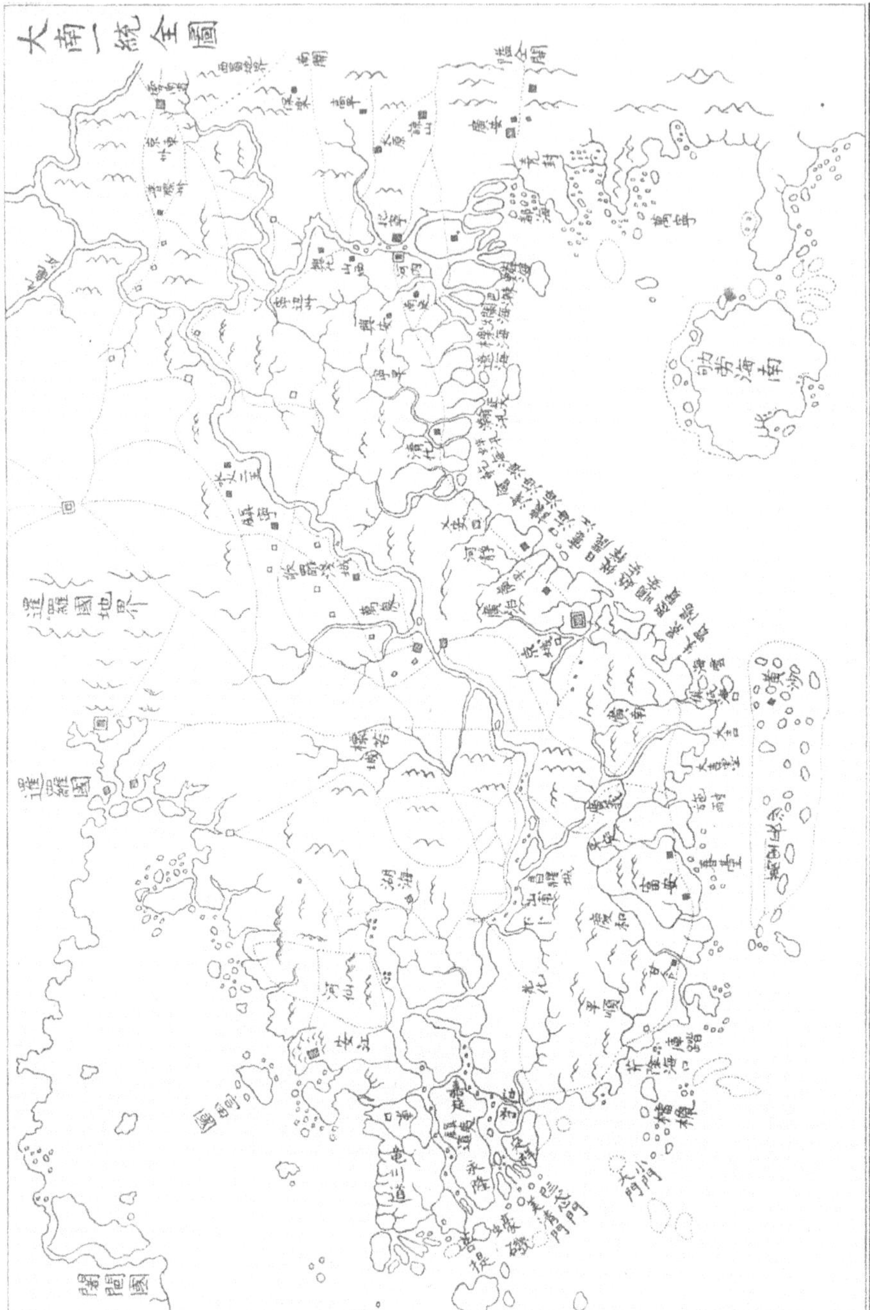

Figure 2.5 Dai Nam Thong nhat Toan do (complete Map of Unified Dai Nam), 1838

This map indicated that "Hoang Sa" and "Truong Sa," which are the easternmost groups of islands off the central coast, are Vietnamese territories. These islands were depicted to be further offshore compared to those near the central coast.

Source: Institute of Han-Nom Studies of Vietnam, Hanoi.

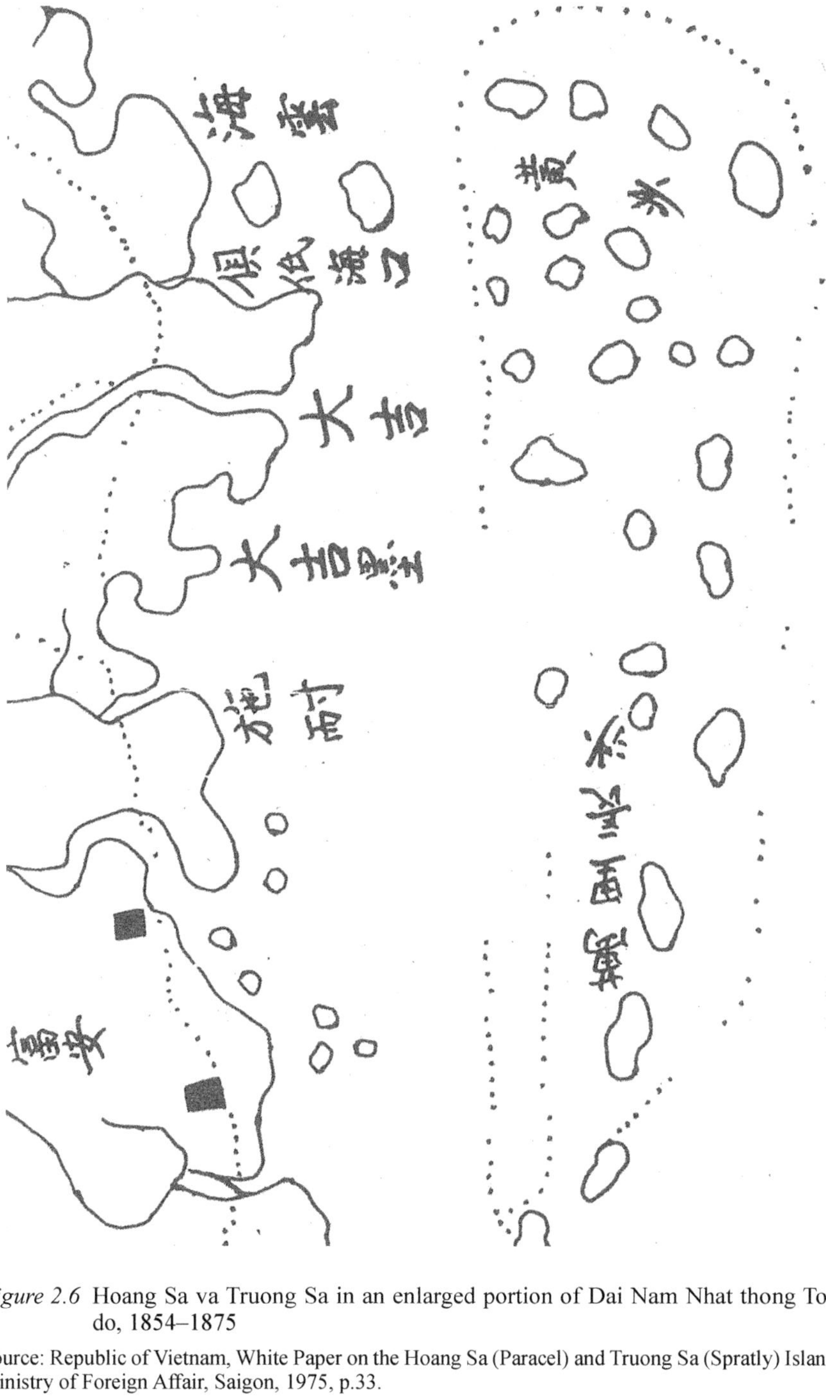

Figure 2.6 Hoang Sa va Truong Sa in an enlarged portion of Dai Nam Nhat thong Toan do, 1854–1875

Source: Republic of Vietnam, White Paper on the Hoang Sa (Paracel) and Truong Sa (Spratly) Islands, Ministry of Foreign Affair, Saigon, 1975, p.33.

Figure 2.7 A geographical *Imeri Anamitic* (Map of the Annam Empire), 1838

The map of the Annam Empire was published in 1838. In the map, Bishop Taberd depicts part of Paracels and notes "Paracel seu Cat Vang" (English: Paracels) for the islands farther than those near the shore of Central Viet Nam, corresponding to the area of the Paracel Islands nowadays.

Source: State Records Management and Archives Department of Vietnam

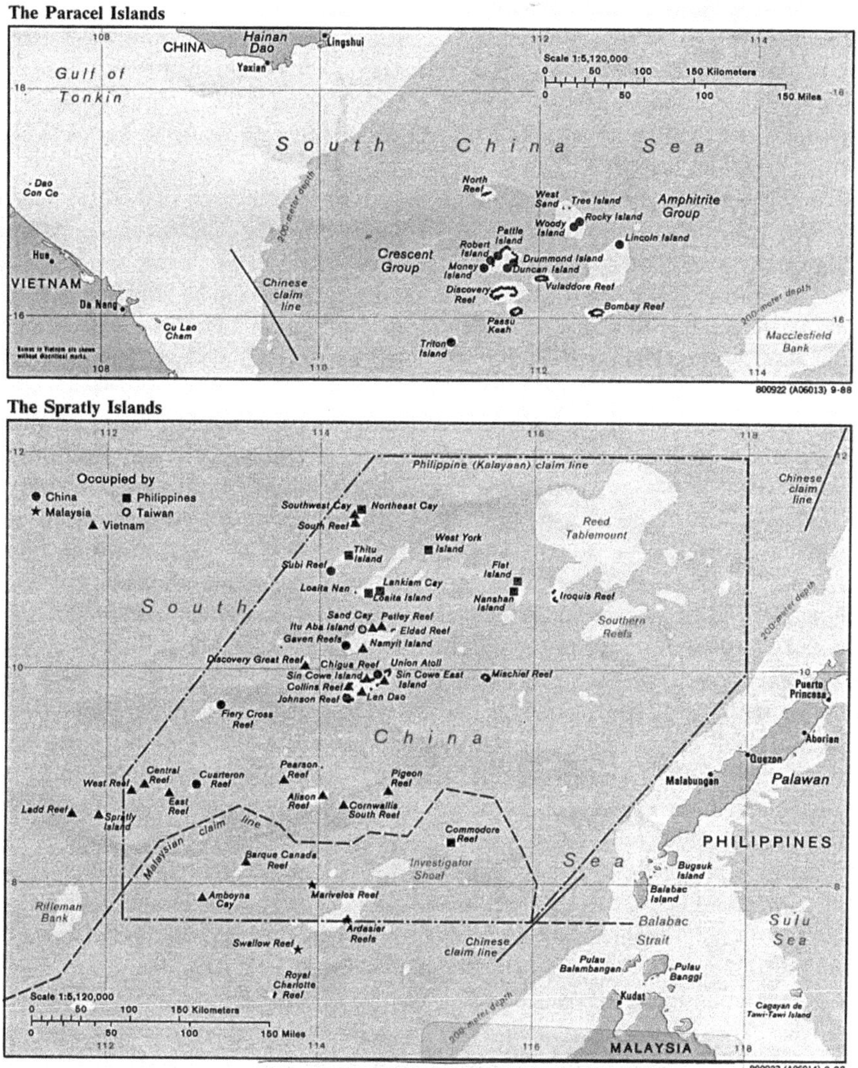

Figure 2.8 The Paracels and Spratlys

Source: CIA Maps.

French Indochina's occupation of the Paracel and Spratlys

France started their colonial quest in Vietnam in 1858 and gained control of the whole country by 1884. On 6 June 1884, the French and the Nguyen emperor signed the Treaty of French Protectorate, in which the state of Dai Nam recognised the protectorate regime of France. From this point of time, the French assumed the responsibility for governing and defending the entire Indochinese Union (including Cambodia and Laos). Although Nguyen rulers, sitting at Hue, were kept in place most of the time (until 1945), their roles were not important because actual military, administrative and diplomatic power was in the hands of French officials in both Indochina and in Paris. The Vietnamese argue that France, as a colonial state, had continued the exercise of sovereignty over the Paracels and Spratlys on their behalf.

The French, like other Europeans, were initially interested in far-off uninhabited and tiny islets of the Paracels and the Spratlys for the purpose of navigation. These areas were long considered as hazardous. In 1899, the governor general of the Indochinese Union, Paul Doumer, ordered a lighthouse to be built on the Paracels. However, due to a lack of funds, the project was halted.[28] The Sino-French Convention on the Delimitation of the Frontier between China and Tonkin, signed on 26 June 1887 as a result of the Sino-French War of 1884–1885, only mentioned the islands in the Gulf of Tonkin without any reference to the Paracels and Spratlys. By that time, Beijing had made no formal claim to the Paracels, and most of the Chinese maps portrayed Hainan Island as China's southernmost territory.

France's inattention of Annam's offshore territories allowed other countries to increase their presence there. Only after the incident of 1907, in which Japanese entrepreneur-adventurer Nishizawa Yoshiji and his subordinates landed on the nearby Pratas Island, did the Chinese become interested in the Paracels.[29] By the end of 1908, the governor general of Kwangtung sent Admiral Li Chun and Vice General Wu Ching-yung on an official expedition to the Paracels. In 1914, the Chinese published a map, titled "the New Geographical Atlas of the Republic of China," which was the first Chinese map drawing a line encompassing the Pratas and the Paracels.[30] Li Chun's expedition to the Paracel Islands was seen as the first formal claim to the Paracels on the part of China. However, the French officialdom did not take notice of this event because it was published only in the local news.[31]

Under the pressures from the Annam court in Hue, since 1925, French Indochina authorities paid greater attention to these offshore islands. A group of scientists from the Oceanographic Institute in Nha Trang was then sent to the Paracels for scientific research from 1925 and to the Spratlys from 1927. Reportedly, they found large guano/phosphate deposits on some islands.[32] France clearly stated its position over the Paracels on 4 December 1931 when its Foreign Ministry filed a protest against China's authorisation of guano mining in the Paracel Islands. In a note to the Chinese legation in Paris, France claimed the Paracels for Indochina on basis of the fact that Emperor Gia Long took possession of the Paracel Islands in 1816 and Emperor Minh Mang built a temple and a stone tablet on one island in 1835.[33] Seven months later, on 15 June 1932, the governor general of the Indochinese Union issued a decree that gave the Paracel Islands the name *Délégation des Paracels* and administratively incorporated them into Thua Thien Province, Annam.[34]

The French kept an eye on the Spratly archipelago when the Japanese consul in Hanoi asked French authorities about the legal status of the reefs and islands off the Philippine islands of Palawan in December 1927.[35] By then, the French were fearful that the Japanese might have some designs for these islands. On 13 April 1930, the French warship *Malicieuse* was sent to the Spratlys. The members of the expedition took formal possession of the islands on France's behalf. At first, the French did not claim over any specific islands but the whole area between the degrees of longitudes 111 East and 117 East, and latitudes 7 North and 12 North.[36] On 26 July 1933, the French government published a proclamation in the *Journal Officiel*, declaring sovereignty over six islands, namely Spratly, Amboyna Cay, Les Deux Iles, Loaita, and Thitu.[37] On 21 December 1933, governor of Cochin China, Mr. J. Krautheimer, officially incorporated the Spratly Islands into Ba Ria Province.[38] On the other side, China showed no interest in the Spratlys before the 1930s. The 1914 map did not include the Spratlys. In 1928, the Chinese authority set up a commission to investigate offshore islands. After surveying the maritime domain in the south of China, the commission issued a report that confirmed: "The Paracel archipelago is our nation's southernmost territory. However our people have paid it little attention."[39]

Since 1937, the French moved to establish a strong physical presence on the islands. In that year, Gauthier, the head of public works, went to the Paracels to examine locations for maritime and air traffic facilities and to explore the feasibility to build a lighthouse on Pattle Island. In 1938, the first detachment of Franco-Annamite civil guards arrived to establish an administrative office and to erect a weather station on Pattle Island. On 5 May 1939, Governor General Jules Brevié decided to divide the existing *délégation* into two compartments: *Délégation du Amphytrite et Dépendences* and *Délégation du Croissant et Dépendences*.[40] Two administrative offices were set up on Pattle and Woody Islands respectively.[41]

The French presence in the Paracel and Spratly Islands was apparently a move to pre-empt Japanese advancement into strategic waters surrounding Indochina. From 1936, there were clear signs that the Japanese were eyeing beyond Manchuria, Formosa and Pescadores to establish its mastery over the entire South China Sea. On 2 July 1937, the British Air Ministry advised that the Japanese were near Itu Aba Island of the Spratlys.[42] In the same month, the Sino-Japanese war broke out. By the end of the year, the Japanese already occupied Nanking, the capital city of Nanjing, China. Given the proximity of the Paracels and Spratlys to the coast of Vietnam, the French authorities in Indochina watched Japanese movements closely. A report written after a French warship's visit to the Paracels stated that although these islands had little commercial values, they could be used as a *jalon* (stepping stone) for Japanese expansion.[43] This drove the French officials in Paris and in Indochina to move quickly to take control of the islands before the Japanese. Indeed, when the Japanese declared to annex the Spratly Islands under the governor general of Taiwan, Paris immediately lodged a diplomatic protest.[44] Because the British shared the French concerns, they quickly joined Paris to oppose the Japanese claim to the Spratly Islands.[45]

The Paracels and Spratlys after the Second World War

During the Second World War, the South China Sea was almost entirely under Japanese control. After Japan's defeat in August 1945, the Paracel and Spratly Islands were left unoccupied. When the French frigate *Escarmouche* visited the

Paracel Islands in May 1946, it found no garrisons or military installations, only mass ruins.[46] After regaining control over Indochina, France quickly reasserted claim to the Paracels and Spratlys. A ministerial meeting held in Paris on 17 October 1946 came to the decision to establish a meteorological station on the Paracels as a sign of reoccupation. On 22 October, the Ministry of Overseas France advised High Commissioner Admiral Georges Thierry d'Argenlieu of the decision, reminding him again one month after, on 28 November.[47] However, beset with the First Indochina War that had broken out between French expeditionary forces and the Democratic Republic of Vietnam in Vietnam,[48] d'Argenlieu decided to defer the operation. On 4 January 1947, the first Kuomintang unit landed on Woody Island to fill the vacuum left after the war. On 10 January, a French reconnaissance plane confirmed the Chinese presence on the island. After being informed of the presence of the Kuomintang troops on Woody Island, the French Foreign Ministry in Paris issued a formal protest, which referred to the sovereign rights France is upholding on behalf of "Viet Nam."[49]

At this point, d'Argenlieu could not make any excuse for further delay. On 13 January 1947, a naval ship, *Le Tonkinois*, was dispatched to the Paracels. As the Chinese had already occupied Woody Island, the French set up a garrison on Pattle Island and tried in vain to persuade the Chinese to withdraw from Woody Island. France again proposed that the dispute should be brought to arbitration, but the government of Chiang Kai-shek refused this option.[50] The French did not proceed with coercive measures, perhaps for the fear that the Chinese would seek revenge by intervening in Indochina. Even when Chiang Kai-shek withdrew his troops from Woody Island in April 1950, France was still hesitant to fill in the vacuum. Woody Island was left unoccupied for five years until December 1955, when a group of soldiers from the People's Republic of China (PRC) landed on it. As for the Spratlys, in October 1946, a French warship, named the *Chevreud*,[51] visited Spratly Island and Itu Aba Island. On this occasion, a stone marker was erected on Itu Aba Island to assert French sovereignty.[52]

On 8 September 1951, the Treaty of San Francisco was concluded. Seven months later, Japan and the Republic of China (ROC) signed the Sino-Japanese Peace Treaty on 28 April 1952. Both texts ruled that Japan abdicated "all rights, title and claim to the Spratly Islands and to the Paracel Islands." Unlike the cases of Hainan and Taiwan, these treaties failed to specify who had sovereignty over the Paracels and Spratlys.[53] However, some developments during the San Francisco Conference shed some light on the position of other nations on the subsequent legal status of the Paracel and Spratly Islands. First, in August 1951, informed of the joint UK/US draft for the treaty, Zhou Enlai, the foreign minister of the PRC made public claims to the Paracels and Spratlys. Second, during the plenary session of the San Francisco Conference on 5 September 1951,[54] the Soviet Union representative Andrei Gromyko proposed an amendment that affirmed Japanese recognition of the PRC sovereignty over the Paracels and other islands further south. This amendment sponsored by the Soviet Union was rejected by forty-six votes to three, with one abstention. Poland and Czechoslovakia were the only other two countries to support the Soviet Union's amendment.[55] Third, during the

Seventh Plenary Session of the San Francisco Peace Conference on 7 September 1951, the State of Vietnam's Prime Minister Tran Van Huu stated: "As we must frankly profit from all the opportunities offered to us to stifle the germs of discord, we affirm our right to the Spratly and Paracel Islands, which have always belonged to Vietnam."[56] No protests were registered after his statement.

South Vietnam took over the Paracels and Spratlys

The Geneva Accords on 21 July 1954 put an end to the First Indochina War. Under the related agreements, all the signatories, including Cambodia, the Democratic Republic of Vietnam (DRV), France, Laos, China, the State of Vietnam (South Vietnam), the Soviet Union and the UK, agreed to the cessation of hostilities and foreign involvements in Indochina.[57] They all were committed to respecting the independence and territorial integrity of the three Indochinese states, namely Vietnam, Laos and Cambodia. The agreements also stipulated that Vietnam was temporarily partitioned at the 17th parallel and awaited reunification on the basis of a nationwide free election to be held in July 1956.[58]

However, the Geneva Accord failed to bring long-lasting peace and reunification to Vietnam. The two Vietnamese regimes, the DRV in the north and the State of Vietnam (later evolving into the Republic of Vietnam) in the south could not reach any agreement on reunification. In August 1959, the Second Indochina War broke out between the DRV-backed National Liberation Front (NLF) and the US-backed Republic of Vietnam (RVN) in the south.[59] As a result, between 1956 and 1975, Vietnam was de facto divided into two states with separate governments. The DRV was diplomatically recognised by the socialist bloc while the RVN gained political support of the United States and other capitalist countries.

During this period, the offshore islands in the Paracels and Spratlys were under the administration of South Vietnam. On 14 October 1950, the administration of the Paracel Islands was officially returned to South Vietnam, though a French garrison was maintained there until 1956. On this occasion, Central Vietnam Governor Pham Van Giao travelled in person to Pattle Island to preside over the ceremony of taking over the offshore territories. In April 1956, when the French troops completely withdrew from Indochina, South Vietnam dispatched a military detachment to Spratly Island to take over the defence of the archipelago.[60]

South Vietnam's occupation of the Paracels and Spratlys did not go unchallenged. In December 1957, Chinese People's Liberation Army's forces quietly landed on Woody Island after the Kuomintang troops deserted. By the time the South Vietnamese noticed Chinese intrusion into the Paracels, the Chinese already controlled Woody and Lincoln Islands.[61] In spite of South Vietnam's official protests, China continued their presence there. Consequently, the Paracels were de facto divided into two parts, the western part (called as the Crescent Group) under the RVN's control and the eastern part (called as the Amphitrite Group) under the Chinese occupation. In the meantime, the situation in the Spratlys became even more complicated with the emergence of a new claimant, the Philippines. In March 1956, a crew of Filipino maritime activists led by two brothers, Thomas and Filemon Cloma, visited a number of Spratly Islands, which they believed to be *res nullius* (nobody's land). They later proclaimed these islands a new *Kalaya'an* (Freedomland). Cloma's map of *Kalaya'an* encompassed the major Spratly Islands, including Spratly, Itu Aba, Nam Yit and Thi Tu, and other reefs and shoals in the south of the Spratlys.[62] In May, Cloma made public his "discovery" and demanded the government of the Philippines support the claim.[63] However, it was not until 1971 that the Philippine government issued a formal claim to the sovereignty over sixty islets, reefs and atolls of the Spratly archipelago on historical, economic and security grounds. They maintained that the Kalaya'an Islands were not part of the Spratlys and therefore, did not belong to any country when the Cloma brothers discovered them.[64]

Alerted by China's creeping occupation of the Amphitrite Group and the Philippine claim to the Spratlys, South Vietnam reasserted its claim and consolidated its control over the Paracel and Spratly Islands. On 1 June 1956, South Vietnam's minister of foreign affairs restated the "rightful position" of Vietnam and referred to the implicit support for Vietnam's statement at the San Francisco Conference in 1951. South Vietnam's naval forces also intensified patrols in the waters around the Paracels and Spratlys to provide a defence for the islands. On 22 February 1959, the South Vietnamese Navy reportedly encountered another Chinese operation, in which more than eighty Chinese "soldiers," disguised as fishermen, covertly disembarked on Cam Tuyen, Duy Mong and Quang Hoa Islands in the Paracel archipelago.[65] The RVN's naval forces arrested these fishermen and took them to Da Nang. In the Spratly archipelago, in 1961, two South Vietnamese warships, *Van Kiep* and *Van Don*, landed on Song Tu Tay, Thi Tu, Loai Ta and An Bang Islands. In 1962, South Vietnamese cruisers *Tuy Dong* and *Tay Ket* visited Spratly and Nam Yit Islands. In 1963, the crews of three ships, *Huong Giang*, *Chi Lang* and *Ky Hoa*, erected the Vietnamese steles of sovereignty on Spratly, An Bang, Thi Tu, Loai Ta, Song Tu Dong and Song Tu Tay Islands. However, the frequency of patrols and visits to the islands were later reduced due to the intensified conflict in South Vietnam.[66]

South Vietnam strengthened its position on the islands by economic activities. Between 1956 and 1960, its authorities granted at least three licenses for phosphate/guano exploitation in the Paracels. However, the phosphate business halted in 1963 because it was unprofitable.[67] In 1961, the first civilian administrator, Nguyen Ba Thuoc, was appointed to the Paracel Islands, which were transferred from the jurisdiction of Thua Thien Province back to Quang Nam just one month later. But, after 1963, all administrative officers assigned to the Paracel Islands had always been military men "due to war condition on the mainland." Accordingly, the headquarters of the Vietnamese administration was transferred to Duncan Island, the island hosting the Regional Forces.[68]

In the early 1970s, tensions over the Spratly Islands increased because of two factors: the "petroleum incentive" and new legal order of the ocean emerging from the United Nations–sponsored negotiations on the law of the sea. From the mid-1950s, British and American oil companies expressed an interest in oil exploration in the Spratly area. Initial seismic surveys carried out in late 1969 revealed the possibility of commercial oil being found throughout the region. While South Vietnam was constrained by war, the Philippines proceeded with test drillings in an area 50 miles west of Palawan Island, or roughly 100 miles from the eastern edge of the Spratlys in March 1971. The test drill results confirmed the existence of tertiary rock formation and suitable reservoir structures on the continental shelf off Palawan.[69] In the broader context, the oil shock in 1973 no doubt heightened the awareness of states of energy security and forced them to seek additional supplies.

The negotiations on the law of the sea started in 1956 and gained momentum in the 1960s and 1970s. Between 1962 and 1968, four conventions took effect, namely the Geneva Convention on Territorial Sea and Contiguous Zones; on the Continental Shelf; on the High Seas; and on Fishing and Conservation of the Living Resources of the High Seas. December 1973 witnessed the opening of the Third United Nations Conference on the Law of the Sea (1973–1982), in which the Second Committee specifically dealt with issues of national jurisdiction, including territorial seas, exclusive economic zones (EEZ), continental shelves, straits, archipelagos and fishing. The discussion within the framework of the Third UN Conference disclosed the possibility of extending national jurisdiction over living and non-living resources within the EEZ and continental shelf. Kenya proposed the creation of a 200 n.m. EEZ as early as 1972.[70] This development increased the value of offshore territories because islands may be entitled to extensive EEZ and continental shelves if the related propositions were adopted.

Significant developments in the negotiations on the Law of the Sea and the possibility of tapping into seabed energy sources elevated the significance of the offshore, tiny and barren islets in the South China Sea and consequently triggered a new round of assertion of sovereignty claims, aggressive actions and reactions. In 1971, the Philippines officially declared that Kalaya'an belonged to the Philippines almost at the same time that the possibility of extracting oil within the area was raised. The Filipino Navy quickly moved to occupy Nanshan (Vinh Vien), Northeast Cay (Song Tu Dong), Loaita (Loai Ta) and Thitu (Thi Tu) Islands in the Spratly archipelago in July of that year.[71] South Vietnam itself conducted oil exploration between 1969 and 1971 and granted some concessions to foreign oil firms in July 1973. In January 1974, China took decisive military action to invade the South Vietnam–held Crescent Group in the Paracels. Caught up by the war against the North, South Vietnam was not capable of regaining these islands. It therefore resorted to the legal instrument to voice official protests over the violation of Vietnamese sovereignty.

South Vietnam's loss of the Paracels in January 1974

Before January 1974, the Paracel archipelago was divided into two parts, the China-controlled Amphitrite Group in the east and South Vietnam–held Crescent Group in the west. In the Amphitrite Group, Chinese command was based in Woody Island, while the Vietnamese headquarters was located on Duncan Island in the Crescent Group. From 1951 to 1972, there were no records of significant skirmishes between Chinese and South Vietnamese forces except the South

Vietnamese navy's arrest of eighty-two Chinese fishermen who secretly landed on Duncan Island. China responded with strong protests and the threat of stiff resistance to defend China's territorial waters.[72] Despite its rhetoric of coercive retaliation, the PRC did not take military action.

On 15 January 1974, Chinese troops landed and hoisted flags on Robert (Huu Nhat), Money (Quang Anh), Duncan (Quang Hoa) and Drummond (Duy Mong) Islands of the Crescent Group.[73] The RVN Ministry of Foreign Affairs held a press conference on the following day to strongly condemn China's violation of Vietnam's sovereignty. South Vietnam's observer at the United Nations also reported the Chinese aggression to the president of the UN Security Council. On 19 January, Chinese naval frigates opened fire at the Vietnamese cruiser Tran Khanh Du. On 20 January, the Chinese forces from Woody Island and reinforcements from Hainan conducted a heavy bombardment of key Paracel islands and moved to occupy them. By the end of the month, China took hold of the entire Crescent Group completely. The South Vietnamese troops had no option but to retreat to the south to reinforce their defence of the Spratlys. Just prior to its fall in April 1975, the RVN government made public a white paper reaffirming its sovereignty over the Paracels and Spratlys and condemning China for its unlawful acts.

On the other side, China blamed the RVN forces for making the first move to attack innocent Chinese fishermen on Robert, Money and Duncan Islands, and claimed that Chinese forces reacted to defend them. The Chinese account seemed less convincing, since these islands had been under full control of the Saigon forces since 1956. Other sources suggested that China's Paracel operations had been premeditated and carefully prepared for some time.[74] Bill Hayton argues that the operation was ordered by Chinese top leaders, Mao Zedong and Zhou Enlai, as a step to strengthen China's defence of the southern coast and open the door for oil exploration around the Paracels.[75]

The timing of the Paracel operation revealed Chinese opportunism. China deliberately took action at a time when the Saigon regime's physical force and spiritual strength were seriously weakened by the withdrawal of the US combat forces and the Viet Cong offensives on almost all fronts. Most importantly, the US abandonment of its South Vietnamese ally after the 1972 Paris Peace Accords resulted in a vacuum in the South China Sea. The Nixon trip to Beijing in February 1972 prevented Washington from taking drastic actions against China. By playing the China card against the Soviet Union and North Vietnam, Richard Nixon and Henry Kissinger chose to play "a neutral game" in the conflict between South Vietnam and China in the Paracels. As a matter of fact, when Saigon asked the US for assistance to counter the Chinese offensives, the Nixon administration refused and ordered the 7th Fleet to move away from disputed area.[76]

For their parts, the DRV and the Provisional Revolutionary Government (PRG) in South Vietnam, whose predecessor was the National Liberation Front, implicitly opposed the Chinese aggression. Given their delicate relations with and reliance on the PRC, they refrained from openly challenging Beijing. In connection with the Paracel incident, Tran Binh, the PRG spokesman based in Beijing, carefully stated:

> The question of sovereignty over territory is a sacred issue for every people. As to problems of conflict over territories bequeathed by history, these are complex questions that need careful examination. This problem – the Paracels incident – must be solved by peaceful negotiations on the basis of equality, mutual respects and friendship.[77]

The DRV representative in New Delhi spoke along the same lines: "the question of sovereignty over the Paracel Islands needed a careful examination of history and ought to be settled on the basis of mutual respect and equality."[78] Though they were carefully worded, these statements expressed an unspoken disagreement with the PRC military actions.

The events of January 1974 prompted animosity in Hanoi towards Beijing. Hanoi's leaders seemed surprised at the Chinese attacks, which occurred on 19 January 1974, just one day after the PRC agreed to negotiate with the DRV on the delimitation in the Gulf of Tonkin.[79] The rift between Hanoi and Beijing could be traced back to the 1954 Geneva Accords negotiations, where Chinese Prime Minister Zhou Enlai supported the French proposal for a divided Vietnam behind Hanoi's back. Hanoi refrained from open criticism of Chinese action since Beijing's support was still indispensable for its cause of reunification. Nevertheless, anti-China nationalism had grown significantly after the "ping-pong diplomacy," in which China reportedly colluded with the US at the expense of its Vietnamese communist ally. Hanoi's leaders realised that North Vietnam had been no more than a pawn in Beijing's game and that China had assisted Vietnam because of its own strategic interests rather than because of the ideal of socialist solidarity.

The Paracels incident shattered Hanoi's illusion of "brothers plus comrades" and awakened its concern of Chinese expansionism.[80] North Vietnamese leaders then came to the conclusion that the Chinese invasion of these islands must have been "premeditated" as part of a master scheme to take control of the entire South China Sea and subdue Vietnam in the long run. They also believed that this unlawful act could not be executed without a green light from the US.[81] On 5–6 May 1975, only five days after the fall of the Saigon regime, the DRV's naval forces rushed to take over six South Vietnamese positions on Spratly Island (Dao Truong Sa), Sandy Cay (Dao Son Ca), Southwest Cay (Dao Song Tu Tay), Nam yit Island (Dao Nam Yet), Sin Cowe Island (Dao Sinh Ton) and Amboyna Cay (Dao An Bang), and deployed troops on some other islands of the Spratly archipelago.[82] It was basically a strategic move to pre-empt Chinese expansionism into the Spratly area.

Unified Vietnam's claims to the Paracels and Spratlys

After the fall of Saigon in April 1975, the northern and southern halves of Vietnam were united under communist rule. The DRV and PRG merged to form a single socialist government, which was officially named the Socialist Republic of Vietnam (SRV). Claiming a leadership role in the unified Vietnam, the CPV then faced the pressing need of forging national unity in the country that had just undergone prolonged war. In this light, defending the country's offshore territories, which belonged to South Vietnam before, became both a strategic and political necessity for consolidating the CPV leadership. That motivated the united Vietnam to reassert South Vietnam's claims over the Paracel and Spratly archipelagos.

After reunification, Hanoi departed from its customary passive position, openly asserting Vietnam's sovereignty over the Paracel and Spratly archipelagos. In an official meeting on 25 September 1975, Vietnamese party chief Le Duan officially raised the status of the Paracel and Spratly Islands with Chinese Vice Premier Deng Xiaoping. During the talk, Deng Xiaoping admitted, "Between us exist the disputes over the Xisha and Nansha . . . Certainly, these issues can be discussed later."[83] Before that, on 5–6 May 1975, the delegation of the Provisional Revolutionary Government in South Vietnam to the Colombo Meteorological Conference requested the World Meteorological Organization to continue to recognise Vietnam's meteorological station, No.48.860, on the Hoang Sa Islands and opposed China's registration for its station there.[84] On 11 November, Hanoi sent a note to Beijing, reaffirming Vietnam's sovereignty over the Paracel and Spratly archipelagos and reminded it of Deng Xiaoping's statement. It also called for a suspension of Chinese publicity campaigns on the Paracel and Spratly issues pending negotiations. Between 1975 and 1976, Vietnam consolidated its grip on the Spratlys by extending its occupation over seven other islands, bringing to thirteen the number of islands under its control. Hanoi also strengthened its defensive posture on five key islands and built an airstrip 500 m long on Spratly Island.[85] At the same time, Hanoi called for negotiations to resolve the disputes and promised not to use force. This position was also articulated in a number of official notes sent by Hanoi to Manila and Kuala Lumpur and in important meetings between its senior officials and foreign counterparts.

The SRV's claims were disputed by other coastal states, of which China appeared the greatest challenger. The disputed status of the islands had produced an intense war of words between Hanoi and Beijing after the DRV took over the South Vietnamese positions in the Spratly archipelago. In the sea, China was reported to increase incursions into the Spratly areas.[86] The disputes made relations worse as the two sides escalated propaganda and rhetoric surrounding their claims. The diplomats of the two sides met each other in October 1977 to discuss the border issues, but apparently the meeting was merely an exchange of charges and irredentist claims. Indeed, at a time when the two countries were on a collision course, the tension over the status of these two archipelagos could not be eased down.

The offshore islands were just one among many disputes between Hanoi and Beijing after 1975, which reinforced one another to strain relations to the point of exploding. Land border clashes became more frequent. Hanoi reported that the number of intrusions along its northern border rose from 179 incidents in 1974, to 294 in 1975, 812 in 1977 and 2,175 in 1978.[87] China's assistance to Vietnam had been cut off since February 1977, even at a time when Vietnam faced a severe scarcity of food in 1976 and 1977 due to harsh weather conditions.[88] This assistance was reportedly diverted to Cambodia in support of the Khmer Rouge regime. China's alleged collusion with Pol Pot's forces, which frequently infringed on Vietnam's southwestern border, worried Hanoi's leaders.

After the border war in early 1979, Vietnam viewed China as an enemy and an expansionist. On 15 March 1979, Hanoi released a memorandum on the facts of the Vietnam-China border issue. Point 9 condemned the Chinese authorities' blatant use of force to take hold of the Paracels illegally in January 1974.[89] In October, Hanoi published a white paper titled "Facts about Vietnam-China Relations over the Past 30 Years," which reviewed the history of Vietnam-China relations from Hanoi's perspective. The paper pointed out three betrayals of the Chinese authorities to the Vietnamese people and sharply criticised China's hegemonic and expansionist policy.[90] At the same time, another white paper specifically covering the issue of the Paracels and Spratlys was released. Under the title "Vietnam's Sovereignty over the Hoang Sa and Truong Sa Archipelagos," the paper presented a full history of the establishment and development of Vietnam's rights over these offshore islands. As Mark Albert Hoyts opined, the paper was "in essence a replica of the South Vietnamese 1975 'White Paper on the Hoang Sa (Paracel) and Truong Sa (Spratly) Islands', with an additional chronology of events listed at the conclusion."[91] In this paper, Hanoi recognised Saigon's actions and claims and took them as evidence of the exercise of Vietnamese sovereignty over the two groups of islands. In January 1980, China published its own white paper, titled "China's Indisputable Sovereignty over the Xisha and Nansha Islands," which presented the Chinese perspectives on historical use and occupation of the South China Sea features. The Vietnamese then answered with a second white paper, titled "The Hoang Sa and Truong Sa Archipelagos: Vietnamese Territories" in 1981. The second white paper refuted China's arguments and evidence.[92]

In the 1980s, Vietnam faced other claimants' expansions in the Spratly area. Though repeating its claims to both Paracel and Spratly archipelagos on several occasions, Taiwan confined its occupation to Itu Aba Island. The Philippines moved to occupy Lamkian Cay (Da Lan Can) in March 1978 and Commodore Reef (Da Cong Do) in August 1980, increasing its holdings from six to eight islands.[93] Malaysia became a disputant in October 1978 when the Malaysian Prime Minister Hussein Onn raised the issue of Amboyna Cay (Dao An Bang) during a meeting with his Vietnamese counterpart, Pham Van Dong.[94] On 21 December 1979, Malaysia published a map of the Malaysian Exclusive Economic Zone and continental shelf, which showed Vietnam-claimed Amboyna Cay, Barque Canada Reef (Da Thuyen Chai) and Commodore Reef within maritime zones claimed by Malaysia.[95] Malaysian troops then moved to occupy Swallow Reef (Hoa Lau) in June 1983, and Mariveles Reef (Da Ky Van) and Ardasier Reef (Da Kieu Ngua) in December 1986.[96] Hanoi responded to these expansions with diplomatic protests.

The 1988 skirmish in the Spratlys

Though a military build-up occurred across the Spratly archipelago throughout the early 1980s, no clashes occurred between Vietnam, Malaysia and the Philippines. In almost all meetings, their leaders vowed to settle the disputes through peaceful means. Since 1984, Vietnam became increasingly concerned as China showed an interest in occupying the Spratly Islands.[97] In December 1985, Chinese Communist

Party (CCP) chief Hu Yaobang made a high-profile visit to the Paracels. Chinese warships reportedly increased patrols and exercises around the Spratlys area.[98] In April 1987, under the pretext of a UNESCO mandate to establish observation posts in the Spratlys, the Chinese organised a scientific expedition to conduct extensive surveys in the area.[99] In June 1987, the Chinese authorities announced it would incorporate Spratly Islands into the new province of Hainan. By the end of 1987, Chinese forces were ready to fight to establish their first foothold in the Spratlys.[100]

Throughout January and February 1988, Chinese warships and construction boats were reportedly present near Fiery Cross Reef (Da Chu Thap) and Cuarteron Reef (Da Chau Vien) and obstructed Vietnam's freighters. Chinese troops also landed on these two reefs to build houses and plant flags.[101] Facing imminent Chinese expansionist attempts, Vietnam proceeded to occupy Barque Canada Reef (Da Thuyen Chai) in April 1987 and four other islets in the first two months of 1988. By February, Hanoi controlled eighteen features of the Spratly archipelago. Two days after the Chinese seized the Cuarteron Reef, just 19 km from the nearest Vietnamese occupation, on 18 February 1988, the spokesman of the Ministry of Foreign Affairs reaffirmed Vietnam's sovereignty over the Spratlys and condemned "China's incursion into Vietnamese waters" and "its acts of provocation." An excerpt of the statement reads:

> Following a series of violations of Vietnamese territory at the Truong Sa archipelago by the Chinese navy in recent years such as reconnaissance, surveying, military exercise and erecting of stone markers, the recent illegal acts have clearly revealed that the Chinese's authorities intention to violate Vietnamese territorial sovereignty, thus seriously jeopardizing the security of Vietnam and other nations on the rim of the South China Sea and creating tension and instability in Southeast Asia. These acts lie in the framework of the Chinese authorities' long-standing scheme of violating Vietnamese territory and expanding in the South China Sea.[102]

Vietnam tried to build up political support for its case internally and externally. A number of Vietnamese organisations, such as the Youth Union, the Vietnam Students' Association and the Vietnam Lawyers' Association, rallied to protest against China's actions. Vietnam also called for support from the UN and its members. A statement on Chinese violation of Vietnamese sovereignty in the Spratlys by the SRV's Foreign Ministry had been distributed at the UN. Cambodia, as Vietnam's closest ally, responded with a statement from the Foreign Ministry, voicing concerns over China's aggressive actions.[103]

All these measures proved insufficient to deter the Chinese Navy from acting. On 14 March 1988, violent clashes were reported. Vietnamese sources stated that Chinese vessels "flagrantly" opened fire on three Vietnamese cargo vessels near Johnson Reef (Da Gac Ma), Collins Reef (Da Co Lin), and Lansdowne Reef (Da Le Dao). The Chinese troops landed on Johnson Reef to remove a Vietnamese flag, planting a Chinese flag in its place. The Chinese troops opened fire on unarmed Vietnamese personnel on the reef.[104] Seventy-four Vietnamese soldiers were killed.[105] The Chinese were also accused of interdicting Vietnamese attempts to rescue survivors and damaged vessels. The Chinese account justified the action by saying that it was the Vietnamese ships that provoked the Chinese ships, which were then "forced to counter-attack in self-defence."[106]

The brief naval skirmish exposed the weakness of Vietnamese naval power vis-à-vis that of China. Much to Hanoi's discontent, its Soviet ally was unwilling to provide more than verbal support despite the November 1978 Treaty of Mutual Defence.[107] The Soviet naval units based in Cam Ranh did not make any intervention during the skirmish. Understandably, the Soviet Union also faced tremendous difficulties at home with its reforms and scaled down its commitments abroad. Without the support of the Soviet Union, Vietnam could not match China in terms of naval power. Consequently, China successfully made headway into the Spratly area, establishing a foothold on six Spratly reefs, namely Fiery Cross Reef, Cuarteron Reef, Johnson Reef, Hughes Reef (Da Tu Nghia), Gaven Reef (Da Gaven) and Subi Reef (Da Xu Bi). Right after occupying these islets, China started to build military installations there.[108]

Though Vietnam was unable to regain these islands, it had shown its determination to block further Chinese expansion. Thirty Vietnamese ships of various sizes were reportedly deployed to the disputed area by early April 1988.[109] In May, Vietnamese Minister of Defence Le Duc Anh sailed to the Spratly Islands to review troops and vowed to defend the islands. He declared:

> We vow before the souls of our ancestors and those carders and combatants who sacrificed their lives for the fatherland, we pledge with compatriots nationwide, and we will tell our posterity that we are determined to defend at all costs our beloved fatherland and the Truong Sa Archipelago – part of our beloved fatherland's sacred land and territorial waters.[110]

This strongly worded statement indicated that "Vietnam was not going to let the disputed islands go without a fight."[111] In the meantime, Vietnam extended its grip to three new islets, bringing the number of islands under its control to twenty-one. Housing facilities for newly reinforced troops on Spratly Island were also constructed.[112]

Yet, Hanoi evidently preferred non-violent alternatives to military confrontation in response to the crisis. While strongly condemning the Chinese authorities' provocative acts and illegal occupation of Vietnamese territories, the Vietnamese Ministry of Foreign Affairs called for self-restraint and proposed talks between two sides on at least three occasions after the clash.[113] As China did not accept its proposal, Hanoi then brought the case to the UN. Four days after the clash, Nguyen Binh Thanh, acting head of the Vietnamese mission to the UN, met with UN Secretary-General Perez de Cuellar to voice Vietnam's protest with the Chinese actions. In April, Thanh sent another statement to the UN secretary-general, opposing China's decision to put the Paracel and Spratly archipelagos under Hainan's jurisdiction and accused China of violating the UN ban on the use or threat to use of force. By the end of April 1988, Hanoi published a white paper, titled "The Hoang Sa and Truong Sa Archipelagos and International Law." The paper again accused Chinese of illegal use of force to occupy Vietnam's offshore islands on three occasions, in 1956, 1974 and 1988. Despite its strong language, the paper called for "the settlement of all disputes between two countries, including the one concerning the two archipelagos, through peaceful negotiation" in its final section.[114]

Vietnam's law-of-the-sea claims

In the post-war period, the sense of insecurity and vulnerability had driven unified Vietnam to seek the control of the littoral areas off the country's mainland coast. The memories of foreign invasions and resistance wars were still fresh. The consecutive struggles for national independence against more powerful adversaries shaped its natural instinct of insecurity. Most importantly, Vietnam was facing extreme hostilities from China, the US and the ASEAN countries after its military interventions into Cambodia in 1979. In addition, Vietnam was also interested in offshore hydrocarbon and fishery to rebuild its economy, which was devastated by the war. Against that backdrop, the defence of the coastal areas and offshore islands became increasingly important. With the assistance by the Soviet Union, Vietnam had a large naval force in Southeast Asia by the mid-1980s. However, its navy was overstretched due to an extensive coastline with ten naval bases from the north to the south. Still, its naval firepower was no match for the Chinese navy.[115]

Given its limited naval capabilities and the lack of strategic depth, Vietnam seized the opportunity brought by the emerging oceanic order to back up its efforts to expand its jurisdiction seaward. In light of the United Nations–sponsored negotiations on the law of the sea, Hanoi issued unilateral law-of-the-sea claims in two key legislations, namely the 12 May 1977 Statement on the Territorial Sea, Contiguous Zone, Exclusive Economic Zone and Continental Shelf (latter referred as the 1977 Statement) and the 12 November 1982 Declaration on Baseline of the Territorial Waters of the SRV (later referred as the 1982 Declaration). The 1977 statement's wording and stipulation closely followed the Revised Single Negotiating Text, which was the product of the fourth UNCLOS session in 1976. The 1982 declaration was adopted just after the closure of UNCLOS negotiations when most of the disagreements among negotiating states had been settled. The signature of UNCLOS 1982 was hailed in Vietnam "as an important turning point that allowed the country expanded eastward vigorously on the basis of international law."[116]

Vietnam's initial maritime claims reflected a maximalist policy that put a premium on to furthering its sovereignty and jurisdiction. Although Vietnam's legislation was generally in line with international law, there were three claims that prompted disapprovals from other states. First, Vietnam claimed a full set of maritime zones, including territorial sea, contiguous zone, EEZ, and continental shelf, not only for its mainland, but also for its offshore islands.[117] If so, this claim could be interpreted that Vietnam considered the Spratlys and Paracel features as full-fledged islands that were entitled to EEZ and continental shelves of their own. It should be noted that article 121 of UNCLOS makes a distinction between islands and rocks. An island, which itself can sustain human habitation or economic life, has capacity of generating the exclusive economic zone and continental shelf of its own. Rocks are only entitled to 12 n.m. territorial sea. It is still very controversial whether remote, barren Spratly and Paracel insular features can be qualified as "islands."

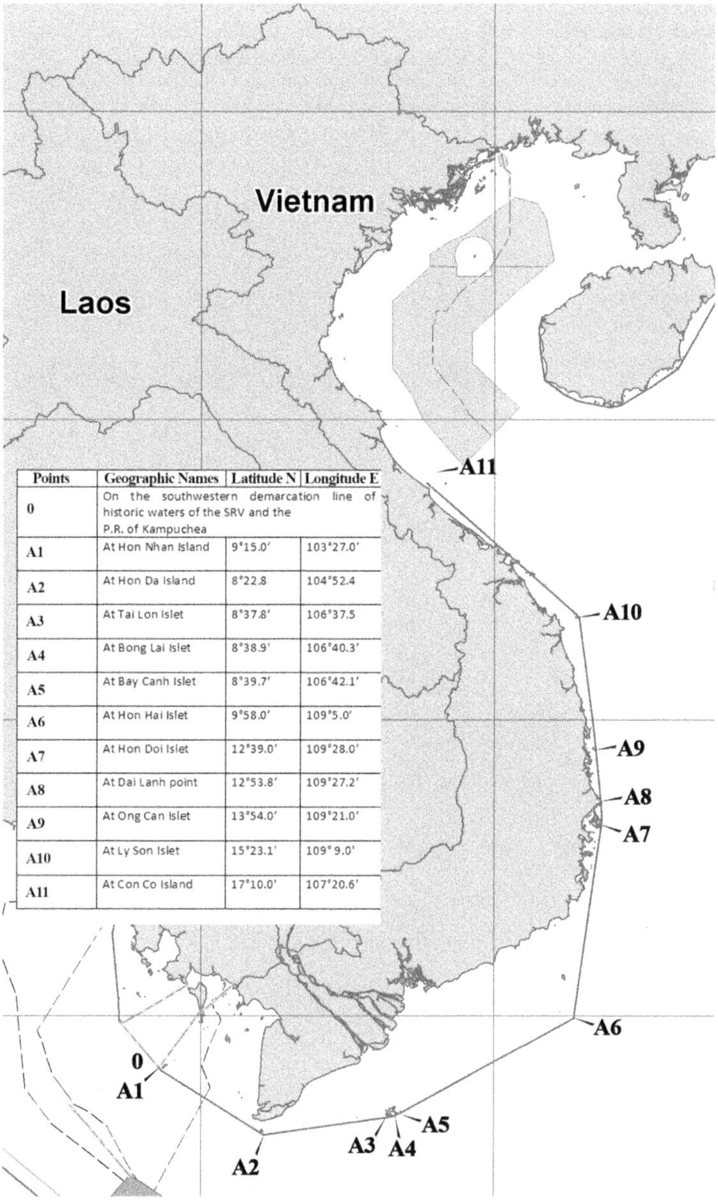

Points	Geographic Names	Latitude N	Longitude E
0	On the southwestern demarcation line of historic waters of the SRV and the P.R. of Kampuchea		
A1	At Hon Nhan Island	9°15.0′	103°27.0′
A2	At Hon Da Island	8°22.8	104°52.4
A3	At Tai Lon Islet	8°37.8′	106°37.5
A4	At Bong Lai Islet	8°38.9'	106°40.3′
A5	At Bay Canh Islet	8°39.7′	106°42.1′
A6	At Hon Hai Islet	9°58.0′	109°5.0′
A7	At Hon Doi Islet	12°39.0′	109°28.0′
A8	At Dai Lanh point	12°53.8′	109°27.2′
A9	At Ong Can Islet	13°54.0′	109°21.0′
A10	At Ly Son Islet	15°23.1'	109° 9.0'
A11	At Con Co Island	17°10.0'	107°20.6′

Figure 2.9 Baselines of Vietnam, 1982

Source: This map is prepared by the East Sea Institute, Diplomatic Academy of Vietnam.

Figure 2.10 Exploration activities in the South China Sea

Map 4 in Roberts, Christopher B., Buszynski, L., *The South China Sea Maritime Dispute* (Routledge, Oxon and New York, 2015).

Source: CIA Maps.

Second, by its 1982 declaration, Vietnam established a system of straight baselines along the central and southeastern coast and southwestern coast of Vietnam. The baseline system proposed in the declaration is a continuous system of ten segments and eleven base points (A1–11), of which nine are on islands, with the closest 7.6 n.m. from the mainland and the farthest 80.7 n.m. from the mainland. With an exception of point A7 on Hoi Doi Islet in Thuan Hai Province and point

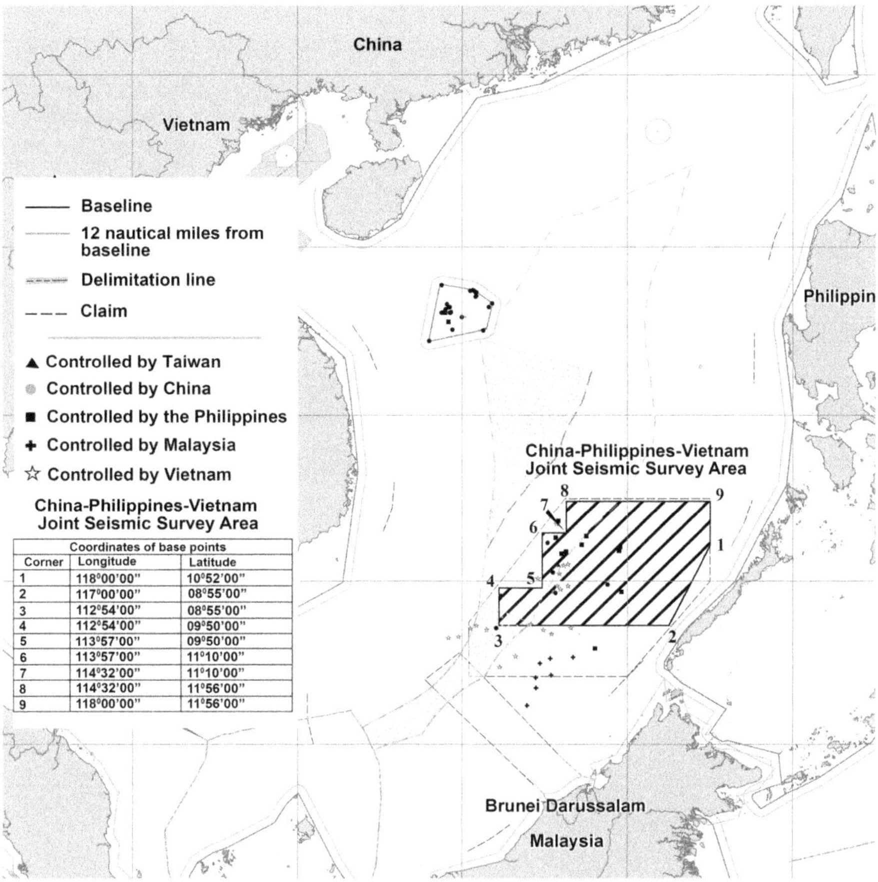

Coordinates of base points		
Corner	Longitude	Latitude
1	118°00'00"	10°52'00"
2	117°00'00"	08°55'00"
3	112°54'00"	08°55'00"
4	112°54'00"	09°50'00"
5	113°57'00"	09°50'00"
6	113°57'00"	11°10'00"
7	114°32'00"	11°10'00"
8	114°32'00"	11°56'00"
9	118°00'00"	11°56'00"

Figure 2.11 Map of Trilateral Joint Seismic Survey Area between China, Philippines and Vietnam, 2005–2008

Source: This map was prepared by the East Sea Institute, Diplomatic Academy of Vietnam.

A8 on Dai Lanh in Phu Khanh Province, all other points are on islands (see Figure 2.9). This straight baseline ran for a total 846 n.m., enclosing nearly 27,000 square n.m. (93 km^2) as internal waters.[118] The northern and southern termini of the baseline located in the Gulf of Tonkin and Gulf of Thailand had not yet been determined, as Vietnam viewed these gulfs as internal waters shared by Vietnam and its two neighbouring countries, China and Cambodia.

Vietnam's baseline position was a point of controversy. As defined by UNCLOS, the baseline is an artificial line from which the breadths of all maritime zones are measured. The US Bureau of Intelligence and Research held that geographical components of Vietnam-claimed straight baseline did not appear to follow related UNCLOS stipulation for three reasons: improper selection of base points on some islands which are distant to the mainland; inappropriate application of straight

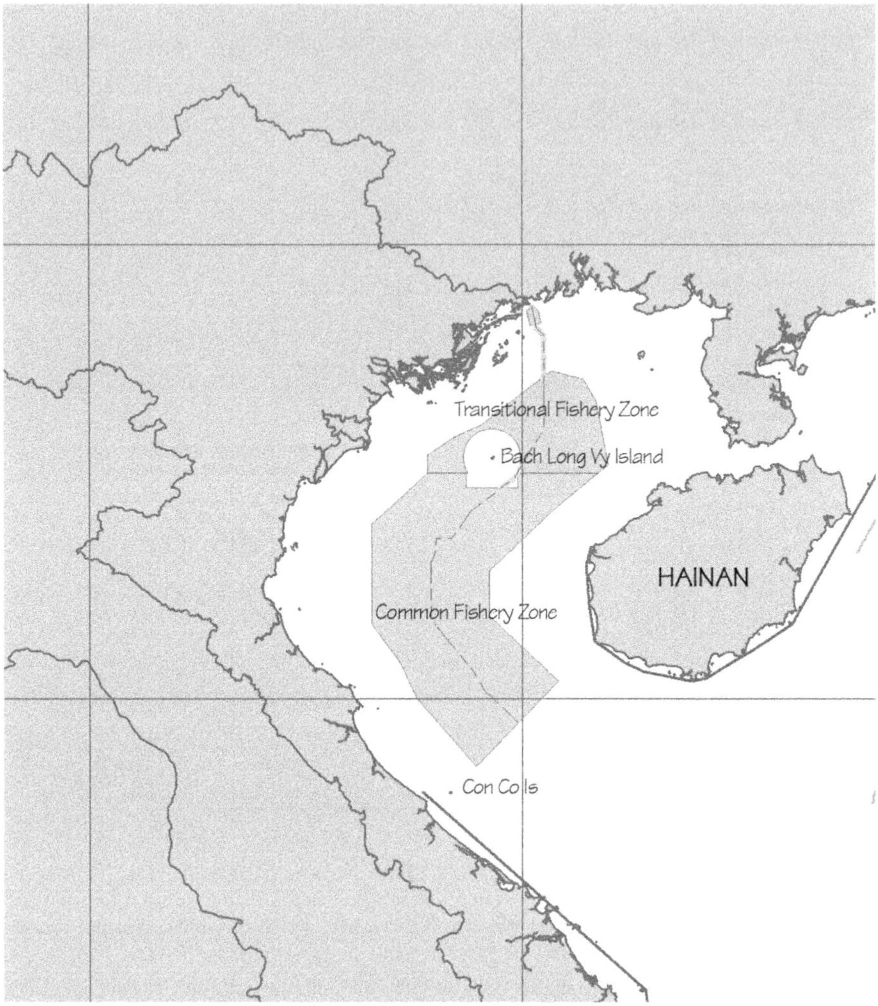

Figure 2.12 The delimitation line and joint fishing zone in the Gulf of Tonkin, 2004
Source: This map was prepared by the East Sea Institute of the Diplomatic Academy of Vietnam.

baseline system in some areas; and deviation between the proposed baseline and the direction of the coastline.[119] Australian law-of-the-sea expert Victor Prescott also claimed that some southern base points on islands couldn't be considered as "a fringe in the immediate vicinity of the coast" as required by UNCLOS to delineating straight baselines. He further claimed that the segments, roughly 160 n.m. each, connecting Bong Lai islet and Hon Doi islet to Hon Hai islet, enabled Vietnam to add to its internal waters 14,000 square n.m. more than the proper use of the normal baseline.[120]

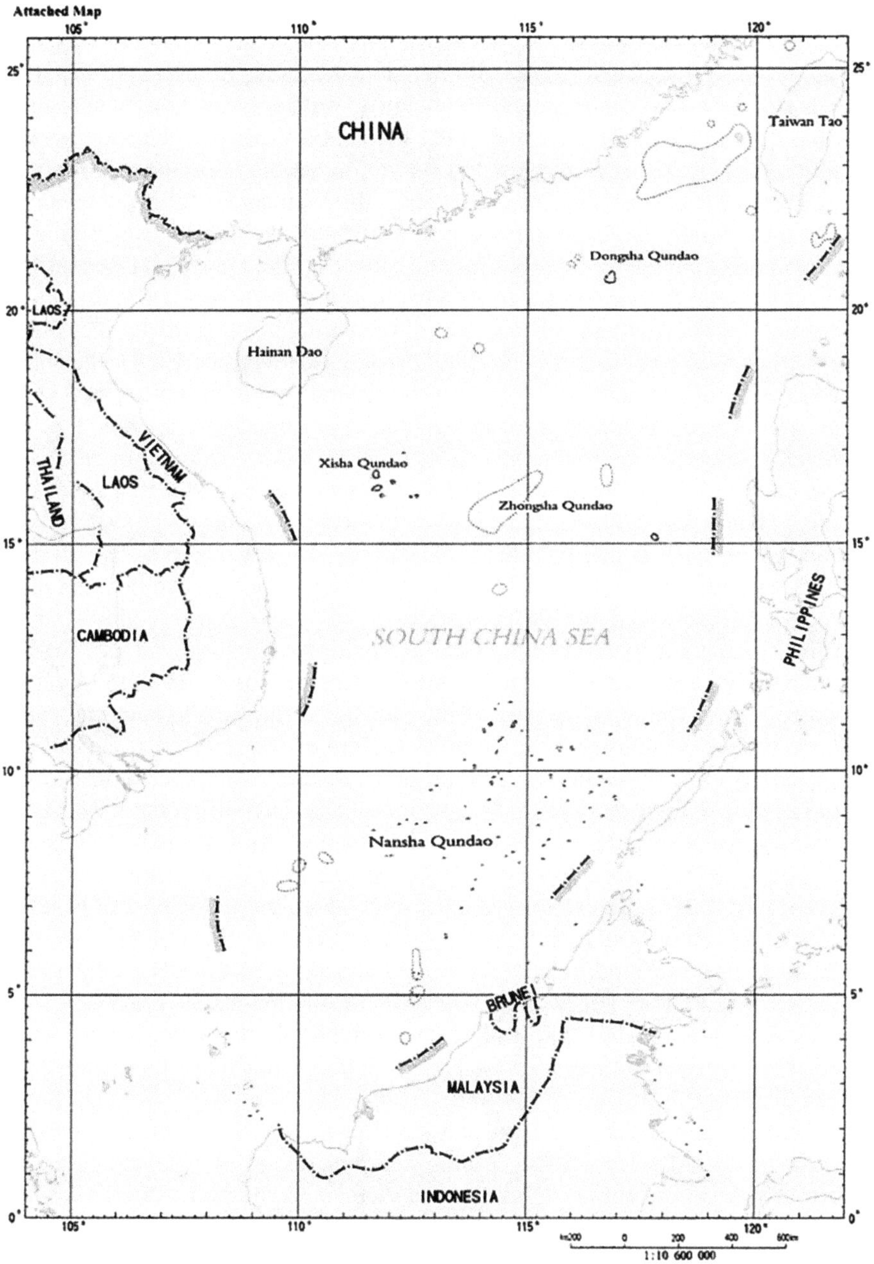

Figure 2.13 China's nine-dash line map attached to its *notes verbales* of 2009

Source: Permanent Mission of the People's Republic of China, *notes verbales* CML/17/2009 and CML/18/2009, 7 May 2009, available from the UN Division for Ocean Affairs and the Law of the Sea (DOALOS) at: www.un.org/Depts/los/clcs_new/submissions_files/mysvnm33_09/chn_2009re_mys_vnm_e.pdf and www.un.org/Depts/los/clcs_new/submissions_files/vnm37_09/chn_2009re_vnm.pdf.

In this regard, Vietnamese analysts insisted that the conditions of the Vietnamese coast met geographical conditions, including deep indentions and a "fringe of islands along the coast in its immediate vicinity," for the use of straight baselines. A *Nhan Dan* article of 15 November 1982 stated that Vietnam's selection of base points did not conflict with the stipulations of international law and custom.[121] In the absence of concrete measurement criteria, the Vietnamese followed the practices of other Southeast Asian states, especially Myanmar, Malaysia and Thailand. They also justified their approach, especially those in Phu Quy, Con Dao and Tho Chu, on national defence and security justifications. With regard to Phu Quy, a Vietnamese publicist noted "on the basis of the *military and security* sides, these island groups serve as frontiers, check points and secure protection for the whole seacoast of South Vietnam."[122] The Con Son island group, in which the A3–A5 points are located and which is located strategically opposite to the mouth of the Mekong River, was reported to have a naval base under construction by Soviet military advisers and technicians.[123] The Vietnamese later admitted that their 1982 baseline system was deliberately delineated to meet the country's "essential *security* and *defense* needs and to defend its legitimate interests in maritime zones." They openly talked about the possibility of adjusting the baseline position after Vietnam's ratification of the 1982 UNCLOS.[124]

Third, Vietnam also claimed the Gulf of Tonkin as "historic waters," explicitly considering the area as its internal waters. Article 3 of the 1988 Declaration specified, "The waters in the part of the gulf belonging to Vietnam constitute *historic waters* pertaining to the judicial regime of the internal waters of the Socialist Republic of Vietnam." The notion of historic waters, or more strictly historic bays, though recognised by customary law, is controversial. The 1958 Geneva Convention and UNCLOS have no provisions for historic waters except some references to historic bays. Article 7 (6) of the 1958 Convention and Article 10 (6) of UNCLOS 1982 exclude "historic bays" from the application of baseline rules to bays. However, some ICJ rulings accepted the status of historic bays under some specific conditions.[125] According to a study by the UN Secretariat in 1962, for a claim to a historic bay to be valid, the claimant state must have seen the bay as internal waters and it must have effectively and continuously exercised authority over the bay with the recognition of other states for a significant period of time.[126]

Vietnam recognised these criteria and used them to justify for its application of the historic water doctrine to the Gulf of Tonkin and Gulf of Thailand.[127] Vu Phi Hoang, a Vietnamese publicist, justified the Vietnamese "historic waters" position on the ground of long usage and control of the gulf on the part of France/Vietnam and China. He stressed the special significance of the gulf for security and defence of both countries, especially Vietnam, by referring to historical use of the gulf as a staging ground by foreign adversaries to launch attacks on the country's mainland.[128] In addition, Vietnam proposed to delimit the maritime boundary of the gulf along the straight north-south line stipulated in Article 2 of the Sino-French Convention on Delimitation of Frontier signed on 27 June 1887.[129] In this convention, the north-south line with no southern terminus was drawn along 108°3′13″

east of Greenwich in the gulf, of which the islands in the east side were to be given to China and those in the west were considered part of Tonkin.

While Vietnam's claim to historic waters in the Gulf of Thailand was supported by Cambodia, its similar claim in in the Gulf of Tonkin was not favoured by China. The Chinese Ministry of Foreign Affairs quickly filed a note on 28 November 1982, which denied the application of the red line without referring to the status of the gulf but made no reference to the claim of "historic waters." Perhaps, China was cautious that the acceptance of "historic waters" doctrine would mean the recognition of the "red line" as a boundary, which distinctly splits the gulf to Vietnam's advantage. It should be noted that France also refused to support the Vietnamese claim to historic waters in the Gulf of Tonkin in a note dated 5 December 1983.[130]

At that point of time, Vietnam's maritime claims reflected the prevailing distrust of international law in Hanoi, which was heavily influenced by socialist ideology and Soviet scholarship. The socialist concept of the contemporary international law focused on state sovereignty, equality of state and self-determination of the people. As such, Hanoi's leaders may have seen the emergence of the law of the sea in the ideological framework of three revolutionary currents, in terms of the struggle of the progressive forces, including the socialist states, the colonised nations and newly independent states, and the progressive people in the capitalist countries, working against the capitalist forces.[131] From this perspective, UNCLOS was seen as a tool for developing nations to restrict imperialist forces' freedom of navigation. Vietnamese war-moulded strategists were quite sceptical about the rule of law and the utility of the international law in controlling aggressions. They saw international law in general and the law of the sea in particular not as a mechanism to handle interstate relations but a foreign policy instrument to advance national interests. Therefore, Vietnam followed other countries' practices to stake maximalist claims. Failing to do so would put Vietnam in a disadvantaged position in negotiations on maritime boundaries with its neighbours.

Conclusion

Vietnam claims both the Paracels and Spratlys in their entirety on both historical and legal bases, though it has not clarified the limits of these claims. It is argued that the Vietnamese states have effectively, continuously and peacefully administered these groups of islands since the Nguyen lord established the original title over the archipelagos. The Vietnamese never relinquished their claim to these archipelagos even after they lost control of the Paracels and a number of Spratly islets. It is widely believed in Vietnam that China's conquests in 1974 and 1988 were illegal acts that did not entitle it to sovereignty over the Paracels and the Spratlys. China's repeated refusals to resort to third-party arbitration are seen as an indication of legal weakness.

While Vietnam's interest in these offshore islands is long-standing, its claim to maritime zones beyond its mainland is a relatively new development. It coincided with the negotiations on the law of the sea within the United Nations framework.

After reunification in 1975, the communist government in Hanoi made a number of claims to define a set of maritime zones as entitlements to its mainland and offshore islands under UNCLOS. Notably, Vietnam claimed a full set of maritime zones for its offshore islands, the status of historic waters for the Gulf of Tonkin, and a straight baseline system to its central and southern coast. Vietnam's intense interest in maritime territories reflected its strategic vulnerability and security concerns in the post-war period.

These claims have caused Vietnam to become involved in a complex, dangerous set of disputes in the South China Sea. Vietnam and China disputed over the Paracels bilaterally. However, the dispute over sovereignty over the Spratly Islands is multilateral and involves six parties: Vietnam, China, Malaysia, the Philippines, Brunei and Taiwan. By the end of 1980s, Vietnam had no presence on the Paracels but reportedly occupied twenty-one to twenty-two islands and atolls. China occupied the entire Paracels and seven to nine features in the Spratlys, where the Philippines were present on eight features since 1978 and Malaysia occupied six (see Figure 2.8). Taiwan held the largest island of the Spratly group, Itu Aba Island.

Vietnam's claims to maritime zones brought it to four disputes over maritime claims with other states bordering the South China Sea. With China, Vietnam had two disputes, the dispute over delimitation in the Gulf of Tonkin and the overlap between Vietnam's claim to an exclusive economic zone and a continental shelf and China's nine-dotted line claim (also referred to as the U-shaped claim). Vietnam and Brunei Darussalam could get involved in a dispute over maritime boundary if Hanoi starts to claim EEZs and continental shelves for the Spratly features. Between Vietnam and Indonesia, there was a dispute over a maritime area of about 12,200 square n.m. north of the Indonesian Natuna Islands.

Notes

1 Quoted from C. Wheeler, "A Maritime Logic to Vietnamese History? Littoral Society in Hoi An's Trading World C.1550–1830," paper presented at the *Seascapes, Littoral Cultures and Trans-Oceanic Exchanges*, Library of Congress, Washington, DC, 12–15 February 2003.
2 S.C. Tucker, *Vietnam*, London: UCL Press, 1999, p.2.
3 In Vietnamese media, offshore insular features are usually called as "dao" (islands) without proper differentiations between different types of features such as reefs, rocks, and islands.
4 L.V. Loi, *Vietnam: Dat, Bien, Troi*, Hanoi: Cong an Nhan dan Publisher, 1990, p.39.
5 Ibid., p.40.
6 Dai Chiem is the present-day Cua Dai, Quang Nam Province.
7 Sa Vinh is the present-day Sa Huynh, Quang Ngai Province.
8 The ly is the traditional Vietnamese length-measuring unit. One ly is approximately 500 m.
9 "The Hoang Sa and Truong Sa Archipelagos: Vietnamese Territories," Ministry of Foreign Affairs (Socialist Republic of Vietnam), Hanoi, 1981, p.19.
10 In Sinicised Vietnamese vocabulary, "Hoang" means "Golden" or "Yellow," and "Sa" means "Sand."
11 L.V. Loi, *Nhung dieu can biet ve Dat, Bien, Troi Viet Nam*, Hanoi: Tuoi Tre Publisher, 2007, pp. 43–4; "White Paper on the Hoang Sa (Paracel) and Truong Sa (Spratly) Islands," Ministry of Foreign Affairs (Republic of Vietnam), Saigon, 1975, p.16.

12 L.Q. Don, *Phu Bien Tap luc*, vol. 2, 1776, pp. 78a–79a, 82b–85b.

13 Le Duy Don's account was recognised and reproduced by a number of ensuing official historical records of the Nguyen Dynasty, such as *Dai Nam Thuc luc tien bien* (Annals of Pre-Dai Nam) (1844), *Lich trieu Hien chuong loai chi* (Classified Rules of Dynasties) (1821), *Hoang Viet Du dia chi* (Geography of the Viet Empire) (1833), and *Viet Su Thong giam Cuong muc Khao luoc* (Outline of the Viet History Chronicles) (1876). For example, *Dai Nam thuc luc tien bien* says nearly the same things: "Offshore of An Vinh Commune, Binh Son District, Quang Ngai Prefecture, there are more than 130 sandbanks. It takes from a few watches to a day to travel from one to another. They span an area of thousands of ly, and are thus called '*Van ly Hoang Sa*.' There are freshwater wells on the sandbanks. Sea products are sea cucumber, sea turtles, volutes, and so forth."

14 See Do Ba, "Toan Tap Thien Nam Tu chi Lo do thu," In: *Hong Duc Ban Do* (reprinted in 1962), Saigon: Archaeologic Institute Library, 1686; Don, *Phu Bien Tap luc*, vol. 2, 1776, pp. 78a–79a, 82b–85a; *Dai Nam Thuc luc tien bien*, History Bureau (Nguyen Court), 1844.

15 N. Nha, N.D. Dau, L.M. Nghia, T.D.M. Thu, and V.Q. Viet, *Hoang Sa, Truong Sa la cua Viet Nam*, Ho Chi Minh: Youth Publisher, 2008; T.D.M. Thu, "Chu quyen tren hai quan dao Hoang Sa va Truong Sa," *Thoi Dai moi* 11, 2007.

16 M. Chemillier-Gendreau, *Sovereignty over the Paracel and Spratly Islands*, The Hague, Boston: Kluwer Law International, 2000, p.35; M.S. Samuels, *Contest for the South China Sea*, New York: Methuen, 1982, p.43; "White Paper on the Hoang Sa (Paracel) and Truong Sa (Spratly) Islands," p.27.

17 The work, which was compiled in 1848, described in detailed the state-sponsored activities under the reign of Emperors Gia Long, Minh Menh, and Thieu Tri with regard to these offshore territories.

18 "Dai Nam Thuc luc Chinh bien," History Bureau (Nguyen Court), 1848, vol. 52, p.15a.

19 Ibid., vol.104, pp. 16a–17a.

20 Ibid., vol.165, pp. 24a–25b.

21 For example, in 1847, Ministry of Public Affairs submitted a petition to Emperor Thieu Tri for a one-year postponement of the Hoang Sa Flotilla's regular sea-route survey for the lack of fund. Emperor Thieu Tri wrote "*đình*" (suspended) on the petition as an approval (see Figure 2.4). In 1867, or 20th year of the reign of Tu Duc, a number of sailors died during the journey to the archipelagos, Emperor Tu Duc conferred upon them the title of hero. Some of these documents bear the seal of the emperor or comments in red ink, a sure sign of the emperor's handwritings.

22 Some notable works are *Su hoc bi khao (Historical Review)*, *Dia du toat yeu (Brief on Geography)*, *Quang Thuan dao su tap (History of Quang Thuan)*, *Trung ky dia du luoc (Geography of the Central Vietnam)* and *Quang ngai tinh chi (Geography of Quang Nghai)*. See N.H. Thao, *Luat Quoc te va Chu quyen tren hai quan dao Hoang Sa va Truong Sa*, Hanoi: Cong an Nhan dan Publisher, 2009, pp. 75–6.

23 The commonly cited map is Bishop Jean-Louis Taberd's "*Note on the Geography of Cochin China*" (1837), which describes "Paracel or Paracels" as part of Cochin China's territory and indicates that Cochin Chinese people refer to Paracels as "Kat Vang." On "*An Nam Dai quoc hoa do*" (Tabula geographica imerii Anamitici – the Map of the Annam Empire) published in 1838, Bishop Taberd portrayed part of Paracels and noted "Paracel seu Kat Vang" (Paracel or Cat Vang) for the islands farther than those near shore of the central Vietnam (see Figure 2.7). J.B. Chaigneau, one of the counsellors to Emperor Gia Long, recorded in his "*Memoire sure la Cochinchine*" (Memory of Cochin China): "the country of Cochin China whose emperor has just ascended to the throne, includes the regions of Cochin China and Tonkin . . . some inhabited islands not too far from the shore, and the Paracel Islands composed of uninhabited small islands, creeks, and cays." In "*On the Cochin Chinese Empire*" published on Journal of the Royal Geographical Society in 1849, Gutzlaff also confirmed that the emperor of Cochin China claimed possession of the Kat Vang archipelago. See "White Paper

on the Hoang Sa (Paracel) and Truong Sa (Spratly) Islands"; "The Hoang Sa and Truong Sa Archipelagos: Vietnamese Territories," Ministry of Foreign Affairs (Socialist Republic of Vietnam), Hanoi, 1981; "The Hoang Sa (Paracel) and Truong Sa (Spratly) Archipelagos and International Law," Ministry of Foreign Affairs (Socialist Republic of Vietnam), Hanoi, 1988.

24 "White Paper on the Hoang Sa (Paracel) and Truong Sa (Spratly) Islands," p.26.

25 See "The Hoang Sa and Truong Sa Archipelagos: Vietnamese Territories," Ministry of Foreign Affairs (Socialist Republic of Vietnam), Hanoi, 1981; "White Paper on the Hoang Sa (Paracel) and Truong Sa (Spratly) Islands."

26 Nguyen Dong, "8 ban do co chung minh Trung Quoc khong co Hoang Sa," *Vnexpress*, 29 July 2012. Online. Available HTTP: <http://vnexpress.net/gl/xa-hoi/2012/07/8-ban-do-co-chung-minh-trung-quoc-khong-co-hoang-sa> (accessed 3 August 2012). Bill Hayton also confirmed that Chinese maps published before 1914 took the Hainan Island as the southernmost point of the Chinese territory. The map of "Map of National Humiliation" published by Central Cartographic Society in Shanghai, which showed territories lost to foreign states, did not include the South China Sea's islands. See B. Hayton, *The South China Sea: The Struggle for Power in Asia*, New Haven: Yale University Press, 2014, pp. 52–3.

27 M. Flecker, "Archaeology Could Wreck China's Sea Claims," *Malay Mail Online*, 6 May 2015. Online. Available HTTP: <www.themalaymailonline.com/what-you-think/article/archaeology-could-wreck-chinas-sea-claims-michael-flecker> (accessed 18 May 2015).

28 Chemillier-Gendreau, *Sovereignty over the Paracel and Spratly Islands*, p.37.

29 China finally agreed to pay Nishizawa of 130,000 silver dollars in exchange for Japanese formal recognition of Chinese sovereignty over the Pratas group.

30 The author of this map was believed to be Hu Jinjie, a Chinese cartographer. The line started from Sino-Vietnamese land border, went downward through the Gulf of Tonkin and the shore of the Vietnamese coast, and ran east near the Luzon Island, then north through the Taiwan Strait and finally rejoined the Chinese boundary in the East China Sea and the Yellow Sea. See Z. Keyuan, "The Chinese Traditional Maritime Boundary Line in the South China Sea and Its Legal Consequences for the Resolution of the Dispute over the Spratly Islands," *International Journal of Marine and Coastal Law* 14, no. 1, 1999, p.32.

31 "White Paper on the Hoang Sa (Paracel) and Truong Sa (Spratly) Islands," pp. 39–40.

32 Samuels, *Contest for the South China Sea*, p.60.

33 S. Tønnesson, "The South China Sea in the Age of European Decline," *Modern Asian Studies* 40, no. 1, 2006, p.4; Samuels, *Contest for the South China Sea*, p.61. In February 1937, France offered to settle the Paracel dispute through international arbitration but China refused.

34 Samuels, *Contest for the South China Sea*, pp. 60–1.

35 "White Paper on the Hoang Sa (Paracel) and Truong Sa (Spratly) Islands," pp. 35–6.

36 Tønnesson, "The South China Sea in the Age of European Decline," p.5.

37 Ibid., pp. 3–8.

38 Chemillier-Gendreau, *Sovereignty over the Paracel and Spratly Islands*, p.38.

39 M.S. Samuels, *Contest for the South China Sea*, p.57.

40 Chemillier-Gendreau, *Sovereignty over the Paracel and Spratly Islands*.

41 Notably, at the same time the French kept their garrisons in Woody and Pattle Islands, there were also about 150 Japanese men already residing on the Woody Island. It is reported that the French, Vietnamese and Japanese co-existed peacefully in the Paracel area. On the Spratlys, the same situation was reported with Japanese-Taiwanese and Franco-Indochinese settlers living side by side on Itu Aba and Spratly Island. The French constructed a radio station and a meteorological station on Itu Aba Island in 1939. See Tønnesson, "The South China Sea in the Age of European Decline," pp. 11–3.

42 Ibid.
43 Ibid.
44 Chemillier-Gendreau, *Sovereignty over the Paracel and Spratly Islands*; Tønnesson, "The South China Sea in the Age of European Decline," p.13.
45 Tønnesson, "The South China Sea in the Age of European Decline," pp. 12–3.
46 Ibid., pp. 22–3.
47 Ibid., p.25.
48 The Democratic Republic of Vietnam is the revolutionary government established by Viet Minh, a Vietnamese independence movement, in September 1945.
49 Tønnesson, "The South China Sea in the Age of European Decline," pp. 25–7.
50 Ibid., p.28.
51 In the book *Contest for the South China Sea* by Marwyn S. Samuels in 1982, the ship name is "Chevreud" (p.76), while in Stein Tønnesson's article "The South China Sea in the Age of European Decline" it is "Chevreuil."
52 See Samuels, *Contest for the South China Sea*, pp. 75–6.
53 Ibid., pp. 79–81. Also see Treaty of Peace between the Republic of China and Japan, signed at Taipei, 28 April 1952, entered into force 5 August 1952.
54 The PRC was absent from the meeting.
55 Samuels, *Contest for the South China Sea*, p.78; Chemillier-Gendreau, *Sovereignty over the Paracel and Spratly Islands*, p.41.
56 "White Paper on the Hoang Sa (Paracel) and Truong Sa (Spratly) Islands," p.86.
57 The United States took note of the final agreements but refused to be a signatory to avoid being legally bound by them.
58 L.V. Loi, *Fifty Years of Vietnamese Diplomacy*, Hanoi: The Gioi Publisher, 2000, pp. 125–31.
59 Tucker, *Vietnam*, pp. 79–109.
60 "White Paper on the Hoang Sa (Paracel) and Truong Sa (Spratly) Islands," pp. 51–2.
61 Ibid., p.57.
62 Samuels, *Contest for the South China Sea*, p.82.
63 Ibid., pp. 82–3.
64 P.M. Chang, "A New Scramble for the South China Sea Islands," *Contemporary Southeast Asia* 12, no. 1, 1990, p.23.
65 "White Paper on the Hoang Sa (Paracel) and Truong Sa (Spratly) Islands," p.57.
66 Ibid., p.82.
67 Ibid., p.54.
68 The Pattle Weather Station regularly provided meteorological reports until its forced closure in 1974. The islands remained under the jurisdiction of Ba Ria Province until September 1973 when they were transferred to Phuoc Tuy Province. In the same year, South Vietnam offered some concessions to US companies to explore for oil in the area west of the Spratlys.
69 Samuels, *Contest for the South China Sea*, p.91.
70 S. Tønnesson, "History of the Dispute," In: Timo Kivimäki (ed.), *War or Peace in the South China Sea?*, Copenhagen: NIAS Press, 2002, p.14.
71 Respective names in the Filipino language are Lawak, Parola, Kota, and Pagasa.
72 Samuels, *Contest for the South China Sea*, p.87.
73 "White Paper on the Hoang Sa (Paracel) and Truong Sa (Spratly) Islands," p.92.
74 C. Lo, *China's Policy towards Territorial Disputes: The Case of South China Sea Islands*, New York: Routledge, 1989, pp. 59–60.
75 B. Hayton, *The South China Sea: The Struggle for Power in Asia*, New Haven: Yale University Press, 2014, pp. 72–8.
76 N.M. Tri and S.L.C. Koh, "The 7th Fleet Was Ordered to Move Away from the Disputed Area," *Diplomat*, 23 January 2014. Online. Available HTTP: <http://thediplomat.com/2014/01/lessons-from-the-battle-of-the-paracel-islands/> (accessed 17 March 2015).

77 M.A. Hoyts, *Sino-Vietnamese Interests Collide in the South China Sea: A Case Study of the Disputed Paracel and Spratly Archipelago*, MA Thesis, Asian Studies Dept., University of Hawaii, Honolulu, 1994, p.40.
78 Ibid.
79 Bo Ngoai giao, *Su that ve Quan he Viet Nam-Trung Quoc trong 30 nam qua*, Hanoi: Su That Publisher, 1979, p.68.
80 See more K. Path, "The Sino-Vietnamese Dispute over Territorial Claims, 1974–1978: Vietnamese Nationalism and Its Consequences," *International Journal of Asian Studies* 8, no. 2, 2011, pp. 191–6.
81 Bo Ngoai giao, *Su that ve Quan he Viet Nam-Trung Quoc trong 30 nam qua*, pp. 69–9. See more "Vietnam stands for a Peaceful Settlement of the Dispute with China over the Truong Sa and Hoang Sa Archipelagos," *Vietnam Courier* 7, 1988, p.11.
82 Hoyts, *Sino-Vietnamese Interests Collide in the South China Sea*, p.71.
83 Bo Ngoai giao, *Su that ve Quan he Viet Nam-Trung Quoc trong 30 nam qua*, p.69.
84 "The Hoang Sa and Truong Sa Archipelagos: Vietnamese Territories," Ministry of Foreign Affairs (Socialist Republic of Vietnam), Hanoi, 1981, p.17.
85 Chang, "A New Scramble for the South China Sea Islands," p.22–3.
86 Path, "The Sino-Vietnamese Dispute over Territorial Claims, 1974–1978," p.198.
87 Bo Ngoai giao, *Van de Bien gioi giua Viet Nam va Trung Quoc*, Hanoi: Su That Publisher, 1979.
88 D.R. SarDesai, *Vietnam: Past and Present*, Los Angeles, CA: Westview Press, 2005, p.180.
89 Bo Ngoai giao, *Van de Bien gioi giua Viet Nam va Trung Quoc*, pp. 15–18.
90 According to the paper, the first betrayal was when the Chinese colluded with the French over the Geneva Accords in 1954 to partition Vietnam. The second happened during the Second Indochina War, when the Chinese at first prevented Vietnam from negotiating with the US and later secretly compromised with the US at the expense of Vietnam. The third was China's use of the Khmer Rouge to sabotage the unified Vietnam. See more ibid.
91 Hoyts, "Sino-Vietnamese Interests Collide in the South China Sea," p.74.
92 "The Hoang Sa and Truong Sa Archipelagos: Vietnamese Territories," p.35.
93 In June 1978, the Philippine President F. Marcos signed Decree No.1596 that annexed the Kalaya'an to the Philippines territory and put it under the jurisdiction of Palawan.
94 N.V. Long, *Hoang Sa-Truong Sa: Cac su kien, tu lieu lich su phap ly chinh (The ky XV-2000)*, vol. 1, Ho Chi Minh City: Tre Publisher, 2013, p.157.
95 Lo, *China's Policy towards Territorial Disputes*, p.155.
96 Long, *Hoang Sa-Truong Sa* 1, pp. 177, 180; "A New Scramble for the South China Sea Islands," p.23.
97 R. Rau, "Present and Future Maritime Security Issues in the Southeast Asian and South China Seas," *Contemporary Southeast Asia* 8, no. 1, 1986, p.48.
98 Chang, "A New Scramble for the South China Sea Islands," p.24.
99 Ibid; Hayton, *The South China Sea*, p.81.
100 Chang, "A New Scramble for the South China Sea Islands," p.24.
101 Hayton, *The South China Sea*, pp. 81–2.
102 Quoted from Hoyts, "Sino-Vietnamese Interests Collide in the South China Sea," p.84.
103 Ibid., pp. 84–5.
104 D. Holley, "Vietnam Seen Preparing for War, China Warns Hanoi to Stop Invading Spratlys," *Los Angeles Times*, 6 April 1988.
105 The recently released footage on YouTube revealed that the Chinese warships opened fire at these defenceless Vietnamese soldiers and killed most of them. The video is available at www.youtube.com/watch?v=Uy2ZrFphSmc (accessed 25 June 2015).
106 Hoyts, "Sino-Vietnamese Interests Collide in the South China Sea," pp. 96–7; Holley, "Vietnam Seen Preparing for War, China Warns Hanoi to Stop Invading Spratlys."

107 J. Clayton, "Conflict in Spratlys Spurs Rift between Hanoi and Moscow," *Christian Science Monitor*, 14 June 1988.
108 Hayton, *The South China Sea*, pp. 83–4.
109 Chang, "A New Scramble for the South China Sea Islands," p.26.
110 Hoyts, "Sino-Vietnamese Interests Collide in the South China Sea," pp. 96–7.
111 Chang, "A New Scramble for the South China Sea Islands," p.27.
112 Ibid.
113 "The Hoang Sa (Paracel) and Truong Sa (Spratly) Archipelagos and International Law," p.26.
114 Ibid.
115 E.C. Farrell, *The Socialist Republic of Vietnam and the Law of the Sea*, The Hague, Boston and New York: Martinus Nijhoff, 1997, pp. 169–70.
116 Quoted from ibid., pp. 29–32, 271.
117 Article 5 of the 1977 Territorial Sea, the Contiguous Zone, the Exclusive Economic Zone, and the Continental Shelf of Vietnam stated:

> The islands and archipelagos, forming an integral part of the Vietnamese territory and beyond the Vietnamese territorial sea mentioned in Paragraph 1, have their own territorial seas, contiguous zones, exclusive economic zones and continental shelves, determined in accordance with the provisions of Paragraphs 1, 2, 3 and 4 of this statement.

118 Bureau of Intelligence and Research (US Department of State), *Limits in the Seas: Straight Baselines: VIETNAM*, Washington, DC, 1983, p.8.
119 Ibid., p.12.
120 J.R.V. Prescott, *Limits of National Claims in the South China Sea*, London: ASEAN Academic Press, 1999, pp. 11–2.
121 Bureau of Intelligence and Research (US Department of State), *Limits in the Seas: Straight Baselines: VIETNAM*, p.12.
122 Farrell, *The Socialist Republic of Vietnam and the Law of the Sea*, pp. 63–6.
123 Ibid., p.66.
124 Bo Ngoai giao, *Gioi thieu mot so Van de co ban cua Luat Bien o Viet Nam*, Hanoi: Chinh tri Quoc gia Publisher, 2004, pp. 45–6; M.J. Valencia, J.M. Van Dyke, and N.A. Ludwig, *Sharing the Resources of the South China Sea*, Boston and Cambridge, MA: M. Nijhoff, 1997, p.32.
125 International Court of Justice in the Cases of Continental Shelf (Tunisia/Libyan Jamahiriya) (1982) and of Land, Island and Maritime Frontier Dispute (El Salvador/Honduras, with Nicaragua intervening) (1992).
126 B.A. Boczek, *International Law: A Dictionary*, Lanham, MD: Scarecrow Press, 2005, p.263.
127 Bo Ngoai giao, *Gioi thieu mot so Van de co ban cua Luat Bien o Viet Nam*, pp. 28–9.
128 V.P. Hoang, "May van de Phap ly trong Tuyen bo cua Chinh phu ta ve Duong Co So ven Luc dia Viet Nam," *Luat hoc* 1, no. 10, 1983.
129 Farrell, *The Socialist Republic of Vietnam and the Law of the Sea*, p.71.
130 Ibid.
131 See ibid.

3 Befriending the Dragon, 1986–1995

Introduction

Before 1991, South China Sea politics was largely dictated by hostilities between Vietnam on one side and China and ASEAN nations on the other over the Cambodia conflict. In 1978, Hanoi signed a treaty of alliance with Moscow and allowed it to establish a naval base in Cam Ranh Bay in return for military and economic support. Though the door to negotiation was always left open, Vietnam scrambled to expand its physical occupation and consolidate its defence system in the Spratly Islands. At the same time, Hanoi engaged in a battle of words and documents to assert its claims and rebuff those of China and other Southeast Asian claimants. By the end of the 1980s, Hanoi gradually moved from a confrontational policy to a conciliatory and cooperative one with neighbours, laying emphasis on status quo maintenance and negotiations to resolve the disputes peacefully. Vietnam also worked to mend its ties with China and ASEAN countries, seriously engaging with them to establish a thick network of bilateral mechanisms for the resolution and management of disputes, and in doing so expanding the scope of cooperation. However, the South China Sea remained an irritant with tensions flaring up periodically due to China's unilateral assertive actions.

From confrontation to conciliation with China, ASEAN

After reunification in 1975, the friendship between Vietnam and China broke down due to worsening disputes over the land border, the Gulf of Tonkin, and especially Vietnam's military intervention in Cambodia. Regarding China as "the most immediate and dangerous danger," Vietnam decided to align with the Soviet Union as the "cornerstone" of its foreign policy.[1] Hanoi also granted the Soviet Union access to its facilities in Da Nang and at the Cam Ranh Bay as a means to deter China's large-scale aggressions. The Vietnamese People's Army (VPA) engaged with Chinese military forces along the land border, sustained their military operations in Cambodia, and vigorously expanded its presence in the Spratlys in a bid to pre-empt China and other claimants.

During the 1980s, Hanoi struggled between the desire to maintain influence over Cambodia and the need to restore normal relations with its neighbours, particularly

China. According to Tran Quang Co, between 1980 and 1988, Hanoi actively extended roughly twenty official requests to Beijing for resumption of talks on the border conflicts and the normalisation of the bilateral relations.[2] Vietnam's desire to improve relations with China was manifest in CPV National Congress' Political Report adopted in December 1986, which stated that Vietnam was "ready to negotiate with China at *any* time, at *any* level and in *any* place to normalise relations between the two countries."[3] Vietnam gradually withdrew its troops from Cambodia to facilitate talks, but China repeatedly denied these requests by setting higher and higher preconditions for the reopening of such meetings.[4] Beijing had little interest in a rapprochement with Hanoi at that time because it took advantage of Vietnam's stalemate in Cambodia to "consolidate (China's) legitimacy as a respectable great power in the Asia-Pacific region" and "expand its strategic influence among the ASEAN states, particularly Thailand."[5]

Since the mid-1980s pressures were mounting on Hanoi from all directions, forcing it to significantly soften its international stance. Inside the country, economic woes in the form of food shortage, production stagnation, high unemployment rate and skyrocketing inflation seriously undermined the legitimacy of the ruling communist party.[6] This dire situation was a result of not only bad economic planning policy but also an economic embargo imposed on Vietnam by the Western world, China and the ASEAN states due to its occupation of Cambodia. Even though the economy had had some signs of improvement after *Doi Moi*, the market-oriented reform package initiated in December 1986, the leading Vietnamese nationalist pragmatist, Foreign Minister Nguyen Co Thach, recognised the need to integrate Vietnam into the "world market."[7]

In terms of national security, Vietnam also faced mounting difficulties. Fighting raged on in the northern border of Cambodia and Vietnam.[8] Also, the Vietnam-controlled Spratly Islands became a serious source of apprehension after the March 1988 clash with China.[9] What was worrying to Vietnam was that its power in relative terms was on the decline, making it more vulnerable to its major adversary, China. Vietnam alone was always overwhelmed by China's economic and military power, and therefore self-defence was not a promising option. However, in the mid-1980s, the Soviet Union suffered serious internal difficulties, which made it turn inward and substantially cut its commitments abroad.[10] As Vietnam was no longer the Soviet Union's strategic priority, Moscow started applying pressure on Hanoi to give the Khmer Rouge faction a part in the final political solution to the Cambodian problem, as Beijing insisted.[11]

In view of the prospect of the gradual decline of the Soviet Union's commitment, Vietnam realised that it would be left alone in the face of China's threatening power. When Chinese warships attacked Vietnamese garrisons and vessels in the Spratly area in March 1988, Moscow took a neutral position, which from the Vietnamese perspective was seen as a clear signal of the Soviet Union's abandonment.[12] At the end of 1989 and early 1990, the Soviet Union withdrew much of its offensive forces from Cam Ranh Bay and reduced the frequency of military transport flights between Cam Ranh and Vladivostok.[13] These circumstances prompted Vietnam either to seek an accommodation with China or look for an alternative to the Soviet Union's deterrent power. The only credible alternative to deter China's expansionism in the South China Sea was the US Navy. However, Vietnam's military occupation of Cambodia blocked all the paths to rapprochement with Western powers and ASEAN countries.

The 1988 Spratly clash marked a turning point in Vietnam's strategic posture. It was a surprise to international observers that Vietnam did not fight back against China during the skirmish. From the military point of view, Vietnam did have some advantages in terms of air power and logistics because these small islets lay within the operating range of Vietnam's air force but outside that of China's.[14] However, Vietnam's naval capabilities were overwhelmed by those of China.[15] In the meantime, Moscow refused Hanoi's request to criticise China and declined to take action to support Hanoi.[16] Vietnam's display of naval power and the consolidation of the defence system in the islands under its control after the skirmish served merely as a warning against any further aggressive actions on the part of China. As mentioned in Chapter 2, instead of challenging China militarily on the islands, Hanoi repeatedly called on to China for talks and peaceful settlement. Hanoi was hesitant to escalate the conflict because it had very little chance to regain China-controlled features while risking further undermining its position in the Spratlys.

Subsequent events, however, indicated that Hanoi's conciliatory approach had been set in motion. Just three months after the 1988 incident, on 28 June 1988, the National Assembly of Vietnam adopted a resolution, drafted by the Foreign Ministry, which removed from the preamble of the Vietnamese Constitution the label that China was "a dangerous, direct enemy of the Vietnamese people."[17] On 15 July, Foreign Minister Thach met with the Chinese ambassador to propose a set of measures to defuse tension and request resumption of talks at any level.[18] Hanoi also toned down its anti-China propaganda. The most credible evidence of departure from the previous position lies in classified Resolution 13 adopted by the CPV Politburo in 20 May 1988, just two months after the March naval battle. This resolution gave priority to three interrelated tasks, namely the settlement of the Cambodian conflict, restored ties with Beijing, and establishment of friendly relations with other countries.[19] This resolution also proposed a more defensive posture and accelerated military withdrawal from Cambodia as an avenue to these ends. Five days after the adoption of Resolution 13, Vietnam's Foreign Ministry announced a major withdrawal of troops from Cambodia and Laos.[20] In September 1989, Vietnam completed its unconditional withdrawal. It was also a strong indication that Vietnam was willing to give up substantial influence abroad for better security at home.[21]

The Spratly clash was perhaps a catalyst for these decisive changes in Vietnam's Cambodia policy. Among the areas of conflict, the Spratlys were Vietnam's most critical vulnerability. The reason was simply that Vietnam's naval and air capabilities did not match with those of China.[22] The gap tended to widen in the near future. In the meantime, there was a standoff in Vietnam's northern border conflict and the Vietnamese forces had an upper hand in the Cambodian battlefields. There were no signs that Hanoi would relinquish its claims to the Paracel and Spratly Islands. Hanoi did not miss any opportunity to restate its sovereignty claim and refute competing claims of other countries through diplomatic channels. Even though it clearly refrained from further provoking, Vietnam signalled a clear message that it would not accept further losses in the Spratlys. Hanoi openly rejected normalisation with China on the terms of recognition of Chinese sovereignty over these island groups.[23] The sequence of Hanoi's actions indicated that maritime insecurity had a strong impact on strategic calculus of the Vietnamese leadership.

As mentioned in Chapter 2, this period witnessed an emerging rift in the Vietnamese leadership in foreign affairs, especially how to deal with the Cambodian issue. The first group led by Foreign Minister Nguyen Co Thach, who saw China essentially an expansionist, advocated improving relations with the Western powers to force China's moderation of its position.[24] In Thach's calculations, Vietnam's complete withdrawal would facilitate talks with the US, Japan and the ASEAN countries because this was the sole condition these countries asked for at that time. If these countries agreed to talk with Vietnam, it helped isolate Beijing in its support of the Khmer Rouge, and China would be under greater pressure to soften its stance.[25] However, Thach had to wait until the mid-1990s to see his policy yield some concrete results. Washington, Tokyo and the ASEAN capitals originally saw Vietnam's withdrawal as a bluff rather than a serious markdown.

The temporary failure of Thach's foreign policy put him into a defensive position before the ideologically conservative elements of the CPV in the military and party apparatus.[26] These elites believed that good relations with China would help protect the communist regime in Vietnam and defuse threats to its sovereignty from its northern neighbour. These conservatives became more vocal and gained more influence during the communist crisis in the Soviet Union, Eastern Europe and China in mid-1989.[27] Since the mid-1990s, they managed to bypass the Foreign Ministry to set up direct communication with Chinese officials. The conservative party and military members communicated directly with Beijing through the Chinese Embassy in Hanoi rather through the Vietnamese Embassy in Beijing.[28] In June 1990, CPV Secretary General Nguyen Van Linh privately talked with the Chinese ambassador in Hanoi to extend a request a meeting with Chinese senior leaders to discuss the "protection of socialism" in the face of "imperialists' peaceful revolution."[29] Linh openly suggested the possibility of Hanoi's recognition of the Khmer Rouge and proposed a "red solution," which prescribed a political coalition between Heng Samrin/Hun Sen and the Khmer Rouge (two communist factions) with the exclusion of other Cambodian political groups.[30]

August 1990 witnessed a decisive change in China's position. When Chinese Premier Li Peng visited Singapore and Indonesia in August 1990, he stated, "Along with the settlement of the Cambodia issue, China would like to normalise relations with Vietnam, and after relations are normalised, China is ready to negotiate and consult with Vietnam to properly settle this matter."[31] Regarding the territorial disputes in the South China Sea, he stated: "China is ready to join efforts with Southeast Asian countries to develop the (Spratly) islands while putting aside for the first time the question of sovereignty."[32] In early September, China abruptly changed its long-standing disregard of Vietnam's request and agreed to hold a high-level meeting to discuss normalisation. But, Beijing insisted that the meeting should be held in China and that "anti-Chinese" Foreign Minister Nguyen Co Thach would be excluded.[33]

The sudden change in China's attitude was definitely not a response to Vietnamese conservatives' proposal for a "red solution," but appeared to be a reaction to a policy change on the part of the United States. On 18 July 1990, US Secretary of State James Baker made it known that the US would discuss the Cambodian settlement with Hanoi and would cease to support the Khmer Rouge's participation in a three-party coalition. The shift in the US position left China as the lone supporter of the Khmer Rouge, and forced it to reassess its "bleeding Vietnam white" policy.[34] That prompted Beijing's quick decision to abandon Pol Pot in exchange for a significant role in the final settlement of the Cambodian conflict. What mattered was that Beijing skilfully took advantage of divisions in the Vietnamese leadership to advance its agenda. Beijing accepted Hanoi's long-standing request for a high-level meeting with a condition that Foreign Minister Thach was excluded.[35]

The conservative ideologues in Hanoi viewed Beijing's more conciliatory response positively and accepted Beijing's conditions. Vietnamese party chief Nguyen Van Linh and the chair of the Council of Ministers, Do Muoi, travelled to Chengdu (China) to have a secret meeting with their counterparts, Jiang Zemin and Li Peng, on 3–4 September 1990. It was reported that though the initial purpose of the meeting was about normalisation of relations, much of the talks focused on the settlement of the Cambodia issue as China wished.[36] To the Vietnamese counterparts' surprise, the Chinese leaders rejected the "red solution" but re-tabled their broad-based formula of a Supreme National Council, which included Cambodia's non-communist factions.[37] Linh and Muoi eventually accepted the Chinese proposal, which was later criticised by Thach. Then, Thach and the Foreign Ministry lost the control of foreign affairs to the Ministry of Defence and the CPV's External Relations Commission. Thach was removed from the Politburo and the Central Committee during the 7th National Party Congress in June 1991 and lost his job in the government later for being critical of the new China policy. After the Congress, Chinese Communist Party (CCP) leaders sent a congratulatory message to the new leadership of Vietnam, which was seen as a sign of pleasure with the removal of Thach.[38] The conservative leaders in Hanoi then not only pushed for normal relations with Beijing but also went further to ask for the restoration of the "alliance" relationship with Beijing.[39] But, they did not yield to China's claims on other issues such as the return of ethnic Chinese, territorial disputes, and repayment of Vietnamese debts.[40]

Official normalisation of the bilateral relations did not occur until comprehensive settlement of the Cambodia problem was finalised in October 1991. Hanoi finally accepted the central role of the United Nations in the Cambodian peace process.[41] In November 1991, the party and government chiefs of Vietnam and China met in Beijing and officially declared normalisation of the bilateral state-to-state and party-to-party relations after more than a decade of hostility. China openly rejected the idea of an "alliance" and made clear that it wanted "comradeship but not a formal alliance."[42] After the summit, the two sides issued an eleven-point joint communiqué, which included the fundamental principles that guided relations of the two countries after the normalisation. Regarding the border and territorial issues, Point 5 of the joint communiqué read:

> The two sides agreed to continue to take the necessary measures to *maintain peace and tranquillity* along the border and encourage the border inhabitants to restore and develop traditional friendly exchanges so as to turn the Sino-Vietnamese border into a border of peace and friendship. The two sides also signed the provisional agreements concerning border affairs. Both sides agreed to settle the boundary and other territorial issues peacefully through negotiations.[43]

As indicated in the joint communiqué, Hanoi secured a minimal gain in terms of China's high-level commitment to avoid military confrontation and peaceful settlements of the territorial disputes. The normalisation shifted the relationship from antagonism to a formal truce, but all key territorial disputes remained unresolved. It is important to note that peace and a normal relationship did not mean any surrender of interests, but the change in attitude and ways to deal with overlapping claims. That ushered in a period of increased interactions to expand cooperation and resolve differences in a non-violent manner. From this point onward, these disputes were considered "remaining issues" or "historical differences" which were supposed to be decided through peaceful negotiations.[44] The nationalist pragmatists in the Vietnamese elites were not pleased with the November 1991 joint communiqué. From their perspective, Vietnam accepted significant concessions on the Cambodian issue and missed the chance to improve relations with the US and ASEAN countries, but gained very little from China. The Chinese skilfully pressed Vietnam on the Cambodian issue in their favour but left all "hard issues," including border and territorial disputes, for future negotiations. Vietnam had lost its most important bargaining chip, which was its influence over Cambodia, and became more dependent on China. Even worse, to the displeasure of most Vietnamese nationalists, China used "normalisation" to press for the removal of a highly prestigious Politburo member and Foreign Minister Nguyen Co Thach.[45]

Developing bilateral mechanisms for management and resolution of territorial and maritime disputes

The signing of the Paris Peace Accords in Cambodia in October 1991 disentangled Vietnam from Cambodia. Although Vietnam lost its client state and its strategic patron as the Soviet Union dissolved, the country became more secure because it managed to move beyond the past to restore friendship with all its neighbours. The Vietnamese nationalist faction did not want to place all hope on China and pushed for a hedging strategy. As a result, in the run-up to the 7th CPV National Congress in June 1991, they pressed for a policy of befriending all the countries in the world regardless of political and ideological differences.[46] They were also behind the adoption of the "Strategy for Socio-Economic Stabilization and Development Up to the Year 2000," which stressed the need for further multilateralising and diversifying foreign economic relations on the basis of independence, sovereignty, equality and mutual benefits.[47] The nationalist leaders, who were also leading reformists, argued that economic development was the most important foundation that enhanced the legitimacy of the ruling communist party and provided resources for stronger defence. Vietnam's Deputy Foreign Minister Vu Khoan stated: "developmental backwardness will reduce the people's belief, cause social problems, and inevitably lead to threats to security, public order and even regime survival."[48]

In this direction, after normalising relations with China, Vietnam's foreign ministry continued to seek diplomatic relations with ASEAN and Western countries. Despite the conservative caveat of "peaceful evolution," pragmatist elites in the foreign ministry argued that relations with ASEAN countries would bring about opportunities for economic development and greater room for manoeuvre against China. In July 1992, Vietnam subscribed to the ASEAN Treaty of Amity and Cooperation (TAC), vowing to adhere to ASEAN normative principles such as mutual respect for sovereignty and territorial integrity, non-interference in the internal affairs of one another, the settlement of disputes by peaceful means, and renunciation of the threat or use of force. Significant progress was also recorded in terms of developing friendly and cooperative relations with the Western world, especially Western Europe, Australia, Japan and the United States.

As the external threats receded, the course to arms was no longer a preferred option for Hanoi. Rapprochement with its neighbours and old foes allowed Vietnam to demilitarise its foreign policy and shift resources to the productive sector. Between 1988 and 1991, Vietnam slashed its armed forces by 600,000 men. This contributed to the reduction in military expenditure from 12 per cent of GDP to 6.6 per cent.[49] Vietnam's arms imports also plummeted about 80 per cent, from USD 200 million in 1991 to nearly zero in 1992 and 1993.[50] This was the clearest indication of a genuine departure in Vietnam's foreign policy from traditional advocacy of socialist internationalism and blatant use of force to a pro-peace and multi-directional approach.

With regard to the sovereignty disputes in the South China Sea, Hanoi was increasingly interested in upholding the status quo, in the name of "maintenance of regional peace and stability." Given the widening gap in their naval capabilities, Vietnam was unable to defend itself in the event of armed conflicts with China. Since the mid-1980s, Beijing embarked on an aggressive program to modernise its navy. By early 1990s, China had sufficient capability to subdue all other claimants in the Spratlys. A simple comparison showed that Vietnamese air and naval forces were dwarfed by the Chinese forces. In 1990, Vietnam had seven frigates and 250 combat aircraft while China possessed ninety-three submarines, fifty-five principal surface combatants and 5,070 combat aircraft.[51] In 1995, Vietnam had seven principal surface combatants and 190 combat aircraft while China operated fifty-two submarines, fifty-five frigates and destroyers, and 4,970 combat aircraft.[52] Though China had not yet acquired an inflight refuelling capability, which was required to control the sky above the Spratlys, its air force had achieved greater reach thanks to the purchase of two squadrons of SU-27 aircraft from Russia in 1992–1993 and the new airstrip in the Paracels.[53] With this balance of force, Vietnam had no interest in going back to confrontation with China.

Though the concern about and suspicion of China's intents persisted after the normalisation of the relations, almost all statesmen in Hanoi no longer viewed China as an imminent threat. Forging a tacit alignment against China would therefore risk exacerbating the problem at hand. After the settlement of the Cambodian conflict, pragmatism prevailed in the broader South China Sea region. Vietnam and its neighbours, China and the Southeast Asian countries, agreed to develop their cooperative relations regardless of the existing disputes. Consequently, they framed these existing disputes as "historical differences," which were no longer considered an "impediment" to the expansion of their bilateral relations.[54] In view of China's growing power and rapid militarisation, there was greater interest on the part of Vietnam and other smaller claimants in stabilising relations with China and taking advantage of peacetime to push for the long-standing resolution of the existing disputes, thus eradicating the roots of conflicts.

Against that backdrop, China enjoyed the status of Vietnam's most important partner. Though Vietnamese nationalist elites considered hedging through diversification was the best way to secure the nation, they supported broader and deeper engagement with China. On the other side, conservative elements in Hanoi still hoped that stronger bilateral ties with Beijing would prevent China from threatening Vietnam and would foster a resolution of the historical differences. Despite the fact that tensions flared up from time to time due to China's assertiveness in the South China Sea, as described in the next section, they persistently worked to develop a wide range of political, military and economic linkages. As a result, Vietnam's party-to-party and mil-to-mil ties with China expanded quickly after normalisation. Between 1990 and 1992, it was reported that there were 219 visits for political purposes.[55] In the second half of 1993, roughly nine delegations were exchanged.[56] Consequently, a dense network of mechanisms at various levels was developed to expand cooperation and deal with "historical differences," particularly the disputes over the land border, maritime delineation in the Gulf of Tonkin and the control of the Paracel and Spratly Islands.

Most importantly, senior leaders of the two countries met every year to keep the relationship on the right track. Between 1991 and 1995, there were five summit meetings, which issued four joint declarations in November 1991, December 1992, November 1994 and November 1995. The summit meeting between President Le Duc Anh and his Chinese counterpart Jiang Zemin in November 1993 did not produce a joint declaration. It was reported that the leaders of the two countries failed to find a common view on the territorial disputes.[57] All these joint statements reaffirmed the aspiration of settling historical differences through negotiations.[58] These commitments were then translated into concrete bilateral mechanisms at the lower levels. During the Hanoi visit of Chinese Foreign Minister Qian Qichen in February 1992, the two sides agreed to establish working groups to discuss the territorial disputes. The first talks on the land border and maritime boundary in the Gulf of Tonkin at the working level took place in Beijing in October 1992 and the second round in Hanoi in February 1993. These interactions yielded preliminary success in the form of an agreement on basic principles for settling the land frontier and demarcation of the sea boundary in the Gulf of Tonkin, signed on 19

October 1993 between two vice foreign ministers. This agreement entailed three principles: no threat or use of force; preventing differences from blocking the development of the bilateral relations; and self-restraint and avoidance of clashes over territorial disputes.[59]

On this occasion, the two sides agreed to establish two separate expert-level working groups on the land border and the Gulf of Tonkin. The first sessions of these two groups took place in February and March 1994 respectively.[60] While talks on these two issues were progressing, no headway was made regarding the Paracel and Spratly disputes until the vice-ministerial meeting in August 1994. In November 1994, during Chinese President Jiang Zemin's visit to Hanoi, the two sides agreed to start up an expert-level forum on the "issue involving the seas" or "maritime issues," which include sovereignty over insular formations and maritime rights in the South China Sea proper (outside the Gulf of Tonkin). There was disagreement between Vietnam and China about which land features and maritime areas should be considered "disputed." Vietnam wanted to consider the Paracels "disputed" while China refuted this proposition. However, they reached a common understanding that it would take "a good deal of time" to resolve the island disputes. The first meeting of this working group took place in November 1995 after its working mechanism was decided at the vice-ministerial meeting four months before.[61]

As Ramses Amer has argued, a structured four-level system of institutionalised bilateral talks was developed to deal with these territorial issues. At the top of the structure were the yearly high-level talks between the party secretary-generals, the heads of states or governments, which adopted the key directions and principles to regulate the bilateral relations and set deadlines for their subordinates to resolve particular disputes. At the governmental level, the foreign ministerial and deputy ministerial meetings were convened on a regular basis to review developments, decide on principles, working procedures and directions for the discussions of the lower-level specialised groups. These expert working groups, each of which was scheduled to meet once or twice a year, were assigned the task of discussing all related technical matters in the light of the agreed principles.[62] Observing this structure, Carlyle A. Thayer is convinced that Vietnam intentionally used party, state and military visits at different levels as diplomatic tools to codify its relations with China. He opines,

> Vietnam has negotiated a web of joint-statements, agreements and treaties in an effort to quarantine contentious issues from intruding on and negatively affecting areas of cooperation and to make Chinese behaviour more predictable and less likely to harm Vietnam's national interests.[63]

From the negotiation point of view, Vietnam as the weaker partner benefited from this structured hierarchy of negotiations and principle-based discussions for three key reasons. First, regular exchanges maintained the interest of China, its stronger partner, in the border and territorial affairs, therefore maintaining the momentum for interactions on the issues. Second, the structured hierarchy of talks stepped up the pace of negotiation because it allowed easy problems to be settled first by the technical working groups, while the more difficult problems would be left to the higher-level meetings to decide. Third, the regular meetings also served to pre-empt assertive acts or to deal with emerging tensions. In any case, Hanoi was always confident that it had a channel to articulate its concerns to the senior Chinese leaders.

By the end of 1995, it was reported that Hanoi and Beijing had finished five rounds of expert-level talks on the land border and the Gulf of Tonkin each, three rounds of government-level talks on border issues, and one expert-level meeting on the sea borders in the South China Sea.[64] Though no major substantive breakthroughs were reported by this point of time, the extensive and structured system of high-level talks, ministerial meetings and specialised working group sessions provided both sides with forums to reaffirm peaceful intentions, discuss mutual understanding of the situation, build up confidence, and slowly but surely bridge the gap between their positions. Perhaps, this period was about the exploration of claims, arguments and counter-arguments, which served as a basis for both sides to map out substantive compromises in the next period.

Regarding the resolution of the disputes, Vietnam had placed premium on peaceful negotiation, self-restraint, compliance with international law and appropriate cooperative activities. During his visit to Thailand on 15 October 1993, the CPV's Secretary General Do Muoi issued a four-point statement, of which Item 4 stated:

> Vietnam advocates peaceful negotiations to resolve interstate disputes, including maritime and territorial disputes in the South China Sea, on the basis of equality, mutual understanding and respect, observation of international law and 1982 UNCLOS, respect for sovereignty of coastal states. With regard to exclusive economic zones and continental shelf, pending fundamental and permanent solutions, all related parties should maintain stability through exercising self-restraint and refraining from taking any action that may further complicate the situation, from using or threatening to use force. They should look for appropriate cooperative programs, including joint-development in the areas and with methods accepted by all the parties.[65]

This position was repeated in many Vietnamese official texts and speeches, especially in the National Resolution on ratification of the United Nations Convention on the Law of the Sea on 23 June 1994.[66] The key features of this position, including self-restraint and no threat or use of force, were included into joint statements and agreements Vietnam signed with other claimants.[67] This stance can be interpreted narrowly as the maintenance of the status quo, which served as a departure point for confidence building, conflict prevention and settlement negotiation. As the weaker party in the asymmetric relationship, the Vietnamese were naturally more concerned about the potential use of force and expansive claim than China because the Vietnamese hold the belief that China's ultimate goal was to "take exclusive control of the South China Sea" for its own strategic and economic purposes. In addition, it was anticipated that China's growing economic and military power would boost its bargaining power in future negotiations. That explained the reason why Hanoi was keen on and actively pressed for institutionalised exchanges on territorial and boundary issues.

There were no signs that Hanoi would surrender its interests in the South China Sea for the sake of its relations with Beijing. In the Gulf of Tonkin, the core issue was the method applied to divide the waters. In this regard, Vietnam disagreed with China on two issues. The first one was whether the 1982 UNCLOS island regime would be applied to Bach Long Vi Island, which was part of the Vietnamese territory.[68] If it applied, as Vietnam claimed, the island would be capable of generating a full set of maritime zones as stipulated by UNCLOS, which effectively impacted on the definition of the equidistance line in case this principle was applied. China definitely sought to reduce the maritime zones of the island, but only to the extent that it would not be counterproductive for its other positions.[69] Second, the two sides continued to pursue different positions on the status of the French-Chinese Treaty in 1887. Vietnam had long argued that the red line defined in the treaty would be used to delimit the boundary of the Gulf of Tonkin because it would divide the gulf in its favour. On the other hand, the Chinese held that this line might define the ownership of the islands not the boundary of the sea area, waters of the islands and seabed in the gulf.[70]

In the meantime, the expert-level talks on "maritime issues" initiated in late 1995 faced an intractable problem of agenda setting at the beginning. On the basis of the Vietnamese and Chinese claims, three disputes should be on the agenda, namely sovereignty over the Paracels, sovereignty over the Spratlys, and the overlapping EEZ claims. The two sides could only reach an agreement to put the Spratly issue on the agenda. However, China disputed Vietnam's proposal to put the Paracels on the agenda. China did not want to talk about the Paracels because Vietnam was not able to challenge it there.[71] On the other hand, Vietnam refused to discuss maritime zones for the Paracel and Spratly features with China, because this could be interpreted as a recognition of the Chinese sovereignty claim over the Paracels and Spratlys.[72] The two sides clearly pursued different lines of argument about the status of the Paracel and Spratly features. Vietnamese legal experts implied that the Spratly features were ineligible for generating exclusive economic zones and continental shelves, while China actions reflected a different line of argument.[73] Hanoi was afraid that the legal regime of the maritime zones derived from the tiny Spratly and Paracel features would overlap with the EEZs and continental shelf Vietnam claimed for its mainland coast.

In terms of existing sovereignty problems in the South China Sea, Vietnam consistently held that the dispute over the Paracels was bilateral, but the disagreement on the Spratlys involved six parties and a final agreement had to be concluded by all six claimants. Vice Foreign Minister Le Mai confirmed on 13 July 1995 that Vietnam supported both bilateral and multilateral talks among claimants on the Spratly issue.[74] Vietnam's conduct of bilateral talks with China on the Spratly dispute did not mean that it subscribed to Chinese bilateralism. In an interview conducted in December 1995 on the sideline of Do Muoi's visit to China, Vietnamese Foreign Minister Nguyen Manh Cam said: "during this process, we can, of course, hold bipartite, tripartite, or multipartite meetings to exchange views . . . Both sides also realised that this issue cannot be resolved quickly."[75] Nonetheless, it should be noted that Hanoi did not consider Taiwan as an official claimant as it was deferential to Beijing's "one-China" policy after the 1991 communiqué.[76] On the other hand, China clearly indicated that it was not in favour of multilateral discussions of the territorial disputes in the South China Sea and protested against any attempts to internationalise them.[77]

Not only did Vietnam talk with China, but it also engaged actively in a number of negotiations with Laos, Cambodia on the land borders, and with Malaysia, Thailand and Indonesia about the delimitation of the overlapping maritime zones in the Gulf of Thailand and in the South China Sea proper. As early as 5 June 1992, Vietnam and Malaysia signed a Memorandum of Understanding to jointly exploit mineral resources in an overlapping area in the Gulf of Thailand. Two months later, PetroVietnam and Petronas, the two countries' state-owned oil and gas groups, reached a bilateral commercial agreement. In August 1997, oil was first extracted from the Bunga Kekwa field. Notable progress was also recorded in the Vietnam-Thailand negotiations on maritime boundary in the Gulf of Thailand, which resulted in the conclusion of an agreement on this issue in 1997. In 1995, Vietnam and the Philippines signed an agreement on a code of conduct which reaffirmed their commitment to settling the Spratly dispute "through peaceful negotiations in the spirit of friendship, equality, mutual understanding and respect."[78] Just one year before, the Vietnamese and Filipino leaders agreed to form a Joint Marine Scientific Expedition in the South China Sea, which conducted several research trips in the following years.[79] These active bilateral engagements were an indication of a real intention and goodwill on the part of Vietnam to look for long-standing settlements of its remaining territorial and maritime disputes.

Progress in Vietnam's territorial and maritime negotiations between 1991 and 1995 was attributed to several factors. First, after decades of consecutive conflicts, there was broadly shared interest in stability around Vietnam's immediate neighbourhood, which encouraged all sides to the negotiating tables. China, the strongest claimant in the South China Sea, was not an exception. Since 1989, China adopted a "good neighbour" policy towards its neighbours and successfully transformed hostile relations with the Southeast Asian countries into cooperative ties, allaying their suspicion of China as a hegemonic power. Second, despite the fact that China's military power was the strongest among the South China Sea claimants, it still lacked the logistical capabilities to project power beyond the Paracel area for a long period of time. From a strategic vantage point, it was said that the Spratly Islands were easy to raid but difficult to occupy permanently.[80] Third, in a broader setting, the negotiations on territorial disputes were supported by increased multifaceted cooperation among South China Sea coastal states.

On the economic front, Vietnam-China bilateral trade grew from USD 32.23 million in 1991 to USD 1.15 billion in 1996, roughly thirty times after five years.[81] China also offered loans and assistance to assist Vietnam's upgrade of China-built factories. On the political front, friendship was restored quickly through frequent exchanges of visits at different levels. Four joint communiqués/declarations were issued in 1991, 1992, 1994 and 1995 after the high-level talks. In addition, a wide range of exchange programs in the field of culture, education, science and technology, and sport were implemented. Relations between Vietnam and ASEAN countries also expanded significantly. Investment from ASEAN into Vietnam increased ten times between 1991 and 1994, equivalent to 15 per cent of total foreign investment. Right before Vietnam joined ASEAN, its trade with the ASEAN region accounted for 60 per cent of the total trade.[82] As agreed by the leaders, the territorial differences and tensions had minimal impact on the development of the bilateral relations. In turn, the state of high interdependence and close cooperation created incentives for the regional governments to manage tensions around the territorial and maritime disputes in a way that would not derail the whole relationship.

Chinese assertiveness exposed the limits of bilateralism

In the early 1990s, Vietnam made marked progress not only in negotiations on frontier areas but also in managing the territorial and maritime disputes with its neighbours. While negotiations on the delineation of its maritime and terrestrial territories were proceeding, Vietnam managed incidents on the ground in various ways, particularly bilateral talks. It also supported proposals for a code of conduct and joint development. As mentioned earlier, Vietnam agreed with Malaysia on joint development in the overlapping area in the Gulf of Thailand in 1992. In 1995, Vietnam and the Philippines reached a consensus on a bilateral "code of conduct" in the South China Sea. Though maintaining the routine claim to sovereignty over the Spratlys, these states repeatedly reassured each other with pledges of self-restraint, peaceful settlement and goodwill in the handling of incidents.[83] However, mini-crises occurred occasionally, since China took advantage of others' inaction to incrementally encroach upon the South China Sea. The policy of bandwagoning in the form of unilateral self-restraint, bilateral engagements, and emphasis on cooperation/interdependence was obviously inadequate to address the fundamental South China Sea problem, or to be precise the China problem.

The relationship between Vietnam and China observably oscillated between constructive bilateral talks and sporadic emergence of tension. On the surface, relations were characterised by friendly meetings and cooperation. Publicly, officials of both countries said that negotiation was the dominant theme of relations between Vietnam and China. However, anxiety regarding ongoing disputes was renewed from time to time around unilateral assertive actions taken by different parties on the ground. Closely following the developments of Sino-Vietnamese relations, Ramses Amer observed that while Vietnam was held accountable in a small number of instances, "a majority of the crisis situations have been caused by Chinese activities."

China's behaviour with regard to territorial disputes was unpredictable with a mixture of cooperative and assertive actions. Not long after formal normalisation of relations between Vietnam and China in November 1991, a chain of troubles regarding territorial and maritime issues arose, dashing Vietnamese ideological conservatives' initial optimism about a benign China. In February 1992, Chinese

Foreign Minister Qian Qichen visited Hanoi, signing an agreement on the establishment of the working group on the territorial disputes. At the same time, China adopted a Law on the Territorial Waters and Contiguous Zone, in which it reasserted the claim to islands in the South China Sea and reserved the right to use force in this area to prevent violations of its sovereignty.[84] This law's promulgation stirred up concerns in China's neighbourhood, as it was indicative of China's uncompromising position over the sovereignty issues and of its willingness to use force to settle the disputes as it did in 1988. It also contradicted previous pledges by Chinese leaders on peaceful settlement of the territorial disputes.

In the same month, the Chinese in a sudden move tried to take over Da Ba Dau (Three-Head Rock) in the Spratlys.[85] On 8 May, during the Beijing visit of former Vietnamese leader Nguyen Van Linh (then senior advisor to the Central Committee), China concluded an agreement with the US Crestone Energy Corporation, offering it the right to explore the Tu Chinh bank (Wan An Bei in Chinese, Vanguard Bank Area), which Vietnam claimed as part of its legitimate continental shelf under UNCLOS.[86] The Tu Chinh area was about 600 n.m. from the mainland of China (almost twice of the maximum distance of 350 n.m. from the baselines as stipulated by 1982 UNCLOS); only 84 n.m. from the Vietnamese coastal islands of Do Long, Do Nho and Hai; and about 50 n.m. from the nearest Spratly Island but separated from it by a trench 2,000 m deep (see Figure 2.10).[87] In the same month, Vietnamese sources revealed that the Chinese also made some intrusions in the land border area. In June, the Chinese military personnel planted a territorial marker on Da Lac Reef of the Spratlys. In August, it was reported that China installed an oil-drilling platform in a disputed area in the Gulf of Tonkin, which the two sides agreed to leave unfilled.[88] In September 1992, it was reported that the Chinese authorities had detained nearly twenty Vietnamese vessels transporting goods from Hong Kong to Hai Phong and Hong Gai ports in Vietnam. It was a deliberate campaign by Chinese armed police because these Vietnam-bound ships were intercepted and seized right after they left Hong Kong waters.[89]

The Vietnamese handled the first two events with care and in a low-key manner. No public protests were recorded. Hanoi chose to state its official positions through bilateral diplomatic communications with the hope that it would not escalate the tension and disturb fragile rapprochement between the two countries. In a note sent on 28 February 1992, Vietnam reasserted its sovereignty claims and reminded China of the November 1991 agreement to settle differences peacefully and refrain from actions that complicate the situation.[90] However, China did not take this warning seriously. Subsequent Chinese actions made Hanoi more vocal in asserting its claims and articulating its protests. Vietnamese officials were reportedly resentful that the Crestone contract was signed with a US diplomat present in Beijing's Great Hall of People, where the Vietnamese leader had just met with General Secretary Jiang Zemin and Premier Li Peng. In their view, this behaviour resembled old-style imperial Chinese conduct.[91] Above all, this concession was also seen as a politically clever calculation to put Vietnam "in a political quandary."[92] The Chinese calculated that Vietnam's desire to normalise relations with the United States and to end the US-led embargo would prevent it from taking drastic actions against a US-involved project, though China's claim to this area was obviously excessive. It was also reported that China's Crestone concession was a response to Vietnam's award of exploration blocks within its EEZs, to companies from Australia, Britain, Canada, France and India.[93] Therefore, the Crestone incident was legally important, as this was the first time that China claimed the Tu Chinh area as part of the "adjacent waters" of the disputed Spratly features. From the Vietnamese perspective, China bent international law to turn Vietnam's legitimately entitled territorial sea and EEZ into disputed waters. The Chinese move effectively put Vietnam in a dilemma, whether to stand up to defend its legitimate rights or to compromise its claim to save its newfound relationship with China and avoid troubles with the United States.

China's Crestone contract prompted the re-emergence of Vietnam's old perception of China as a long-term threat to Vietnam's national security. At the third plenary session of the 7th Central Committee of the CPV at the end of June 1992, the question of China's designs in the South China Sea was tabled. Some old, ideologically conservative party leaders insisted that Vietnam should discount the small rows with China because the two countries shared the greater goal of building socialism. At the other end of the table, some younger, nationalist Central Committee members expressed deep distrust with China and argued that China used "socialism as a rope to tie Vietnam's hands."[94] It was reported that even the CPV Secretary General Do Muoi, the leading conservative who led the efforts to normalise relations with China, actually called China "expansionist," a label that was dropped from the CPV vocabulary from the early 1990s. The sharp division prevented the meeting from reaching any concrete conclusions on Chinese intention. Yet, ostensibly, after the plenum the Ministry of Foreign Affairs was given the green light to make strong public protests. An official in Vietnam's Foreign Ministry said, "We realize that we also need to make public protests and try to mobilise international opinion, or China will keep expanding in the South China Sea."[95] Consequently, the Foreign Ministry was enabled to play greater role in handling of relations between Vietnam and China.

As a result, on 10 May 1992, a spokesman from Vietnam's Foreign Ministry publicly stated that the Tu Chinh area was located "fully" within Vietnam's undisputed exclusive economic zone and continental shelf, and outside the periphery of the Spratly Islands.[96] On 19 May, the Vietnamese Permanent Mission to the United Nations lodged a note to all state members to reaffirm this position.[97] It was noted that Vietnam prudently escalated its response vis-à-vis China's behaviour. On 5 September, Hanoi even warned Beijing of the possibility of using force to ward off two Chinese vessels exploring for oil in the Gulf of Tonkin.[98] In a press conference on 8 September, Vietnam's Foreign Minister Nguyen Manh Cam accused China of "impeding the smooth normalisation of relations" by sending an oil rig to Vietnamese waters in the Gulf of Tonkin. He strongly warned, "We are determined to normalise relations with China but at the same time, we are determined to protect our sovereignty and territorial integrity."[99] By this statement, Vietnam sent a strong message to China that it treasured its cooperative relationship with China but would not tolerate China's infringements.

The tension gradually waned on the eve of Chinese Premier Li Peng's watershed visit to Hanoi from 30 November to 4 December 1992, the first by a Chinese premier in twenty-one years. Just three weeks before that landmark visit, China withdrew its drilling vessels from the Gulf of Tonkin. Li Peng brought to Hanoi reassurance that "China will never seek hegemony nor practise expansionism and at the same time it is opposed to hegemony and power politics of all descriptions."[100] He also stressed the principles of peaceful settlements of disputes and no resort to force or the threat of force and commitments to efforts to narrow differences. During his visit, four major agreements on investments, economics, technical cooperation, science and technology, and culture were signed. It remained unclear how Li Peng's diplomacy affected Vietnam's perception of China, but reportedly at the end of 1992 the CPV Central Committee adopted a classified resolution that defined Vietnam's foreign relations along a list of priorities. China, Cuba and North Korea were put in the first priority category.[101] However, suspicion of China stayed within Vietnamese nationalist pragmatist elites. Foreign Minister Nguyen Manh Cam openly said, "Premier Li Peng has stated his views in our discussions. We took note of the statements. It is our hope that it will be translated into reality."[102] Cam's statement indicated that Hanoi was aware of the difference between China's rhetoric and actions.

In Hanoi, Li Peng proposed to shelve the disputes to focus on joint development in disputed maritime areas of the Spratlys, implying an initial experiment in the Tu Chinh area.[103] However, Vietnam rejected that proposal, regarding it as a Chinese tactic to turn its EEZ and continental shelf into disputed areas. Vietnam's foreign minister argued, "Tu Chinh (the concession China awarded to the Crestone Corporation) is neither a disputed area nor an outstanding problem left by history but a new problem arising after the normalisation of the relations."[104] Hanoi did not rule out the idea of joint development. In fact, it accepted joint development in the overlapping area with Malaysia as early as 1992. However, Hanoi stood firm to oppose any joint development proposals in the EEZ and continental shelves that it claimed in the light of UNCLOS 1982. As mentioned earlier, Hanoi refuted China's claim to "adjacent waters" of the Spratly Islands because such acceptance may be interpreted as recognition of China's claim to sovereignty over them. In addition, it was China's condition for joint development that other countries should acknowledge China's sovereignty first.[105] As Leszek Buszynski commented, the Chinese defined "joint development" as foreign involvement in exploiting China's resources.[106] From the Vietnamese point of view, joint development was only possible in the actual disputed areas where overlap occurs between legitimate maritime claims derived from undisputed land features.

Throughout 1993 and 1994, there were no significant incidents in the South China Sea. In the meantime, the two countries signed an agreement on principles to guide the settlement of border territory disputes. Specialised working groups were set up. However, uneasiness lingered and Vietnam's nerve was constantly put to the test. Two cases of intrusion by Chinese oil exploration ships into Vietnamese territorial waters near the central coastline were reported in February and May 1993. Also in that year, it was reported that China had secretly built an airstrip on the Woody Island of the Paracels. Though the Chinese official held that the airfield was for transportation purpose, military analysts believed that it had a military function that helped extend China's reach into the South China Sea.[107] It should be remembered that in the 1988 Spratly skirmish, Chinese naval forces did not have air cover because Chinese fighter jets could not reach the region without air refuelling capabilities.

In April 1994, the Vietnamese were alarmed by Crestone seismological surveys in the Tu Chinh area. On 5 May, Vietnam issued a statement through the spokesman of the Foreign Ministry, reiterating its long-standing position that the Tu Chinh area was located "fully" within Vietnam's EEZ and continental shelf and was not a disputed area. A war of words began on 10 May with China's denunciation of Vietnam's exploration contract with American Mobil Oil Company in Thanh Long (Blue Dragon) oil field, which China claimed was "part of *adjacent waters* of Nansha islands" (emphasis added) (see Figure 2.10). Vietnam quickly refuted China's accusation and asserted that both Tu Chinh and Thanh Long areas were located in its legitimate EEZ and continental shelf where Vietnam was entitled to sovereign rights to explore and exploit natural resources.[108] The situation calmed down in June when the second round of the joint working groups on the land border and the Gulf of Tonkin was convened. The issues were brought to the meetings between Vietnamese and Chinese foreign ministers on the sidelines of ASEAN meetings in July. In this context, China's proposal for joint-development resurfaced. In this regard, in the interview with *Sankei Shimbun* on 22 August, Vietnam's deputy foreign minister bluntly criticised China's proposal for joint development as no more than a justification of Chinese presence in Vietnamese waters under the "name of joint development."[109]

As China pushed for its expansive claims, Vietnam gradually aligned its claims and arguments with international law. In terms of sovereignty over the Paracels and Spratlys, Vietnamese legal experts utilised historical evidence and highlighted legal principles and norms such as "effective sovereignty" (acquisition of sovereignty should be effective, uninterrupted and peaceful occupation), and wide range of modern ICJ cases to defend their claims and counter China's doctrine of discovery and sovereignty since ancient times.[110] The Vietnamese also indicated that they were willing to submit the case to the ICJ while the Chinese were not.[111] In terms of maritime rights, Hanoi moved to align its claims to the spirit and letter of UNCLOS 1982. On 23 June 1994, Vietnam's National Assembly adopted the Resolution on the Ratification of UNCLOS. According to Thao, UNCLOS 1982 has constituted "a *firm international legal ground* for the struggle to protect Vietnam's seas and continental shelf, as well as its legitimate rights and interests on the sea and its sovereignty over the Hoang Sa and Truong Sa archipelagos."[112] In 1992, Hanoi started granting a large number of oil and gas exploration contracts to foreign companies within the exclusive economic zones as authorised by UNCLOS.

Obviously, the headache for the Vietnamese in the South China Sea was not about the disputes themselves and the complexities of the claims, but primarily about China's behaviour. In the Vietnamese perspective, China was unpredictable, inconsistent, ambiguous in its claims, and legally dubious. There seemed to be big gaps between Chinese rhetoric and actions on the ground. On the one hand, China's leaders vocally declared their policy of self-restraint and peaceful settlements of the disputes and repeatedly advised the Vietnamese counterparts to handle bilateral relations with care. Despite this rhetoric, most of the incidents that heightened tension were initiated on the Chinese side. The common pattern was that incidents often occurred on the eve of important visits or meetings and tension then declined when these events took place as a show of China's "goodwill." As the pattern persisted, the Vietnamese were prone to think that these mini-crises were deliberately orchestrated rather than accidental. Dao Huy Ngoc, Vietnam's former ambassador to the United Nations, said straightaway, "We watch China's actions, not her words."[113] Given the confusing signals that the Chinese authorities sent out, the Vietnamese kept questioning China's underlying motives.

From the Vietnamese point of view, China's claims to the Tu Chinh and Thanh Long areas, which were about 600 n.m. from Hainan, were legally unacceptable and unjustifiable. China claimed these areas without indicating precisely the meaning of "adjacent waters" and legal regime applied to the disputed islands. In contrast, the Vietnamese argued strictly on the basis of UNCLOS 1982 that the entire Thanh Long and most of the Tu Chinh area fell within Vietnam's 200 n.m. EEZ.[114] Second, both areas are located within Vietnam's extended continental shelf as a natural prolongation from its mainland. Third, it is argued that even if China owned the westernmost island of the Spratlys, the application of the principle of equidistance, proportionality, and mainland priority would give these areas to Vietnam. In addition, most of the Spratly islets are small, insignificant and remote from China's mainland, making it incapable of generating EEZs and continental shelves. In this case, China's claim to Tu Chinh and Thanh Long was untenable from the legal point of view. To solve the sovereignty dispute, Vietnam indicated several times that it is willing to go with China to the international court to resolve the disputes or discuss the matters multilaterally.[115] Yet, China consistently insisted on bilateral processes, in which it could leverage its military, political and economic power.

In 1995, while the western part of the South China Sea was relatively calm, the eastern part was unsettled by an incident on the Mischief Reef, roughly 135 n.m. from Palawan but 559 n.m. from China's Hainan. In January, the Filipino fishermen discovered China's newly built stilted complex in the unoccupied Mischief Reef. Eight Chinese vessels were reportedly near the reef. The Philippines quickly lodged a protest, condemning the Chinese act as inconsistent with international law and against the 1992 ASEAN Declaration on the South China Sea in Manila. In response to an uproar from the Philippines, Beijing explained that the structure was built as a shelter for fishermen and that "the occupation was ordered by low-level personnel acting without the knowledge and consent of the Chinese government."[116] However, satellite photographs revealed that this structure was solid and firm and was built for military purposes rather than for civilian uses. The Mischief Reef incident was a watershed because this was the first time China moved to challenge the claim of an ASEAN member in the South China Sea. Prior to the event, the clashes in the South China Sea happened between China and Vietnam only.

The crisis had two broad implications not only for the Philippines but for the whole of Southeast Asia also. First, the Mischief Reef incident set off an alarm across Southeast Asia about regional vulnerabilities to China's growing maritime power and ambition. As Paul Godwin argued in his book published in 1997, "Force projection in the South China Sea to enforce China's sovereignty claims is now more plausible than it was a decade ago."[117] Regional balance of power was tilting in favour of China because both the United States and Russia scaled down their military commitments to Southeast Asia. Russia withdrew all its forward combat forces from Cam Ranh Bay. Though it retained a base in the first decade after the Cold War, Russian presence was minimal with the main focus on surveillance and intelligence.[118] In 1992, the US withdrew its military bases in Subic in the Philippines. The withdrawals of the United States and Russia from the region created a power vacuum for other powers to fill in. The Philippines' military weakness prompted China to expand at its expense.

Second, the crisis rekindled the scepticism about China's strategic intents and perception of China as a potential threat. Though it was unclear whether the decision came from Beijing or not, the Mischief Reef incident represented an indication of a revisionist China. Putting the Mischief Reef incident in a line with the 1974 Paracel and 1988 Spratly crises, some analysts and politicians in Southeast Asia argued that China's creeping occupation of the Mischief Reef was merely another stepping stone towards China's ultimate goal to turn the South China Sea into a "Chinese lake" and establish its hegemony in the region.[119] Upon the passage of the Chinese Territorial Waters Law, B.A. Hamzah held that

> China's intentions in the South China Sea are very much more than settling old scores with Vietnam. Peking's recent action strongly suggests that its ultimate aim is to replace the United States and Russia in the region.[120]

As China's decision-making remained so opaque, there were no clear insights into the key actors that took the lead in the Mischief Reef operation. Whatever factors triggered China's action, the Mischief Reef incident sent out a shockwave across Southeast Asia because from now on, no South China Sea claimants would be immune to Chinese territorial ambitions. It should be recalled that Southeast Asian claimants adopted a deferential approach, staying nearly silent when the Chinese invaded the Vietnamese positions in the Paracels and Spratlys in January 1974 and March 1988 respectively. This time, ASEAN as a group did manage to raise the issue at an informal meeting between ASEAN-China officials in Hangzhou in April 1995.[121] However, divisive ASEAN was reluctant to push the issue further. In spite of Manila's forceful advocacy, other ASEAN members refused to bring the issue to the ASEAN Regional Forum (ARF) with a fear of antagonising China.[122]

Suffering from recurring Chinese invasions and assertive actions, Vietnam had no illusion of China's design for the South China Sea. On this occasion, Hanoi sent its foreign minister to Manila to discuss the Spratly dispute.[123] Hanoi then announced its intention to reinforce its outposts in the Spratlys.[124] Unlike other ASEAN claimants,

Vietnam issued a public statement accusing China's expansion and Mischief Reef occupation of complicating the situation and undermining peace, stability and cooperation in the region.[125] For the Vietnamese, it was also another case that China's actions did not match its words. A dense web of bilateral engagements and increased economic interdependence proved to be insufficient to constrain China's assertiveness. Chinese occupation of Mischief Reef provided a strong reason for Vietnamese nationalist pragmatist leaders, notably Prime Minister Vo Van Kiet and Foreign Minister Nguyen Manh Cam, to press for increased engagement with the West and the ASEAN countries to curb China's hegemonic ambitions.

Expanding the range of options

After normalisation, conservative ideologues in Hanoi were keen on developing a network of bilateral talks with their counterparts in Beijing to promote political and security dialogues, economic interdependence, and multifaceted cooperation. Through this web of bilateral engagements, Vietnam sought a long-standing resolution of territorial and boundary disputes, and also tried to prevent tension from escalating on the ground. However, the series of South China Sea incidents in the early 1990s also had a broader impact on Vietnam-China relations. As Carlyle A. Thayer put it, they effectively undermined the argument of the Vietnamese conservatives that deference and bandwagoning could be rewarded with China's protection and benign behaviour.[126]

Taking stock of the South China Sea developments, Vietnamese pragmatist nationalists came to realise that Vietnam was involved in a whole new game with China. In feudal times, the Vietnamese emperors accepted the tributary relationship with China in exchange for peace and stability. During the fight for independence, the Vietnamese communists had "as close as lips and teeth" relationships with the Chinese communists. With these relationships, the Vietnamese political elites felt secure, at least temporarily, in front of its imperial neighbour. Now, Vietnam and China were two sovereign states, two comrades but not allies, and each has its own national interests. One Vietnamese official elaborated:

> There are three possible ways of organising our relations with China: (1) confrontation; (2) satellite status similar to North Korea or (3) a median position between the two. Satellite status provides no guarantees. North Korea was sacrificed by China when it turned to South Korea. Also, even if Vietnam were to be a good satellite, China would not leave us alone. They will always pressure us and try to dominate Southeast Asia. We tried for a full year to forge new relations with China but we failed. Take its occupation of Bai Tu Chinh and the Crestone affair. Okay, we distrusted China but it was only with Bai Tu Chinh that we understood that China follows its national interest. That game is in the nature of international politics.[127]

It implies that China would not compromise its claim in the South China Sea for the sake of a good relationship with Vietnam. Therefore, Vietnam needed a new approach to defend sovereignty and territorial integrity without provoking hostilities on the part of China. In this regard, Vietnamese pragmatic nationalist leaders pushed for a hedging strategy by deepening bilateral relationship with China while at the same time balancing this relationship by increased cooperation with other powers. But, it should be noted that they did not oppose cooperation with China. To protect Vietnam's interests in the face of China's future assertiveness, they saw the need for a hedging strategy in the form of defence build-up, ASEAN membership and increased involvement of external stakeholders.

The first option was to boost national defence capabilities. In the mid-1993, the downward trend in the military budget was reversed. It was reported that the approved military budget in 1994 was increased by 49 per cent more over the previous year.[128] This increase was said to satisfy the newly emerging needs of national defence and security. This increase was enabled by the strong growth of the Vietnamese economy that allowed Vietnam to purchase advanced weapons from Russia. There was a heavy focus on naval and air power. In March 1994, Vietnam placed three orders with Russian weapon manufacturers to acquire six Su-27 Flanker fighter-bombers, four defence radar systems, and two Type 1241 RA corvettes, with options for further purchase. These contracts represented Vietnam's largest military purchase in the post–Cold War. In the same year, Vietnam reached an agreement with Russia to co-produce the BPS 500-type missile boat. These purchases indicated that Vietnam aimed to upgrade its naval and maritime air capabilities to defend its waters.[129] Reportedly, Vietnamese military delegations were sent to a number of countries, including Russia, Ukraine, Australia, Israel, India, Malaysia and Singapore, to explore the possibilities of military supplies, especially ships, radar systems and fighters, and training agreements. Not surprisingly, Vietnam did not look to China as an arms supplier, though the exchanges between two militaries increased.[130]

The second option was political alignment with ASEAN countries. Though Vietnam became a member of the United Nations in 1975, Hanoi's experience of multilateralism was near zero before 1991. At that time, some leaders in Hanoi were antagonistic to ASEAN, considering it no different from the US-led SEATO.[131] However, Vietnam's relations with ASEAN as a group and its members individually improved significantly in the post–Cold War period. Between 1991 and 1992, Vietnam hinted at its desire to be part of ASEAN. In 1992, Vietnam subscribed to the Treaty of Amity and Cooperation and participated in ASEAN processes as an observer. As Carlyle A. Thayer pointed out, it was China's forceful actions in the Spratlys in 1992 that pushed Vietnam to consider ASEAN's membership.[132] Two years later, Vietnam was formally invited to join the group. Also in this year, Vietnam became one of the founding members of the ARF. Vietnam was accepted as a full member of the group in July 1995.

China and the South China Sea disputes figured significantly in Vietnam's calculation to seek ASEAN membership.[133] This is not to argue that the concern about China's assertiveness in the South China Sea was the only impulse for Vietnam to join the group. ASEAN membership no doubt provided Vietnam with other benefits such as improved relations with its neighbours, favourable external conditions for economic renovation, a better bargaining position with other states, especially China and the United States, and broader access to international markets and investments.[134] As far as the South China Sea disputes are concerned, though ASEAN was not an alliance that had military teeth to deter China, the organisation could be an effective medium to restrain the Middle Kingdom. From the Vietnamese perspective, China would refrain from assertive actions if Southeast Asian countries banded together. ASEAN appeared to be a resilient and strong grouping that played an effective part in putting pressure on Vietnam in the Cambodian issue.[135] It was hoped that when all the members united, the group could exert considerable political and diplomatic weight against big powers.

In addition, Hanoi quickly realised that Vietnam and other Southeast Asia claimants had the same concerns about China and shared the need to engage China to maintain regional peace and stability through self-restraint and preservation of the status quo in the disputed areas.[136] When China adopted the Law on the Territorial Waters and Contiguous Zone and moved on to Da Ba Dau Reef in 1992, ASEAN foreign ministers adopted a five-point Declaration on the South China Sea calling for peaceful resolution self-restraint.[137] This ASEAN position, enshrined in the South China Sea declaration and the Treaty of Amity and Cooperation in Southeast Asia, was largely in conformity with the principles of Vietnam's foreign policy in the *Doi Moi* period. Therefore, Vietnam fully endorsed the ASEAN Declaration on the South China Sea. It was clear that the pragmatist nationalists in Hanoi saw increased cooperation with ASEAN countries as a means to enhance its position vis-à-vis big powers, especially China, and to curb their aggressive intents.[138] Hoang Anh Tuan argued,

> Vietnam as a member of ASEAN would have some effect on Hanoi-Beijing relations. Particularly in the conflict over the Spratly Islands, China would find it *more difficult* to isolate Vietnam, as it would no longer treat Vietnam separately from other ASEAN claimants to the islands. This would temper any Chinese intentions to put military pressures on the Vietnamese presence in those islands which Hanoi concurrently hold.[139]

Clearly, ASEAN was viewed as a good platform for Hanoi to forge a common understanding and position on the South China Sea disputes. Jörn Dosch argued that ASEAN membership somehow converted bilateral Sino-Vietnamese issues into multilateral ones involving China and ASEAN as a group.[140] Plugging itself to the ASEAN circuit might help Vietnam to borrow the strength of ASEAN as regional grouping to increase its bargaining position vis-à-vis China and other big powers. Last but not least, ASEAN was the most practical option because it afforded a measure of deterrence without provoking confrontation from China. Suffice it to say, ASEAN was by no means a perfect option, but it is a good supplement to bilateral engagements and self-defence as a means to constrain China. Vietnamese commentators explained,

> Vietnamese history shows that one-sided relations have led to political isolation and economic difficulties . . . Therefore, Vietnam's ASEAN membership

should be achieved in a way that would strengthen instead of harm Vietnam's relations with China.[141]

However, Vietnamese analysts saw no prospect for a military alliance between Vietnam and other Southeast Asian. Vietnam did not intend to take ASEAN as a balancer against China.[142] Rather, the Vietnamese diplomats framed ASEAN as part of the policy of multilateralisation and diversification of foreign relations.[143] They also worked to reposition Vietnam from a socialist outpost in Southeast Asia to an Asia-Pacific country and a member of the regional community. Right after normalisation with China, in early 1992, they engineered Prime Minister Vo Van Kiet's groundbreaking visits to key ASEAN states, namely Thailand, Singapore and Indonesia. In 1993, they successfully arranged the historic trips of party chief Do Muoi to Thailand and Singapore on the eve of Le Duc Anh's visit to Beijing. As a result, Vietnam's interaction with ASEAN expanded and ASEAN invited Vietnam to join the group earlier than expected. ASEAN members largely saw Vietnam's admission as strengthening the association. Reportedly, a considerable percentage of the CPV, mostly the conservatives, questioned the impact of ASEAN membership on Vietnam's socialist orientation. Some Politburo members argued that Vietnam could have relations with ASEAN but should not join ASEAN. Dao Duy Tung, a conservative Politburo member, opined that ASEAN was merely reincarnation of anti-communist SEATO.[144] There was little available information on how the intra-party debate on ASEAN membership played out. However, Vietnam's admission to ASEAN in July 1995 implied that conservative argumentation lost ground.

The third option was to get external stakeholders involved in the maintenance of rule-based order that enabled Vietnam to advance its rights. The most direct way to do this was to offer joint-exploration and exploitation of resources to foreign companies in Vietnam's legitimately claimed EEZ and continental shelf. As the economy grew, Vietnam became more interested in offshore resources within its EEZ and continental shelf. However, China was the main obstacle with expansive claims and assertive actions. Defying China's objections and countering China's Crestone undertaking, on 19 April 1994 PetroVietnam entered a production-sharing contract to grant the American corporation Mobil Oil the rights to explore the Thanh Long area and promised to protect foreign partners against acts of aggression. This type of joint production venture with Western oil companies benefited Vietnam in a number of ways. First, it allowed Vietnam to take advantage of Western technologies to tap into the resources within its continental shelf. Second, the presence of foreign oil firms was a signpost that marked Vietnam's legitimate maritime zones. It was a way to legitimate Vietnam's claims in line with UNCLOS 1982 and denounce other countries' excessive claims. Third, through this strategy Vietnam was clearly "seeking to tie its fate in the South China Sea to that of Western oil companies, hoping thereby to add to its strength and deter China."[145] The Vietnamese leadership tended to believe that political support would follow economic interest. It is worth recalling that Tran Quang Co, former Vietnamese deputy foreign minister, saw the presence of an oil rig of Mobil Oil (US) as valuable as the Seventh Fleet of the US Navy.

The indirect way to limit China's influence was to expand Vietnam's international relations, especially its ties with the world's major powers. The Vietnamese had learned a good lesson about the cost of political isolation after the March 1988 Spratly incident. A Vietnamese diplomat argues that Vietnam should look for and utilise "as many spider webs as possible to tie up the elephant."[146] The whole idea was to restrain China without directly confronting it. As a result, in the early 1990s Vietnam successfully established multifaceted relations with Japan, India, European countries, South Korea and Australia. Despite conservative concerns about "peaceful evolution," the Ministry of Foreign Affairs pushed for normalisation of relations with the old enemy, the United States, which finally came in July 1995. It is interesting to note that after the Mischief Reef incident in 1995, a Vietnamese foreign ministry official proposed a bigger role for the US in the Spratly dispute.[147]Though normalisation with the United States was justified mainly on economic grounds, the strategic aspect could not be ignored.

By the end of 1995, outreach bore fruit, gaining Hanoi more friends and improving its international footing. After being a politically isolated country in most of the 1980s, Vietnam secured diplomatic relations with 163 countries, including all five permanent members of the UN Security Council, by the end of 1996.[148] Vietnam's openness to the global market helped it survive the collapse of the Eastern European socialist bloc at the end of the 1980s and the demise of the Soviet Union in 1991. At the same time, it was hoped that relations with multiple powers would help constrain China, as Sino-Vietnamese relations would be entangled within a regional network of interlocking economic and political interests.[149] Anyway, this pathway effective reduced threats and risks from its Southeast Asian neighbours and big powers, helping Hanoi focus on coping with China, its principal foreign policy problem in the post–Cold War.

Conclusion

After the 1988 skirmish with China in the Spratlys, Vietnam was more determined to withdraw from Cambodia to seek peace and acceptance from the international community. It aimed to pacify its neighbourhood and maintain the status quo in the South China Sea. This approach was manifest in Politburo Resolution 13 adopted in May 1988, which prescribed a complete withdrawal from Cambodia, normalisation with China and expanded international relations. Though the process was initiated by a group of pragmatic nationalist decision-makers, it was then dictated by ideologically conservative elements within the CPV. As a result, in September 1989 Vietnam finally conducted a complete withdrawal from Cambodia in a way that facilitated normalised relations with China. After the normalisation of Vietnam-China relations in 1991, Vietnamese conservative leaders continued to push for closer political and security ties with China, though China rejected its proposal for a revived military alliance between the two countries. A dense web of regular bilateral meetings at various levels was established to deal with the disputes over land borders, the delimitation in the Gulf of Tonkin and so-called maritime issues. In addition, the two countries agreed to develop cooperative relations regardless of the resolution of these so-called historical differences. However, normal relations, expanded cooperation and bilateral mechanisms did not bring an end to Vietnam's concern about the South China Sea disputes. Tension erupted from time to time, mostly due to unilateral acts by China. From the Vietnamese perspective, China intentionally created disputes in Vietnam's legitimate EEZ and continental shelf. All this disquiet prompted inner-party circles in Hanoi, especially the pragmatic nationalist elites, to expand Vietnam's policy options in view of the prospect of China becoming a revisionist power. As a result, they pushed for a defence build-up, ASEAN membership and increased involvement of external stakeholders to place more constraints on China, to preserve the status quo over the island groups and to advance Vietnam's maritime interests in light of international law.

Notes

1 Dang Cong san Viet Nam, *Van kien Dai hoi Dai bieu Toan quoc lan thu VI*, Hanoi: Su That Publisher, 1987, p.99.
2 T.Q. Co, *Hoi uc va Suy nghi* (*Memoir and Reflection*), Hanoi, 2003, Chapter 4, p.36.
3 Dang Cong san Viet Nam, *Van kien Dai hoi Dai bieu Toan quoc lan thu VI*, p.107 (emphasis added).
4 Co, *Hoi uc va Suy nghi*, Chapter 4, pp. 33–4.
5 G. Klintworth, "The Outlook for Cambodia: The China Factor," In: Gary Klintworth (ed.), *Vietnam's Withdrawal from Cambodia: Regional Issues and Realignments*, Canberra: Strategic and Defense Studies Center, ANU, 1990, p.49.
6 M.C. Williams, *Vietnam at the Crossroads*, New York: Council on Foreign Relations Press, 1992, p.55.
7 S. Tomoda, "Detaching from Cambodia," In: James William Morley and Masashi Nishihara (Eds), *Vietnam Joins the World*, Armonk, NY: M. E. Sharpe, 1997, p.144.
8 R. Amer, "Sino-Vietnamese Relations: Past, Present and Future," In: A. Thayer and Ramses Amer Carlyle (eds.), *Vietnamese Foreign Policy in Transition*, Singapore: Institute of Southeast Asian Studies, 1999, pp. 72–3; R.K. Betts, "The Strategic Predicament," In: James William Morley and Masashi Nishihara (eds.), *Vietnam Joins the World*, Armonk, NY: M.E. Sharpe, 1997, p.105.
9 Betts, "The Strategic Predicament," pp. 105–07.
10 Williams, *Vietnam at the Crossroads*, p.66.
11 L. Buszynski, "The Soviet Union and Vietnamese Withdrawal from Cambodia," In: Gary Klintworth (Ed), *Vietnam's Withdrawal from Cambodia: Regional Issues and Realignments*, Canberra: ANU Strategic and Defense Studies Center, 1990, p.41.
12 H. Viet, "Tu Hoang Sa nghi ve tuong lai Bien Dong," *BBC Tieng Viet*, 13 January 2014. Online. Available HTTP: <www.bbc.co.uk/vietnamese/forum/2014/01/140113_bien-dong_hoangsa> (accessed 23 March 2015).
13 I.C. Storey and C.A. Thayer, "Cam Ranh Bay: Past Imperfect, Future Conditional," *Contemporary Southeast Asia* 23, no. 3, 2001, p.456.
14 R.K. Betts, "The Strategic Predicament," p.102.
15 "Gac Ma-1988: Goi dung ten 'cuoc chien xam luoc cua Trung Quoc," *Bao Dat Viet*, 15 March 2016.
16 "CQ-88: Vi sao Lien Xo lam ngo Trung Quoc xam luoc Truong Sa," *Bao Dat Viet*, 21 March 2016.
17 Co, *Hoi uc va Suy nghi*, p.31.
18 Ibid., p.159.
19 Ibid.
20 Ibid.

21 Tomoda, "Detaching from Cambodia," p.143.
22 Betts, "The Strategic Predicament," p.207.
23 Claude Pomonti, "Le contentieux entre le Vietnam et la Chine: Hanoi refuse les conditions mises par Pékin à une normalisation de leurs relations," *Le Monde*, 21 June 1991.
24 C.A. Thayer, "Vietnam: Coping with China," *Southeast Asian Affairs*, 1994, p.354.
25 B. Womack, *China and Vietnam: The Politics of Asymmetry*, Cambridge and New York: Cambridge University Press, 2006, p.205.
26 A.L. Vuving, "Strategy and Evolution of Vietnam's China Policy: A Changing Mixture of Pathways," *Asian Survey* 46, no. 6, 2006, p.812.
27 See Williams, *Vietnam at the Crossroads*.
28 Co, *Hoi uc va Suy nghi*, pp. 65–7, 109.
29 Ibid., p.65.
30 Ibid.
31 J. Gouxing, "The Spratly Islands: China's Dispute with Vietnam," *Indochina Report* 24, no. Jul–Sep, 1990, p.1.
32 Ibid.
33 Thayer, "Vietnam: Coping with China," p.353.
34 Womack, *China and Vietnam*, p.208; C.A. Thayer, "Sino-Vietnamese Relations: The Interplay of Ideology and National Interest," Asian Survey 34, no. 6, 1994, p.516; L. Sun, "Leaders of Vietnam, China Held Secret Talks," *Washington Post*, 19 September 1990.
35 Thayer, "Sino-Vietnamese Relations," p.516.
36 Co, *Hoi uc va Suy nghi*, p.86.
37 Ibid.
38 Thayer, "Vietnam: Coping with China," p.354.
39 Ibid.
40 Thayer, "Sino-Vietnamese Relations," p.523.
41 T. Okabe, "Coping with China," In: James William Morley and Masashi Nishihara (Eds), Vietnam Joins the World, Armonk, NY: M. E. Sharpe, 1997, pp. 112–3.
42 Co, *Hoi uc va Suy nghi*, p.94.
43 Quoted from Womack, *China and Vietnam*, p.119.
44 L.T. Lee, *China and the South China Sea Dialogues*, Westport, CT: Praeger, 1999, p.93.
45 N. Trung, "Phai chan dung nguy co tai dien kich ban Thanh Do 1990," 11 August 2012. Online. Available HTTP: <www.viet-studies.info/NguyenTrung/NguyenTrung_ChanDungThanhDo.htm> (accessed 26 October 2012).
46 Dang Cong san Viet Nam, *Van kien Dai hoi Dai bieu Toan quoc thoi ky Doi Moi*, vol. 1, Hanoi: Chinh tri Quoc gia Publisher, 2010, p.403.
47 Ibid., pp. 426–72.
48 N.V. Tung, "Vietnam's Security Challenges: Hanoi's New Approach to National Security and Implications to Defense and Foreign Policies," In: Eiichi Katahara (Ed), Asia Pacific Countries' Security Outlook and Its Implications for the Defense Sector, Tokyo: NIDS Joint Research Series No.5, 2010, p.108.
49 C.A. Thayer, *The Vietnam People's Army under Doi Moi*, Singapore: Institute of Southeast Asian Studies, 1994, p.36.
50 C.A. Thayer, "Force Modernization: The Case of the Vietnam People's Army," *Contemporary Southeast Asia* 19, no. 1, 1997, p.3.
51 *The Military Balance, 1990–1991*, London: International Institute for Strategic Studies, 1990, pp. 148–9, 80–1.
52 *The Military Balance, 1995–1996*, London: International Institute for Strategic Studies, 1995, pp. 176–9, 97–8.
53 S. Simon, "Vietnam's Security: Between China and ASEAN," *Asian Affairs* 20, no. 4, 1994, p.195.

54 Lee, *China and the South China Sea Dialogues*, p.93.
55 J.Y.S. Cheng, "Sino-Vietnamese Relations in the Early Twenty-First Century," *Asian Survey* 51, no. 2, 2011, p.382.
56 Thayer, "Vietnam: Coping with China," pp. 364.
57 Ibid., p.363.
58 N.H. Thao, "Vietnam and the Code of Conduct for the South China Sea," *Ocean Development and International Law* 32, no. 2, 2001, p.111.
59 A.C. Guan, "Vietnam-China Relations since the End of the Cold War," *Asian Survey* 38, no. 12, 1998, p.1130.
60 R. Amer, "Sino-Vietnamese Relations: Past, Present and Future," In: A. Thayer and Ramses Amer Carlyle (Eds), Vietnamese Foreign Policy in Transition, Singapore: Institute of Southeast Asian Studies, 1999, p.76.
61 Guan, "Vietnam-China Relations since the End of the Cold War," pp. 1128–29.
62 Amer, "Sino-Vietnamese Relations," pp. 108–10.
63 C.A. Thayer, "The Tyranny of Geography: Vietnamese Strategies to Constrain China in the South China Sea," *Contemporary Southeast Asia* 33, no. 3, 2011, p.352.
64 Amer, "Sino-Vietnamese Relations," pp. 81–2.
65 Quoted in *Nhan Dan Newspaper*, 16 October 1993; N.V. Long, *Hoang Sa-Truong Sa: Cac su kien, tu lieu lich su phap ly chinh (The ky XV-2000)*, 1, pp. 196–97.
66 N.H. Thao, "Vietnam's Position on the Sovereignty over the Paracels and the Spratlys: Its Maritime Claims," *Journal of East Asia International Law* 1, 2012, pp. 207–8.
67 Thao, "Vietnam and the Code of Conduct for the South China Sea," p.111.
68 Bach Long Vi Island is in the middle of in the Gulf of Tonkin, halfway between Hai Phong (Vietnam) and Hainan Island (China). The island has an area of 2.5 km^2 and is 62 m above the sea level. It is about 50 n.m. from the nearest Vietnamese coastal island.
69 R. Amer, "Assessing Sino-Vietnamese Relations through Management of Contentious Issues," *Contemporary Southeast Asia* 26, no. 2, 2004, pp. 331–2.
70 Ibid.
71 L.T. Lee, *China and the South China Sea Dialogues*, p.97.
72 See more Amer, "Assessing Sino-Vietnamese Relations through Management of Contentious Issues."
73 M.J. Valencia, J.M. Van Dyke, and N.A. Ludwig, *Sharing the Resources of the South China Sea*, p.31; N.H. Thao, "Vietnam's Position on the Sovereignty over the Paracels and the Spratlys: Its Maritime Claims," p.198.
74 M.J. Valencia, J.M. Van Dyke, and N.A. Ludwig, *Sharing the Resources of the South China Sea*, p.94.
75 Guan, "Vietnam-China Relations since the End of the Cold War," p.1131.
76 Joint-Communiqué between Vietnam-China issued on 10 November 1991.
77 See Lee, *China and the South China Sea Dialogues.*
78 Thao, "Vietnam and the Code of Conduct for the South China Sea," pp. 112–3.
79 Thao, "Vietnam's Position on the Sovereignty over the Paracels and the Spratlys," p.209.
80 Betts, "The Strategic Predicament," pp. 102–3.
81 J.Y.S. Cheng, "Sino-Vietnamese Relations in the Early Twenty-First Century," p.393.
82 C.A. Thayer, "Vietnamese Foreign Policy: Multilateralism and the Threat of Peaceful Evolution," In: Carlyle A. Thayer and Ramses Amer (Eds), *Vietnamese Foreign Policy in Transition*, New York: St. Martin's Press, 1999, pp. 4–5.
83 Amer, "Sino-Vietnamese Relations," p.110.
84 S.S. Kim, "China as a Regional Power," *Current History* 91, no. 566, 1992, p.249.
85 Thayer, "Sino-Vietnamese Relations," p.525.
86 Ibid.
87 Lee, *China and the South China Sea Dialogues*, p.94; "Vietnam's Position on the Sovereignty over the Paracels and the Spratlys," p.199.

88 Thayer, "Vietnam: Coping with China," p.358.
89 Amer, "Sino-Vietnamese Relations," p.75; P. Goodspeed, "China Resorts to Gunboat Diplomacy," *Toronto Star*, Toronto, 20 September 1992.
90 Thayer, "Vietnam: Coping with China," p.356.
91 Ibid.
92 Lee, *China and the South China Sea Dialogues*, p.94; S. Simon, "Vietnam's Security: Between China and ASEAN," p.196.
93 S. Simon, "Vietnam's Security: Between China and ASEAN," Asian Affairs 20, no. 4, 1994, p.196.
94 Thayer, "Sino-Vietnamese Relations," p.525.
95 Quoted from Thayer, "Vietnam: Coping with China," p.357.
96 Thao, "Vietnam and the Code of Conduct for the South China Sea," p.106.
97 Thao, "Vietnam's Position on the Sovereignty over the Paracels and the Spratlys," pp. 198–9.
98 Thayer, "Vietnam: Coping with China," p.357.
99 "Vietnam Says It Will Keep Reducing Size of Its Military," *Reuters*, 8 September 1992.
100 Quoted from Thayer, "Vietnam: Coping with China," p.359.
101 Ibid., p.361.
102 Thayer, "Sino-Vietnamese Relations," p.526.
103 Thayer, "Vietnam: Coping with China," p.360.
104 Ibid.
105 Lee, *China and the South China Sea Dialogues*, p.140.
106 L. Buszynski, "ASEAN Security Dilemmas," *Survival* 34, no. 4, 1992, p.94.
107 Lee, *China and the South China Sea Dialogues*, p.67.
108 Thao, "Vietnam and the Code of Conduct for the South China Sea," p.106.
109 Amer, "Sino-Vietnamese Relations," p.79.
110 See Thao, "Vietnam's Position on the Sovereignty over the Paracels and the Spratlys."
111 Valencia et al., *Sharing the Resources of the South China Sea*, p.33.
112 Thao, "Vietnam's Position on the Sovereignty over the Paracels and the Spratlys," p.196 (emphasis added).
113 Quoted from Valencia et al., *Sharing the Resources of the South China Sea*, p.92.
114 Vietnam signed the Convention in 1982 and ratified it in 1994.
115 Valencia et al., *Sharing the Resources of the South China Sea*, p.91.
116 D.J. Dzurek, "The Spratly Islands Dispute: Who's on First?," *Maritime Briefing* 2, no. 1, 1996.
117 Quoted from A.C. Guan, "The South China Sea Dispute Revisited," *Australian Journal of International Affairs* 54, no. 2, 2000, p.205.
118 See more Storey et al., "Cam Ranh Bay."
119 D. Zha and M.J. Valencia, "Mischief Reef: Geopolitics and Implications," *Journal of Contemporary Asia* 31, no. 1, 2001, p.87; I.J. Storey, "Creeping Assertiveness: China, the Philippines and the South China Sea Dispute," *Contemporary Southeast Asia* 21, no. 1, 1999, p.105.
120 B.A. Hamzah, "China Strategy," *Far Eastern Economic Review*, 13 August 1992.
121 Storey, "Creeping Assertiveness," pp. 107–8.
122 Ibid., p.108.
123 Dzurek, "The Spratly Islands Dispute," p.35.
124 "Hanoi Reinforces Troops on Spratlys," *Kyodo*, Tokyo, 28 February 1995.
125 "Vietnam Slams Chinese Move in the Spratlys," *Reuters*, Hanoi, 10 February 1995.
126 Thayer, "Vietnam: Coping with China," pp. 364–65.
127 Ibid., p.365.
128 Thayer, "Force Modernization," p.7.
129 Ibid., p.14.
130 Ibid., p.16.

131 Interview with an official of Vietnam's Ministry of Foreign Affairs, 18 March 2014.
132 C.A. Thayer, "Vietnam and ASEAN: A First Anniversary Assessment," p.367.
133 K. Bolton, "Domestic Sources of Vietnam's Foreign Policy," In: Carlyle A. Thayer and Ramses Amer (eds.), *Vietnamese Foreign Policy in Transition*, New York: St. Martin's Press, 1999, pp. 184–5.
134 C.A. Thayer, "Vietnamese Foreign Policy: Multilateralism and the Threat of Peaceful Evolution," pp. 7–10.
135 D. Zagoria, "Joining ASEAN," In: James William Morley and Masashi Nishihara (eds.), *Vietnam Joins the World*, Armonk, NY: M.E. Sharpe, 1997, p.157.
136 J. Dosch and T.M. Tuan, "Recent Changes in Vietnam's Foreign Policy," In: Martin Gainsborough (ed.), *Vietnam: Rethinking the State*, London: Zed Books, 2010, p.206.
137 ASEAN Declaration on the South China Sea adopted by the Foreign Ministers at the 25th ASEAN Foreign Ministers' Meeting (AMM) in Manila, Philippines on 22 July 1992.
138 Co, *Hoi uc va Suy nghi*, Chapter 21, p.138.
139 H.A. Tuan, "Vietnam's Membership in ASEAN: Economic, Political and Security Implications," *Contemporary Southeast Asia* 16, no. 3, 1994, p.269 (emphasis added).
140 J. Dosch, "Vietnam's ASEAN Membership Revisited: Golden Opportunity or Golden Cage?"; Thayer, "Vietnam and ASEAN: A First Anniversary Assessment," p.367.
141 Thayer, "Vietnam and ASEAN: A First Anniversary Assessment," p.368.
142 Tuan, "Vietnam's Membership in ASEAN," p.269.
143 D. Zagoria, "Joining ASEAN," pp. 155–7; Vuving, "Strategy and Evolution of Vietnam's China Policy," pp. 813–5.
144 Huy Duc, *Ben thang cuoc*, vol. 2, Quyen Binh, E-book: Osinbook 2012, p.247.
145 G. Segal, "East Asia and the 'Constrainment' of China," *International Security* 20, no. 4, 1996, p.119.
146 Interview with officials of Vietnamese Ministry of Foreign Affairs in Hanoi, 7 April 2014.
147 Lee, *China and the South China Sea Dialogues*, p.98.
148 Thayer, "Vietnamese Foreign Policy," p.5.
149 Thayer, "Vietnam: Coping with China," p.365.

4 ASEANising the South China Sea issue, 1995–2002

China's creeping assertiveness in the Mischief Reef resulted in a new dynamics in the South China Sea. Anxieties in Southeast Asia about a revisionist China activated a collective attempt to seek a multilateral mechanism to prevent China's subsequent actions that would alter the status quo in the area. Political elites in Southeast Asia pragmatically understood that there would be no prospect of any complete and permanent settlement of the disputes over offshore islands in the foreseeable future. Therefore, they invested more energy in designing a code of conduct, which focused on conflict avoidance, dispute management and functional cooperation, to induce cooperation and mitigate strategic risks from China. As a new ASEAN member, Vietnam quickly familiarised itself with the ASEAN processes and started utilising it as a platform to advance its interests in the South China Sea. At the same time, Hanoi continued to engage its neighbours bilaterally to manage the existing disputes and find solutions to them.

Competitive pursuits of maritime rights

In the post-Mischief Reef crisis period, tensions were still simmering in the South China Sea. Though generally agreeing to the principle of self-restraint, all South China Sea claimants sought to substantiate their claims in one way or another, thus prompting reactions from other claimants. The Philippines disappointed because China not only refused to vacate Mischief Reef but also quietly upgraded its structures there. The Scarborough Shoal also became a source of tensions as China intensified its activities around this area.[1] Since mid-April 1996, Vietnam-China relations became strained. Vietnam asserted its UNCLOS rights, authorising a consortium led by Conoco Vietnam Exploration and Production BV, a unit of Houston-based Conoco Inc., to explore Blocks 133 and 134, which encompassed three million acres of the South Con Son basin, about 200 miles off Vietnam's southern coast.[2] These offshore acreages were also situated within Tu Chinh area (Vanguard Bank) that overlapped with the northwestern part of the South China Sea area China National Offshore Oil Corporation (CNOOC) and Crestone referred to as Wan'an Bei-21 (WAB-21; see Figure 2.10). As compared with its production-sharing agreement with Mobil Oil in 1994, Hanoi's Conoco enterprise made an even deeper inroad into the WAB-21 area that China claimed.

Beijing immediately lodged a protest, reiterating its "indisputable sovereignty" over the Spratlys and its "adjacent waters" and charging that Hanoi's Conoco contract violated China's sovereignty, marine rights and interests. The Vietnamese responded with a statement from the Foreign Ministry claiming sovereign rights and jurisdiction over these two blocks as part of Vietnam's continental shelf by UNCLOS. "No one else has the right to intervene into the contract," Vietnam's Foreign Ministry stated.[3] Failing to dissuade Hanoi from the project, Beijing then turned to threaten DuPont Co., which owned Conoco Inc. and which was involved in eight projects in China.[4] This contract was Hanoi's second defiant action, the first being with Mobil Oil, against China's claim to the WAB-21 area, and was indicative of a propensity in Hanoi to lay more emphasis on national economic interest than on socialist fraternity with China. It was also a sign that Hanoi was determined to advance its maritime interests in light of international law, particularly UNCLOS.

Vietnam's active partnership with Western oil corporations to develop offshore hydrocarbon resources was pushed by its government, headed by progressive Prime Minister Vo Van Kiet. Kiet was a nationalist pragmatist leader who championed performance-based legitimacy and greater integration into the world's economy. Hanoi's first oil and gas undertaking in the South China Sea dates back to the establishment of the joint venture Vietsopetro in 1981 to explore the acreage off the southeast coast near Ho Chi Minh City. The first oil barrel came out from the Bach Ho (White Tiger) field in June 1986. Since then, oil became vital to Vietnam's economic development as the major source of hard currency and the most attractive area for foreign investment. After the promulgation of the Law on Foreign Investment in 1988, Vietnam was keen on drawing upon Western oil companies to prospect for oil and gas and develop its energy sector. Between 1988 and 1994, Vietnam Oil and Gas Corp., which reported directly to the prime minister, signed twenty-seven production-sharing agreements to allow foreign oil groups from dozens of countries to explore its offshore blocks.[5] Most of these transactions went largely unchallenged except Hanoi's partnership with a consortium led by US-based Mobil Oil to carry out drills in the Thanh Long (Blue Dragon), part of the WAB-21 area China ambiguously claimed as "adjacent waters of the Spratlys." Vietnam showed resolve by deploying an exploratory oil rig in this area in defiance of China's diplomatic protests and physical harassment of a Vietnamese logistic ship in 1994.[6] In August 1995, Mobil moved on with the second exploratory drill in the Thanh Long area.[7]

As the economy picked up momentum in the mid-1990s, Vietnam's interest in offshore oil exploration and exploitation grew quickly. By the end of 1994, Vietnam started oil production in two more fields, Dai Hung (Big Bear) (Block 05–1) and Rong (Dragon) (Block 16). However, the big increase in oil production and exports could not match soaring imports of gasoline and oil products. In 1995, the trade deficit reached a record of USD 2.2 billion – roughly 40 per cent of total exports – as the need for imported oil products and cement increased due to the construction boom.[8] Two refineries were planned to reduce reliance on imported gasoline, diesel and other refined products, adding more pressures to look for additional crude supplies.[9] Thus, Vietnamese industrial and economic ministries eagerly looked for new reserves to raise earnings from crude oil exports. As most potential near-shore blocks had been leased out in the early 1990s, the Vietnamese energy industry was prompted to explore further acreages of their continental shelves, the area that China also eyed.[10]

Though hydrocarbon was clearly an important source of competitive actions in the South China Sea, basic commercial motives were perhaps not compelling enough for Hanoi's leaders to involve American oil companies to the point of straining their relations with China. If so, they might have seriously considered the idea of joint development that China put forward in several occasions. Randall C. Thompson, the chairman of Creston, visited Hanoi in 1995 to discuss the possibility of joint development, but Hanoi publicly rejected the proposal on the basis that China-proposed joint development was seen as an inroad into Vietnam's legitimate rights granted by UNCLOS. Mobil attorney N. E. Maryan Jr. disclosed Vietnam's underlying logic, "after Vietnam's unhappy experience with the Russians, the Vietnamese wanted superior American technology and a *buffer* against the Chinese. The Vietnamese think we (the United States) have the keys to unlock the South China Sea."[11] So for Hanoi, sovereign rights over the EEZ and continental shelf under UNCLOS were its core interests and giving concessions to foreign oil companies was a means to advance them.

Anxieties about China were manifest in Vo Van Kiet's confidential letter to the Politburo (latter published online) to advise the drafting of the Political Report to the 8th National Party Congress in 1996. In the letter, Kiet maintained that relations among the existing socialist countries, including those between Vietnam and China, were not driven by shared ideology but national interests. He then warned of the potential conflicts in some "hot spots" in Vietnam-China relations, a vague reference to Chinese assertiveness in the South China Sea. On the other hand, Kiet downplayed the potential confrontation between socialism and imperialism, highly valued the Vietnam's outreach beyond the socialist bloc, and maintained that Vietnam should "go down this path."[12] Kiet's perspective revealed the primary reason why the Vietnamese government eagerly pushed for greater integration in general and stronger presence of international corporations in the South China Sea in particular as a means to curb China's assertiveness.

Hanoi's approach in couching its arguments in UNCLOS terminology and engaging international companies to defend its rights in the South China Sea effectively put China in a dilemma. China consistently rejected any proposals and efforts to internationalise the disputes or bring them to the courtroom. It was Hanoi's hope that international companies' participation would validate Vietnam's claims, and if Beijing protested loudly or took action forcefully, the disputes would be automatically internationalised against its will. Also, the involvement of foreign companies helped draw attention to the legal aspect of the dispute in which Hanoi thought that it had a stronger case. In mid-1994, Hanoi reportedly hired Washington-based law firm Covington & Burling to assess Vietnamese and Chinese claims to Thanh Long (Blue Dragon) and Tu Chinh (Vanguard Bank) areas. By mid-1995, the firm provided it with one 100-page document confirming the legal strength of the Vietnam's claim over that of China for three reasons. First, Blue Dragon and the "great majority" of the Tu Chinh area is situated in the 200-mile EEZ to which Vietnam is entitled under UNCLOS. Second, the entire Tu Chinh and Thanh Long areas lie well within Vietnam's legitimate continental shelf, because the natural prolongation of Vietnam's mainland allows it to claim more than a 200 n.m. continental shelf seaward. Third, the delimitation of the continental shelf boundary on the principle of equidistance and proportionality would give Vietnam all of the Thanh Long and Tu Chinh areas.[13] International experts and lawyers were also sceptical about the validity of China's claim to WAB-21, as based on its historical U-shaped line or as the "adjacent waters" of the Spratly Islands under UNCLOS 1982.[14]

Despite lots of fanfare, no drilling was reported after the signature of the contract between Conoco and PetroVietnam.[15] Not all political elites in Hanoi applauded the presence of the American oil companies in Vietnamese waters and were reluctant to go to great lengths with them for energy interests. The conservative elements within the Vietnamese leadership considered Kiet's stance as "a deviation from socialism," though avoiding attacking him directly and personally.[16] They countered with a ten-page classified report, titled "American Strategies to Transform Socialist Vietnam after the Normalisation of United States-Vietnam Relations."[17] Most significantly, the report denied ASEAN membership and normalisation with the US as diplomatic victories but regarded them as elements of the US strategy of "selective economic development" which was designed to undercut the communist rule in Vietnam. Though there were no references to China in the report, the emphasis on ideology indicated that the conservative scepticism about the US's investment and economic designs served as a check on the pragmatic nationalist efforts to strengthen Hanoi's relations with the Western world. One party conservative even asserted that ideology, particularly Marxism-Leninism and Ho Chi Minh's Thoughts, needed defending as much as the country's territorial integrity.[18]

The tension over the Conoco incident was followed by China's ratification of UNCLOS and its controversial delineation of straight baseline systems for its mainland coast and an archipelagic-state baseline system around the Paracels on 15 May 1996. While China's endorsement of UNCLOS was supposedly good news to its neighbours, the delimitation of its baselines caused outright concerns in the region. This claim was estimated to increase the sea area under China's jurisdiction from 370,000 km^2 to around 3 million km^2 (1.16 million square n.m.).[19] A number of international legal experts and governments quickly voiced concerns about China's baseline systems, especially the Paracel baselines, considering this action a violation of UNCLOS 1982.[20] Indonesia sent an aide-memoire asking for clarification of China's new claims.[21] Vietnam's Foreign Ministry issued a statement on 16 May that contested the Chinese claim to the Paracel Islands, deliberately avoiding any comment on the legality of the Chinese baselines.[22] As usual, Vietnam was afraid that any discussion of such an issue might be mistaken as Vietnam's acceptance of China's claim to the island group. The ASEAN countries reportedly raised the issue at the second China-ASEAN forum held in Bukittingi, Indonesia, in June 1996.[23] Seemingly, Vietnam was left alone with its protests regarding the Chinese claim over the Paracels. Other states were mostly concerned about the application of UNCLOS provisions. However, Vietnam toned down its protest against the Chinese baseline declaration on the eve of Chinese Prime Minister Li Peng's visit to Hanoi in June 1996.[24] In early July 1996, the second meeting of the Vietnam-China working group on "maritime issues" was convened in Beijing.

One of the most serious challenges to Vietnam came on 7 March 1997. China responded to Vietnam's Conoco contract by sending an oil-drilling platform, known as KANTAN-03, to the sea area at the entrance of the Gulf of Tonkin, between Da Nang (Central Vietnam) and Hainan Island. It was reported that the KANTAN-03 was towed by two tugboats to an area about 64 n.m. off the Vietnamese coast (Chan May Cape) but 71 n.m. off the nearest point of China's Hainan Island. The drilled area overlapped with Vietnam's Block 113, roughly midway between Da Nang and Hainan but beyond the median line on the side of Vietnam.[25] China's oil drilling was a strategically and politically calculated move. The physical presence of the oil rig was seen as "an exercise of political muscle" to feed rising nationalism in China.[26] However, this time the Chinese intentionally chose an area nearly halfway between Vietnam and China, which was of little interest to international oil companies. By intruding on Vietnam only, Beijing deliberately avoided dragging other ASEAN countries into the dispute.[27]

The KANTAN-03 incursion angered the Vietnamese. One Vietnamese official stated that this action was another piece of evidence that the Chinese still pursued an expansionist policy.[28] A Vietnamese foreign affairs analyst disclosed that this "unfriendly" maritime gesture happened just before the "friendly" visit by Lou Gan, the secretary general of China's State Council to Hanoi. He pointed out that KANTAN-03 was the *ninth* instance of coincidence of this type and accused China of purposely abusing its common socialist cause with Vietnam.[29] Initially, Hanoi complained privately in the meeting between the representatives of Vietnam's Foreign Ministry and China's embassy and in a diplomatic note to the Chinese ambassador in Hanoi. It cited the 1993 Vietnam-China agreement on the principles for the settlement of the territorial and border disputes, calling for self-restraint and demanding the immediate departure of the rig from the area. The Chinese denied Hanoi's claim and refused to withdraw the drilling platform. Since two-week quiet diplomacy fell on Beijing's deaf ears, Vietnam finally went public to protest against China. On 20 March, Vietnam's minister of foreign affairs sent a letter to his Chinese counterpart to voice Vietnam's disapproval of China's action and proposed a meeting between the two countries' legal experts to clarify, discuss and settle the incident in line with international law. On the same day, in an unprecedented move, Vietnam's Deputy Foreign Minister Vu Khoan met with the ambassadors of seven ASEAN members to inform them of the oil-drilling dispute and explain Vietnam's position. The day after, Hanoi held a press conference to condemn China's violation of its EEZ and continental shelf.[30] On 22 March, at the height of the spat, Hanoi received Admiral Joseph Prueher, commander-in-chief of the US Pacific Command. He was the highest-ranking US military officer who had visited Vietnam since normalisation of relations.[31] Admiral Prueher disclosed that top leaders in Hanoi firmly supported a continued US military presence in the Asia-Pacific region.[32] Reportedly, Prueher talked about a "nascent military relationship" between the two old foes and brought up the proposal for US naval ships to visit Cam Ranh Naval Base.[33]

In response to Hanoi's protests, China again floated the idea of joint development in the area China had positioned the oil rig. However, Vu Van Mao, a senior official of PetroVietnam, rejected the possibility of a production-sharing contract with China in this area.[34] Finally, by late March China agreed to hold talks with Vietnam on the KANTAN-03 problem.[35] Just two days before the talks, China announced the withdrawal of KANTAN-03 for a vague reason that the rig had completed the assigned job. The question remains, however, as to which of the measures Hanoi had taken laid most pressure on China. Vietnam's diplomatic victory was largely the result of Hanoi's bold play of the ASEAN card. Hanoi won ASEAN's support for its approach.[36] One senior ASEAN diplomat said, "We don't recognize any Chinese rights to Vietnam's continental shelf, nor do we recognize the right of the Chinese to do what they did. Now, we're in this together."[37] Reportedly, the ASEAN countries privately raised South China Sea issues with China during an ARF conference on regional security and asked China to abide by the 1992 Manila ASEAN Declaration on the South China Sea.[38] However, no countries publicly expressed their concerns about China's oil exploration in Vietnam's continental shelf except the Philippines. David Wurfel argues that the more discernible impact of Vietnam's ASEAN strategy was seen in the outcome of annual China-ASEAN dialogue held in mid-April 1997 in Huangshan (China). There, the South China Sea problem were raised so forcefully that China for the first time accepted the invitation to discuss the issues in a multilateral setting and offered to negotiate a code of conduct to regulate its relations with ASEAN countries.[39]

Vietnam's increased military contact with the United States was also a factor that compelled Beijing to reconsider its assertive posture in the South China Sea. Alexander L. Vuving argued that the watershed shift in China's approach was part of Beijing's grand strategy to keep Vietnam at arm's length and prevent it from moving closer to Washington.[40] Rapprochement between Vietnam and the US and the initiation of military exchanges as seen in Admiral Joseph Prueher's groundbreaking visit to Hanoi may have alerted China as to the possibility of the US return to Cam Ranh Bay. Leszek Buszynski adopts the same argument that the US increased relations with the Philippines, notably the Philippines-US talks on the signature of a Visiting Forces Agreement (VFA),[41] compelled Beijing to reconsider its aggressive posture in the South China Sea after the Mischief Reef crisis. Worried about the United States' return to regional ports and bases, China became more responsive to its neighbours' preoccupations over some pressing issues.[42] A Chinese official stated that Beijing desired to promote a benign image of China across Southeast Asia and that China should not be viewed as a threat or a potential aggressor.[43] Perhaps, it was not a coincidence that, at an ASEAN meeting in 1997, China formally introduced the "New Security Concept," which advocated cooperative security, multilateral dialogue, confidence-building measures and peaceful settlement of international disputes. With its tenets similar to

ASEAN's fundamental values and norms, Beijing's New Security Concept aimed to promote a benevolent picture of China in Southeast Asia.[44]

This logic also helps to explain the subsequent conciliatory and cooperative gestures from China towards Vietnam. Though the talks in April 1997 did not yield any concrete agreements on the KANTAN-03 dispute, just three months after the crisis Chinese President Jiang Zemin invited CPV General Secretary Do Muoi to Beijing. At this summit, the two sides agreed to accelerate talks on land borders and maritime boundary in the Gulf of Tonkin. The two leaders informally reached a consensus to conclude the negotiations of these outstanding historical differences by the turn of the century.[45] This commitment was made public during Prime Minister Phan Van Khai's visit to China in October 1998 and Chinese Vice President Hu Jintao's visit to Vietnam two months later. As power disparity between China and Vietnam was widening, Beijing presumably had the advantage if settlements were delayed. In this way, securing China's high-level commitment to set a deadline for negotiation regardless of its goals would be considered a diplomatic success for Hanoi. The shift in China's strategy paved the way for agreements on the land border and the Gulf of Tonkin between Vietnam and China in December 1999 and December 2000, which will be discussed in the next section.

In 1998, the state of affairs in the South China Sea became markedly calmer. Some minor incidents happened, but tensions were mostly short-lived and the number of public protests was reduced significantly. In 1998, Vietnam complained about China's tourism plan in the Paracels, the intrusion of Chinese ship *Discovery 08* into Vietnamese waters in April, and China's scientific survey in the Spratly area in September. In September 1998, the Chinese issued a protest against Vietnam's construction of "two economic-scientific technological service stations" in the Ba Ke submerged reefs that China claimed as part of the Spratlys.[46] As regards Chinese accusation, Hanoi claimed that the reefs lay well within its continental shelf without any connection to the Spratlys. During these rows, there were no prolonged public displays of discontent, and all the responses to one another's activities were confined to rhetoric.[47] This state of affairs continued. In 1999, the only protest on the part of Vietnam was against China's imposition of a fishing ban (for the first time) in the disputed waters in the South China Sea. In 2000, no major incidents were reported. In 2001 and 2002, tensions emerged on several occasions because of China's fishing ban and sea bans for live fire drills. However, tensions did not rise to the same level as during the Mobil Oil, Mischief Reef, Conoco or KANTAN-03 incidents.[48] There was also some tension between Vietnam and other ASEAN claimants in the same period. In June 1999, Hanoi lodged two protests against Malaysia's tourism plan for the Spratly Islands. It also accused Malaysian naval ships of opening fires on Vietnam's fishing boats going through the area. In early 1999, Vietnam protested Malaysia's move to occupy Erika and Investigator Reefs in the Spratlys. In October, Vietnam complained about Philippines aircraft flying over Vietnam's controlled sites in the Spratlys. Reportedly, the Vietnamese force stationed in the Spratlys fired warning shots.[49]

This calmer situation in the South China Sea was perhaps the direct effect of greater restraints and the more cooperative attitudes of all claimant states, especially China. In this period, China actively pursued its "charm offensive" to drive away the myth of "China threat" connected to China's rise, and to expand its influence in its immediate neighbourhood. As part of this strategy, China did not devalue the yuan during the Asian financial crisis, proposed a free trade agreement to ASEAN in 2001 and collaborated with ASEAN during the SARS outbreak. In 2003, China became the first dialogue partner to join the ASEAN Treaty of Amity and Cooperation (TAC).[50] Also, since 1998, China pleased Vietnam by speeding up the pace of negotiations on the land border and the Gulf of Tonkin as guided by the high-level agreement between Do Muoi and Jiang Zemin in July 1997. Against this backdrop, the two countries deliberately refrained from provocative actions and tit-for-tat responses that could derail the negotiation process.

Vietnam-China settlements on the land border and the Gulf of Tonkin maritime boundary

In spite of sporadic tensions about disputed territories, Vietnam patiently engaged China to seek a final settlement of existing territorial disputes. Most importantly, Vietnam managed to maintain annual high-level dialogues with China through rotating visits of the two countries' senior leaders to each other's capitals. In November 1995, CPV Secretary General Do Muoi visited Beijing and held talks with his Chinese counterpart Jiang Zemin. In June 1996, Chinese Premier Li Peng travelled to Hanoi where he attended the 8th National Congress of the CPV and met with Vietnam's top leaders. In July 1997, Do Muoi paid an official visit to Beijing. In 1998 Vietnamese Prime Minister Phan Van Khai visited Beijing in October, and Chinese Vice President Hu Jintao visited Hanoi in December. CPV Secretary General Le Kha Phieu visited Beijing and held talks with Jiang Zemin in February 1999. During this meeting, the two leaders agreed on a guideline for Vietnam-China relations: "*lang gieng huu nghi, hop tac toan dien, on dinh lau dai, huong toi tuong lai*" ("friendly neighbourliness, comprehensive cooperation, long-term stability, and future-oriented relationship"). In December 2000, Jiang Zemin made a trip to Hanoi for a summit with President Tran Duc Luong, during which they adopted a Joint Statement for Comprehensive Cooperation. Boundary issues figured significantly in these meetings. Through the joint statements, the Vietnamese and Chinese leaders pledged to seek basic, long-term settlements by peaceful means, renounce the use or the threat of use of force, and refrain from "any actions" that could further complicate the disputes. At the very same time, the governmental level meetings and three joint working groups on the land border, the Gulf of Tonkin and "maritime issues" in the South China Sea proper met as planned to discuss specific developments in the light of the high-level leaders' agreements.[51]

Vietnam's bilateral engagements with China yielded some concrete results in terms of resolving historical differences. On 30 December 1999, after six rounds of government-level negotiations and sixteen rounds of technical-level negotiations, Vietnam and China signed an agreement on the land border demarcation.[52] Almost one year later, on 25 December 2000, Vietnam and China signed an Agreement on

Delimitation of the Territorial Seas, Exclusive Economic Zones and Continental Shelves in the Gulf of Tonkin, which mapped out a single line (defined by coordinates) for both the EEZ and continental shelf boundaries. This agreement was the result of seven rounds of governmental-level talks, eighteen rounds of negotiations at the working level and forty-nine meetings of the joint working team and the mapping team between 1993 and 2000.[53] On the same day, the Agreement on Fishery Cooperation in the Gulf of Tonkin between Vietnam and China was also concluded. However, the talks on "maritime issues" in the South China Sea area outside the Gulf of Tonkin made no progress because the aforementioned incongruities persisted. It is worth mentioning again that the level of tension between Vietnam and China in the South China Sea, measured in terms of rhetoric and duration of public display of discontent, had decreased significantly since 1998, when their diplomats entered the phase of substantive negotiation on the land border and the Gulf of Tonkin.

Settling territorial disputes with its neighbours was obviously a priority of Vietnam's foreign affairs. Before the Gulf of Tonkin agreement, Hanoi already signed an agreement with Thailand on the delimitation of the EEZ and the continental shelf in the Gulf of Thailand on 9 August 1997. This agreement also adopted a straight line as the single boundary for both the EEZ and the continental shelf.[54] On 26 June 2003, Vietnam and Indonesia reached an agreement on the delimitation of their continental shelf boundary in the area to the north of the Natuna Islands.[55] While Vietnam's maritime delimitation with Thailand and Indonesia had never been sources of domestic controversy, its maritime settlement with China in the Gulf of Tonkin drew a good deal of criticism from dissidents and overseas Vietnamese. They accused that the negotiating process had neither been adequately published or undergone proper public scrutiny. Vietnamese legal analysts held that the Gulf of Tonkin agreement was a fair and equal deal from the legal point of view.[56] The assessment of the coordinates stipulated in the agreement indicated that the two sides must have agreed on a line of equidistance with some slight modifications, reflecting the impact of some islands on the delimitation. It meant that the Vietnamese negotiators finally dropped their long-standing claim to apply the north-south red line in the 1887 Franco-Chinese Treaty to delineate the boundary in the Gulf. It was also evident that the Vietnam-controlled islands ultimately had limited weight on the delimitation of the Gulf.

Vietnamese legal analyst Nguyen Hong Thao revealed that the Bach Long Vi Island was given 25 per cent effect on the delimitation line, equivalent to an entitlement of 12 n.m. territorial sea and a 3 n.m. EEZ and continental shelf. Con Co, a small island near the Vietnamese coastline, was given 50 per cent impact. There were different views on the fairness of the delimitation. An international source estimated that with this delimitation line, China was likely to gain about 3,200 square n.m. beyond a strict median line.[57] However, Allen Carlson argues that the agreement was the product of compromise in the spirit of reciprocity in which Vietnam conceded on its claims to waters derived from the islands under its control and China accepted a less expansive territorial approach in return.[58] A Vietnamese calculation revealed that the net result of the settlement was that Vietnam secured

53.23 per cent of the sea area subject to delimitation in the gulf, representing a margin of 8,000 km^2 over China's entitlement, which accounted for 46.77 per cent. The ratio of the areas allocated to each state closely follows the ratio of the Vietnamese and Chines coastlines in the gulf.[59]

Though signed separately, the Vietnam-China Agreement on Fishery Cooperation in the Gulf of Tonkin was clearly connected to the aforementioned maritime delimitation settlement. The agreement is the first one that established fishery cooperation in the South China Sea within permanent maritime boundaries.[60] It was revealed that this fishery regime was negotiated hastily during six rounds of negotiations between April and December 2000 before the final deal was struck.[61] However, the fishery regime needed a supplemental protocol to be completed. The agreement on the supplementary protocol, which was signed in April 2004, enabled the national assemblies of both countries to ratify the Agreement on the Delimitation of Waters, Exclusive Economic Zones and Continental Shelves in the Gulf of Tonkin in June 2004. It took this agreement nearly three and a half years to be ratified while the Land Border Treaty took only six months after its signing. Under the fisheries agreement, the two sides agreed to designate a four-year transitory fishery zone, a fifteen-year common fishery zone and a "buffer zone" for small fishing vessels. Though the agreement was believed to generate opportunities for both sides, Vietnam clearly faced more challenges because its fishing fleets were weaker in terms of quantity, capacity and technology vis-à-vis those of China.[62]

The land border agreement was also a highly contentious issue among the Vietnamese. Even after Vietnam's National Assembly ratified the agreement on 9 June 2000, its text was not made public until August 2002. When demarcation started in December 2001, there were claims that some Vietnamese villages were situated on the other side of the border. Some political dissidents and Vietnamese overseas accused Hanoi of making excessive concessions to China. However, Vietnamese Deputy Foreign Minister Le Cong Phung made it known that, out of 227 km^2 Vietnam and China disputed, 113 km^2 were annexed to Vietnam and 114.9 km^2 went to China.[63] In the light of roughly equal division of the contested area, he concluded that the negotiation outcome conformed to the principle of "ensuring fairness and satisfaction for both sides."[64] Obviously, it was very difficult to judge whether the negotiation outcomes were an equal or fair deal given the complex natural condition of the terrain, history of conflict and control over different areas, the settlements and movements of population, and the interventions of local authorities between the two sides.[65] In the process of bargaining and negotiation, closing the deal on a range of complex and high-stakes issues requires both sides to make concessions, and the balance of gains and losses should be calculated on the overall package base and in the long-term perspective.

Arguably, leaders in Hanoi were keen on settling the territorial disputes with their neighbours because they badly needed stability in their neighbourhood. Unresolved border disputes are generally seen as potential sources of tension and conflict. Thus, stable and clearly defined borders would enhance national security, facilitate multifaceted cooperation with neighbours, and allow Hanoi's leaders to reallocate its limited resources to domestic developmental issues, which were more critical to regime security in peacetime.[66] This thinking drove Vietnam to simultaneously conduct a number of bilateral dialogues with China and Cambodia on land borders and with China, Indonesia, Thailand and Malaysia on maritime delimitation and other related issues. These efforts were systematically carried out as a priority of Hanoi's omni-dimensional foreign policy, which was aimed at "creating external conditions more favourable to foster socio-economic development, national industrialisation and modernisation."[67] Because of asymmetry of power between the two, Vietnam usually needs a cooperative China more than China needs a cooperative Vietnam.

However, regime security and the strategic objective, which stress the need for a peaceful and stable environment, is insufficient to explain the timing of and the nature of the deal decided. A closer look into different actors in Vietnam's domestic politics will bring some valuable insights into how these agreements were decided on the part of Vietnam. The Foreign Ministry was the lead negotiator of the land border and Gulf of Tonkin agreements but the final decisions were supposed to be decided collectively within the Politburo. Domestic manoeuvres in Hanoi reflected the contest of different opinions on how to negotiate with China. Le Kha Phieu, who replaced Do Muoi as CPV Secretary General at the 4th (mid-term) Plenum of the 8th Central Committee in December 1997, was reportedly accused of making an unprincipled decision on territorial concessions to China. The lost area was estimated to be the same size of Thai Binh province, roughly 1,500 km^2.[68] An indication of Phieu's overuse of his power was his discussion with Jiang Zemin in Beijing without the presence of Foreign Minister Nguyen Manh Cam and Politburo member Tran Dinh Hoan during his visit to Beijing in late February 1999. Surprisingly, Cam was not allowed to enter the meeting room with an excuse that he was not on the list, while Chinese Foreign Minister Tang Jiaxuan was allowed to accompany Jiang Zemin.[69] Phieu was also blamed for endorsing China's preference for bilateralism in dealing with the territorial disputes in the South China Sea. Phieu purportedly argued that raising the South China Sea issue in multilateral forums, especially the dispute over the Tu Chinh area, would adversely affect Vietnam's sovereignty there.[70] At a summit in Beijing in 2001, Phieu allegedly conceded to China's demands with regard to the delimitation of the Gulf of Tonkin. Making the matter worse, he did so without the consent of the Vietnamese Politburo, the Central Committee or the Foreign Ministry.[71]

What Phieu did during his leadership showed that he was the strongest driver for closer ideological relations with China and finalisation of the border negotiation between the two countries. Perhaps, Phieu's deference was rewarded with the Chinese pledge of "friendly neighbourliness, comprehensive cooperation, long-term stability, and future-oriented relationship." Phieu was known as the most ideologically conservative figure among the then Vietnamese leaders. He was apparently a strong critic of Vo Van Kiet and Nguyen Manh Cam's call for expanding Vietnam's ties with ASEAN and the US.[72] During his visit to Beijing in February 1999, which was some days prior to US Secretary of Defense William Cohen's trip to Hanoi, Phieu assured the Chinese that Hanoi was not seeking alignment with Washington to contain China.[73] As indication of his anti-imperialist stance, Phieu manoeuvred to delay the signature of the trade pact with the US in 1999 and gave US President Bill Clinton an undiplomatic talk about imperialism during Clinton's historic visit to Vietnam in November 2000. On the other hand, Phieu was enthusiastic about consolidating ideological ties with China. He proposed to initiate regular consultations on ideology between the two countries.[74]

However, Le Kha Phieu should not be the only one who was accountable for the controversial border deals with China. The then Vietnamese leaders collectively saw a rare opportunity for wrapping up the land border negotiation, thus putting an end to that long-lasting dispute. Phieu lost his job as party chief to Nong Duc Manh at the 9th National Party Congress in April 2001. Apparently, the prime reason was not only because he was too much deferential to Beijing.[75] Even though the meeting between Le Kha Phieu and Jiang Zemin occurred in February 1999, no real effort to reopen the border deal was reported before the agreement was officially signed in December. The political campaign against Phieu peaked in the run-up to the 9th National Party Congress, during which different factions fought for the key posts in the party and government. This implied that Phieu's compromises with Chinese leaders were largely tolerated because the Vietnamese political leadership as a whole needed a peaceful and stable border with China. However, his political ambitions and manoeuvres were not acceptable in the eyes of other leaders. Phieu was reportedly under fierce criticisms for many other problems such as corruption, poor economic management, love affairs and manipulation of secret agencies.[76] Most importantly, Phieu allegedly advocated abolishing the status of Advisor to the Central Committee (Co Van), which was granted to retired but influential top leaders such as Do Muoi, Le Duc Anh and Vo Van Kiet. Phieu's conspicuous bid to consolidate his power and his misuse of authority were intolerable within the Vietnamese political culture of collective leadership. Consequently, Phieu lost supports from both ends of the political spectrum and was removed from both the Politburo and the Central Committee after half a term.[77] The demise of Le Kha Phieu significantly weakened the power base of the conservative ideologues, which gave way to further outreach to Western powers in the next period.

There was a consensus among political elites in Hanoi that settling the land border and the Gulf of Tonkin boundary with China was a strategic necessity. Even the most liberal minds in the Vietnamese leadership expressed support for sensible flexibilities and concessions to secure a border deal package with China. Vietnamese Prime Minister Phan Van Khai admitted, "We could not annex the whole Ban Gioc Waterfall. General Vo Nguyen Giap did not accept the proposed division of Ban Gioc but a lengthy quarrel on this disputed point only would deprive us of a *border deal package*."[78] As with the concessions on Height No.1509, Foreign Minister Nguyen Manh Cam explained,

> everyone knows that giving up an inch of territory is already a wrongdoing. However, as China is a big country, the disputes with China ought to be settled to achieve a *peaceful border*. Before the agreement, no single day passed by without provocative acts on the Chinese side.[79]

Vu Khoan, Vietnamese deputy foreign minister, revealed that China's repeated assertive actions threatened stability that the Vietnamese government desired. Therefore, Vietnamese leaders were not willing to make reservation as regards sensitive areas, such as Ban Gioc and Huu Nghi Quan. "Reservation means continued living in nervousness," Khoan added.[80] The statements unveil the difference between the logic of the pragmatic nationalists and that of the conservative ideologues. The latter were willing to yield to China in exchange for China's recognition and solidarity to defend socialism. Though the motives of those groups diverged, their goals converged. The former wanted to settle the border affairs with China because they knew that Vietnam was negotiating from weakness and were therefore willing to accept the minor territorial concessions for long-term security of the frontier. At the end of the day, they understood that the land border and the Gulf of Tonkin disputes were by all means bilateral and could not be handled in the same way as those in the South China Sea. This paved the way to the finalisation of the agreements on the land border and the delimitation of the Gulf of Tonkin.

The signature of the agreements effectively reduced the risk of conflicts in the areas, though tensions may arise occasionally. In the follow-up to the land border agreement, Vietnam and China started on-the-ground demarcation and the erection of land markers. The two sides set up a Joint Committee for this purpose. Its first meeting was held from 19 November to 1 December 2000. The first land marker was erected on 27 December 2001. After the Gulf of Tonkin and fishery cooperation agreements, Vietnam and China started negotiations on a supplementary protocol to the agreement. It was by no means an easy task. It took the two countries roughly eight years to finish the land border demarcation process and four years to reach consensus on the supplementary protocol on fisheries. Obviously, the implementation phase was no less troublesome and required political will from both sides to complete. In June 2002, it was reported that Vietnam's coast guards arrested nine Chinese fishing vessels and 179 crewmembers for illegal fishing in the Vietnamese side of the Gulf of Tonkin.[81] However, overall state of affairs in the regions was much calmer and more stable than before.

Multilateralism and Declaration on Conduct of the Parties in the South China Sea (DOC), November 2002

Vietnam, ASEAN multilateralism and the South China Sea issue

ASEAN gradually gained importance in Vietnam's foreign policy. In 1996, Vietnam established the National ASEAN Committee chaired by a deputy prime minister. This body was responsible for coordinating all agencies that engaged with ASEAN or ASEAN-affiliated organisations. An ASEAN Department was also established within the Ministry of Foreign Affairs to deal with ASEAN processes specifically and work with the departments in charge of bilateral relations with ASEAN countries.[82] Despite much scepticism on the part of the conservatives, foreign policy elites considered Vietnam's entry to ASEAN as the right decision and a diplomatic success and called for deep engagement with ASEAN.[83] Membership in ASEAN was seen as a gate to overcome political isolation abroad and a means to increase the legitimacy of the CPV at home.

ASEAN membership assisted Vietnam to manage the South China Sea disputes in three ways. First, though ASEAN was not a mechanism to resolve disputes, its norms and processes effectively prevented differences among its members from evolving into conflicts. The establishment of ASEAN first helped control the Malaysian-Philippine dispute over Sabah, which had long obstructed cooperation between them.[84] ASEAN convened thousands of meetings at all levels every year, helping its members develop and maintain cordial relations and discuss ways to defuse tensions. As a result, ASEAN members' bilateral relationships with one another were less troublesome than their relationship with China in terms of territorial disputes. It was argued that ASEAN's quiet diplomacy and principle of self-restraint served as an effective dispute management mechanism that not only reduced distrust and suspicion among its members but also generated greater understanding and increased cooperation among ASEAN claimants.[85]

Second, ASEAN offered an avenue for its member states to forge common ground on any specific issue and decide on subsequent coordinated actions. ASEAN's processes are considered as important bloc building efforts, which could exercise considerable international influence and strengthen its member states' bargaining position vis-à-vis external powers. This influence was seen in ASEAN opposition to Vietnam's military intervention in Cambodia during the 1980s. ASEAN members also managed to come up with a unified standpoint on the South China Sea issue on a number of occasions. The best examples of the ASEAN action in South China Sea affairs were the ASEAN Declaration on the South China Sea of 1992, the Statement of ASEAN Foreign Ministers on Recent Developments in the South China Sea of 15 March 1995, the joint-communiqués of the 29th and 35th ASEAN Foreign Ministers' Meetings of 1996 and 2002 respectively, and the Hanoi Declaration of the 6th ASEAN Summit of 1998. ASEAN also provides a place for its members to work collectively. An example is the ASEAN common effort to develop a multilateral code of conduct in the South China Sea between 1996 and 1999 and engage with China in the process between 1999 and 2002. However, even in these instances, the effects of ASEAN's collective statements and actions were always dependent on how far ASEAN as a group could go. Regarding the South China Sea, ASEAN members agree on general principles of no threat or use of force and conflict avoidance through self-restraint. However, it is usually difficult for them to reach a consensus on a specific problem, especially if it involves direct criticism of Beijing's approach. No doubt, ASEAN's lack of cohesion and solidarity undermines its ability to develop common position on contentious issues.

Third, ASEAN also developed dialogues with external powers, including China. In July 1994, ASEAN and China established two joint committees on science and technology and on economic and trade cooperation. The first ASEAN-China Senior Officials Meeting (SOM) was held in Hangzhou in April 1995. ASEAN member states raised the issue of the Mischief Reef incident in an informal gathering prior to that meeting. In 1996, China became an official dialogue partner of ASEAN. Since then, China has taken part in the annual ASEAN Post-ministerial Conference consultation process. This process includes a meeting between ASEAN and its ten dialogue partners (ASEAN+10) and a separate meeting between ASEAN and each of its dialogue partners (ASEAN+1). At the 2nd Informal ASEAN Summit in Kuala Lumpur in December 1997, ASEAN adopted a new dialogue with heads of state/government from three Northeast Asian countries (China, Japan and South Korea), known as ASEAN Plus Three. Dialogue between ASEAN and China created various chances for ASEAN members to raise and discuss their security concerns in the South China Sea with the strongest claimant, China.

ASEAN also convenes and sets agenda for the ASEAN Regional Forum (ARF), which was established in 1994. The ARF constituted a multilateral forum for ASEAN to discuss common defence and security issues with major countries in the world. Its meetings are often organised back to back with the ASEAN Foreign Ministers' Meeting (AMM) each year to review the past work and adopted cooperative programs. The ARF is the extension of the "ASEAN Way" to the outer world as the process is centred on constructive consultation and consensus building dialogue to promote mutual understanding and build confidence among the participants. ARF discussions focused on natural disasters, search and rescue, maritime security, international terrorism, transnational crime, transparency in defence policies and defence education.[86] The South China Sea disputes are potential items on the ARF agenda. After the Mischief Reef incident in 1995, the Philippines proposed to take the issue to the ARF, which was scheduled to hold the first working session in May 1995. However, the Chinese made it clear that they opposed any attempt to put the Mischief Reef problem on the ARF agenda. Though Vietnam supported the Philippines' suggestion, other ASEAN members declined because they were afraid that such action would turn China away from the ARF process.[87]

The diplomatic arenas created by ASEAN and its offspring offered a whole new experience to Vietnam's foreign affairs. Up until joining ASEAN, Vietnam's exposure to multilateralism had been rather limited. First, Vietnamese officials had never been exposed to such great diversity of interests and opinions before. Its participation in the Soviet Union-led Council for Mutual Economic Assistance (CMEA) was a totally different experience because that organisation was composed of countries that had the very same ideological, political and economic systems. The ASEAN setting obligated Hanoi to find new alignments and new strategies to seek advantages. Second, as a member of ASEAN and the ARF, Vietnam had to play by a new set of rules, procedures and norms. There was no place for socialist solidarity, only the "ASEAN Way." Third, in the ARF and ASEAN forums, there was a greater room for Hanoi's diplomatic manoeuvre but it had to act on its own to advance its national interests. Vietnam's previous experience with the United Nations was of no help either. During the Cold War, Hanoi had absolutely no chance to speak up against the Soviet Union or adopt a position markedly different from the common position of the socialist group on key international affairs. But at the ARF and ASEAN meetings, Vietnam did not have any ideological colossus or strategic patron to rely on. These properties made multilateralism a new arena for Vietnam, in which its national interests were best displayed.

Development of the South China Sea code of conduct

The idea of a code of conduct for the South China Sea first appeared in the 1992 ASEAN Declaration on the South China Sea. The declaration called on all parties to develop a code of international conduct for the South China Sea on the basis of the Treaty of Amity and Cooperation in Southeast Asia (TAC).[88] The Mischief Reef incident prompted the Philippines to develop bilateral codes of conduct with other claimants as a means to manage their relations in the South China Sea and prevent further occupation of its features. Subsequently, the Philippines reached two joint statements on the principles for a code of conduct in the South China Sea with China and Vietnam in August and November 1995 respectively. At the same time, the Philippines put forward the idea of a multilateral code of conduct (COC) for the South China Sea region at the second ARF annual meeting, held in Brunei in August 1995. In this regard, Filipino Secretary of Foreign Affairs Domingo L. Siazon argued:

> Pending a final resolution of the fundamental question of sovereignty in the South China Sea, all concerned countries should strive to arrive at an informal arrangement, a modus vivendi, a code of conduct, which could give all of us clearer idea of what to expect from one another in terms of our behaviour in the sea.[89]

ASEAN foreign ministers at the 29th ASEAN Foreign Ministers' Meeting (AMM) in July 1996 reached a consensus on the formation of a code of conduct for the South China Sea region, which aimed to "lay the foundation for long-term stability in the area and foster understanding among claimant countries."[90] This agreement was made possible perhaps by widespread anxieties around China's occupation of Mischief Reef in early 1995 and its controversial baseline statement published in May 1996. According to Leszek Buszynski, a code of conduct in the South China Sea setting had two aims. Its first purpose was to promote unity within ASEAN given existing divergence among the members on how to deal with China and to approach particular South China Sea disputes. Non-claimant members such as Thailand and Singapore did not want the disputes to adversely affect their ties with China. There were also visible divisions among the ASEAN claimants about the geographical limits of ASEAN intervention. Malaysia did not see the Mischief Reef clash as an ASEAN problem. In the same way, some ASEAN members did not want to entangle ASEAN with the Vietnam-China dispute over the Paracels. The second intent was to use norms and rules to impose verifiable limits on China's freedom of action, thereby increasing predictability in the area.[91] It should also be noted that the individual ASEAN countries had harboured different expectations on the code of conduct. The states most exposed to Chinese power, particularly the Philippines and Vietnam, would envisage that the norms and rules enshrined in the code of conduct to protect the status quo over the offshore territories and their rights of access against the dominant power of China. Meanwhile, the ASEAN non-claimants might just want an instrument of conflict prevention that would not alienate China. This may explain why some ASEAN states, particularly the Philippines and Vietnam, were very forceful in pushing the idea while others were less enthusiastic.

The idea of a code of conduct was then deliberated at the Second Meeting of the Technical Working Group in South China Sea in Chiang Mai, Thailand, 13–17 May 1997. The participants agreed on the necessity of a code of conduct as an important confidence building measure (CBM) and a tool to uphold the status quo in the South China Sea. At the 6th ASEAN Summit in Hanoi in December 1998, the ASEAN leaders again pledged to "promote efforts to establish a regional code of conduct in the South China Sea."[92] In March 1999, ASEAN assigned the Philippines and Vietnam the task to prepare draft codes of conduct.[93] The issue was tabled at the 5th ASEAN-China Senior Official Meeting, held in Kunming, China, in April, in which China rebuffed the necessity of a code of conduct, arguing that the existing joint statements between ASEAN and China were enough to maintain stability in the South China Sea.[94] In spite of Chinese disapproval, ASEAN proceeded with its own agenda to discuss the Vietnamese and Philippine drafts at the ASEAN SOM in May. At this point, ASEAN officials failed to forge a consensus on the geographical scope of application and the formality of the text.

Vietnam advocated the inclusion of the Paracels into the geographical scope of the code, an opinion with which some other ASEAN members disagreed. Malaysia and Indonesia were said to turn down the Philippines' draft on the basis of improper design of the text. The former insisted on a political document, not a legally binding treaty that the latter lobbied.[95] The SOM meeting in July then decided to refer the matter to a working group.[96] On 24 November 1999, ASEAN officials unanimously adopted the draft code prepared by the Philippines and Vietnam, which was then sent to China for consideration.[97] The approved code of conduct was designed more as a political statement that expressed a desire for peaceful resolution of the disputes rather than an obligation-based legal document. As regards the geographical scope of the code, ASEAN leaders finally agreed on the use of general term "Disputed Area" without referring specifically to either the Spratlys or Paracels. This represented a compromise among different definitions of geographical scope of the code. The Philippines also gained ASEAN's approval of the commitment to "refrain from action of inhabiting or erecting structures in presently uninhabited islands, reefs, shoals, cays and other features in the so-called Disputed Area."[98]

At first, the Chinese either refuted or disregarded ASEAN's endeavour to develop the South China Sea code of conduct. They repeatedly stated that China saw bilateralism as the only avenue to settle and manage territorial disputes with its neighbours. Beijing long resisted any attempts to raise the South China Sea issues in formal multilateral settings such as the ARF meetings and China-ASEAN dialogues. However, Beijing markedly reversed its position in May 1999, agreeing to explore the possibility of a code of conduct in the South China Sea.[99] China circulated its own code of conduct proposal by the end of October, rebuffing the ASEAN-drafted code in doing so.[100] China's change in position was seemingly prompted by ASEAN's determined and fast-paced efforts to achieve a consensus on the code of conduct. Asia-Pacific powers, especially the US, Japan, Australia and Canada, strongly backed this ASEAN initiative, creating more pressure on China.[101] Beijing came to realise that if it continued to stand outside the forum, it risked either being isolated or being a laggard that had no other choice but to accept the previously settled formalities and principles. As mentioned earlier, the Chinese were concerned about the increased involvement of external powers in the South China Sea situation. Beijing eventually went out of its way to engage ASEAN multilateralism, as staying outside the process was more harmful than not. The code of conduct discussion would be a platform to impose Chinese will and discourage ASEAN countries from internationalising the disputes and from strengthening their strategic ties with external powers. While agreeing to talk with ASEAN countries on the code of conduct, Beijing stressed that relevant discussions should only be held between China and the ASEAN countries.[102]

An analysis of the Chinese version showed more evidence for this point. In its draft, Beijing limited disputes to the Spratly Islands and advocated joint development while shelving all disputes. The draft also demanded that all the parties avoid actions that would "complicate or magnify the disputes," a subtle reference to the Philippines-US Visiting Force Agreement (VFA).[103] Beijing also proposed that the parties "refrain from use or threat of force, or taking coercive measures, such as seizures, detention or arrest of fishing boats or other civilians engaged in normal operation."[104] This suggestion referred to the Philippines' assertive actions against Chinese fishermen. In subsequent negotiations, China expressed more clearly its strategic preoccupations. The Chinese-drafted code of conduct called on the claimants to "refrain from conducting any military exercises directed against other countries in the Nansha Islands and their adjacent waters, and from carrying out any dangerous and close in military reconnaissance."[105] Beijing also proposed a ban on military patrols in the areas and a limitation of the code of conduct only to the Spratlys.[106] At the ASEAN-China SOM meeting, held in March 2000 in Cha-am, Thailand, a Chinese senior official cautioned ASEAN member states against joint military exercises in the South China Sea and strengthened military ties with external powers, such as the United States. The warning was spelled out during US Secretary of Defense William Cohen's tour throughout a number of regional capitals.[107] This was indicative of Beijing's concerns about the US military activities in its southern sea, which was considered as a buffer area for China.[108]

The ASEAN-China working group held its first meeting on 15 March 2000 in Hua Hin, Thailand. At this meeting, China's opening position was based on the draft it already circulated at the end of 1999, while ASEAN made two revisions to the draft it had agreed to four months beforehand. The first revision was that the Spratlys and Paracels were referred as disputed areas. The second was the removal of the phrase referring to the exploration and exploitation of resources in the disputed areas out of the list of potential areas of cooperation.[109] The group met again in Kuching, Malaysia in May; in Da Lian, China, in August; and in Hanoi in

October. These meetings built up a consensus on the necessity of the code and the key elements of the code, including the basic principles, the set of CBMs, and areas of cooperation. However, ASEAN and China failed to agree on the geographical scope of the code and the question of occupation and construction of facilities on the disputed islands.

The stalemate caused by these differences resulted in negotiators adjusting their positions to find a compromise. Prior to the 34th ASEAN Foreign Ministers' Meeting (AMM) held in Hanoi on 23–24 July 2001, the Philippines suggested the removal of the references to specific island groups. At the same time, China signalled flexibility on geographical scope: either the Spratlys only or the entire South China Sea could be accepted. Later, the Filipinos and Chinese tried to find a compromise in regards to the provision of occupation and construction of new structures on islands or reefs. Finally, they arrived at an agreement to "refrain from action of inhabiting on the presently uninhabited islands, reefs, shoals, cays and other features."[110] China still resisted any binding effect of the code. During the preparation for the 35th ASEAN Foreign Ministers' Meeting (AMM) in Brunei in July 2002, Malaysia suggested a watered-down option that was a non-binding political statement, titled "Declaration on the Conduct of Parties in the South China Sea" instead of a legal instrument. China endorsed Malaysia's proposal. In the face of China's insistence, the other ASEAN members had to give in, accepting a political declaration as a stepping-stone towards a formal code of conduct.[111] The joint communiqué of the 35th AMM indicated that ASEAN foreign ministers decided to "work toward a Declaration on the Conduct of Parties in the South China Sea."[112] Beijing was also concerned about any obligation, which might arise from the declaration, to work on a formal code of conduct later. Therefore, it pressed for the insertion of the words "on the basis of consensus" into Article 10 of the Declaration to keep all possibilities open.[113] After three years of negotiation, ASEAN and China adopted the Declaration on the Conduct of Parties in the South China Sea at the 8th ASEAN summit, held in Phnom Penh, Cambodia, in November 2002. Though the final outcome was just a political statement, falling short of a binding code as projected initially, ASEAN negotiators felt it was satisfactory. They converged on the idea that "it's all that is possible at the moment."[114]

Vietnam's involvement in the negotiation on the South China Sea code of conduct

Vietnam, like other Southeast Asian claimants, viewed the code of conduct largely as a political and legal measure to constrain China. Disputes among ASEAN countries had been well managed through the ASEAN mechanism.[115] As China was increasingly assertive, ASEAN claimants found each other as natural allies in the face of China's territorial ambition. Six ASEAN countries supported the ASEAN Declaration on the South China Sea in 1992, which was then endorsed by Vietnam. The Mischief Reef crisis was a region-wide alert that prompted them into collective action. ASEAN member states converged on the idea of the code of conduct would strengthen ASEAN solidarity and draw a red line on China's maritime expansion. As the most exposed to China's assertiveness, Vietnam and the Philippines were naturally enthusiastic to put this initiative forward.[116]

Since July 1996, Vietnam joined other ASEAN members to develop a multilateral code of conduct for the South China Sea region. Initially, the Vietnamese quietly supported the Philippines-led effort to call for deliberation of the key contents of the code. They just became more engaged when hosting the 6th ASEAN Summit, held in Hanoi in December 1998. In the aftermath of that meeting, Vietnam and the Philippines played a leading role in developing a draft code of conduct for ASEAN consideration, as noted earlier. Hanoi's initial low-key approach to the Philippines' initiative was perhaps an outcome of the apprentice mentality typical of a newcomer. Justifiably, modest experience with multilateralism in general and ASEAN in particular meant that the Vietnamese leadership required some time to understand how the organisation works and how ASEAN politics affects its sovereignty and independence. During this period Hanoi held its first bilateral talks with Beijing on the maritime issues in the South China Sea. It was the first time Beijing sat down to talk with Hanoi specifically on the complex and sensitive disputes. Vietnamese leaders knew that Beijing preferred to deal bilaterally, protesting against any third party's involvement in the South China Sea disputes. As a result, Hanoi was not willing to take the lead in an initiative that would disappoint Beijing.

Vietnam's public support for the code of conduct was voiced by Nong Duc Manh, Chairman of Vietnam's National Assembly during an address to the General Assembly of the ASEAN Inter-Parliamentary Organisation (AIPO) on 20 September 1999. He stated that the early formation of the code of conduct in the South China Sea would serve as a useful confidence-building measure in the region.[117] Two months later, Prime Minister Phan Van Khai reiterated this stance at the third ASEAN Informal Summit held in Manila on 28 November 1999.[118] From the Vietnamese perspective, a multilateral code of conduct represented the most viable, promising alternative, in addition to bilateralism, to manage the existing disputes. There was no prospect that the disputes over the Paracels and Spratlys would be resolved through negotiation or arbitration in the near future. Also, all the paths to bypass the sovereignty issue such as joint development and authority sharing were not effective given China's expansive claims.[119]

Also, Vietnamese leaders became increasingly comfortable with ASEAN ways and gained confidence about its possible influence. Vietnamese officials reportedly maintained that ASEAN's support was the key factor that forced China to withdraw its KANTAN-03 oil rig in April 1997.[120] Hanoi now looked at ASEAN as an important platform to manage its relations with external powers, including China. The grouping may bear significant political power if its member states united. Working through ASEAN, Hanoi opted for a step-by-step but all-round approach and envisaged a kind of a half-political and half-legal instrument. Thao made it clear that the code of conduct should not be "a treaty involving obligations," but an avenue for the parties to express their desire to settle the disputes peacefully.[121] At the same time, he maintained that the final document must touch upon broader issues concerning peace, stability and security in the South China Sea, and would include detailed commitments to good neighbourliness.[122] This position indicates that Hanoi had not worked out any concrete preferences or projections for the final settlement of the disputes.

Hanoi eventually took a leading role alongside the Philippines in drafting the code of conduct because the Vietnamese came to understand divisions within ASEAN and wanted other ASEAN members to discuss their own terms. The geographical parameter of the code was the most difficult point for ASEAN and for China as well. Hanoi insisted on the inclusion of the Paracel archipelago, which was disputed bilaterally between Vietnam and China, into the geographical scope of the code of conduct and refused to accept the limitation to the Spratlys. The other ASEAN claimants, who clearly did not want to be involved in the Vietnam-China spat over the Paracels, were reluctant to endorse Vietnam's proposal.[123] Although failing to have the reference to the Paracels inserted into the code of conduct adopted by ASEAN in November 1999, Hanoi managed to get it through in the ASEAN version presented in the ASEAN-China consultation held in Hua Hin, Thailand, on 15 March 2000.[124] China proposed to exclude the Paracels, which were under its control, out of the scope of the code. Hanoi's insistence on the inclusion of the Paracels was indicative of an apprehension that its claim over the Paracels had become generally unnoticed and ignored. Though in the final text, there was no reference to the Paracels specifically, through the negotiation of the code of conduct Hanoi hoped to have its claims to the Paracels recognised by the ASEAN state members.

On the other hand, Vietnam, like other ASEAN claimants, did not expect the scope of the code to expand beyond the contested areas of the Paracels and Spratlys. Defining a geographical scope for the code not only meant pinpointing disputed areas but also drawing a line in the sand for China's freedom of action. The Vietnamese argued that the disputes over the Paracels and Spratlys should be distinguished from the EEZs and the continental shelves of the coastal states under UNCLOS.[125] Hanoi had Kuala Lumpur's support for the idea that the scope of the code should be confined to the disputed island groups only. In the same way, Jakarta maintained that the code should not include the Natuna area. It is clear that Hanoi was concerned that China aimed to turn the Tu Chinh and Thanh Long areas into disputed zones. These areas should be outside the scope of the code because they are not part of the Spratlys, as the Vietnamese often argued.

The provision of self-restraint was similarly a contentious point. Self-restraint was a key CBM in the South China Sea since the early 1990s. However, there had been no clear-cut definitions and clarifications. The ASEAN Declaration on the South China Sea of 1992 called on "all parties concerned to exercise restraint with the view to creating a positive climate for the eventual resolution of all disputes." This principle had been spelled out in almost all joint statements of the Vietnamese and Chinese high-level leaders since 1991, in the Philippines-Vietnam code of conduct of 1995, and in the ASEAN-China Joint Statement of December 1997. However, it was clear that such political assertions were insufficient to prevent the claimants from taking unilateral actions and risked triggering protests from other coastal states. Tensions in the South China Sea were mostly caused by various unilateral activities, such as occupying reefs and rocks, erecting markers and structures for fishery, scientific research and military purposes. On some occasions, relations between claimants were strained when one side carried out unilateral civilian activities, such as maritime research, hydrocarbon development, tourist visits, circulation of historical testimonies to assert claims, and enforcement of domestic laws in the contested sea areas. There emerged a strong need for specifying prohibited actions and for developing mechanisms to monitor activities in the South China Sea region.

In this regard, Chinese and ASEAN negotiators pursued different definitions of the sets of action that should be banned or discouraged. Vietnam and the Philippines strongly pushed for the clearer definition of the specific actions that should be forbidden and those that should be encouraged.[126] Vietnam supported the Philippines' proposal to prohibit the occupation of the new islands, reefs or shoals and construction of new structures, as a means to maintain the status quo and avoid conflicts. They strongly protested against China's occupation of Mischief Reef in 1995 and Malaysia's presence on Erika and Investigator Reefs in 1999. Nguyen Hong Thao proposed a list of prohibited actions, specifically

> military exercises without prior consultation, introduction or stationing of offensive long-range weapons and platforms (for instance, nuclear ships, missiles, attack submarines, naval combatants, fighter aircraft, etc.); encouraging fishers go near occupied positions without consultation, low-flying aircraft over occupied; and stopping and seizing other parties' ships sailing outside the 12-mile area around occupied positions.[127]

On the other hand, China did not recognise the Philippines' and Vietnam's concerns about new occupations or constructions but pushed for a prohibition on joint military exercises and close-in military reconnaissance with external powers in the Spratly area, which could nullify the Philippines-US Visiting Force Agreement. Though Vietnam had no intention of conducting joint military activities with the United States, Hanoi quietly supported its greater military presence in the South China Sea region.[128]

The Declaration on Conduct of the Parties in the South China Sea (DOC) signed in November 2002 was clearly a product of compromise. Regarding geographical scope of the declaration, all the parties agreed not to mention specific disputed areas, but to use the South China Sea generally. The declaration had ten points. The first point reaffirms the parties' commitment to the principles of the Charter of United Nations, UNCLOS, ASEAN Treaty of Amity and Cooperation, and the Five Principles of Peaceful Coexistence. The second point commits all parties to exploring ways for building trust and confidence. The third point assures freedom of navigation in and overflight above the South China Sea. The fourth reaffirms the principle of no threat or use of force to resolve the disputes. The fifth lists prohibited actions, such as inhabiting on presently uninhabited islands, reefs, shoals, cays and other features, but does not mention the construction of new structures. It also presents a list of desired CBMs such as holding dialogues, humane treatment of all persons in danger or distress, notifications of joint/combined military exercises and information exchange. The sixth specifies possible cooperative activities, such as marine environment protection, marine scientific research, safety of navigation and communication at sea and so on. The seventh commits all the parties to further consultation and dialogues on relevant issues. The eighth and the ninth encourage the parties and other countries to respect the principles of the DOC. The last point restates the goal of a code of conduct and commits all the parties to work towards this goal on the basis of consensus.[129] This non-binding text was largely a statement of intent by all signatories to restrain from activities that might complicate or escalate disputes and affect peace and stability.

In spite of limited results, all parties seemed content with the process and optimistic about the progress. Beijing was satisfied at a non-binding and ambiguously written text, which would not obligate China to any specific set of actions. In public, Chinese Vice Foreign Minister Wang Yi stated that the DOC would not resolve the territorial conflicts, but would help to preserve peace.[130] ASEAN countries, including Vietnam, were hopeful that the DOC was an indication of China's subscription to multilateralism and was a stepping-stone to the ultimate goal of a binding code of conduct in the South China Sea region. Chem Widhya, permanent secretary to the Cambodian Ministry of Foreign Affairs said "we (ASEAN and China) want to show the world that we are politically committed to establishing peace, stability and security, and to establishing friendly relations."[131] Reportedly, after the DOC the Vietnamese prime minister urged, "ASEAN should establish a code of conduct in the East Sea (the South China Sea) to lay a fundamental and long-term foundation for disputes in the sea."[132] A closer look into the substance of the text indicated that Hanoi managed to block the possibility of exclusive application to the Spratlys, which would give it a further disadvantaged position in dealing with China over the Paracels dispute. However, the geographical scope of "the South China Sea" would allow a variety of interpretations according to the interests of the signatories. The Vietnamese interpretation would permit the scope of application of the DOC to include the Paracels. The Chinese later argued that much of the South China Sea could be "disputed areas," including maritime zones which are considered "undisputed" from other claimants' perspectives. No doubt, the DOC's ambiguity in geographical scope is not a solution but a problem, which may give rise to newfound tensions in the future.

Conclusion

The period between 1995 and 2002 witnessed Vietnam's continued bilateral talks with its neighbours to resolve the differences among them about territorial issues. The most important outcomes of this process were the signature of the land border agreement and Gulf of Tonkin delimitation agreement with China in 1999 and 2000 respectively. The agreements were principally facilitated by the shift in China's approach to become more receptive to its Southeast Asian neighbours' pressing concerns to prevent increased US involvement in the region. China agreed to speed up these negotiations and reached agreements on these outstanding issues before the turn of the century. Also, leaders in Hanoi converged on the imperative to settle land borders and on the Gulf of Tonkin with China as the earliest possible date, though their motives may not be the same.

However, the disputes in the South China Sea proper remained intractable. Vietnam-China dialogue on maritime issues made no substantive progress primarily because of disagreement on the status of the Paracels. In the same time, the competitive assertions of maritime rights and actions of claimants to substantiate their claims strained relations among them from time to time. The most challenging crisis involving Vietnam occurred in March 1997 when China sent the KANTAN-03 oil rig to the waters off Vietnam's central coast. As bilateral diplomacy failed to persuade China to remove the oil rig, Vietnam resorted to public protests and sought support from other ASEAN members.

In this period, Vietnam also engaged with other ASEAN members to develop a multilateral binding code of conduct, which was aimed to prevent attempts to change the status quo. Hanoi forcefully advocated the inclusion of the Paracels into the geographical scope of the code. However, it hesitated to expand the scope to extend beyond these two disputed archipelagos for fear that their legitimate EEZ and continental shelf could be turned into "disputed areas" by excessive Chinese claims. Being afraid of leaving behind, China finally moved beyond its bilateral preference to talk with the ASEAN countries collectively. However, the rigid positions of some ASEAN claimants and China prevented them from reaching a consensus on the outcome of a binding document and on the geographical scope of application. They finally accepted a watered-down political statement of intent, the Declaration on Conduct of the Parties in the South China Sea, in November 2002.

Notes

1 B. Wain, "Loggerheads with Beijing," *Asian Wall Street Journal*, 6 October 2000, p.12.
2 "Accord Seen Possible off China, Vietnam," *Oil & Gas Journal*, 22 April 1996, p.36.
3 T. Gred, "Deal to Escalate Row over Spratlys," *South China Morning Post*, 13 April 1996, p.12.
4 D. Ivanovich, "The Risky Business of Petroleum Politics/U.S. Oil and Gas Firms Must often Weigh Instability in Some Areas with the Lure of Rich Reserves," *Houston Chronicle*, 28 July 1996; M.J. Valencia, "Asia, the Law of the Sea, and IR," *International Affairs* 73, no. 2, 1997, p.270.
5 "Vietnam Finds Success in Program Aimed at Building Oil and Gas Capacity," *Oil and Gas Journal*, 28 November 1994; "Vietnam Oil Output Sets Quarterly Record," *Asian Wall Street Journal*, 7 April 1995, p.17.
6 See more C. Snyder, "The Implication of Hydrocarbon Development in the South China Sea," *International Journal* 52, no. 1, 1996/1997, pp. 142–58.
7 M.J. Valencia, J.M. Van Dyke, and N.A. Ludwig, *Sharing the Resources of the South China Sea*, Boston and Cambridge, MA: M. Nijhoff, 1997, p.95.
8 "Vietnam Revises '95 Trade Deficit to a Record Level of 2.2 Billion," *Asian Wall Street Journal*, 17 January 1996, p.4.
9 "Vietnam Plans Refineries," *Globe and Mail*, 21 June 1994, p.B7.
10 M. Richardson, "Oil Rush Is Fuelling Fears on Spratlys," *International Herald Tribune*, 6 June 1994, p.13. The most significant discovery was made by Japan Vietnam Petroleum Co. Ltd (JVPC), a subsidiary of Mitsubishi near the Bach Ho oil field, about 75 miles east of Vung Tau Port.

11 S. Raymer, "Oil Company Rush to Develop Vietnam," *Journal Record*, Oklahoma, 22 March 1995 (emphasis added).
12 V.V. Kiet, "Thu gui Bo Chinh tri," 9 August 1995. Online. Available HTTP: <www.diendan.org/tai-lieu/bao-cu/so-048/thu-vo-van-kiet-1995Hanoi> (accessed 29 June 2015). On 9 August 1995, in the run-up to the 8th National Party Congress of the Communist Party of Vietnam, Prime Minister Vo Van Kiet sent this letter to the Politburo, discussing four key issues: (1) the assessment of current international conjuncture; (2) deviation from socialism or not; (3) improvement of state management capacity; and (4) party building.
13 B. Wain, "Sea Battle: Vietnam Fires New Weapon in Oil Dispute: The Law," *Asian Wall Street Journal*, Hong Kong, 16 June 1995, p.1.
14 B. Wain, "Maritime Manoeuvres: Lawyer Say Vietnam Has a Strong Case," *Asian Wall Street Journal*, Hong Kong, 20 July 1994, p.5.
15 D. Wurfel, "Between China and ASEAN," In: C.A. Thayer and R. Amer (eds.), *Vietnamese Foreign Policy in Transition*, Singapore: Institute of Southeast Asian Studies, 1999, p.156.
16 N.C. Trung, "Thuc chat tu Dai hoi Dang IX tro ve truoc (tu thap ky 90 TK 20) la van de gi?," 4 August 2009. Online. Available HTTP: <www.danluan.org/tin-tuc/20090804/thuc-chat-tu-dai-hoi-dang-ix-tro-ve-truoc-tu-thap-ky-90-tk20-la-van-de-gi> (accessed 15 March 2015). This is a memoir by Nguyen Chi Trung who was personal assistant to former Secretary General Le Kha Phieu when he was in power.
17 C.A. Thayer, "Vietnamese Foreign Policy: Multilateralism and the Threat of Peaceful Evolution," In: C.A. Thayer and R. Amer (eds.), *Vietnamese Foreign Policy in Transition*, Singapore: Institute of Southeast Asian Studies, 1999, pp. 11–2.
18 Ibid.
19 "Sea of Troubles," *Economist*, 339, 25 May 1996, p.36.
20 B. Wain, "China Snubs the Law of the Sea," *Asian Wall Street Journal*, 1 November 1996, p.8; "Sea of Troubles," p.36.
21 J. Leahy, "Indonesia Seeks Clarification on Extension of Territorial Waters Into Disputed Area," *South China Morning Post*, 22 July 1996, p.11.
22 N.V. Long, *Hoang Sa-Truong Sa: Cac su kien, tu lieu lich su phap ly chinh (The ky XV-2000)*, 1, pp. 213–14.
23 "China Backs Further Dialogue But Proves Wary About Change," *Bangkok Post*, 14 June 1996.
24 R. Amer, "Sino-Vietnamese Relations: Past, Present and Future," In: C.A. Thayer and R. Amer (eds.), *Vietnamese Foreign Policy in Transition*, Singapore: Institute of Southeast Asian Studies, 1999, pp. 84–6.
25 P.P. Nguyen, "Oil Search Fuels Rising Tension in South China Sea," *Inter Press Service*, 21 March 1997, p.1.
26 W.J. Dobson, "Now Vietnam Needs America to Ward off China," *Christian Science Monitor*, 17 April 1997, p.19.
27 Ibid.
28 Wurfel, "Between China and ASEAN," p.156.
29 "A Rig Too Near," *Economist*, 29 March 1997, p.36.
30 Nguyen, "Oil Search Fuels Rising Tension in South China Sea," p.1.
31 A.L. Vuving, "Strategy and Evolution of Vietnam's China Policy: A Changing Mixture of Pathways," *Asian Survey* 46, no. 6, 2006, p.815.
32 J. Grant, "US-Vietnam Military Ties," *Financial Times*, 22 March 1997, p.2.
33 I.J. Storey, "Living with the Colossus: How Southeast Asian Countries Cope with China," *Parameters* 29, no. 4, 1999/2000, p.123.
34 "China and Vietnam to Hold Maritime Dispute Talks on April 9," *AFP*, 3 April 1997; "Chinese Oil Drilling Sparks Vietnam's Ire," *Asian Wall Street Journal*, 25 March 1997, p.7.

35 T. Gred, "Beijing Agrees to Talks on Drilling," *South China Morning Post*, 1 April 1997, p.6.
36 J. Grant, "China Rig Leaves Disputed Zone Oil Exploration Move Surprises Diplomats before Talks with Vietnam Next Week," *Financial Times*, London, 5 April 1997.
37 Quoted in Wurfel, "Between China and ASEAN," p.159.
38 Ibid.
39 Ibid.
40 A.L. Vuving, "Turning Points in China-Vietnam Relations," In: Tang Shipping, Li Mingjiang, and Acharya Amitav (eds.), *Living with China: Regional States and China through Crises and Turning Points*, New York: Palgrave Macmillan, 2009, pp. 222–3.
41 The agreement stipulated the resumption of joint military exercises.
42 See more L. Buszynski, "ASEAN, the Declaration on Conduct, and the South China Sea," *Contemporary Southeast Asia* 25, no. 3, 2003, pp. 343–62.
43 Ibid., p.354; S. Simon, "ASEAN and Multilateralism: The Long, Bumpy Road to Community," *Contemporary Southeast Asia* 30, no. 2, 2008, pp. 281–82.
44 See D. Roy, "China's Pitch for a Multipolar World," *Asia-Pacific Security Studies* 2, no. 1, 2003, pp. 1–4.
45 B. Womack, *China and Vietnam: The Politics of Asymmetry*, Cambridge, NY: Cambridge University Press, 2006, p.222; R. Amer, "Sino-Vietnamese Relations: Past, Present and Future," pp. 90–1.
46 R. Amer, "The Sino-Vietnamese Approach to Managing Boundary Disputes," *IBRU Maritime Briefing* 3, no. 5, 2002, p.25.
47 Amer, "Sino-Vietnamese Relations," pp. 95–6.
48 R. Amer, "Assessing Sino-Vietnamese Relations through Management of Contentious Issues," *Contemporary Southeast Asia* 26, no. 2, 2004, pp. 322–23.
49 N.H. Thao, "Vietnam and the Code of Conduct for the South China Sea," pp. 106–7.
50 A. Acharya, "China's Charm Offensive in Southeast Asia," *International Herald Tribune*, Paris, 8 November 2003, p.8.
51 See more Womack, *China and Vietnam*, pp. 212–25; Amer, "Assessing Sino-Vietnamese Relations through Management of Contentious Issues," pp. 328–37.
52 N.H. Thao, "Viet-Trung va duong bien gioi phap ly, cong bang, huu nghi," *Vietnamnet*, 2 January 2009. Online. Available HTTP: <http://vnn.vietnamnet.vn/chinhtri/2009/01/821775/> (accessed 17 January 2013).
53 Hong Chuyen, "Hiep dinh phan dinh Vinh Bac Bo quy dinh dieu gi?," *Infonet*, 8 April 2014. Online. Available HTTP: <http://infonet.vn/hiep-dinh-phan-dinh-vinh-bac-bo-quy-dinh-dieu-gi-post124151.info> (accessed 30 March 2015).
54 N.H. Thao, "Vietnam's First Maritime Boundary Agreement," *IBRU Boundary and Security Bulletin*, Fall 1997.
55 N.H. Thao and R. Amer, "Managing Vietnam's Maritime Boundary Disputes," *Ocean Development and International Law* 38, no. 3, 2007, pp. 309–10.
56 See N.H. Thao, "The Settlement of Disputes in Bac Bo (Tonkin) Gulf," *Vietnam Law and Legal Forum* 7, no. 77, 2001.
57 S. Tønnesson, "Sino-Vietnamese Rapprochement and the South China Sea Irritant," *Security Dialogue* 34, no. 1, 2003, p.63.
58 A. Carlson, *Unifying China, Integrating with the World: Securing Chinese Sovereignty in Reform Era*, Singapore: NUS Press, 2008, p.88.
59 Thao, "The Settlement of Disputes in Bac Bo (Tonkin) Gulf," p.17.
60 D. Rosenberg, "China, Neighbours Progress in Fishery Agreements," *Asia Times*, 19 August 2005. Online. Available HTTP: <www.atimes.com/atimes/China/GH19Ad02.html> (accessed 17 February 2013).
61 Amer, "Assessing Sino-Vietnamese Relations through Management of Contentious Issues," p.332.
62 "Vietnam-China Tonkin Gulf Fishing Agreement Opens Way for Cooperation," *BBC Monitoring Asia Pacific*, 2001, p.1.

63 Tra Mi, "Dai su VN tai My tra loi phong van ve van de Bien gioi Lanh hai voi Trung Quoc," *RFA–Dai A Chau Tu Do*, 25 September 2008. Online. Available HTTP: <www.rfa.org/vietnamese/SpecialTopic/ChinaVietnamBorder/interview-with-VN-amb-in-the-US-on-Sino-Vietnamese-borders-issues-TMi-09252008115350.html> (accessed 12 March 2013).
64 Quoted in R. Amer, "Assessing Sino-Vietnamese Relations through Management of Contentious Issues," p.331.
65 Ibid., p.330.
66 R. Amer and H.T. Nguyen, "The Management of Vietnam's Border Disputes: What Impact on Its Sovereignty and Regional Integration?," *Contemporary Southeast Asia* 27, no. 3, 2005, p.439.
67 Dang Cong san Viet Nam, *Van kien Dai hoi Dai bieu Toan quoc lan thu VIII*, Hanoi: Chinh tri Quoc gia Publisher, 1996, p.120.
68 D. Koh, "The Politics of a Divided Party and Parkinson's State in Vietnam," p.540.
69 Huy Duc, *Ben thang cuoc*, 2 – Quyen Binh, p.517.
70 Trung, "Thuc chat tu Dai hoi Dang IX tro ve truoc (tu thap ky 90 TK 20) la van de gi?"
71 Z. Abuza, "The Lessons of Le Kha Phieu: Changing Rules in Vietnamese Politics," *Contemporary Southeast Asia* 24, no. 1, 2002, p.140.
72 See Trung, "Thuc chat tu Dai hoi Dang IX tro ve truoc (tu thap ky 90 TK 20) la van de gi?"
73 Z. Abuza, "The Lessons of Le Kha Phieu: Changing Rules in Vietnamese Politics," p.139.
74 Vuving, "Strategy and Evolution of Vietnam's China Policy," p.816.
75 Abuza, "The Lessons of Le Kha Phieu," p.138.
76 Ibid., pp. 134–38.
77 See D. Koh, "The Politics of a Divided Party and Parkinson's State in Vietnam."
78 Huy Duc, *Ben thang cuoc*, 2 – Quyen Binh, p.496 (emphasis added).
79 Ibid., p.498.
80 Ibid.
81 Tønnesson, "Sino-Vietnamese Rapprochement and the South China Sea Irritant," p.65.
82 Thayer, "Vietnamese Foreign Policy," p.7.
83 K.C. Lee, "Vietnam Had No Regrets about Joining ASEAN," *Strait Times*, 10 September 1996.
84 R. Lim, "The ASEAN Regional Forum: Building on Sand," *Contemporary Southeast Asia* 20, no. 2, 1998, p.118.
85 See more M. Caballero-Anthony, "Mechanism of Dispute Settlement: The ASEAN Experience," *Contemporary Southeast Asia* 20, no. 1, 1998, pp. 38–66.
86 R.C. Severino, "ASEAN Beyond Forty: Towards Political and Economic Integration," *Contemporary Southeast Asia* 29, no. 3, 2007, p.413.
87 I.J. Storey, "Creeping Assertiveness: China, the Philippines and the South China Sea Dispute," p.108.
88 ASEAN Declaration on the South China Sea of 1992.
89 Quoted from Y.H. Song, "The South China Sea Declaration of Conduct of Parties and Its Implication: Taiwan's Perspective," *Maritime Studies*, March–April 2003, p.13.
90 Z. Othman, "Disputed Areas: ASEAN Calls for Self-Restraint," *Business Times*, Kuala Lumpur, 22 July 1996, p.1.
91 See more Buszynski, "ASEAN, the Declaration on Conduct, and the South China Sea."
92 ASEAN, Hanoi Plan of Action at the 6th ASEAN Summit, 1998.
93 M. Dickie and T. Tassel, "Manila Set to Propose Code of Conduct for Spratlys," *Financial Times*, London, 15 July 1999, p.6.
94 Thao, "Vietnam and the Code of Conduct for the South China Sea," p.114.
95 Buszynski, "ASEAN, the Declaration on Conduct, and the South China Sea," pp. 354–55.
96 M. Richardson, "On Eve of Annual Talks, ASEAN Members Are Split over Spratly Dispute," *International Herald Tribune*, 23 July 1999, p.6; R. Nambia and R. Said,

"Regional Code of Conduct Now Referred to Working Group," *New Straits Times*, 21 July 1999, p.4.

97 V. England, "Spratlys Behaviour Code Hinges on China," *South China Morning Post*, 26 November 1999, p.13.

98 Regional Code of Conduct in the South China Sea, Adopted by the Member States of ASEAN, November 1999.

99 Buszynski, "ASEAN, the Declaration on Conduct, and the South China Sea," p.355.

100 B. Porter, "Beijing Still Wants to See Spratly Code: Pragmatic Approach Urged in Developing Islands," *South China Morning Post*, 30 November 1999, p.10; "China Agrees to Talks with Southeast Asian Group on South China Sea Code," *BBC Monitoring Asia Pacific*, London, 25 November 1999, p.1.

101 "Canada Warns of Rising Asian Conflict," *Spectator*, 26 July 1999, p.C4; C. Skehan, "Canberra Condemns ASEAN's Failure to Back Code," *Age*, 29 July 1999, p.9; J.M. Van Dyke and M.J. Valencia, "How Valid Are the South China Sea Claims Under the Law of the Sea Convention," *Southeast Asian Affairs*, 2000.

102 "China Agrees to Talks with Southeast Asian Group on South China Sea Code," p.1.

103 Buszynski, "ASEAN, the Declaration on Conduct, and the South China Sea," p.355.

104 Ibid.

105 B. Wain, "A Code of Conduct in the South China Sea?," *Asian Wall Street Journal*, 10 March 2000, p.10; Wain, "Loggerheads with Beijing," p.12.

106 Buszynski, "ASEAN, the Declaration on Conduct, and the South China Sea," p.356.

107 "Bully in the South China Sea," *Asian Wall Street Journal*, Hong Kong, 17 March 2000, p.10; J. East, "Beijing Warns against Joint Military Games," *South China Morning Post*, 16 March 2000, p.10.

108 M.J. Valencia, "South China Sea Beijing's Buffer?," *Washington Times*, 24 August 2001, p.A14.

109 Y.H. Song, "The South China Sea Declaration of Conduct of Parties and Its Implication: Taiwan's Perspective," *Maritime Studies*, March–April 2003, p.15.

110 L. Buszynski, "ASEAN, the Declaration on Conduct, and the South China Sea," p.356.

111 Song, "The South China Sea Declaration of Conduct of Parties and Its Implication," p.16.

112 Joint Communiqué of the 35th ASEAN Foreign Ministers' Meeting, Bandar Seri Begawan, 29–30 July 2002.

113 Buszynski, "ASEAN, the Declaration on Conduct, and the South China Sea," p.357; B. Wain, "Taking Charge," *Far Eastern Economic Review* 165, no. 45, 2002, p.26.

114 Wain, "Taking Charge," p.26.

115 See Simon, "ASEAN and Multilateralism."

116 Buszynski, "ASEAN, the Declaration on Conduct, and the South China Sea," p.354.

117 "Vietnam Assembly Chairman Speaks on South China Sea Disputes," *BBC Monitoring Asia Pacific*, London, 21 September 1999, p.1.

118 "Vietnamese Premier Calls for South China Sea Code of Conduct," *BBC Monitoring Asia Pacific*, London, 29 November 1999, p.1.

119 N.H. Thao, "Vietnam and the Code of Conduct for the South China Sea," *Ocean Development and International Law* 32, no. 2, 2001, pp. 108–9.

120 Wurfel, "Between China and ASEAN," p.160.

121 Thao, "Vietnam and the Code of Conduct for the South China Sea," p.113.

122 Ibid., pp. 113–14.

123 Wain, "A Code of Conduct in the South China Sea?," p.10.

124 Song, "The South China Sea Declaration of Conduct of Parties and Its Implication: Taiwan's Perspective," p.14.

125 Thao, "Vietnam and the Code of Conduct for the South China Sea," pp. 115–16.

126 Ibid., p.114.

127 Ibid., p.118.

128 L.T. Lee, *China and the South China Sea Dialogues*, Westport, CT: Praeger, 1999, p.98.
129 Declaration on Conduct of the Parties in the South China Sea, signed on 24 November 2001 in Phnom Penh, Cambodia.
130 "ASEAN, China Sign Pact on Disputed Spratlys," *CNN*, 4 November 2002.
131 V. England and S. Meixner, "China and ASEAN Reach Agreements on Sea Disputes," *South China Morning Post*, 2 November 2002, p.10.
132 "Vietnamese Premier Calls for Regional Pact on South China Sea," *BBC Monitoring Asia Pacific*, London, 7 October 2003, p.1.

5 Shaping the regional balance of influence, 2003–2007

Introduction

The signing of the Declaration on the Conduct of Parties in the South China Sea (DOC) in November 2002 was seen as a significant milestone, as it prescribed a range of conflict avoidance mechanisms through self-restraint, dialogues and cooperative activities. However, as the implementation of the DOC and work towards a code of conduct faced deadlocks, optimism about fruitful ASEAN multilateralism receded. Beijing's "charm offensive" helped increase its influence across Southeast Asia, basically neutralising ASEAN as a means to constrain China. In the same time, China renewed its maritime assertiveness, using its physical force as well as its economic power to deny Vietnam's rights to maritime control and resources under UNCLOS. China's growing economic and military power as well as increased trend of bandwagoning with China in Southeast Asia then created a serious challenge to Hanoi's foreign policy, which has been primarily centred on bilateralism with China and ASEAN multilateralism. The chapter examines the South China Sea developments and Vietnam's security predicament in the context of China's rise in the period 2003–2007.

The loopholes of the DOC

The signing of the DOC in November 2002 kindled hopes across Southeast Asia for a long-lasting end to hostilities arising from disputes in the South China Sea. In spite of being short of the original goal of a legally binding code of conduct, the DOC was hailed as evidence of substantial progress in managing the disputes in the South China Sea. Obviously, the ASEAN countries viewed the DOC not as an end in itself, but an important provisional confidence-building measure and a step forward towards a binding code of conduct. The key reason for optimism was not the substance of the DOC document, but the hint of a shift in China's approach in three dimensions. First, the DOC represented China's commitment to maintain the status quo and its readiness to renounce the use of force to settle existing territorial disputes. Second, China's subscription to the multi-party arrangement of the DOC was viewed as its acquiescence to ASEAN multilateral process and norms. Third, China observably moderated its posture in the South China Sea after the

Mischief Reef crisis in 1995 and worked to expand its cooperation with Southeast Asian countries.

As for Vietnam, the code of conduct constituted a critical component of Hanoi's engagement with its neighbours to ensure the status quo in the South China Sea. Addressing the opening session of the ASEAN Summit in Bali, Vietnamese Prime Minister Phan Van Khai continued to press for the development of a code of conduct in the South China Sea as "a fundamental and long-term foundation for the peace and stability in the region."[1] Vietnamese officials appeared hopeful that ASEAN could be a good medium to constrain China's territorial irredentism. Deputy Director General of MOFA Policy Planning Department Bui Thanh Son informed a US diplomat that China's foreign policy had shifted in 2002, moving away from security issues – like the South China Sea – and instead towards economic issues with renewed attention to Southeast Asia. He added that the best hope of Vietnam and ASEAN was to continue to ensure China's "integrated interests" within the region through the ASEAN Plus Three process, free trade agreements (with expected concessions for countries like Vietnam, he added), and other contacts.[2]

However, the process of operationalising DOC quickly reached an impasse because of a disagreement in drafting the guidelines to implement the DOC provisions. Not until December 2004 was the first ASEAN-China Senior Official Meeting (SOM) on the implementation of the DOC held in Kuala Lumpur, Malaysia. The meeting decided to set up a Joint Work Group (JWG) to study and recommend cooperative activities as confidence building measures.[3] The ASEAN foreign ministers endorsed the proposal in July 2005.[4] According to its Terms of Reference, the ASEAN-China JWG was tasked with working out recommendations on: (1) guidelines and action plan for the implementation of the DOC; (2) specific cooperative activities in the South China Sea; (3) a register of experts and eminent persons who may provide technical inputs, non-binding and professional views or policy recommendations to the ASEAN-China JWG; and (4) the convening of workshops, as the need arises.[5] ASEAN tabled a seven-paragraph draft of the Guidelines for the Implementation of the DOC for discussion at the first meeting of the ASEAN JWG in August 2005 in Manila. Seven points were outlined:

1 The implementation of the DOC should be carried out in a step-by-step approach in line with the provisions of the DOC.
2 ASEAN will continue its current practice of consulting among them before meeting China.
3 The implementation of the DOC should be based on activities or projects clearly identified.
4 The participation in the activities or projects should be carried out on a voluntary basis.
5 Initial activities to be undertaken under the ambit of the DOC should be confident building measures.
6 The decision to implement concrete measures or activities of the DOC should be based on consensus among parties concerned and lead to the eventual realization of a COC.

7 In the implementation of the agreed projects under the DOC, the service of the experts and eminent persons if deemed necessary will be sort to provide specific inputs on the project concerned.[6]

Point 2 of the draft was focal controversy. China disagreed with the ASEAN consultation formula and insisted on consultations with "relevant parties" because it did not want to deal with ASEAN as a bloc. Vietnam was on the other side.[7] This sticking point stalled the whole process for six years although twenty-one successive drafts were exchanged.[8] No guidelines to implement the DOC were adopted until late 2011. In the meantime, there were no consultations between ASEAN and China on the specific steps to be taken towards a binding code of conduct until January 2012. During the second meeting of the Technical Working Group, the Philippines put forth a proposal to convene a seminar on elements of the regional code of conduct in the South China Sea. China expressed no interest in that proposal, as it did not want its hands to be tied.[9] When asked by journalists about the future of the code of conduct, a spokesman of Chinese Foreign Ministry ambiguously answered, "When conditions are ripe China would like to discuss with ASEAN countries the formulation of the COC."[10]

The DOC failed to stabilise the South China Sea because of its three major shortcomings. First, the DOC was not inclusive because Taiwan, which controlled the largest island in the Spratly group, was not a party to the political compromise.[11] In March 2004, Taiwan built a bird-watching stand on Ban Than Reef of the Spratly group. Hanoi strongly protested the Taiwanese move and called it "an act of land grabbing expansion that seriously violated Vietnam's territorial sovereignty."[12] It was a concern that if it were not regarded as a legitimate party to the Spratly dispute, Taiwan would be inclined to act to spoil the DOC.[13]

Second, though requiring all parties to refrain from activities that would complicate the dispute, the DOC did not specify geographical scope and type of actions what would not be accepted with only the exception of "inhabiting on the presently uninhabited islands, reefs, shoals, cays, and other features." This ambiguity failed to stop all claimants to undertake measures, one way or another, to bolster their claims. China continued to repeat its unilateral fishing bans annually and conduct marine research in the areas near the coasts of other countries without their consent.[14] On 7 November 2003, the Philippines announced that it discovered China-built markers on a number of uninhabited islands in the Spratlys.[15] In April 2004, Hanoi announced a controversial plan to open a boat tour for civilians to one of the Spratly Islands, which it described as "normal civil activity."[16] These undertakings were stimulated by the ICJ's ruling in December 2002 to award ownership of the Celebes Sea islands of Ligitan and Sipadan to Malaysia over Indonesia on the basis of continuous administration and the control of Malaysian authorities over these islands.[17] "It is naïve to believe that the parties ceased activities that complicate the disputes," Vietnamese analyst Nguyen Hong Thao predicted.[18] Hanoi clearly anticipated that DOC would not end activities to bolster their claims by disputants.

Third, though outlining some sort of confidence building measures (CBMs), the DOC failed to specify methods and areas for such cooperative schemes. Not until

February 2006 could the parties concerned agree on a list of cooperative projects. However, proposed cooperation was limited to conducting seminars, workshops or training in less sensitive areas such as search and rescue exercises, marine ecosystem, biodiversity, oceanography and maritime climate projects; and disaster prevention. The contribution of these projects to confidence building among the claimants was rather limited.

Trust eroded quickly when Beijing used its influence to seek bilateral deals with individual ASEAN countries. In August 2003, during his visit to Manila, Chairman of the Chinese National Assembly Wu Bangguo proposed to the Philippines a joint development project in the Spratly area.[19] In spite of their long suspicion of China's intentions, the Philippines appeared unusually receptive to the Chinese proposal. Jose de Venecia, the Speaker of the Philippine Congress, said, "If we in the Philippines and China take a joint initiative in the Spratlys, this can constitute a breakthrough. We take seriously proposals on how to undertake joint development in the South China Sea with all others."[20] However, the details of China's proposal were kept confidential. One year later, in September 2004, it was reported that China and the Philippines signed a three-year deal to jointly gauge prospects for oil and gas exploration and production in the Spratlys. The area designated for the joint survey was not published. The deal came out as a shock to other South China Sea claimants, particularly Vietnam. It was later revealed that the Philippine government had been persuaded to participate by offers of Chinese aid for projects such as North Luzon Railway, Southern Luzon Railway, and National Broadband Network, in return for Philippine support for the joint survey project in the South China Sea. It should be noted that China's overseas development assistance was attractive to Filipino officials because they were not accompanied by any condition of governance accountability.[21]

Though the Sino-Philippine joint survey project might be an instance of functional cooperation as suggested by the DOC, the problem was that other claimants had not been consulted before the deal was concluded. Secrecy clouded the agreement, as the exact sites for joint survey were not disclosed. China's bilateralism appeared effective. Leaders in Hanoi were clearly shaken by the Philippines' silent bandwagoning with China given the two countries' long-standing oceanographic cooperation in the Spratly area and their previous coordinated efforts to push for a regional code of conduct. The spokesperson for the Vietnamese Ministry of Foreign Affairs, Le Dung, stated "we are very concerned by the suggestion that a deal on South China Sea has been signed by China and Philippines on 1 September without consultation with any relevant parties."[22]

Hanoi initially denied the invitation to participate in the project with the view that the Sino-Philippine agreement would be a breach of the Declaration on Conduct of the Parties in the South China Sea. Vice Foreign Minister Nguyen Phu Binh told an US diplomat that Hanoi "did not want to be seen making side deals on the Spratly Islands when all parties were supposed to be committed to a solution that involved all claimants."[23] As usual, Hanoi tried to approach high-level Chinese leaders bilaterally to persuade them to withdraw from the contract with the Philippines. The issue was raised in the meeting between Vietnamese PM Phan

Van Khai and Chinese Premier Wen Jiabao during his visit to Hanoi for the 5th Asia-Europe Meeting Summit in Hanoi in October 2004. Khai asked Wen to stop the joint-survey project. Wen refused, however, with a blunt response that that Sino-Philippine joint exploration agreement did not run against the DOC and did not at all hurt Vietnam's national interests.[24] Vietnamese officials also approached their Philippine counterparts to ask them to stop the controversial deal without any success.

Six months later, Hanoi abruptly reversed its previous position and agreed to take part in the project prepared by China and the Philippines. Though Hanoi did not explain its shift, it was later revealed that the designated zone for joint survey was beyond the waters it claimed. It was a 142,886 km^2 area off Palawan, jutting into the Spratlys and the Philippines' Malampaya oil field. Its closest point is just 25 km to the southern tip of Palawan, and one-sixth of the zone lies within Philippine territorial waters, outside the claims of both Vietnam and China (see Figure 2.11).[25] This paved the way to the signature of the tripartite agreement between the Vietnam Petroleum Corporation (PetroVietnam), Philippine National Oil Company (PNOC) and China National Offshore Oil Corporation (CNOOC), called Joint Marine Seismic Undertaking (JMSU), in March 2005. Its purpose was to conduct seismic surveys in the Spratly Islands for oil and gas resources over a three-year time frame starting from 1 July 2005.[26] Vietnamese Foreign Minister Nguyen Dy Nien joined his Philippine and Chinese counterparts to laud the trilateral agreement as a significant measure of ASEAN-China cooperation. Vietnam's participation in the China-led JMSU did not mean that Vietnam had compromised its maritime claims and long-standing view on joint development. However, the development forced Vietnam to seriously reconsider the role of ASEAN as a platform to manage and resolve the South China Sea disputes. The Philippines' mini-lateral agreement with China implied a new strategic setting in the region, in which the Southeast Asian claimants compete for the most favourable bilateral agreements with China.[27] In other words, ASEAN was now of little help in enhancing Vietnam's position in the South China Sea dispute.[28]

China's rising influence and Vietnam's indirect balancing

Beijing's extensive engagement with the ASEAN countries quickly increased its influence over Southeast Asia. On the economic front, at a time when the DOC was concluded, ASEAN and China also signed a Framework Agreement on Comprehensive Economic Cooperation in Phnom Penh in November 2012. The agreement laid out a roadmap for the establishment of an China-ASEAN Free Trade Area (CAFTA), which aimed to liberalise 99 per cent of bilateral trade between China and ASEAN's six more advanced members by 2010 and for the rest of ASEAN by 2015.[29] One of the main features of CAFTA was "early harvest" provision, which granted tariff-free access to the Chinese market for goods from individual ASEAN countries three years before reciprocity applied.[30] An analyst explained, "Within ASEAN China is perceived as an engine of growth, a distinction that previously belonged to Japan." He argued that CAFTA, especially the Early Harvest Program, promoted China's image as "a benevolent regional leader."[31]

As economic relations between China and ASEAN countries expanded, there was a commonly shared belief within the ASEAN circle that economic interdependence between ASEAN and China would work to constrain China's unilateralism. Increased economic interdependence between China and ASEAN was expected to defuse possible political tensions. One Southeast Asian analyst argued,

> From a political angle, the realization of a China and ASEAN trade agreement indicates that historical feuds and political clashes between ASEAN member states and PRC are no longer one of the most important factors influencing ASEAN-PRC relations.[32]

Commenting on the disputes in the South China Sea, one ASEAN official said "We have higher stakes elsewhere."[33] In addition to trade liberalisation, Chinese leaders also promised to facilitate Chinese foreign direct investment (FDI) into Southeast Asia and support Mekong River Basin development and the building of rail and road links in the region.[34] China also wrote off ASEAN countries' debts while providing aid to the less developed ones. Without governance and human rights conditions attached, Chinese aid allowed Beijing to exert leverage over Southeast Asian capitals to achieve its political goals. Examples of this are China's success in forcing Singapore to succumb to Beijing's "one-China policy," bringing the Philippines into the joint survey project in the Spratlys, and gaining access to key locations in the Indian Ocean in Myanmar.[35]

In the political and security realm, China took another step to show it was a status quo power by submitting an application to join the Treaty of Amity and Cooperation (TAC) in early 2003.[36] The TAC was a fundamental document of ASEAN, which promoted peaceful settlement of disputes and renounced the threat or use of force. At the Ninth ASEAN Summit in Bali, Indonesia, in October 2003, China's application was endorsed and China became the first non-Southeast Asian nation to formally subscribe to the TAC. On the same occasion, ASEAN and Chinese leaders signed a Joint Declaration on a Strategic Partnership for Peace and Prosperity, which was aimed "to foster friendly relations, mutually beneficial cooperation and good neighbourliness" between ASEAN and China.[37] China also pledged to continue discussion with ASEAN on an early accession to the 1995 Southeast Asian Nuclear Weapons Free Zone Treaty.[38]

Thanks to these "charm offensive" engagements, China gained more influence over Southeast Asia at the expense of the US.[39] While being disappointed at US unilateralism, officials from ASEAN member states appreciated new developments in ASEAN-China relations as a symbol of "deeper political trust and higher level of cooperation."[40] They even said that cooperation with China helped maintain peace "while upholding the authority and the central role of the UN" – a clear contrast with US military interventions in Iraq.[41] It should be noted that ten years after the establishment of China-ASEAN dialogue, China managed to put in place twenty-seven separate ASEAN-China mechanisms, while during the twenty-eight years since the inception of US-ASEAN dialogue, only seven US-ASEAN mechanisms were set up.[42] China's growing economic clout and intensive interactions with ASEAN countries individually enabled Beijing to influence ASEAN's agenda setting and discussions.

By 2002, the bilateral relationship between Vietnam and China was probably the best ever, with a comprehensive established network of institutionalised bilateral talks. The land border disputes had been settled and the boundary in the Gulf of Tonkin had been delimited. Cross-border trade was booming. This state of affairs created little incentive for Hanoi to antagonise Beijing. Nevertheless, Vietnamese nationalist leaders were not convinced by China's rhetoric of "peaceful rise" or "peaceful development." They always believed that China's ultimate realpolitik intention was to exercise hegemony over Southeast Asia and gain exclusive control of the South China Sea.[43] China's increased influence over Southeast Asia simply undermined Vietnam's ASEAN card and prompted Hanoi to look for other means to expand the room for manoeuvrability. Given its modest capabilities vis-à-vis those of China, Vietnam did not have other viable options to deter China but to seek military cooperation with the United States. This time, the pragmatist nationalists faced little opposition from the conservative ideologues.

It should be noted that the conservative camp in Vietnam's politics was seriously weakened by the removal of Le Kha Phieu and the rift among leading conservative figures, specifically Le Kha Phieu, Do Muoi and Le Duc Anh, in the Ninth Party Congress in June 2001.[44] After the Congress, Le Kha Phieu was replaced by a politically moderate leader, Nong Duc Manh, who had previously chaired the National Assembly. Phan Van Khai, who was also a reformist and nationalist southerner, later succeeded Vo Van Kiet as prime minister. The new political configuration allowed Vietnamese pragmatist nationalists to move away from Phieu's ideologically driven foreign policy and push for further multilateralisation and diversification of Vietnam's international relations.[45] On the economic front, the danger of lagging behind economically continued to be highlighted. The new leaders forged a consensus on the need to further integrate into the world's economy. On 27 November 2011, the CPV Politburo adopted a resolution that affirmed international economic integration, which implied deeper incorporation into the US-led global economic system.[46]

Consequently, Vietnam's foreign and security policy was adjusted to reflect greater emphasis on national interests. During its Eighth Plenum in July 2003, the CPV Central Committee held a discussion on national defence strategy, which was initially prompted by the concerns about the US invasion of Iraq in April 2003. Vietnamese conservative leaders were fearful about the US-dominated unipolar world and American unilateralism. However, there were also concerns about China as a major challenge to Vietnam's sovereignty and territorial integrity. The final resolution, titled "Strategy for the Defence of the Fatherland in the New Situation," allowed greater engagement with Washington rather than more reliance on China and other communist countries to defend socialism.[47] This resolution, usually referred to as Resolution 8, signalled fundamental changes in the way Vietnam defined "friends" and "foes." It appeared that ideology no longer was the most important criterion for Hanoi to determine partners and adversaries. Instead, the resolution put premium on national interests by the introduction of two new concepts: *doi tac* (objects of cooperation or partners) and *doi tuong* (objects of struggle). The former was defined as "anyone who respects our independence and sovereignty, establishes and expands friendly, equal and mutually beneficial relations with Vietnam." The latter referred to "any force that plans and acts against the objectives we (Vietnam) uphold in the course of national construction and defence."[48] It should be noted that the resolution did not see any country as purely *doi tac* or *doi tuong*, but argued that a country could be both partner in some policy areas and an object of struggle to Vietnam in the others:

> With the objects of struggle, we can find areas of cooperation; with the partners, there exist interests that are contradictory and different from those of ours. We should be aware of these, thus overcoming the two tendencies, namely lacking vigilance and showing rigidity in our perception, design, and implementation of specific policies.[49]

In essence, the resolution stressed national interests and downplayed the danger of "peaceful evolution," which referred to the non-violent means that the United States and other capitalist countries used to facilitate regime change inside Vietnam As a result, Vietnam started cooperating with the United States in the field of security. Hanoi accepted America's long-standing invitation to send its Minister of Defence Pham Van Tra to Washington.[50] Tra made a landmark visit to Washington between 9 and 12 November 2003, which was the first visit of a Vietnamese military chief to the US. One week later, Vietnam allowed the US Navy ship, the USS Vandergrift FFG 48, to visit Ho Chi Minh City, which was also the first-ever visit of a US Navy vessel to Vietnam since 1975. Moreover, Vietnam approved low-key cooperation with the United States in counter-terrorism, anti-drug smuggling, de-mining, search and rescue, and disaster relief.[51] In the second half of 2003, Vietnamese ministers of trade, planning and investment, and foreign affairs, and the Vietnamese deputy prime minister travelled to Washington.[52] Interestingly, after the Eighth Plenum resolution, a new pattern of Vietnamese diplomacy emerged. Whenever Hanoi sent a senior leader to Washington, it also dispatched another to Beijing. Based on these observations, Alexander Vuving argued that the Eighth Plenum resolution set forth a shift in Vietnam's strategy from solidarity with China towards a more balanced position, or "equidistance," between China and the United States. He further explained that the resolution prioritised national interests over ideology, which provided the rationale for Hanoi to move to a more balanced geopolitical position between Beijing and Washington.[53]

However, the terms "equidistance" and "balancing act" used by Vuving and other scholars failed to reflect the subtlety of Vietnam's strategy. Though Vietnam stepped up its security relations with the US, the position of the US in Vietnam's foreign affairs hierarchy was not equal to that of China. In fact, military cooperation between Vietnam and the US was quite nascent, and could not be compared with the extensive, regularised institutional links between the armed forces and high-level leaders of Vietnam and China. Also, Vietnam was always mindful to calibrate its military cooperation with the United States to the extent it did not hurt relations with China. Since 2003, Hanoi allowed port calls from American warships to Vietnamese ports, but has set the limit of one visit per year.[54] It deliberately avoided the impression that Hanoi was colluding with the United States to contain China.[55]

Vietnam's newfound enthusiasm for engaging strategically with other powers, especially the United States, was arguably part of its hedging strategy to indirectly balance Chinese power and deny its domination. In spite of initial optimism about the signature of the DOC and other progresses in ASEAN-China relations, Hanoi watched the rise of its socialist neighbour with anxiety. US diplomatic sources revealed that Vietnamese leaders became increasingly concerned about the rise of China. Since mid-2003, a number of authoritative Vietnamese officials spoke in private about China's growing ties with Southeast Asia in threatening terms. In October 2003, the chief of a Vietnamese think tank, which was affiliated to the Ministry of Public Security, claimed at a conference in Washington that the United States had become "naïve about China."[56] In December 2003, Deputy Prime Minister Vu Khoan told Secretary of State Condoleezza Rice that the United States should keep an eye on Southeast Asia. He warned that the US focus on the war on terrorism had left Southeast Asia dominated by "others."[57] In the same month, Vietnam's Vice Foreign Minister Nguyen Van Bang warned the US ambassador in Hanoi that the Chinese Communist Party's (CCP's) 16th Party Congress devised a reaching-out strategy to expand Chinese influence over Southeast Asia, Northeast Asia, Latin America and Africa. He described China's comprehensive engagement with Southeast Asia, in terms of the ASEAN-China dialogue, a free trade agreement, and admission to the Treaty of Amity and Cooperation as "aggressive" rather than simply "active."[58] It should be noted that these opinions were opposite from the image that Beijing wanted to project around the world. In 2004, China's official Xinhua News reported Chinese Premier Wen Jiabao's declaration that that China's rise "will not come at any cost of any other country, will not stand in the way of any other country, nor pose a threat to any other country."[59] In 2005, China's State Council published a white paper on China's peaceful development.[60]

Despite these concerns, Vietnam continued to engage China through the extensive web of institutionalised dialogues at all levels and expand economic cooperation, especially trade relations. Vietnam saw a rising China as enormous opportunities for developing its economy. As a result, it actively sought closer trade ties through upgrading linking roads and rail routes and establishing an economic corridor between the two countries' economic hubs.[61] Vietnam's trade with China grew more quickly than its total trade, from its share of 6.1 per cent in 1999 to 14.3 per cent in 2007, though Vietnam suffered big deficits.[62] China's FDI into Vietnam reached USD 710 million by August 2005, ranked 14th among countries investing in Vietnam.[63] Still, Vietnam kept an eye on China, trying to reach out to the United States and other powers to keep open alternatives for uncertain strategic contingencies. To get the balance right between economic and security needs, Hanoi deliberately restricted military cooperation with the United States because it was afraid of sending "a wrong signal" to Beijing.[64] Also, while sending a senior leader to Washington, Hanoi also arranged a visit by other senior leaders to Beijing. The reason was not to maintain a position of equidistance between China and the United States, but to reassure the leaders in Beijing that Vietnam would not work with the United States against China if its interests were respected.

Clearly, economic reasons figured significantly in Hanoi's rapprochement with Washington.[65] Hanoi had to win the support of Washington to be admitted to the World Trade Organization (WTO).[66] Resolution 8 showed that the change was not confined only to the economic sphere. Hanoi also increasingly saw the United States as a critical security actor, thinking that a better relationship with Washington could enhance Vietnam's position vis-à-vis China. Hanoi evidently overcame fear of "peaceful evolution" to expand cooperation with Washington. In September 2004, the US State Department put Vietnam in the list of "countries of particular concern" (CPC) under the US Religious Freedom Act.[67] Though Hanoi was overtly unhappy with this designation and vocally protested against so-called US biases, it continued to deepen its economic and military engagement with Washington. In June 2005, the Vietnamese prime minister made a high-profile historic visit, the first by a high-level Vietnamese leader, to Washington. He was accompanied by a large delegation, including the deputy prime minister, five ministers, ten vice ministers and over 100 business people.[68] During the trip, the two sides concluded an Agreement on International Military Education and Training and agreed to increase intelligence sharing and cooperation in the struggle against terrorism and transnational crimes such as smuggling and human trafficking.[69]

As pressures from China were mounting, Vietnam strengthened its security cooperation with other major powers. In 2001, Vietnam established the first strategic partnership with Russia, an important partner in energy development and the major provider of armament to Vietnam. Between 2003 and 2006, Vietnam engaged in extensive talks with Japan and India to boost security cooperation. These efforts resulted in the signature of strategic partnership agreements with Japan and India in October 2006 and July 2007 respectively. Vietnam agreed to upgrade its relations with China to strategic partnership in 2008, and comprehensive strategic partnership in 2009. Since then, this policy of strategic partnership gained momentum. Until 2015, Vietnam managed to establish fifteen strategic partnerships and ten comprehensive partnerships. In Vietnam's foreign affairs vocabulary, the word "strategic" means important in the long term without military implications. The terms "comprehensive strategic partnerships," "strategic partnerships," and "comprehensive partnerships" are used to categorise different levels of mutual trust as well as the breadth and depth of bilateral cooperation. Strategic partnerships do not amount to military alliances, but represent commitments to a broad-based scope of cooperation, including political, security and military areas, and establishment of mechanisms to manage bilateral relations.[70]

How does these partnerships work for Vietnam? Thayer described this policy as "multi-polar balancing," which equates to diversification and multilateralisation of relations.[71] Evelyn Goh termed it complex balancing, which meant diversifying its security ties with other major actors in regional politics to balance its relations with China. Unlike normal balancing, where one state seeks additional capabilities through forming alliances with other countries to counter a specific threat, complex balancing is aimed at expanding room for manoeuvring while preserving strategic autonomy.[72] Essentially, strategic and comprehensive partnerships were part of Vietnam's indirect balancing policy, which was aimed to balance interests as well as the influences of multiple big powers in Vietnam without making it a threat to China. Former Deputy Prime Minister Vu Khoan explained that these partnerships are helpful in four ways: (1) by strengthening Vietnam's international stance; (2) by supporting Vietnam's position in international forums; (3) by increasing mutual interdependence with multiple countries as a way to bolster independence; and (4) by paving the way to greater economic cooperation to strengthen Vietnam itself.[73] David Elliot provided the best explanation for the logic behind Vietnam's relationship with big powers. In his view, Hanoi avoids being drawn into explicit strategic relationships through either bandwagoning or balancing, but uses "the self-balancing dynamic of big power to provide them with what they most want from these countries – stability and peaceful interactions on the world scene."[74] If examining carefully, it is important for Vietnam to establish a solid framework of bilateral relations, most importantly channels of regular dialogue and expanded substantive cooperation, so that it could make the offsetting system of big power rivalry work for its interests.

In the broader region, the Vietnamese leadership increasingly believed that the United States had an indispensable role as a strategic stabiliser. In other words, they saw the United States as the only power that was able to keep a rising China in check. The WikiLeaks-released US diplomatic cables in late 2004 and early 2005 revealed that Vietnamese officials in the Foreign Ministry consistently complained about Washington's neglect of Southeast Asia due to the wars in Afghanistan and Iraq.[75] They were particularly agitated by America's tough approach towards Myanmar, arguing that this pattern of behaviour would push the country towards China.[76] In February 2005, Deputy Prime Minister Vu Khoan told US National Security Council Member Michael Green that Vietnam acknowledged the United States as a legitimate actor in the region. He added that Vietnam wanted the United States to play a constructive role in the region based on mutual understanding and respect.[77]

Clearly, Hanoi was afraid that its position in the South China Sea disputes was undermined by the bandwagoning behaviour of other claimants such as Malaysia and the Philippines. Vietnam also felt threatened by China's increased influence over its near abroad, particularly Laos, Cambodia, Myanmar and Thailand.[78] A Vietnamese strategist elaborated in an interview with a foreign researcher:

> Vietnam is concerned about China's rising influence in Laos and Cambodia. China is the strategic backbone of Cambodia security and China and ASEAN are seen by the Cambodian and Laotian governments as credible forces to counterbalance Thailand and Vietnam. Though Laos still sees Vietnam as its closest ally, the former's generational transfer of political power could lead to a preference of China as a security guarantor and an economic partner in the midst of competition for influence in Laos between China, and Vietnam, and Thailand to a lesser extent.[79]

At the regional level, Vietnam's concern about Chinese hegemony was reflected in its position over the formation of an East Asian Summit (EAS). The idea of a summit for East Asia first appeared in a report by East Asia Vision Group (EAVG), a Track-II task force composed of representatives from ASEAN Plus Three (APT) countries. The report recommended upgrading the annual APT summit into the EAS as a pathway to the East Asian Community. China generally supported the proposal and pressed for an EAS composed of the APT countries only.[80] In the Chinese perspective, this East Asia-only arrangement would exclude the US, Australia and India, giving Beijing a dominant voice within the group. China criticised Japan for "trying to drag countries outside this region such as Australia and India into the community to serve as a counterbalance to China."[81] Clearly, Beijing viewed Japan, Australia and India as an extension of US influence in the region.[82]

Within the ASEAN group, Malaysia and Thailand supported China's position while Vietnam and Indonesia supported open, inclusive form of regionalism. Hanoi viewed the EAS as an attempt by China to undermine ASEAN solidarity and its centrality. Hanoi obviously worried about Chinese domination and preferred a balance of influence in East Asia. As a result, Vietnam and Indonesia privately expressed their objection to the exclusion of the United States in this regional multilateral structure.[83] However, when Indonesia changed its stance, Hanoi found it difficult to block a China-backed enterprise. It then supported the idea of an inclusive EAS to embrace non-East Asian states, notably Australia, New Zealand and India, to build a counterweight to China.[84] "We will need to balance China in the EAS," one Vietnamese official stated.[85] Despite China's lobby, ASEAN countries finally agreed to invite non-APT countries, particularly Australia, New Zealand and India, into the EAS.

Relations between Hanoi and Washington continued to improve with Vietnamese Prime Minister Phan Van Khai's first visit to Washington in June 2005. The issue of China came up indirectly in the joint statement issued after this visit. The two countries indicated they shared a strategic goal:

> The President and the Prime Minister shared the vision of peace, prosperity, and security in Southeast Asia and the Asia-Pacific region, and they agreed to cooperate bilaterally and multilaterally to promote these goals.[86]

The reference to "Southeast Asia" alongside the term "Asia-Pacific" in the statement was particularly important. As the United States is not a Southeast Asian country, this statement implicitly acknowledged the role of the United States in maintaining peace and stability in the region. Hanoi's diplomatic manoeuvre around the EAS initiative and Phan Van Khai's message in Washington indicated that Hanoi had attempted to step out of the Chinese shadow. However, Hanoi remained extremely vigilant in calibrating its security and defence relations with the United States so as not to provoke China. A clear example was Defence Minister Phung Quang Thanh's cautious answer to the request of Admiral William J. Fallon, Commander of the US Pacific Command for joint exercises in July 2006. Thanh was afraid that "other countries" might misread this type of activity.[87] Deputy Head of the National Assembly's External Relations Committee, Ton Nu Thi Ninh, made it clearer: "Everyone knows that we have to keep a fine balance neither leaning over toward the United States or bow to China."[88]

Vietnam's push for maritime development

Vietnam's integration into the world's economy, metaphorically called "a plunge into the big ocean" (*vuon ra bien lon*), set the stage for a more expansive and comprehensive oceanic policy. Hanoi's maritime aspiration was manifest in the adoption of Resolution 09–NQ/TW, titled Vietnam's *Maritime Strategy toward 2020*, at the Fourth Plenum of the Ninth CPV Central Committee on 9 February 2007. The resolution could be seen as an amendment to the CPV Politburo's Directive 20–CT/TW on the industrialisation and modernisation of the Vietnamese maritime economy[89] adopted on 22 September 1997. The General Secretary of the CPV Nong Duc Manh stated, "A correct ocean strategy is the foundation and condition for the further exploitation of the role of the ocean in the construction and defence of the Motherland, and the realization of the industrialization and modernization causes."[90]

Though the details of the document have not been published, its key principles and goals were broadly discussed in the media. Three guidelines were put forth. First, the long-term goal was to develop Vietnam into a maritime power that prospers by unlocking all oceanic potential. Second, the development of the maritime economy should be closely linked to national defence and security, international cooperation, and environmental protection. Third, maritime development and maritime environment protection should be implemented by mobilisation of all resources and international cooperation.[91] Importantly, the new strategy called for an expansion of marine-based activities by setting the target that the share of maritime economy would constitute 53–55 per cent of Vietnam's GDP and 55–60 per cent of its exports by 2020.[92] The marine-based economy made up for 48 and 49 per cent of the GDP of the country in 2005 and 2007 respectively.[93] The goal signalled a shifting emphasis in economic development from the rice fields in the deltas of Red and Mekong Rivers to marine-based development.

Resolution 09–NQ/TW represented both an outlook for the future and recognition of the rapid growth of maritime economic activities. Oil and fish as the backbone of the marine-based economy recorded strong growth over the last decade. In particular, Vietnam's oil production nearly doubled from 200,000 barrels a day in 1997 to 400,000 barrels a day in 2004. However, production peaked in 2004 with 400,000 barrels per day and slowly declined thereafter. In the meantime, energy consumption soared as a result of rapid economic growth and industrialisation. Between 1997 and 2007, oil consumption increased twofold.[94] Facing the prospect of becoming a net oil importer, Vietnam accelerated exploratory efforts to look for new reserves to offset the decline in the established oil fields. In September 2004, PetroVietnam offered international oil firms nine offshore blocks covering a 7,000 km^2 area in the Phu Khanh Basin off the central and south coast of Vietnam. It should be noted that almost all previous offerings were in the Song Hong Basin in the north and Cuu Long Basin and Nam Con Son Basin in the south. The exploration rights for three blocks were awarded to energy companies from the United States, Canada and India.[95] In 2007, PetroVietnam offered seven oil blocks in the Song Hong Basin offshore the northern coast of Vietnam. Up to

2007, PetroVietnam had concluded thirty-seven production-sharing agreements, one business operation contract and seven joint operating contracts with more than fifty foreign energy firms.[96]

The marine fishing industry expanded rapidly during the *Doi Moi* period. The total yield of capture fisheries increased from 709,000 tons in 1990 to 1,062,000 tons in 1997, 1,280,590 in 2000, 1,798,600 tons in 2006 and 2,280,000 tons in 2010. In the same period, the number of fishing vessels fell from 72,723 in 1990 to 71,500 in 1997 but rose again to 85,758 in 2007 and 130,000 in 2011.[97] In spite of small increase in the number of vessels, total engine capacity rose much higher, increasing roughly twice between 1990 and 1997 and six times between 1990 and 2005. This growth was the result of the upturn in the number of vessels with capacity over 90 horsepower (hp). It was also attributed to the implementation of the policy on development of the offshore fishing, the impact of coastal exploitation subsidies, and credit programs for building offshore vessels after 1997.[98] By 2008, 17,000 vessels with capacity over 90 hp were deployed. As a result, the offshore fishing production significantly increased, from 192,000 tons in 2000 to 546,000 tons in 2006 and 750,000 tons in 2010.[99] This augmented capacity enabled Vietnamese fishermen to sail further afield and increase their presence in the South China Sea. The depletion of fish stocks near and around coastal areas and the implementation of the Vietnam-China agreement on fisheries in the Gulf of Tonkin also forced them to sail to further afield. As a result, since 2004, there has been an increased presence of Vietnamese fishing vessels in the areas around the Paracel Islands, which resulted in a greater number of confrontations with Chinese fishery administration vessels.[100]

Other areas of the maritime economy of Vietnam have also grown significantly over the last two decades. In particular, the size of the Vietnamese fleet for maritime transport expanded quickly. Its tonnage capacity rose twenty-one times between 2000 and 2011, around ten times more than the average increase of Southeast Asian countries.[101] The shipping industry grew with a rate of over 30 per cent annually in terms of total output in late 1990s and early 2000s before the GFC.[102] In 2010, Vietnam was the world's fifth largest shipbuilders in terms of orders.[103] Vietnam has so far established three marine-based economic zones, thirty export-oriented industrial zones and eighty ports with the capacity of 100 million tons annually.[104] The shipping and shipbuilding industries have been key sectors in Vietnam's developmental plan. However, marine-based incomes primarily came from oil and fisheries, which account for 64 per cent and 14 per cent respectively.[105]

Incentives for maritime development came from two sources. The first was the need to accelerate the growth of the Vietnamese economy. It was widely believed that the country is entitled to 1 million km^2 sea area (three times larger than the size of the Vietnamese land) under UNCLOS 1982. This area was estimated to hold a reserve of 1.2 billion barrels of oil, a fish stock of 2,744,900 tons (allowable catch of 1,372,400 tons), and a great deal of other resources.[106] In addition, a 3,000 km coastline and thousands of islands create natural advantages for shipbuilding, shipping and tourism. Between 2001 and 2005, Vietnam managed to achieve relatively high economic growth with an annual rate of 72 per cent. The rate peaked at

8.5 per cent in 2005.[107] Vietnam benefited from a high tide of foreign capital with pledged investments amounting to USD 7 billion in 2006 and USD 20 billion in 2007.[108] This fact laid the groundwork for an overly optimistic forecast of 7–8 per cent GDP growth for the period 2006–2010.[109] To this end, the Vietnamese elites looked to the vast expanse of maritime space that was believed to have enormous untapped potential.

Second, Hanoi's leaders viewed the physical presence of fishing vessels and oil rigs as an effective way to assert and protect Vietnam's legitimate rights under UNCLOS in the face of what may be regarded as illegal Chinese claims. Vietnam's *Maritime Strategy toward 2020* called for measures to encourage people to settle on the offshore islands and to support business operations at sea and pilot projects to build economic defence zones in islands, the Spratly Islands and other maritime zones of the country.[110] Vietnamese leaders attempted to extend their doctrine of all people's national defence from land domain over to sea arena. The idea was that the defence of legitimate maritime rights of the country should require the involvement of all people, not only the armed forces, and that a strong oceanic economy constitutes a solid ground for maritime defence.

China's discreet, tailored assertiveness and Vietnam's defiance

Vietnam's sea development activities were met with punitive reactions on the part of China. Two months after Vietnam launched the first licensing round for hydrocarbon resource exploration in September 2004, China installed the KANTAN-03 oil-drilling platform in the area that was just 63 miles from the Vietnamese coast and 67 miles from the Hainan coast.[111] The location of the drilling rig obviously lay on the Vietnamese side of the Gulf of Tonkin demarcation line. A spokesperson for the Foreign Ministry of Vietnam stated that this area "lies entirely within the Exclusive Economic Zone and continental shelf of Vietnam" and called on China to withdraw.[112] Eventually, China withdrew the platform. Chinese civilian maritime forces also harassed Vietnamese fishing vessels. On 8 January 2005, Chinese Maritime Police opened fire on Vietnamese fishing vessels just south of an island about halfway between Hainan Island and the Vietnamese port city of Hai Phong. Nine Vietnamese fishermen were killed, some injured, and eight others arrested in the incident. Chinese and Vietnamese accounts of the incident were markedly different. The Chinese asserted that these Vietnamese were pirates who were carrying automatic weapons.[113] On the other hand, Vietnam's Foreign Ministry went public to criticise China in an usually strong language for killing and injuring honest Vietnamese fishermen who were legally fishing in the western side of the Gulf of Tonkin delimitation line in the common fishing area. The Vietnamese Foreign Ministry's spokesperson denounced China for violating the Vietnam-China Tonkin Gulf Delimitation Agreement and Fishery Cooperation Agreement.[114] Vietnamese officials revealed that the skirmishes over fisheries happened every day, but this case was unusually violent.[115]

While overseas Vietnamese roared against what they called a "Chinese massacre," Hanoi's response was largely restrained. Hanoi was obviously reluctant to engage in a lengthy exchange of diplomatic accusations or take any significant retaliatory actions.[116] Rather, the Vietnamese leaders chose to work bilaterally with China to control the incidents and dissuade the Chinese authorities from subsequent provocative actions. Hanoi also dampened popular outrage to avoid negative impacts on Vietnam-China relations while it allowed anti-Japan protests by the Chinese outside the Japanese embassy in Hanoi at the same time.[117] Vietnam showed some gestures of deference in a public statement issued after a meeting between senior Vietnamese and Chinese leaders just a few days after the incident. The statement, while not mentioning the serious incident, boasted: "the friendship and comprehensive cooperation between the two countries [Vietnam and China] are developing well."[118]

A new round of Chinese assertiveness was linked with Vietnam's adoption of *Maritime Strategy toward 2020*. This time, Beijing consistently exercised a more determined and assertive posture than ever before to block Vietnam's activities to explore and exploit marine resources, even in maritime zones near the Vietnamese coasts. Vietnam's fishing activities faced intensified harassment and intimidation from China's maritime enforcement units. Chinese assaults on and detainments of Vietnamese fishermen were reported in February, April, June, July and October 2007.[119] Certainly, the number would have been much higher had Hanoi published all incidents.[120] Perhaps, Hanoi feared that public anger might strain its bilateral relations with Beijing and escalate the conflicts. A serious incident, disclosed by the *Strait Times*, took place on 9 July 2007 in the area near the Spratly Islands. Chinese naval vessels opened fire on Vietnamese fishing boats, causing one death and several injures. One boat was sunk.[121] As tensions rose, Vietnamese naval and coast guard forces were put on alert but were ordered to exercise restraint. Hanoi could not afford prolonged strain and thus dispatched Vice Foreign Minister Vu Dung to Beijing to discuss these incidents with Chinese officials. Dung and his Chinese counterpart reportedly conducted "frank and detailed exchanges," and both sides agreed not to take further actions to deteriorate the situation.[122] Yet, the diplomatic pledge did little to calm the situation.

Tensions were more serious in the energy domain. In April 2007, during the goodwill visit to China of the chairman of the National Assembly of Vietnam, Nguyen Phu Trong, Beijing lodged a strong protest against a gas pipeline project by PetroVietnam and British Petroleum (BP) to bring gas from two new fields, Lan Tay and Lan Do, off the Vietnamese south coast. Beijing also protested against Hanoi's decision to hold local elections in the Spratly Islands. A spokesperson in the Chinese Foreign Ministry said that Vietnam's new actions infringed on China's sovereignty, sovereignty rights and administrative rights on the Nansha Islands.[123] A Vietnamese Foreign Ministry spokesperson rebuked China's accusation and pointed out that the aforementioned project had been running since 2000 without any protests from China. He added that the area designated for the project was entirely within Vietnam's EEZ and continental shelf.[124] In June, BP executive David Nicholas confirmed that the company suspended its planned seismic activities to prospect for oil in Blocks 5.2 and 5.3, about 370 km from the Vietnamese south coast.[125] US-leaked cables revealed that Beijing threatened unspecified economic penalties against BP's business activities in China. Having heavily invested in China, particularly in the downstream sector, BP had no other choice but to concede and advise its partners, ConocoPhillips and PetroVietnam, to halt the project.

Between April and September 2007, it was reported that five Vietnamese energy projects, which involved four American companies (Chevron, ConocoPhillips, ExxonMobil and Transocean) and other international energy companies, were suspended.[126] A Chevron executive disclosed that in August, China's political councillor in the Chinese embassy to the United States, Xiu Dong Jia, summoned Chevron managers in Washington and demanded a halt to the company's project in Block 122.[127] The block lay in Phu Khanh Basin, roughly 250 km from Vietnam's Quy Nhon port. In one Vietnamese account, besides Chevron, BP and ConocoPhilips, China also exerted pressure on other energy consortiums headed by Marina Neptuna (Russia) in Blocks 112, 113; PGS (Norway) in Block 145, SK (South Korea) and Santos (Australia) in Block 123; CGG Veritas (France) in Block 04–3; Pearl Energy (UK) in Block 06–1; and Nippon Energy (Japan) in Blocks 5–1b and 5–1c.[128] The number of publicised incidents was just the tip of the iceberg. Then, in July 2008, Beijing publicly called for ExxonMobil to stop its production-sharing contract with PetroVietnam.[129]

There was some speculation about the rationale behind China's determined actions to thwart Vietnam's oil and gas activities. The first argument was that China's actions were no more than a tactical posture in the run-up to the coming CCP Congress. The second theory held that China's coercive measures reflected a long-term shift in Beijing's foreign policy to assert its primacy in the region. The third view was that China eagerly jumped into a competition for hydrocarbon resources because of its thirst for energy.[130] Ian Storey proposes two other theories. He argued that China either tactically flexed its muscle to press Vietnam to accept joint-development in the areas off its coast or wanted to show displeasure at improved Vietnam-US relations.[131] Vietnamese officialdom held that China's assertive actions might be prompted by a shift to a revisionist policy characteristic of a rising power, and that Beijing's fear of threats emanated from the presence of other powers in the South China Sea, and Chinese domestic politics.[132]

Hanoi was angered of China's arbitrary claim and assertive behaviour. Vietnamese Deputy Minister of Foreign Affairs Vu Dung held that, given their proximity to the Vietnamese coast, all the parcels awarded to foreign companies lay within Vietnam's EEZ and continental shelf as stipulated by UNCLOS 1982.[133] Some of these blocks lay too far from the offshore islands and could not be considered as "adjacent maritime zones" of the Spratly Islands. According to Greg Torode, international oil companies were convinced that Vietnam's maritime claims were in line with UNCLOS 1982.[134] However, China's quiet, coercive campaign exposed Vietnam's vulnerabilities in the face of China's superior economic and military power. Clearly, Vietnam did not possess comparable political and economic weight to persuade international companies to challenge China. Hanoi could not tell China how it should do business with a third party. Hanoi also found it hard to rally other South China Sea claimants, let alone ASEAN as a whole, against China.[135] The US embassies in the Philippines, Indonesia and Malaysia reported that China had not protested against concession agreements between these countries and international oil firms in the areas China claimed.[136] Though the companies were confident of the legal basis of Vietnam's claims, they were reluctant to publicly criticise China for fear of reprisals. Certainly, Vietnam was reluctant make the case public because it would expose its weaknesses. In short, China's new strategy not only exposed the fundamental flaws of Vietnam's bilateralism but also barred it from using multilateral leverage to defend its interests. Its strategy of using international oil companies to assert rights in the South China Sea was seriously undermined by China's determination and heavy-handed approach. Therefore, in order to pursue its interests in the South China Sea, Vietnam had to think of other options to fend off China's powers.

In reply, Hanoi took four countermeasures. First, it applied a tit-for-tat response. On 6 August 2007, Vietnam officially demanded the US ocean drilling company, Transocean, to cancel its concession agreement with CNOOC for Block 2–4 west of the Paracel Islands, which overlapped with Vietnam's Block 141.

Second, various Vietnamese leaders promised foreign energy companies and relevant diplomats that Vietnam would take all measures possible to protect their exploration activities in the Vietnamese waters. They also tried to coax these companies into resuming their work in defiance of Chinese threats.

Third, authoritative Vietnamese leaders actively approached US officials to ask for assistance. Hanoi again recognised the role of the United States in maintaining stability in the region. As stated earlier, on 10 September, Deputy Foreign Minister of Vietnam Vu Dung called in the US Ambassador in Hanoi and asked him to persuade Chevron to resume its work. Dung argued that China's assertive behaviour was destabilising the South China Sea and that giving in to China's threats would send a "wrong message" to Beijing.[137] On 18 September, Deputy Prime Minister Hoang Trung Hai conveyed a similar appeal to the US ambassador, asking him to urge ConocoPhillips to accelerate its exploration in Block 5–3.[138] In March 2008, Deputy Foreign Minister of Vietnam Dao Viet Trung made the same request to US Assistant Secretary for East Asia and Pacific Affairs Christopher R. Hill. He went even further to request a statement on the part of the US government to endorse peace and stability in the area and urge countries to refrain from threats and to respect the DOC.[139]

Despite its long-standing position of neutrality with regard to South China Sea claims, the US officials were receptive to Vietnamese requests because they were concerned about Chinese behaviour. In a press conference in Hanoi in August 2008, the US ambassador to Vietnam Michael Michalak stated,

> We certainly don't like anybody interfering in the commercial operations of companies that are trying to carry out commercial contracts. I think that it is up to the companies where they would like to work and with whom they would like to work.[140]

The ambassador also referred to a recent statement by the US and Vietnamese leaders which stressed "the US government's *support* for Vietnam's national sovereignty, security and territorial integrity."[141] In September, during his visit to Vietnam, US Deputy Secretary of State John D. Negroponte declared,

> The question of maritime jurisdiction between countries, especially when there are disagreements, is something that ultimately must be settled by those countries themselves in accordance with United Nations Law of the Sea.[142]

Negroponte also asserted that American companies such as ExxonMobil had the right to sign a business agreement with a sovereign state as Vietnam.[143]

Fourth, when foreign companies stepped back, Vietnam undertook the work on its own to show its will to defy China's pressure. In early 2008, BP transferred operatorship of its Block 5–2 and 5–3 to PetroVietnam Exploration and Production Company (PVEP), a subsidiary of PetroVietnam. PVEP was said to carry out all exploratory works planned by the BP in 2008.[144] Interestingly, unlike the way it dealt with fisheries incidents, when it came to hydrocarbon resources, Hanoi was determined to assert its rights in defiance of Chinese threats. Hanoi's obstinacy showed that rights to offshore hydrocarbon are Vietnam's vital interest and it was determined to stand up against any Chinese assertive actions.

Vietnam carefully calibrated its acts of defiance and conducted these countermeasures without fanfare. This indicated that Hanoi was determined to defend its legitimate interests in the South China Sea in defiance of China's threats, but at the same time, it did not want to let the fight for resources sour the bilateral relationship. Pragmatism really dictated Vietnam's China policy. The years of 2006 and 2007 were a critical time for Hanoi and Beijing to complete the land border demarcation. Therefore, Vietnam-China relations looked stable on the surface with hundreds of meetings and exchanges of delegations at low levels every year. This high-intensity interaction led to several accomplishments, of which the most important was the completion of land border demarcation at the end of 2008. Vietnam and China agreed to upgrade their relationship from a comprehensive cooperation framework, which was established in 1999, to a "strategic partnership" in June 2008 and to a "comprehensive strategic cooperative partnership" in March 2009. There are no official definitions of these terms, but these designations are used to describe relationships that are deemed important to Vietnam's security and development.[145] Concretely, the Vietnam-China strategic partnership has been underpinned by regular meetings between party and government leaders of the two countries, a Joint Steering Committee on Bilateral Cooperation, and a wide range of cooperative activities in multiple realms of politics, defence, security, economy and culture.[146] Also in 2008, a hotline was established for better communication between the leaders of the two countries. However, the pattern of Vietnam-China high-level exchange observably moved to asymmetry in 2007 and 2008. During these years, no visits of Chinese high-level leaders were reported while Hanoi sent State President of Vietnam Nguyen Minh Triet and Secretary General Nong Duc Manh to Beijing in May 2007 and May 2008 respectively. Prime Minister Nguyen Tan Dung also met with Premier Wen Jiabao in October 2008 in Beijing. However, underneath the cordial surface of the relationship, Vietnamese officials were not happy about China's claims and coercive behaviour in the South China Sea.[147]

Conclusion

The period between 2002 and 2008 witnessed increased uncertainties in Vietnam's strategic environment because of the rise of China. China's growing capabilities and increasing influence over Southeast Asia had several important implications for disputes in the South China Sea. First, the DOC and COC processes lost steam and no significant progress was made in terms of managing the South China Sea disputes through the ASEAN framework. In September 2004, China even managed to break ASEAN's unity when it involved the Philippines in a joint seismic survey project in the Spratly area at the expense of Vietnam. Realising that its ASEAN card was rather weak in the face of China's growing political and economic clout, Vietnam had to reach out to other powers, seeking greater involvement from other big powers, particularly the United States, to negate China's domination in Southeast Asia. Second, China tried to prevent Vietnam from developing its maritime zones. Since 2006, Vietnam found it increasingly defenceless in the face of China's growing assertiveness in the South China Sea. Chinese maritime forces increased harassment and intimidation against Vietnamese fishermen. At the same time, Beijing used its economic power to prevent international oil firms from working with Vietnam to develop its continental shelf. China's assertiveness tailored against Vietnam in the South China Sea prompted Hanoi to quietly court Washington for support to resist China's maritime expansions.

Notes

1 Thanh Giang, "ASEAN summit 9: ASEAN, China Sign Strategic Partnership Declaration," *Vietnam Business Forum*, Hanoi, 25 October 2003.
2 US Embassy in Hanoi, "MFA Goals for 2004 and Beyond," *Cable (Released by WikiLeaks)*, 11 February 2004. Online. Available HTTP: <http://wikileaks.org/cable/2004/02/04HANOI377.html> (accessed 19 August 2013).
3 ASEAN-China Senior Official Meeting on the Implementation of the Declaration on Conduct of the Parties in the South China Sea Kuala Lumpur, *Press Release*, Kuala Lumpur, 7 December 2004.
4 "ASEAN Endorses Establishment of ASEAN-China Joint Working Group on South China Sea," *Xinhua News*, 26 June 2005.
5 Terms of Reference of the ASEAN-China Joint Working Group on the Implementation of the Declaration on Conduct of the Parties in the South China Sea, adopted on 7 December 2004 in Kuala Lumpur, Malaysia. Online. HTTP: <www.aseansec.org/16885.htm> (accessed 16 August 2013).
6 T.T. Thuy, "Recent Development in the South China Sea: From Declaration to Code on Conduct," paper presented at *The 2nd International Workshop, Titled "The South China Sea: Cooperation for Regional Security and Development,"* Ho Chi Minh City, 11–12 November 2010.
7 T. Fravel, "Maritime Security in the South China Sea and the Competition over Maritime Rights," In: Patrick M. Cronin (ed.), *Cooperation from Strength: The United*

States, China and the South China Sea, Washington, DC: Center for a New American Security, 2012, p.44.

8 T.T. Thuy, "Recent Developments in the South China Sea: From Declaration to Code of Conduct," In: Tran Truong Thuy (ed.), *The South China Sea: Towards a Region of Peace, Security and Cooperation*, Hanoi: The Gioi Publisher, 2011, p.104.

9 N.H. Thao, "The Declaration on Conduct of Parties in the South China Sea: A Vietnamese Perspective, 2002–2007," In: Sam Bateman and Ralf Emmers (eds.), *Security and International Politics in the South China Sea: Toward a Cooperative Management Regime*, London and New York: Routledge, 2009, p.215.

10 "China Willing to Discuss South China Sea Code," *Agence France-Presse*, 7 September 2012.

11 B. Wain, "More Claims," *Far Eastern Economic Review*, 15 April 2004, p.20.

12 "The Treasure Island of Southeast Asia," *South China Morning Post*, Hong Kong, 28 May 2004, p.13.

13 R.A. Rodriguez, "Conduct Unbecoming in the South China Sea," *PacNet*, 21 May 2004. Online. Available HTTP: <http://csis.org/files/media/csis/pubs/pac0422a.pdf> (accessed 21 May).

14 Thao, "The Declaration on Conduct of Parties in the South China Sea," p.122.

15 L. Breckon, "China-Southeast Asian Relations: A New Strategic Partnership Is Declared," *CSIS Comparative Connections*, 1 Jan 2004. Online. Available HTTP: <http://csis.org/files/media/csis/pubs/0304qchina_seasia.pdf> (accessed 25 May 2015).

16 "Vietnamese Spokesman Comments on US Diplomats' Visit, Tour to Spratlys," *Voice of Vietnam*, Hanoi, 8 April 2004.

17 In this case, the Court cited ordinary measures by British colonial authorities, specifically collection of turtle eggs, the formation of fishing in the area, and the designation of a bird sanctuary, erection of light towers, as evidence of effective control and regulation of the islands. See D.A. Colson, "Sovereignty over Pulau Ligitan and Pulau Sipadan (Indonesia/Malaysia)," *American Journal of International Law* 97, no. 2, 2003, pp. 398–406.

18 Thao, "The Declaration on Conduct of Parties in the South China Sea," p.122.

19 "China's Top Legislator, Philippine House Speaker Holds Talks," *Xinhua News*, 31 August 2003.

20 "Spratly Plan Proposed," *Oil Daily*, Washington, DC, 3 September 2003.

21 E. Bower, "The JMSU: A Tale of Bilateralism and Secrecy in the South China Sea," *CSIS Paper* 1, no. 23, 27 July 2010, p.3; I.C. Storey, "Conflict in the South China Sea: China's Relations with Vietnam and the Philippines (Part II)," *Asia-Pacific Journal: Japan Focus* 8, no. 9, 2008.

22 "Vietnam Comments on China-Philippines Spratly Islands Oil Survey," *BBC Monitoring Asia Pacific*, London, 10 September 2004, p.1.

23 US Embassy in Hanoi, "Chinese Missteps in Vietnam Are a U.S. Opportunity," *Cable (Released by WikiLeaks)*, 28 January 2005. Online. Available HTTP: <http://wikileaks.org/cable/2005/01/05HANOI247.html> (accessed 12 August 2013).

24 US Embassy in Hanoi, "PRC PM Wen's Visit to Hanoi: Trade Takes the Front Seat," *Cable (Released by WikiLeaks)*, 21 October 2004. Online. Available HTTP: <http://wikileaks.org/cable/2004/10/04HANOI2857.html> (accessed 12 August 2013).

25 Y.T. Chua and E. Tordesillas, "Six RP-Occupied Islands Covered in Controversial Spratlys Deals," *Vera Files*, 9 March 2008. Online. Available HTTP: <http://verafiles.org/six-rp-occupied-islands-covered-in-controversial-spratlys-deals/> (accessed 3 August 2013).

26 I.C. Storey, "Maritime Security in Southeast Asia: Two Cheers for Regional Cooperation," *Southeast Asian Affairs*, 2009, pp. 36–58.

27 J. Dosch, "Managing Security in ASEAN-China Relations: Liberal Peace of Hegemonic Stability," *Asian Perspective* 31, no. 1, 2007, p.221.

28 J. Dosch, "Vietnam's ASEAN Membership Revisited: Golden Opportunity or Golden Cage?," p.248.
29 "China, ASEAN See Closer Economic, Political Cooperation," *Xinhua News*, 19 August 2003.
30 D. Dillion and J.J.J. Tkacik, "China's Quest for Asia," *Policy Review* 134, December 2015/January 2006, p.34.
31 Dosch, "Managing Security in ASEAN-China Relations."
32 Quoted from A. Acharya, "Seeking Security in the Dragon's Shadow: China and Southeast Asia in the Emerging Asian Order," *IDSS Working Papers*, March 2003.
33 Wain, "More Claims," p.20.
34 Breckon, "China-Southeast Asian Relations," p.2.
35 Dillion and Tkacik, "China's Quest for Asia," pp. 40–3.
36 "China to Accede to ASEAN Amity Treaty in June," *Kyodo News Service*, Tokyo, 29 April 2003.
37 "China, ASEAN Sign Joint Declaration, Forge Strategic Partnership," *Xinhua News*, 8 October 2003.
38 "ASEAN Appreciates China's Position on Regional Nuclear Weapons Treaty," *Xinhua News*, Phnom Penh, 15 June 2003.
39 B. Vaughn and W. M. Morrison, "China-Southeast Asia Relations: Trends, Issues, and Implications for the United States," *CRS Report for Congress*, 4 April 2006. Online. Available HTTP: <www.fas.org/sgp/crs/row/RL32688.pdf> (accessed 6 December 2015).
40 Breckon, "China-Southeast Asian Relations," p.2.
41 Ibid.
42 C.T. Goh, "Constructing a New East Asia," *Address at Asia Society Conference*, Bangkok, 9 June 2005.
43 D. Roy, "Southeast Asia and China: Balancing or Bandwagoning?," *Contemporary Southeast Asia* 27, no. 2, 2005, p.315; I.C. Storey, "Vietnam and the United States 2004–2005: Still Sensitive, but Moving Forward," *Asia-Pacific Center for Security Studies*, February 2005, pp. 6–7.
44 D.W.P. Elliot, *Changing Worlds: Vietnam's Transition from Cold War to Globalisation*, New York: Oxford University Press, 2012, p.201.
45 See Z. Abuza, "The Lessons of Le Kha Phieu: Changing Rules in Vietnamese Politics," p.141.
46 Politburo (CPV), *Resolution No.07-NQ/TW on International Economic Integration*, Hanoi, 27 November 2001. The resolution stated:

> Active international economic integration is to expand markets and attract capitals, technologies and management knowledge to foster socialist-oriented industrialisation and modernisation and to achieve the goal of rich people, strong country, and equitable, democratic and civilised society.

47 Interview with officials of Vietnam's Ministry of Foreign Affairs in Hanoi, 7 April 2014.
48 M.X. Ba, "Van de doi tac-doi tuong trong chien luoc bao ve To quoc," *Tap chi Cong san*, 31 January 2015. Online. Available HTTP: <www.tapchicongsan.org.vn/Home/Nghiencuu-Traodoi/2015/31758/Van-de-doi-tac-doi-tuong-trong-chien-luoc-bao-ve.aspx> (accessed 25 May 2015).
49 C.A. Thayer, "Upholding State Sovereignty through Global Integration: Remaking of Vietnamese National Security Policy," paper presented at the *Workshop on Vietnam, East Asia and Beyond*, City University of Hong Kong, Hong Kong, 11–12 December 2008, p.27.
50 C.A. Thayer, "Vietnamese Diplomacy, 1975–2015: From Member of the Socialist Camp to Proactive International Integration," paper presented at the *International Conference on Vietnam: 40 Years of Reunification, Development and Integration (1975–2015)*, Thu Dau Mot University, Binh Duong, 25 April 2015, p.10.

51 Storey, "Vietnam and the United States 2004–2005," p.6.
52 A. L. Vuving, "Strategy and Evolution of Vietnam's China Policy: A Changing Mixture of Pathways," p.818.
53 Ibid., pp. 817–18.
54 See L. M. Stern, U.S.-Vietnam Defense Relations: Deepening Ties, Adding Relevance, *Strategic Forum*, Institute for National Strategic Studies, National Defense University, No.245, September 2009.
55 Storey, "Vietnam and the United States 2004–2005," pp. 6–8.
56 US Embassy in Hanoi, "Final Thoughts from Hanoi," *Cable (Released by WikiLeaks)*, 4 September 2004. Online. Available HTTP: <http://wikileaks.org/cable/2004/09/04HANOI2438.html > (accessed 12 August 2013).
57 Ibid.
58 US Embassy in Hanoi, "Following up on DPM Khoan Visit with VFM Bang," *Cable (Released by WikiLeaks)*, 29 December 2003. Online. Available HTTP: <www.wikileaks.org/plusd/cables/03HANOI3351_a.html> (accessed 3 December 2013)
59 Quoted from E. Pan, "The Promise and Pitfalls of China's Peaceful Rise," *Council on Foreign Relations*, 14 April 2006. Online. HTTP:www.cfr.org/china/promise-pitfalls-chinas-peaceful-rise/p10446 (accessed 16 March 2016).
60 China's Peaceful Development Road, China's State Council, 22 December 2005.
61 "Vietnam Seeks Closer Economic Ties with China's Western Region," *Xinhua News*, 21 July 2004.
62 B. Womack, "Managing an Asymmetric Relationship in an Era of Economic Uncertainty," *Asian Politics and Policy* 2, no. 4, 2010, p.585.
63 "VIETNAM/CHINA: Relations Firm Amidst Problems," *Oxford Analytica Daily Brief Service*, 21 December 2005.
64 US Embassy in Hanoi, "ASEAN Partnership, Human Rights Dialogue, Embassy Compound Discussed with Assistant Foreign Minister," *Cable (Released by WikiLeaks)*, 27 October 2005. Online. Available HTTP: <http://wikileaks.org/cable/2005/10/05HANOI2857.html> (accessed 11 August 2013).
65 US Embassy in Hanoi, "Final Thoughts from Hanoi."
66 Elliot, *Changing Worlds*, p.211.
67 See Z. B. Frederick, "Rapprochement between Vietnam and the United States," *Contemporary Southeast Asia* 32, no. 3, 2010, pp. 317–42.
68 US Embassy in Hanoi, "Scene-Setter for the Prime Minister's Visit," *Cable (Released by WikiLeaks)*, 13 June 2005. Online. Available HTTP: <http://wikileaks.org/cable/2005/06/05HANOI1394.html> (accessed 13 August 2013).
69 E. Nakashima, "Vietnam, U.S. to Improve Intelligence, Military Ties: Premier Discusses Goals before Visit," *Washington Post*, 17 June 2005.
70 C.A. Thayer, "Vietnam on the Road to Global Integration: Forging Strategic Partnership through International Security Cooperation," paper presented at the *Fourth International Vietnam Studies Conference*, Vietnam Academy of Social Sciences and Vietnam National University, Hanoi, 26–28 November 2012, pp. 30–4.
71 C.A. Thayer, "Why Vietnam's Foreign Policy Won't Change after Its Party Congress," *Diplomat*, 8 December 2015.
72 E. Goh, "Great Powers and Hierarchical Order in Southeast Asia: Analyzing Regional Security Strategies," *International Security* 32, no. 3, 2007/2008, pp. 139–44.
73 H. Phan, "Viet-Trung: Song gio chang loi cho ai," *Vietnamnet*, 20 December 2013.
74 Elliot, *Changing Worlds*, p.261.
75 US Embassy in Hanoi, "Congressman Chabot Meets with Foreign Ministry, National Assembly Representatives," *Cable (Released by WikiLeaks)*, 13 December 2004. Online. Available HTTP: <http://wikileaks.org/cable/2004/12/04HANOI3301.html> (accessed 11 August 2013).
76 US Embassy in Hanoi, "Chinese Missteps in Vietnam Are a U.S. Opportunity."

77 US Embassy in Hanoi, "NSC Senior Director Michael Green Discusses China, Country of Particular Concern Designation, APEC, Prime Minister's Visit with Deputy Prime Minister Vu Khoan," *Cable (Released by WikiLeaks)*, 7 February 2005. Online. Available HTTP: <https://wikileaks.org/cable/2005/02/05HANOI315.html> (accessed 11 August 2013).
78 R. Burghardt, "US-Vietnam: Discreet Friendship under China's Shadow," *YaleGlobal*, 22 November 2005. Online. Available HTTP: <http://yaleglobal.yale.edu/content/us-vietnam-discreet-friendship-under-china%E2%80%99s-shadow> (accessed 12 August 2013).
79 Dosch, "Vietnam's ASEAN Membership Revisited," p.250.
80 J.C. Kim, "Politics of Regionalism in East Asia," *Asian Perspective* 34, no. 3, 2010, pp. 121–4.
81 "East Asia Summit: In the Shadow of Sharp Divisions," *People's Daily*, 7 December 2005. Online. Available HTTP: <http://en.people.cn/200512/07/eng20051207_226350.html> (accessed 25 May 2015).
82 M. Malik, "China and the East Asian Summit: More Discord Than Accord," *Asia-Pacific Centre for Security Studies*, February 2006. Online. Available HTTP: <http://apcss.org/Publications/APSSS/ChinaandEastAsiaSummit.pdf> (accessed 15 December 2015).
83 Dosch, "Vietnam's ASEAN Membership Revisited," p.251.
84 US Embassy in Hanoi, "Vietnam Unenthusiastic about East Asia Summit," *Cable (Released by WikiLeaks)*, 6 January 2005. Online. Available HTTP: <http://wikileaks.org/cable/2005/01/05HANOI42.html> (accessed 13 August).
85 Ibid.
86 See Burghardt, "US-Vietnam: Discreet Friendship under China's Shadow."
87 S. Blagov, "US, Vietnam Scratch Each Other's Back," *Asia Times*, 21 July 2006.
88 Quoted from J. Perlez, "U.S. Competes with China for Vietnam's Allegiance," *International Herald Tribune*, 19 June 2006.
89 The maritime economy is defined as a combination of fish, ships, shipping, natural resources, tourism and related services.
90 N.D. Manh, "Phat bieu của Dong chi Nong Duc Manh be mac Hoi nghi lan thu 4 Ban Chap hanh Trung uong Dang khoa X," *Tap chi Cong san*, 25 January 2007. Online. Available HTTP: <http://dangcongsan.vn/cpv/Modules/News/NewsDetail.aspx?co_id=30397&cn_id=136235> (accessed 12 January 2014).
91 T.H. Quynh, "Tiem nang Bien Viet Nam va nhung Dinh huong Chien luoc co ban de xay dung va phat trien," *Tap chi Cong san*, 25 July 2008. Online. Available HTTP: <http://dangcongsan.vn/cpv/Modules/News/NewsDetail.aspx?co_id=30463&cn_id=239397> (accessed 25 November).
92 N.V. Tung, "Vietnam's Security Challenges: Hanoi's New Approach to National Security and Implications to Defense and Foreign Policies," p.116.
93 Ngoc Bach, "Nam 2020, Kinh te Bien dong gop khoang 53–55% GDP," *Bo Tai nguyen Moi truong*, 16 May 2011. Online. Available HTTP: <www.monre.gov.vn/v35/default.aspx?tabid=428&CateID=53&ID=101068&Code=0YDK101068> (accessed 12 December 2013).
94 US Energy Information Administration, "Vietnam," *Country Analysis Brief*, 9 May 2012. Online. Available HTTP: <www.eia.gov/countries/cab.cfm?fips=VM> (accessed 15 August 2013).
95 "Vietnam Invites Bids for 9 Oil/Gas Blocks, Boosts Investment," *Reuters*, 2 August 2011. Online. Available HTTP: <http://uk.reuters.com/article/2011/08/02/vietnam-energy-licensing-idUKL3E7J20A720110802> (accessed 14 August 2013).
96 L. Buszynski and I. Sazlan, "Maritime Claims and Energy Cooperation in the South China Sea," *Contemporary Southeast Asia* 29, no. 1, 2007, p.157.
97 Vietnam Directorate of Fisheries, "Stages in the Development of Vietnam Fisheries Sector," 12 July 2012. Online. Available HTTP: <www.fistenet.gov.vn/introduction/

about-directorate-of-fisheries/history-of-fisheries-development> (accessed 14 September 2013).
98 UNEP, VIEP, and WWF, "Fisheries Subsidies, Supply Chain and Certification in Vietnam: Summary Report," September 2009. Online. Available HTTP: <www.unep.ch/etb/areas/fisheries%20country%20projects/vietnam/Final%20Summary%20Report%20Vietnam.pdf> (accessed 12 August 2013).
99 D. V. Toan, "Trien vong Kinh te bien Viet Nam," *Nhan Dan*, 192/4, 22 April 2013.
100 T. Fravel, "Maritime Security in the South China Sea and the Competition over Maritime Rights," pp. 37–8.
101 T. X. Tinh, "Van tai bien Viet Nam doi mat voi nhieu thach thuc," *Vietnam News Agency*, 18 December 2013. Online. Available HTTP: <www.vietnamplus.vn/van-tai-bien-viet-nam-doi-mat-voi-nhieu-thach-thuc/235851.vnp> (accessed 19 January 2014).
102 "Vietnamese Shipbuilding," *Global Security*, June 2009. Online. Available HTTP: <www.globalsecurity.org/military/world/vietnam/shipbuilding.htm> (accessed 19 January 2014).
103 Norwegian Agency for Development Cooperation, "Study of the Vietnamese Shipbuilding/Maritime Sector," *Final Report*, June 2010.
104 N. H. Son, "Vietnam: A Case Study in Naval Modernization," In: Geoffrey Till and Jane Chan (eds.), *Naval Modernization in South-East Asia: Nature, Causes and Consequences*, London and New York: Routledge, 2014, p.122.
105 P.T.T. Binh, "Thuc trang Phat trien Kinh te bien Viet Nam," *Dang Cong san Viet Nam*, 22 October 2009. Online. Available HTTP: <www.cpv.org.vn/cpv/Modules/News/NewsDetail.aspx?co_id=0&cn_id=366824> (accessed 20 January 2014).
106 D. T. Tich, *Dau khi Viet Nam*, Ho Chi Minh City: Dai hoc Quoc gia TP Ho Chi Minh, 2001, p.56.
107 C. A. Thayer, "Vietnam: The Tenth Party Congress and After," *Southeast Asian Affairs*, 2007, p.388.
108 "Vietnam Attracts Record Amount of Foreign Direct Investment," *Voice of America*, 1 November 2009.
109 Thayer, "Vietnam: The Tenth Party Congress and After," p.388.
110 Communist Party of Vietnam, *Documents of the Fourth Plenum of the Ninth Central Committee*, Hanoi: National Political Publishing House, 2007, p.85.
111 "Nanhai 215 Vessel Has Hauled Oil Drilling Platform KANTAN 3 of China to the Continental Shelf of Viet Nam," *Vietnam News Agency*, 19 November 2004.
112 US Embassy in Hanoi, "Chinese Missteps in Vietnam Are a U.S. Opportunity."
113 Ibid.
114 "Ve viec tau Trung Quoc tan cong ngu dan Viet Nam: Yeu cau Trung Quoc giai quyet moi hau qua," *Vietnam Ministry of Foreign Affairs*, 16 January 2005. Online. Available HTTP: <www.mofa.gov.vn/vi/nr040807104143/nr040807105001/ns050117170913> (accessed 13 January 2016).
115 US Embassy in Hanoi, "Chinese Missteps in Vietnam Are a U.S. Opportunity."
116 Thi Lam, "Massacre in the Gulf of Tonkin," *National Catholic Reporter* 41, no. 19, 11 March 2005.
117 Vuving, "Strategy and Evolution of Vietnam's China Policy," p.819.
118 "Vietnamese Prime Minister Calls for Further Cooperation with China," *Vietnam News Agency*, 13 January 2005.
119 R. Mitton, "Vietnam Blasts China's Plans for Paracels," *Strait Times*, 18 August 2007; N. Trung, "Loi ke cua ngu dan bi tau Trung Quoc ban," *BBC Tieng Viet*, 23 October 2007; N. Trung, "Doi cho ngu phu tro ve nha," *BBC Tieng Viet*, 23 October 2007.
120 US Embassy in Hanoi, "Vietnam MFA Disputes Details of Article on Clash with China over Spratlys," *Cable (Released by WikiLeaks)*, 20 July. Online. Available HTTP: <http://wikileaks.org/cable/2007/07/07HANOI1283.html> (accessed 14 August 2013).
121 According to Roger Mitton in his article "Vietnam, China Clash Again over Spratlys," *Strait Times*, 19 July 2007, the incident took place on 9 July 2007, near the Spratlys.

However, according to the WikiLeaks-released cable sent on 20 July 2007 from Hanoi, a MOFA official confirmed the occurrence of the incident but corrected the report, saying that the incident occurred at the end of June 2007 in the Paracels and no Vietnamese vessels were sent to the scene.

122 R. Mitton, "Vietnam, China Hold Crisis Talks over Territorial Spats," *Strait Times*, 28 July 2007.

123 "Spokesman Says Vietnam's Gas Pipeline Infringes on China's Sovereignty," *Xinhua News*, 10 April 2007.

124 "Viet Nam phan hoi canh bao cua Trung Quoc," *BBC Tieng Viet*, 12 April 2007. Online. Available HTTP: <www.bbc.co.uk/vietnamese/vietnam/story/2007/04/070412_vncnoil updates.shtml> (accessed 15 August 2013).

125 "BP ngung Tham do o Truong Sa," *BBC Tieng Viet*, 14 June 2007. Online. Available HTTP: <www.bbc.co.uk/vietnamese/vietnam/story/2007/06/070614_bp_china.shtml> (accessed 13 August 2013).

126 US Embassy in Hanoi, "Sino-Vietnam Territorial Dispute Entangles Multiple Multinational Energy Firms," *Cable (Released by WikiLeaks)*, 7 September 2007. Online. Available HTTP: <http://wikileaks.org/cable/2007/09/07HANOI1599.html> (accessed 14 August 2013).

127 Ibid.

128 T.T. Thuy, "South China Sea and the Disputes," paper presented at the *Presentation at CSIS*, April 2010.

129 "Trung Quoc ep Cong ty Dau lua cua My," *BBC Tieng Viet*, 20 July 2008. Online. Available HTTP: <www.bbc.co.uk/vietnamese/vietnam/story/2008/07/080720_exxonmobil_warning.shtml> (accessed 13 August 2013).

130 US Embassy in Hanoi, "Conoco Philippines and BP Concerns about Projects in the South China Sea," *Cable (Released by WikiLeaks)*, 15 June 2007. Online. Available HTTP: <http://wikileaks.org/cable/2007/06/07HANOI1119.html> (accessed 13 August 2013).

131 Storey, "Vietnam and the United States 2004–2005," pp. 51–2.

132 US Embassy in Hanoi, "Foreign Ministry Summons Ambassador to Discuss Sino-Vietnam South China Sea Dispute," *Cable (Released by WikiLeaks)*, 11 September 2007. Online. Available HTTP: <http://wikileaks.org/cable/2007/09/07HANOI1623.html> (accessed 14 August 2013).

133 Ibid.

134 G. Torodc, "Diplomatic Balancing Act for Oil Exploration," *South China Morning Post*, 23 August 2008.

135 US Embassy in Hanoi, "2008 Recap of the Sino-Vietnam South China Sea Territorial Dispute," *Cable (Released by WikiLeaks)*, 20 January 2009. Online. Available HTTP: <www.wikileaks.org/plusd/cables/09HANOI52_a.html> (accessed 20 July 2014).

136 US Embassy in Hanoi, "Sino-Vietnam Territorial Dispute Entangles Multiple Multinational Energy Firms."

137 US Embassy in Hanoi, "Foreign Ministry Summons Ambassador to Discuss Sino-Vietnam South China Sea Dispute."

138 US Embassy in Hanoi, "Newly-Appointed DPM Hai nixes Gannon Project," *Cable (Released by WikiLeaks)*, 20 September 2007. Online. Available HTTP: <http://wikileaks.org/cable/2007/09/07HANOI1681.html> (accessed 15 August 2013).

139 US Embassy in Hanoi, "Assistant Secretary Hill Visit to Vietnam," *Cable (Released by WikiLeaks)*, 7 March 2008. Online. Available HTTP: <http://wikileaks.org/cable/2008/03/08HANOI277.html> (accessed 15 August).

140 Torode, "Diplomatic Balancing Act for Oil Exploration."

141 "Joint Statement between the United States of America and the Socialist Republic of Vietnam," 25 June 2008. Online. Available HTTP: <http://vietnam.usembassy.gov/jointstatement_.html> (accessed 20 August 2013).

142 "US Deputy Secretary of State John D. Negroponte's Press Conference," 12 September 2008. Online. Available HTTP: <http://merln.ndu.edu/archivepdf/EAP/State/109503.pdf> (accessed 20 June 2013).

143 Ibid.

144 US Embassy in Hanoi, "BP Transfers Operatorship of South China Sea Blocks to PetroVietnam; Exploration Work Resumes," *Cable (Released by WikiLeaks)*, 16 May 2008. Online. Available HTTP: <http://wikileaks.org/cable/2008/05/08HANOI579.html> (accessed 15 August).

145 L.H. Hiep, Viet Nam bi "lam phat" doi tac chien luoc, *BBC Tieng Viet*, 18 April 2013.

146 C.A. Thayer, Vietnam on the Road to Global Integration: Forging Strategic Partnership through International Security Cooperation, *Presentation to Opening Plenary Session, Fourth International Vietnam Studies Conference*, Hanoi, 26–39 November 2012, pp. 14–19.

147 US Embassy in Hanoi, "Despite Popular Resentment, Vietnam's China Policy Marked by Pragmatism, Cautions, and Modest Gain," *Cable (Released by WikiLeaks)*, 23 September 2008. Online. Available HTTP: <https://search.wikileaks.org/plusd/cables/08HANOI1094_a.html> (accessed 13 December 2015).

6 Riding on nationalism, 2007–2009

Since the mid-2000s, the South China Sea became a hostile ground for the Vietnamese. There had been more reporting about the Chinese coast guard's aggressive actions against Vietnamese fishing vessels. Due to discreet threats from Beijing, international oil firms ceased to cooperate with Vietnam to explore hydrocarbon in the area off the Vietnamese coast. As other Southeast Asian countries increasingly believed in China's "peaceful rise" rhetoric, the South China Sea became less relevant on the ASEAN agenda. While China effectively overwhelmed Vietnam at sea and in regional forums, its assertive behaviour unintentionally released the nationalist genie in Vietnam out of the bottle. Increased anti-Chinese sentiment at home added more complexity to Vietnam's management of the territorial disputes with China. Though being aware of the risk of domestic stability and escalated inter-state tensions associated with the use of the nationalist card, the Vietnamese political elites were increasingly willing to accept some degree of nationalist manoeuvre to signal its resolve and draw international attention.

Rising anti-Chinese nationalism

Since the mid-2000s, popular resentment against China in Vietnam silently augmented as a result of increased reportage about grievances Vietnamese fishermen suffered in confronting Chinese maritime forces at sea. As mentioned in Chapter 5, China's more determined efforts to bolster its claims led to greater number of incidents between Vietnamese fishermen and Chinese coast guard vessels. In July 2007, a Chinese warship opened fire on a Vietnamese fishing trawler, injuring five.[1] November 2007, the PLA conducted high-profile military exercises near the Paracel Islands to simulate offensives on the islands in the South China Sea.[2] In December 2012 Beijing upgraded the status of its Paracel Islands Office to the county-level city of Sansha.[3] These two events stimulated angst in Vietnam and prompted unprecedented street demonstrations in front of the Chinese Embassy in Hanoi and Chinese Consulate General in Ho Chi Minh City. There was no evidence that these public gatherings, participated by mostly the youngsters and students, were organised by the Vietnamese government. However, two demonstrations for two weekends in a row indicated that there was some degree of toleration within the government towards these "patriotic" expressions.[4]

Distrust of China in Vietnam increased in August 2008 when an alleged Chinese plan to invade Vietnam was posted on four Chinese language websites, which were usually under strict censure from the Chinese authority. Though Vietnam summoned Chinese senior diplomats to raise concerns and request the removal of the post, the offending document was kept online for more than a month. One observer commented that Chinese authorities kept this document online for a period of time indicated that they truly intended to intimidate Vietnam.[5] Anti-Chinese sentiment in Vietnam rose amid the rhetoric of the Vietnam-China strategic partnership. It prompted Secretary General Nong Duc Manh to highlight the need to protect Vietnam's sovereignty and territorial integrity when he addressed the All-Army Political Military Convention in December 2008.[6] These circumstances gave the nationalists in the military and top leadership reasons to push for drastic military modernisation at a time when the economy was hit severely by the global financial crisis. As Vietnam pursued a non-alignment defence policy, strengthening its self-help capabilities was necessary to maintain the country's strategic independence amid the uncertainties of China's rise.

In 2008, the South China Sea spats gradually spilled over the officialdom into the public. In June, the trilateral agreement in Joint Marine Seismic Survey among China, the Philippines and Vietnam expired without being renewed. When the survey area was leaked to the public, it was clear that one-sixth of the survey area lay within the Philippines' territorial waters, beyond the claims by both China and Vietnam. It caused political outrage in Manila, in which the Arroyo administration was charged with trading the Philippines' territory for Chinese development aid.[7] For its part, Vietnam also faced a reality that foreign oil firms were much more likely to stop their projects because of Chinese pressures. As said in Chapter 5, in 2006 and 2007, China repeatedly issued private warnings to a dozen of international oil companies against their collaboration with Vietnam in prospecting for hydrocarbon resources off the Vietnamese coast. Chevron ceased its activities in Block 122 in July 2007. BP quietly withdrew from its exploration project in Blocks 5–2, 5–3 in Nam Con Son Basin in May 2008. In July, the strain between Vietnam and China over maritime resources rose to the surface as Chinese diplomats in Washington asked ExxonMobil executives on several occasions to terminate their exploration contract with PetroVietnam in Blocks 117–8–9.[8] Beijing no longer hid its fist as a spokesman of the Chinese Foreign Ministry confirmed the request.[9] In October 2008, a Vietnam-hired Norwegian vessel conducting exploration off Vietnamese coast (Block 5–2) was intercepted by Chinese naval ships and ordered to leave the area; otherwise it would be fired upon. Beijing clearly indicated that it would take action forcefully and rigorously rather than resort merely to verbal threats.[10] Frustrated with China's actions, Hanoi reportedly requested the American naval ship, the USS *Mustin*, to re-route its port call to Da Nang's Tien Sa port instead of to Ho Chi Minh City as previously arranged.[11] The resentment against China's consistently assertive actions was amplified and overshadowed the positive developments in Vietnam-China relations, namely completion of final land border demarcation, progress in cooperative oil and gas exploration in the Gulf of Tonkin, and the elevation of the relationship to a comprehensive strategic partnership.

The Vietnamese government was also concerned about China's expansive claims and presence in the South China Sea. Beijing protested against Vietnam's major oil development projects in the areas very close to the Vietnamese coast. The locations of these incidents indicated that the Chinese saw an extensive swathe of waters within the nine-dash line, stretching 1,000 miles beyond its border, as belonging to China. Vietnamese authorities lamented the intrusions of Chinese fishing, oil exploration, and maritime surveillance vessels into their territorial waters. It was reported that Chinese craft crossed the agreed boundary in the Gulf of Tonkin to conduct oil exploration in the Vietnamese part. These Chinese vessels usually left only after being confronted by the Vietnamese navy.[12] In November 2008, Vietnam was alarmed by a plan by China National Offshore Oil Corporation (CNOOC), worth USD 29 billion, to acquire deep-water drilling capabilities to explore the South China Sea, including the Paracel and Spratly areas.[13] In early 2009, it protested against the China Oceanographic Bureau's proposal to encourage the habitation and exploitation of unoccupied islands in China's Southern Sea.[14] Hanoi's quiet but no less significant distress was about China's expanded military presence in the South China Sea with the construction of the Yulin Naval Base in Hainan. From a strategist perspective, the base, which would house China's Jin-class submarines, was designed with the purpose of asserting dominance over the South China Sea.[15] Hanoi was also concerned about actions of other claimants. It protested against the Philippine revised Baseline Law, which stipulated an archipelagic baseline enclosing the main archipelago and "regime of islands" for the Kalaya'an Island Group and Scarborough Shoal.[16]

In early 2009, anti-China sentiment turned into extensive popular disapproval of the government-backed plans to develop bauxite mining in the Central Highland with the investment of China Aluminium Company (Chalco). Anxieties about this project were related to economic inefficiency, adverse environmental and social impacts, and potential danger to national security. The matter became a national controversy when General Vo Nguyen Giap, the last standing national hero of the Indochina Wars, published his three letters to the Politburo. Giap voiced grave concerns that such projects would seriously undermine national security as well as harm the sustainable development of the entire country.[17] The retired general further pointed out that Central Highlands are the "Achilles heel" of Vietnam, to which no foreigners, implying the Chinese, should be granted access.[18] Facing widespread public discredit, the CPV Politburo requested a major review of these bauxite development plans and eventually decided to start with two pilot projects in Tan Rai Lam Dong Province and Nhan Co, Dak Nong Province, in which Vietnam National Coal-Mineral Industries Group (Vinacomin) was the investor and China Chalco just the main subcontractor.[19] The discourse about the bauxite development in the Central Highlands revealed that public concerns about China had increased significantly and the perception of China as an existential threat to Vietnam slowly and surely revived.

Forging elitist consensus on nationalist stance

China's aggressive pursuit in the South China Sea not only revived age-old fear of Chinese imperialism in the population but also provided a ground for a convergence to nationalist stance among Vietnamese political elites. Such a hard-earned consensus was exhibited in the first National Conference on the East Sea Studies, themed *East Sea Disputes: History, Politics, and International Law*, in Hanoi on

17 March 2009.[20] Roughly one hundred leading Vietnamese experts and academics in the fields of maritime security, international relations and international law participated in this symposium. It should be noted that this was the first high-profile public debate of the South China Sea issues since 1991 when Vietnam and China normalised their relations. Normally, Hanoi refrained public discussion of controversial and sensitive issues of the bilateral relations.[21] Vietnamese conservative leaders were afraid that such public discussions would unnecessarily damage the fraternal front of Vietnam-China relations.

The timing of the conference also represented Hanoi's hardened stance. It was organised on the eve of the official visit of Chinese State Councillor Dai Bingguo to Vietnam and the annual meeting of the Vietnam-China Steering Committee on 19 and 20 March 2009.[22] Customarily, before important meetings like this, Hanoi tended to avoid events, statements and broadcasts that would cause tensions and complicate bilateral conversations. Against that backdrop, the initiation of a series of high-profile national conventions on the South China Sea theme, which must have secured a green light from the high-level leadership in Hanoi, signalled subtle changes in the way Hanoi approached the issue. This event also reflected the tipping of the power equation in Hanoi in favour of nationalist voices. The public debate was aimed at testing the waters and preparing the ground for the upcoming shifts in Vietnam's handling of the South China Sea disputes.

A number of articles, which summed up the major points raised during the conference, were published on *Vietnamnet*, one of the most popular and progressive online newspapers in Vietnam, upon the arrival of Dai Bingguo in Hanoi. The discussions at the conference brought about some radical assessments and bold recommendations for better management of territorial and maritime disputes in the South China Sea. First, it was agreed that China's ultimate and consistent goal was to turn the South China Sea into a "Chinese lake."[23] Though this assessment was not new to the Vietnamese, it revealed some defiance as it was published on the special occasion as mentioned. Second, there was a consensus at the conference that Vietnam had strong claims to the Paracels and Spratlys, supported by ample historical evidence of Vietnam's continuous, effective administration of these archipelagos since the Nguyen lords in the seventeenth century. On the other hand, it was argued that China's nine-dash line claim (usually called the U-shaped line or cow-tongue line) was legally groundless and indicated China's ambition to gain exclusive control of the South China Sea.

Vietnamese scholars were convinced that international law stood on their side, but admitted that Vietnam lagged behind China in academic discourse and propaganda about sovereignty over the South China Sea features. However, they considered the legal options such as an appeal to the international court of justice or arbitration as "impracticable" as these measures required the consent of both parties, though the advisory opinions of international bodies may have certain political and legal implications.[24] Last but not least, the participants argued that the South China Sea was important to China's broader geopolitical strategy to subdue regional rivals such as Japan, South Korea and Taiwan, and expel the United States out of the region. However, the dominant view was that China was not ready to use force. At this time, China's top priority was still "peaceful development" and Beijing cared about its national image and international prestige as a "responsible stakeholder."[25]

The conference proposed to view Vietnam's South China Sea policy as a part of its overall foreign policy and international politics in Asia and the Pacific.[26] A number of specific recommendations were tabled as follows:

1 It is important to build a complete *legal file* for the case of Vietnam in the South China Sea dispute, and make full use of it for political struggle, information warfare, negotiation and legal adjudication if necessary.
2 The National Assembly of Vietnam should adopt a *law* on sovereignty over the Paracel and Spratly archipelagos and the government must have a *comprehensive, multidimensional, and cohesive maritime strategy* with emphasis laid on military modernisation to strengthen the country's *deterrent power*.
3 It is necessary to embark on "four transformations," namely socialisation (*xa hoi hoa*), publication (*cong khai hoa*), internationalisation (*quoc te hoa*), and de-sensitisation (*phi nhay cam hoa*) of the South China Sea issue.
4 The struggle to protect sovereignty over the archipelagos and jurisdiction in the South China Sea must take advantage of the power of *national unity* (all Vietnamese in and outside the country) and the time (international law and Vietnam's righteousness).
5 It is of strategic importance to support *scholarly works* and strengthen capabilities of Vietnam's South China Sea experts by granting scholarships; educating, and increasing awareness of, young people about the South China Sea; and nurturing patriotism and will to protect national integrity for the next generation.[27]

These strategies represented a more nationalist approach to the South China Sea dispute, which aimed at putting Vietnam in a more advantageous position in the legal and information feud with China. National unity and international public support were seen as additional sources of leverage to enhance Vietnam's footing in the face of China's overwhelming military and civilian power. Clearly, these activities were outside the framework of bilateralism and the ASEAN-led multilateral framework that Hanoi had long favoured. At that time, it was not clear whether the political leaders in Hanoi would adopt these measures, recommended by a quasi-academic conference. However, it was clear that a green light was given to publicise them to the wider audience. The open appeal to national unity and international public opinion on the South China Sea issue was indicative of the fact that nationalist elites and intellectuals gained more ground in the making of Vietnam's policy towards the South China Sea disputes. Obviously, deference, in terms of silence before continuous Chinese assertiveness, not only failed to restrain China but also undermined the legitimacy of the CPV domestically.

Hanoi needed to find additional leverage to curb China's creeping assertiveness at sea because bilateralism and ASEAN-led multilateralism was no longer instrumental in managing the South China Sea dispute. Despite the progress in land border demarcation and joint development in the Gulf of Tonkin, the technical-level working group between Vietnam and China on "maritime issues" in the South China Sea proper had effectively been stalled after the eleventh round in 2006. Such meetings were clearly fruitless because the negotiators could not even agree on the agenda.[28] Still Vietnam was keen on continuing such meetings because they gave it access to Chinese policy making circles and provided a tool to defuse tensions if necessary. However, Chinese officials repeatedly refused to return to the table with an excuse of being "too busy." It should be noted that between December 2006 and September 2010, no top Chinese leader paid an official visit to Hanoi while their Vietnamese counterparts came to China at least on one or two occasions a year.[29] It was indicative that Beijing undervalued the importance of bilateral dialogue with Hanoi. ASEAN-China negotiations on the Guidelines on DOC Implementation also faced deadlock over the question of the status of ASEAN in dealing with China. The Vietnamese officials clearly had no illusion about any prospect for a COC that China would oppose anyway.[30] They were well aware of the difficulties in forging an ASEAN common stance in a consensus-driven decision-making system in the context of highly divergent interests among members.[31] Vietnamese scholars also doubted the prospect of reaching a negotiated settlement of the sovereignty dispute because no country was willing to compromise. And, if the sovereignty issues were not resolved, shelving disputes for joint development was unrealistic.[32]

Promoting national awareness of the country's maritime territories

One significant change in Vietnam's approach to the South China Sea was its information strategy. Before 2009, there was limited coverage in the Vietnamese media about the bitter history of the Vietnam-China relations or contemporary tensions over disputed territories. In most circumstances, the government-controlled media only covered statements by spokesmen of the Foreign Ministry without further analysis or commentary. They sometimes provided broadcasts on historical and archaeological evidence of Vietnam's occupation of the Paracels and Spratlys. However, they hardly broadcast reports on incidents at sea, or reported analyses or scholarly debates on Vietnam-China relations. There were two reasons for the strict censorship. First, the leaders of the ruling communist parties of Vietnam and China agreed to "educate the two countries' peoples about the traditional friendship between Vietnam and China."[33] In other words, they implicitly pledged to calm nationalist voices, or avoid negative portrayals of one another in the public space. Though criticisms of Vietnam appeared on Chinese media quite often, Chinese diplomats usually referred to the previously mentioned agreement when complaining about, or even demanding the cancellation or removal of any public discourse or publication that may taint China's image. Conservative leaders in Hanoi argued for the need to preserve the cordial face of socialist solidarity and avoid public outcries that would displease China and negatively affect rapprochement between the two countries. Second, from the pragmatist point of view, the Vietnamese officials were afraid that the coverage of such stories would result in strong public outcries, which would undermine their control of policies of national importance.[34] In most cases, Vietnamese authorities refused to feed information about the South China Sea clashes to the media. They preferred bilateralism as an access to Chinese high-level leaders to raise concerns and discuss ways to manage them properly.

China's tailored and quiet assertiveness in the South China Sea proved that Vietnam's deference was not rewarded with China's benevolence. The first half of 2008 witnessed relative calm in the South China Sea, perhaps thanks to the Olympic Games in Beijing in July. In the run-up to the Olympic games, China inserted the U-shaped line (nine-dash line) in the official online map of the torch relay and only removed it after Vietnam lodged a protest to the president of the International Olympic Committee.[35] After the groundbreaking anti-China demonstrations in December 2007, Vietnamese bloggers and political activists continued to mount criticisms of the Communist Party and government of Vietnam for its soft handling of the disputes over the Paracels and Spratlys and its relations with China. They also planned to stage a demonstration against China's Olympic torch relay in Ho Chi Minh City in April 2008. In a gesture of deference to China, Vietnam's prime minister vowed to ensure a trouble-free relay as a way to show "the Vietnamese nation's love for sports and peace and its amity with China."[36] Reportedly, behind closed doors, China told Vietnam and a number of countries that there should be no interference with the torch relay.[37] Consequently, the public security forces moved to detain fourteen persons before the event.[38]

Nonetheless, after the successful Olympic Games, China became more straightforwardly assertive, openly demanding ExxonMobil to terminate its project with Vietnam. Against that backdrop, there was a strong demand among the Vietnamese intelligentsia and political elites for building awareness among ordinary people of the need to protect their ancestors' maritime legacies.[39] Some scholars even advocated de-sensitising the issues, informing the public of actual happenings (or China's bullying behaviour and unreasonable claims), and socialising the struggle to defend sovereignty and territorial integrity. Phieu and Huy argued,

> We need to actively build up a South China Sea consciousness. From there, we need a strong legion of scholars on sea-related issues, maritime strategy to boost national will and awareness of the South China Sea . . . Vietnam has failed to make full use of combined strength of the entire nation in a bid to safeguard its sovereignty in the South China Sea.
>
> . . . Today, Vietnam is confronted with a threat to the long-term future of the nation. Different from those of the part, this threat is evolving slowly throughout decades, even the course of a century, but is increasingly graver day in day out.[40]

It was also said that, though having stronger claims supported by solid historical evidence, Vietnam had not paid adequate attention to information sharing, publication and propaganda. Vietnam faced "an asymmetric war" with China in terms of the quantity and quality of researchers and publications, the support of the governments and the participation of non-state actors.[41] Doan Trang held that few Vietnamese works had been published in the English language and in internationally accredited journals. Meanwhile, China had heavily invested in research and publication. The Chinese scholars had published at least sixty major works on the field.[42] She also complained about censorship, lack of incentives and access to "sensitive" sources, and a low-level public awareness of the territorial issues and of the actual events at sea.[43]

Major changes in Vietnam's information policy in the maritime domain came by the end of 2008. On 26 November, the CPV's Central Commission for Publicity and Education (*Ban Tuyen giao Trung uong*) issued an instruction which said: "increased publicity of sea and island issues is to boost awareness of and actions of all party executives, state agencies, and people from every walk of life with regard to the strategic importance of the country's seas and islands."[44] In March 2009, a conference to review propaganda on the sea, islands, border demarcation, and foreign affairs in 2008 was held in the city of Hai Phong. It was disclosed that the theme of seas and islands was regarded as one of the three key priorities for the state's publicity program.[45] In the same month, the Vietnamese government issued a decree on the management of maritime resources management and environment protection, which designated the week between 1 and 8 June as "Vietnamese Seas and Islands Week" (*Tuan le Bien dao Viet Nam*) in honour of the World Oceans Day (8 June) and World Environment Day (5 June).[46] The first Vietnamese Seas and Islands Week was held in June 2009. In November, the National Assembly approved the 2010 budget appropriation that added VND 38 billion to the South China Sea and Island Program.[47] It was likely that this amount was dedicated to propaganda programs to boost publicity on the seas and islands.

Since then, there has been a long list of state-funded nation-wide propaganda campaigns, titled "Turning to the Country's Seas and Islands" (*Huong ve Bien Dao Que huong*) in various forms (musical performances, public lectures and fund-raising events) aimed to increase the people's awareness of the maritime sphere. Contests, involving the themes of the seas and islands, were held across the country in many locations, for all types of people, from pupils and students, to music composers, writers and photographers, to public servants and military officers.[48] These campaigns had clearly run wide and deep. As instructed, publicity on the country's maritime domain is integrated into the work plans of all central departments and agencies and local authorities under the centralised command of the State Steering Committee on the South China Sea and Islands. Specifically, the Ministry of Foreign Affairs, the Naval Central Command, the General Department for Maritime Police, and the Ministry of Public Security were tasked to provide appropriate information to the media and the public. The Ministry of Information and Communications was mandated to instruct and monitor central and local media. The Ministry of Education and Training was tasked with developing the education materials and integrating the sea and island content into the curricula and exams.[49] In 2009, Vietnamese educators introduced Vietnam's sovereignty and jurisdiction in the South China Sea into syllabuses for high-school and university students. In June 2012, for the first time, questions related to the South China Sea were included in the nationwide high-school graduation examination.[50]

Vietnam's new information strategy has two components. First and foremost, Hanoi adopted a more active posture using information to indoctrinate maritime patriotism in the population to forge national unity on the maritime front. It is indicative of more reliance placed on the power of public opinion and national unity to defend the country's offshore interests. Vietnamese Seas and Islands Week was in essence a nation building campaign. That was reflected in the symbolic designation of the Vietnam Seas and Islands Week. Nguyen Chu Cong, Vice Director General of National Bureau for Vietnamese Seas and Islands, said:

> Our seas are rich in resources, provide the livelihood for tens of millions of Vietnamese people, constitute the *living space* for the nation and a *strategic realm for the national defence and construction*, and represent *sacred part* of the Fatherland in the context of international integration.
>
> . . . It is necessary to step up propaganda to enhancing awareness of the society, the entire political system, and all peoples about the importance of the seas and oceans to the sustainable development of the oceans and the efforts to reduce impacts of climate change to the world in general and to Vietnam in particular. It is also to promote in each everyone an awareness of the need to protect maritime resources and environment, *pride and national consciousness about national sovereignty* over the country's maritime space, about the lifeline of the community and the long-term economic development of the country for the sake of making Vietnam a prosperous maritime power.[51]

After that point, a green light was given to news agencies to increase coverage of the sea and island issues. The frequency of editorials and commentaries on these issues quickly increased.[52] The South China Sea has become one of the most popular topics in the public discourse in Vietnam since 2009. Almost all newspapers have their own corners for the themes related to the country's seas and islands. Most importantly, reporters and academics were allowed to be much more critical of China. In the past, the Vietnamese media narrowly focused on historical evidence of Vietnam's sovereignty over the Spratlys and Paracels, and made public the statements of high-level leaders or spokespersons of the Foreign Ministry. Since 2009, the focus shifted to analyses and commentaries on the claims of other coastal states in light of international law, and international politics around maritime security. There was a flood of editorials, analyses, and commentaries critical of China's nine-dash line claim.[53] They also provided up-to-date reportage on contemporary activities by Vietnam, other claimants and big powers. A major share of their reporting covered the struggle of Vietnamese fishermen to counter China's unilateral fishing ban, harassments by Chinese law enforcement vessels, and maltreatment by Chinese authorities.[54] Clearly, news agencies enjoyed greater level of disclosure from the state agencies and greater freedom to approach domestic and international researchers to look for sources on the related topics.

It should be noted that increased space for the South China Sea coverage has never meant an indulgence in xenophobia. The CPV has cautiously kept tight control on the public discourse on the South China Sea disputes and aimed to use it to enhance the legitimacy of the regime and serve its pragmatist policy. The Central Commission for Publicity set the guidelines for propaganda activities in 2009 as follows:

> Propaganda should articulate the Party and State's policy to persistently settle the disputes with countries concerned, including the South China Sea issue, through peaceful negotiations, and to dialogue and collaborate with all the parties to resolve all emergent problems for the sake of regional peace and cooperation. These activities are designed to educate people on mindfulness to protect national sovereignty and territories, and increase their knowledge of national borders and maritime sovereignty. They should be aware that safeguarding national sovereignty and territorial integrity is a long-term, complicated and comprehensive task. It is required that defence of national sovereignty would not be detrimental to maintenance and development of comprehensive cooperative relations with countries concerned.[55]

It was disclosed that the editors in chief received strict guidelines on what should be covered and how far their reportage should go. Some articles, which were too critical of China, were removed. At 11:52 a.m. on 6 December 2008, *Vietnamnet* posted an article that called China's South China Sea strategy as "hawkish." It was removed several hours later.[56] The Vietnamese leaders clearly did not want anti-China emotion to get out of hand. Since the eruption of the first mass demonstration in December 2007, Vietnamese authorities suppressed any calls for or in support of street protests. Tough sanctions were applied on non-compliance. In April 2009, *Du Lich* Newspaper was suspended because it published an article honouring the anti-China demonstration in late 2009.[57] However, it is clear that government censorship is largely a cat-and-mouse game, which is increasingly difficult in the era of information technology. As events unfolded, newswires usually followed occurrences and tried to satisfy the audience's taste rather than comply with ambiguous rules. Besides, the government does not have effective control of discussions mushrooming in cyberspace such as the blogosphere, Facebook and Twitter. One Vietnamese analyst held that rising nationalism was a tiger that will cause "endless troubles" if uncaged.[58]

The second component of Vietnam's information strategy is international. As mentioned earlier, the Vietnamese believed that the Chinese scholars, supported by the Chinese government, have long used scientific publications as platforms to assert China's territorial claims and to compensate for their inherent historical and legal weaknesses.[59] Vietnamese scholars on the South China Sea were outnumbered by Chinese experts based in dozens of research institutions across China. Most importantly, Chinese researchers managed to achieve greater outreach by publishing their works in English and in internationally accredited journals such as *Marine Policy*, *Marine Custom Management*, *Marine and Coastal Law Journal*,

American Journal of International Law and so on, while Vietnamese publications were mostly in the Vietnamese language and were released in domestic outlets. A preliminary count showed that China has published around sixty books on the Paracels and Spratlys in English and Chinese, apart from works by overseas Chinese around the world. Vietnamese scholars were seen as not active enough in Track II dialogue, which include think tankers, scholars and academics on regional affairs. On this basis, a Vietnamese reporter recommended:

> In the modern times, to win the complicated struggle such as sovereignty disputes, the key is to win the support of international community, not merely military primacy.
>
> Therefore, internationalising the issue of land and water territories, the Paracels and Spratlys is indispensable for Vietnam. It should start with introducing Vietnamese views to the world.[60]

The first National Conference on the South China Sea Studies in March 2009 also laid emphasis on the importance of research and publication as an avenue to defend Vietnam's claims in the South China Sea. Le Minh Phieu and Duong Danh Huy opined,

> Through communication and diplomacy, it is necessary to draw attention and support of international public opinion on a fair and peaceful settlement of sovereignty disputes in the South China Sea. The world will support us if justice and righteousness stands on our side, and they also have an interest in this fair and peaceful resolution.[61]

In this light, Hanoi took steps to shift the game to its strengths, namely legality, transparency and fairness, and the virtue of righteousness, to gain the higher moral ground in the face of China's military might and its salami-slicing tactics. Apart from regular statements by Ministry of Foreign Affairs' spokespersons, Hanoi launched a campaign on Track II to defend its position and exposed China's weaknesses with the hope of winning the support of international public opinion. Vietnamese scholars became more active and more candidly engaged in regional and international forums to raise and discuss the South China Sea issues. They also appeared more frequently in the international media to present their views and analyses of the related subjects. Vietnam also sent its officials and leading experts on a regular basis to key countries to provide first-hand information on developments at sea and to explain Vietnam's stance and policy towards the disputes.

One of the important actors in the scholarly realm was the Diplomatic Academy of Vietnam (DAV), a think-tank under the Ministry of Foreign Affairs. In November 2009, the DAV, in collaboration with the Vietnam Law Association, launched a series of high-profile annual international conferences on the South China Sea issues. The most important feature of this series of Track II workshops is that it focuses on recent developments and does not avoid controversial issues, especially security, political and legal questions, which are deemed "sensitive" to China, implications and possible avenues for cooperation and resolution. This made the DAV workshop series different from the workshop process on Managing Potential Conflicts in the South China Sea hosted by Indonesia since 1989. These Indonesia-hosted workshops, which were informal meetings of the claimant parties' officials, mostly focused on cooperative programs, dialogue between directly involved parties, and confidence building measures while avoiding contentious issues of sovereignty and jurisdiction.[62]

Chinese scholars were invited to these workshops to present their views and participate in the discussions. As seen from the programs, from the first (2009) and third one (2011), time slots for discussion were increased incrementally, allowing participants to debate more with one another rather than just presenting their views. The workshop won credits and managed to attract a large number of international scholars in the field. However, Chinese participants were sceptical of the workshop. Chinese scholar Su Hao criticised the DAV's initiative as having a "political design" as a pathway to "internationalise" the South China Sea issue.[63] The DAV also developed an in-house research unit focusing on the South China Sea. Its East Sea Studies project has recently become an Institute for East Sea Studies, reflecting growing importance and size of the tasks assigned. The DAV hosts a feature website, *nghiencuubiendong.vn*, which is among the biggest collections of research works on the South China Sea and Vietnam's policies, and provides up-to-date reproduction of related news and feeds. Most importantly, the website is in three languages, Vietnamese, English and Chinese. It serves as an important database for research as well as a platform for the Vietnamese scholars to publish their views to the world.

Vietnamese academics, in and outside the country, became watchful of international publications, especially by Chinese scholars, and vocal to protest what they deemed "inappropriate" or "abuse of science." In March 2010, the Vietnamese sent a petition to National Geographic Society (US) to demand the removal of a map which indicated that the Paracels was as part of China.[64] In October 2011, they also demanded *Google Maps* (Chinese version) to remove the nine-dash line map.[65] A number of incidents in which Chinese scholars inappropriately introduced the controversial nine-dash line map to prestigious journals were found out. In April 2011, they contested the irrelevant intrusion of a cow-tongue (U-shaped line) map, in an article by Chinese scholars, to the *Journal of Waste Management*. In August, a group of 57 Vietnamese scientists, engineers and professionals lodged a protest to *Science* about the article "China's Demographic History and Future Challenges" with the insertion of the infamous map.[66] Reportedly, they also sent warnings against the publication of such maps to hundreds of journals to pre-empt similar abuses in the future. In the communication with editors of *Nature*, Nguyen Van Tuan, a Sydney-based Vietnamese scientist said:

> They (Chinese authors) include the line around the South China Sea even when this region, and the islands within it, have absolutely zero relevant to the topic . . . The publication of such a map represents an abuse of science.[67]

In October, the co-editor of *Climatic Change*, Michael Oppenheimer, also received a number of requests by scientists from Vietnam, Finland and Canada to remove a Chinese map in one of its publication four years ago. In review of the publication, Michael Oppenheimer concluded that the map was irrelevant to the contents of the paper and forwarded the opinion to the Chinese lead author, Xuemei Shao of the Institute of Geographic Sciences and Natural Resources Research in Beijing. Xuemei Shao refused to amend the figure, and indicated that he did so as "*requested* by the Chinese government." The author of the publication in *Nature* confirmed that the insertion of "Chinese seas" was a matter of following "China's law."[68] Though *Science*, *Nature* and *Climatic Change* finally decided to keep the maps, they were clearly informed about politics of territorial claims behind such maps thanks to the protests by Vietnamese scholars. After these map controversies, *Nature* warned scientists away from "inflammatory remarks, contentious statements and controversial map designations."[69]

Vietnam's development of naval capabilities

Vietnamese officials usually stress the need for defending the country's long coast and 1 million km^2 of maritime area under its jurisdiction. Since the early 2000s, Vietnam's ministers of defence expressed an interest in high-level technology weapon systems, particularly new submarines, landing craft and missile gunboats for the Vietnamese People's Navy (VPN) to defend the country's coastal areas and offshore oil fields.[70] However, Vietnam's force structure was slow to change and most of the annual military budget was allocated to the army. Due to the shortage of funding, Vietnam could only afford piecemeal air and sea defence modernisations. Between 2002 and 2006, it was reported that Vietnam acquired twenty-seven combat aircraft and two S-300P PMU1 air defence systems.[71] In March 2004, Vietnam reached an agreement with Russia for two Russia-built Tarantul V/Molniya corvettes armed with SS-N-25 (Kh-35 Uran-E) missiles and another six, with the option of four more, to be built in Vietnam.[72] The Kh-35 Uran-E is an anti-ship cruise missile with a range of 130 km. In 2005, Vietnam ordered two Bastion-P mobile coastal defence systems armed with Yakhot ramjet-powered supersonic sea-skimming cruise missiles (delivered in 2011). The systems were designed to attack sea-surface and land targets with a maximum range of 300 km.[73] In December 2006, Hanoi signed a USD 300 million deal with Russia's Rosoboronexport to acquire two Gepard-class frigates armed with guided anti-ship missiles.[74]

Since 2008, Vietnam embarked on a broader and more expensive upgrade for its naval and air arsenals. In early 2008, Vietnam reportedly reached a USD 600 million agreement with Russia for the delivery of several shipbuilding kits and related weapons for assembly in its Hong Ha shipyard. The kits were said to be a mix of naval and coast guard vessels.[75] In the same year, Vietnam was determined to acquire underwater capabilities and expressed an interest in a number of used conventional submarines from Serbia at a time when Yugoslavia disintegrated, but it failed to seal a deal. Hanoi then approached Moscow for new submarines.[76] In April 2009, Vietnam was reportedly near a deal to purchase a set of six diesel-electric Project 636 Kilo-class fast attack submarines armed with Novator Club-S (SS-N-27) cruise anti-ship missiles. The Novator Club-S was effective within a range of 300 km. The value of the submarine package amounted to USD 1.8 billion.[77] By December 2009, it was confirmed that the order was placed and the total cost later jumped to USD 3.2 billion with the inclusion of armaments and Russian-built maintenance facilities at Cam Ranh Bay.[78] At the same time, Vietnam also placed a USD 500 million order for eight Su-30 MK2 warplanes (first reported as twelve), delivered in 2011.[79] In 2010, Vietnam agreed to buy a batch of twelve more Su-30MK2, which would be delivered in 2012 and 2013. In May 2010, Canadian Viking Air of Victoria signed a contract to provide Vietnam with six amphibious DHC-6 Twin Otter Series 400 aircraft, which was supposed to form the first air arms of the VPN and was used for maritime patrol.[80] In the same month, it was reported that Vietnam was near a deal to upgrade its missile capability with Extended Range Artillery Munitions (EXTRA) from Israel. The EXTRA rockets, which can carry a warhead of 125 kg and has a range of 150 km with high precision, can be launched from multiple platforms.[81]

The arrangements with Canada's Viking and Israel indicated that Vietnam had started looking beyond Russia, its traditional weapon provider. In September 2011, Vietnam ordered two additional Gepard-class frigates armed with antisubmarine weapons (to be delivered in 2016 and 2017).[82] In late 2011, it was reported that Vietnam was negotiating to procuring up to four SIGMA frigates from Netherland and P-3ASW aircraft from the United States.[83] In August 2013, Vietnam signed a contract with Russia to acquire another batch of twelve Su-30MK2 multirole fighter aircraft, raising its SU-30MK numbers to forty-eight.[84] Vietnam's long list of arms procurement since 2008 represented an aggressive attempt to bolster land-based and underwater capabilities to defend its maritime areas and offshore islands.

Vietnamese officials maintained that the armed forces were modernised to the extent necessary to defend their sovereignty and as far as the economic conditions allowed. These officials also denied that Vietnam was in an arms race or actively preparing for conflicts in the South China but stressed the need for defending its long coast and maritime zones.[85] Vietnam had a long-standing interest in underwater capabilities. In the late 1980s Hanoi attempted to obtain its first submarine from the Soviet Union and sent a crew to be trained in a Project 641 diesel submarine of the Soviet Pacific Fleet. The project was suspended by the Soviet leaders, who were concerned that it may provoke China.[86] Hanoi bought two Yugo-class mini submarines from North Korea in 1997. In 2002, it requested India's assistance to train its naval cadets and officers. However, the acquisition of Kilo submarines and other expensive sophisticated hardware was unusually big in terms of funding given to the Navy. The timing of the deals also revealed some level of urgency. Hanoi made big investments in expensive hardware at a time of economic austerity caused by the GFC. The acquisition, together with additional costs for maintenance of these platforms and systems, would seriously impair their state budget balance in the years to come. This was indicative of a critical and urgent situation in the South China Sea.

Though officials in Hanoi repeatedly denied any links between its naval modernisation and those of other regional countries, it was clearly linked to its insecurity in the face of China's newfound maritime ambitions. Chinese maritime ambition and its assertive actions in the South China Sea constituted direct triggers of this urgent naval modernisation. In December 2006, addressing a meeting of top military officers, Chinese President Hu Jintao said China would build a powerful navy to protect "the nation's authority and security and maintaining maritime rights."[87] Hu's speech unveiled China's dream to become a major power, which explained its consistent efforts for naval modernisation. Since 1990, when most countries in region cut their military spending, China's defence budget increased by double digits annually and reached 17.8 per cent in 2007.[88] In spite of a relatively benign security environment, the PLA added to its arsenal more than thirty new submarines and a large number of advanced destroyers and deployed over one thousand ballistic missiles and hundreds of modern fighters between 1995 and 2006.[89] Most importantly, in early 2008, it was revealed that China was constructing Yulin naval base, a harbour with underground facilities able to house nuclear submarines, near the city on the southern tip of Hainan Island.[90] Beijing usually referred to Taiwan as a justification for its ambitious military modernisation but it did not explain the reasons for the Yulin base. An analyst observed that the development of Yulin base, alongside the development of an airfield in Woody Island (Paracels), and the reinforcement of facilities at Fiery Cross Reef (Spratlys) clearly enhanced China's power projection in the South China Sea and beyond.[91] In 2008, it was reported that China was developing its first aircraft carrier. A senior Chinese military officer confirmed its country's plan to acquire aircraft carriers for blue water missions.[92] The rapid growth of Chinese power projection capabilities aroused concerns among Southeast Asian countries, including Vietnam. In response, these countries rushed to develop or boost their underwater capabilities. Malaysia placed an order for two submarines built by a Franco-Spanish consortium in 2007 and 2009.[93] Indonesia is considering an order for two Kilo-class submarines from Russia.[94]

Vietnam's expansion of naval capabilities was not competitive in nature. Simply speaking, Hanoi wanted to develop an affordable, viable deterrent against any attempts to encroach upon its maritime zones and the offshore islands under its control.[95] Though Vietnam's firepower would never match that of China, its development of maritime capabilities made it more difficult and costly for the Chinese to start a short and limited war against Vietnam in the Spratlys. It meant that China now faced greater difficulties and higher costs for any military actions against Vietnam's positions in the Spratlys. From the operational and tactical point of view, the deployment of Kilo submarines in interoperation with surface warships, Bastion coastal defence systems, and advanced Sukhoi multirole aircrafts, can effectively increase the strength and operational range of its firepower for coastal and littoral combat and for the defence of the Spratly Islands. It was not clear for what purposes the Vietnamese would use the newly built submarines and how they would be integrated into its force structure. However, a military analyst pointed out that those Russian-made Kilo submarines, which are dubbed "black holes" because of their improved stealth feature, could be effective for anti-submarine warfare, anti-surface ship warfare, and general reconnaissance and patrol missions.[96] Vietnam could deploy its submarines to undertake offshore defence and pose a threat to PLA Navy submarines in Chinese Yulin naval station when they are entering or leaving the port.[97] A Vietnamese analyst argues that the operational quietness of the ordered Kilo submarines featured well into Vietnam's traditional asymmetric and guerrilla warfare against superior power. The squadron of Kilo submarines constituted a core component of Vietnam's preparedness to counter a prospective Chinese aircraft carrier and support its air force to provide an effective cover for the Spratlys in case of crisis.[98] It was clear that if the aforementioned air, land, and underwater-based platforms were put in place, Vietnam would be able to impose a credible blockade on the major sea lanes through the South China Sea between its southern coast and the Spratlys in case of crisis.

Conclusion

The period between 2007 and 2009 witnessed a rise in anti-China nationalism in Vietnam as a result of China's increased coercions against Vietnam's fishing and oil exploration activities in the South China Sea. The expression of popular resentment took to the street with two unprecedented weekend demonstrations in Hanoi and Ho Chi Minh City and widespread objections to the bauxite development project involving Chinese companies in the Central Highland. For nearly a decade and half after normalisation, Hanoi tried to dampen the flame of nationalism and engage in quiet diplomacy to manage controversial and sensitive issues with Beijing to avoid a serious rupture with Beijing. However, as China was more determined to thwart its maritime rights under UNCLOS, political elites in Vietnam, especially nationalist pragmatists, increasingly saw the benefits of popular patriotism to show tenacity against China's creeping expansions and attract international attention. Hanoi placed more emphasis on the publication of information and mobilisation of people to defend the country's maritime sovereignty and jurisdiction. China's growing naval power and more aggressive posture at sea prompted Hanoi to upgrade its own defences. In this period, Vietnam acquired a handful of multi-role strike aircraft, coastal defence systems, and frigates and placed an order to purchase six Kilo-class submarines from Russia. These platforms, armed with anti-submarines and anti-ship weapons, were intended to impose higher costs on any Chinese attempts to encroach upon its maritime zones and islands.

Notes

1 "Chinese Navy Fires at Vietnamese Fishing Ship, Injuring 5," *Kyodo*, 21 July 2007.
2 J. Manthorpe, "China Is Rolling Up Its Sleeves and Showing Off," *Vancouver Sun*, 21 December 2007.
3 R. Mitton, "Vietnam Sees Second Weekend of Anti-China Protests," *Strait Times*, 17 December 2007.
4 G. Torode, "Dispute at Sea Rocks the Boat in Vietnam," *South China Morning Post*, 15 December 2007.
5 Trong Nghia, "Ke hoach Tan cong Viet Nam la mot qua bong tham do?," *RFI Tieng Viet*, 16 September 2008.

6 J. Dosch, "Vietnam in 2008: Foreign Policy Successes but Daunting Domestic Problems," *Southeast Asian Affairs*, 2009, p.383.
7 International Crisis Group, "Stirring Up the South China Sea (II): Regional Responses," *Asia Report No. 229*, 24 July 2012, pp. 6–7.
8 "China Warns Exxon over Vietnam Deal," *Reuters*, 20 July 2008.
9 L. Xian, "China Angered over Exxon Mobil Oil Agreement," *China Daily*, 23 July 2008.
10 J. Crickton, "China Threatens Neighbours in South China Sea," *Global Geopolitics*, 24 October 2008.
11 R. Mitton, "China-Vietnam Ties Remain More Sour Than Sweet," *Asia Sentinel*, 14 November 2008.
12 J. Crickton, "China Threatens Neighbours in South China Sea."
13 "Vietnam lai bay to quan ngai," *BBC Tieng Viet*, 29 November 2008.
14 N.V. Long, *Hoang Sa-Truong Sa: Cac su kien, tu lieu lich su phap ly chinh (2000–2013)*, vol. 1, Ho Chi Minh City: Tre Publisher, 2014, pp. 92–3.
15 R.D.J. Fisher, "China's Naval Secrets," *Wall Street Journal*, 5 May 2008.
16 I.C. Storey, "Recent Developments in the South China Sea: Cause for Concern," In: Tran Truong Thuy (ed.), *The South China Sea: Cooperation for Regional Security and Development*, Hanoi: Diplomatic Academy of Vietnam, 2010, pp. 160–6.
17 "Tu lieu lien quan den ban Kien nghi 2009 — Ba la thu cua Dai tuong Vo Nguyen Giap gui den cac nha lanh dao ve van de khai thac bauxite o Tay Nguyen," *Bauxite Viet Nam*, 6 March 2013. Online. Available HTTP: <http://boxitvn.blogspot.com.au/2013/03/tu-lieu-lien-quan-en-ban-kien-nghi-2009_6.html> (accessed 6 June 2014).
18 "Tuong Giap gui thu nua ve bauxite," *BBC Tieng Viet*, 27 May 2009. Online. Available HTTP: <www.bbc.co.uk/vietnamese/vietnam/2009/05/090527_vonguyengiap_bauxite.shtml> (accessed 6 June 2014).
19 C.A. Thayer, "Political Legitimacy of Vietnam's One Party-State: Challenges and Response," *Journal of Current Southeast Asian Affairs* 28, no. 4, 2009, pp. 49–52.
20 East Sea (Bien Dong) is the name for the South China Sea in Vietnam. The conference was held by the East Sea Studies Program of the Diplomatic Academy of Vietnam, a think tank affiliated to the Ministry of Foreign Affairs.
21 "Hoi thao dau tien ve Chu quyen Bien Dong," *BBC Tieng Viet*, 18 March 2009. Online. Available HTTP: <www.bbc.co.uk/vietnamese/vietnam/2009/03/090318_biendong_conference.shtml> (accessed 6 March 2014).
22 R. Sutter, "South China Sea: Economic Issues," *CSIS Comparative Connections*, April 2009.
23 T.T. Thuy, "Nhung khuyen nghi sau Hoi thao Bien Dong," *Tuan Viet Nam*, 19 March 2009. Online. Available HTTP: <www.tuanvietnam.net/2009–03–19-nhung-khuyen-nghi-sau-hoi-thao-bien-dong> (accessed 9 July 2014).
24 Ibid.
25 Ibid.
26 Phuong Loan, "Khong the giu chu quyen bang cam tinh," *Vietnamnet*, 18 March 2009. Online. Available HTTP: <http://vnn.vietnamnet.vn/chinhtri/2009/03/836677/> (accessed 9 July 2014).
27 See Thuy, "Nhung khuyen nghi sau Hoi thao Bien Dong" (emphasis added).
28 US Embassy in Hanoi, "Some in GVN Apparently Unworried about Situation in South China Sea," *Cable (Released by WikiLeaks)*, 22 April 2008. Online. Available HTTP: <https://search.wikileaks.org/plusd/cables/08HANOI464_a.html> (accessed 22 July 2014).
29 L. Hiep, "Vietnam's Hedging Strategy against China since Normalisation," *Contemporary Southeast Asia* 35, no. 3, 2013, pp. 347–48.
30 US Embassy in Hanoi, "ASEAN-China Negotiations on South China Sea 'Guidelines' Stalled by Dispute over ASEAN's Negotiating Status," *Cable (Released by*

WikiLeaks), 17 April 2009. Online. Available HTTP: <https://search.wikileaks.org/plusd/cables/09HANOI362_a.html> (accessed 17 July 2014).

31 US Embassy in Hanoi, "2008 Recap of the Sino-Vietnam South China Sea Territorial Dispute," *Cable (Released by WikiLeaks)*, 20 January 2009. Online. Available HTTP: <www.wikileaks.org/plusd/cables/09HANOI52_a.html> (accessed 20 July 2014).

32 See Thuy, "Nhung khuyen nghi sau Hoi thao Bien Dong."

33 US Embassy in Hanoi, "Uneventful, Unpublicized, but Not Unnoticed : 30th Anniversary of 1979 China-Vietnam Border War," *Cable (Released by WikiLeaks)*, 18 February 2009. Online. Available HTTP: <www.wikileaks.org/plusd/cables/09HANOI134_a.html> (accessed 20 July 2014).

34 US Embassy in Hanoi, "Covering the Spratlys: Silence Is Officially Golden," *Cable (Released by WikiLeaks)*, 5 February 2008. Online. Available HTTP: <https://search.wikileaks.org/plusd/cables/08HANOI133_a.html> (accessed 20 July 2014).

35 L.M. Phieu and D.D. Huy, "Viet Nam truoc chu truong cua Trung Quoc doi voi Bien Dong," *Tuan Viet Nam*, 11 January 2009. Online. Available HTTP: <http://tuanvietnam.net/2009–01–11-viet-nam-truoc-chu-truong-cua-trung-quoc-doi-voi-bien-dong> (accessed 20 July 2014).

36 "Vietnam PM Warns of Olympics Torch Relay Disruptions," *Reuters*, 20 April 2008.

37 G. Torode, "The Closer to China, the Cooler It Becomes," *South China Morning Post*, 26 September 2009.

38 C.A. Thayer, "Political Legitimacy of Vietnam's One Party-State: Challenges and Responses," *Journal of Current Southeast Asian Affairs* 4, 2009, p.58.

39 V.V. Thanh, "Can khoi day y thuc giu gin bien dao cua cha ong," *Tuoi Tre*, 23 March 2009. Online. Available HTTP: <http://tuoitre.vn/Chinh-tri-Xa-hoi/307537/can-khoi-day-y-thuc-giu-gin-bien-dao-cua-cha-ong.html#ad-image-1> (accessed 27 July 2014).

40 Phieu and Huy, "Viet Nam truoc chu truong cua Trung Quoc doi voi Bien Dong."

41 Doan Trang, "Cuoc chien khong can suc giua hoc gia VN va TQ," *Tuan Viet Nam*, 11 March 2009.

42 Doan Trang, "Van de Truong Sa-Hoang Sa: Can mot no luc tong hop," *Tuan Viet Nam*, 7 December 2008.

43 Ibid.

44 Instruction No.65 HD/BTGTW, titled "Instruction on Propaganda on the Sea and Island Issues in 2009," dated 28 November 2008 by Communist Party of Vietnam's Central Commission for Publicity and Education.

45 Huong Giang, "Giao duc nhan dan neu cao y thuc bao ve chu quyen, lanh tho quoc gia," *Thanh Nien*, 22 March 2009. Online. Available HTTP: <www.thanhnien.com.vn/news1/pages/200912/20090322005039.aspx> (accessed 31 July 2014).

46 "To chuc 'Tuan le bien va hai dao Viet Nam'," *Tap chi Cong san*, 26 May 2009.

47 "VN day manh tuyen truyen bien dao," *BBC Tieng Viet*, 11 November 2009.

48 A simple Google search of "Huong ve bien dao que huong" exposed a long list of contests and competitions held by various party and state agencies, universities, youth unions, and popular organisations under the Fatherland Front.

49 See Instruction No.65 HD/BTGTW, titled "Instruction on Propaganda on the Sea and Island Issues in 2009," dated 28 November 2008 by Communist Party of Vietnam's Central Commission for Publicity and Education.

50 "Chu quyen Bien dao vao De thi," *BBC Tieng Viet*, 3 June 2012. Online. Available HTTP: <www.bbc.co.uk/vietnamese/vietnam/2012/06/120603_geography_graduation_question.shtml> (accessed 27 July 2014).

51 Khiet Hung, "Tien ra khai thac 'mat tien' bien," *Tuoi Tre*, 1 June 2009. Online. Available HTTP: <http://tuoitre.vn/Chinh-tri-Xa-hoi/319257/tien-ra-khai-thac-mat-tien-bien.html#ad-image-0> (accessed 28 July 2014) (emphasis added).

52 "Vietnam 'coi trong' thong tin lanh hai," *BBC Tieng Viet*, 23 March 2009.

53 T.C. Truc, "Khong the banh truong 80% dien tich Bien Dong," *Tuan Viet Nam*, 13 June 2009. Online. Available HTTP: <www.tuanvietnam.net/khong-the-banh-truong-

80-phan-tram-dien-tich-bien-dong> (accessed 9 July 2014); Quoc Phap, "Ban do 'duong luoi bo' tren Bien Dong: Duong yeu sach phi ly cua Trung Quoc," *Thanh Nien*, 18 August 2009. Online. Available HTTP: <www.thanhnien.com.vn/news1/pages/200934/20090818003413.aspx> (accessed 9 July 2014); Quoc Phap, "Truoc yeu sach 80% dien tich Bien Dong cua Trung Quoc: Khong chap nhan duong luoi bo," *Tuoi Tre*, 18 August 2009. Online. Available HTTP: <http://tuoitre.vn/Chinh-tri-Xa-hoi/332309/truoc-yeu-sach-80-dien-tich-bien-dong-cua-trung-quoc—khong-chap-nhan-duong-luoi-bo.html> (accessed 9 July 2014).

54 N. Luu, "Nhung viec lam di nguoc tinh huu ngh," *Cong an Nhan dan*, 1 July 2009. Online. Available HTTP: <www.cand.com.vn/vi-VN/thoisu/2009/7/115633.cand> (accessed 9 July 2014).

55 Huong Giang, "Giao duc nhan dan neu cao y thuc bao ve chu quyen, lanh tho quoc gia," *Thanh Nien*, 22 March 2009.

56 T. Du, "Bien Dong va Chien luoc Dieu hau cua Trung Quoc," *Tuan Viet Nam*, 6 December 2008. Online. Available HTTP: <www.viet-studies.info/kinhte/BienDong_DuTran_VNN.htm> (accessed 27 July 2014).

57 "Bao Du lich bi dinh ban," *BBC Tieng Viet*, 15 April 2009.

58 J. Bellaqua, "The China Factor in US-Vietnam Relations," *CNA Analysis & Solutions*, March 2012, p.23.

59 Phieu and Huy, "Viet Nam truoc chu truong cua Trung Quoc doi voi Bien Dong."

60 Doan Trang, "Cuoc chien khong can suc giua hoc gia VN va TQ."

61 Phieu and Huy, "Viet Nam truoc chu truong cua Trung Quoc doi voi Bien Dong."

62 I. Townsend-Gault, "Preventive Diplomacy and Pro-Activity in the South China Sea," *Contemporary Southeast Asia* 20, no. 2, 1998, pp. 182–7.

63 "Bao Trung Quoc: Viet Nam dang 'quoc te hoa' van de Bien Dong," *VOA Tieng Viet*, 2 March 2010.

64 "Vietnamese Citizens Protest National Geographic Mapping Error," *Thanh Nien News*, 2 March 2010. Online. Available HTTP: <www.thanhniennews.com/politics/vietnamese-citizens-protest-national-geographic-mapping-error-17482.html> (accessed 31 July 2014).

65 L. V. Ut, "Google Maps can go bo 'duong luoi bo'," *Thanh Nien*, 16 October 2011.

66 L. V. Ut, "Thuyet phuc Science dang thu phan doi duong luoi bo the nao?," *Tia Sang*, 4 January 2012.

67 N. D. Hung, "Tap chi Nature se noi khong voi ban do luoi bo," *Tuan Viet Nam*, 22 October 2011 (emphasis added).

68 D. Cyranoski, "Angry Words over East Asian Seas," *Nature* 478, no. 20, 2011, p.293.

69 "Uncharted Territory," *Nature*, 478, 20 October 2011, p.285.

70 J. Goldrick and J. McCaffrie, *Navies in South-East Asia: A Comparative Study*, London and New York: Routledge, 2013, p.208.

71 C.A. Thayer, "Vietnam's People Army: Development and Modernisation," *Research Monograph*, 30 April 2009, pp. 12–4.

72 J. Goldrick and J. McCaffrie, *Navies in South-East Asia: A Comparative Study*, p.208.

73 "Nga giao ten lua phong thu cho Viet Nam," *BBC Tieng Viet*, 19 October 2011. Online. Available HTTP: <www.bbc.co.uk/vietnamese/vietnam/2011/10/111019_russia_missiles.shtml> (accessed 20 September 2013).

74 I. Zarembo, "Russia Floats out Second Gepard Class Frigate for Vietnam," *RIA Novosti*, 16 March 2010. Online. Available HTTP: <http://en.ria.ru/military_news/20100316/158215375.html> (accessed 20 September 2013).

75 Thayer, "Vietnam's People Army," pp. 14–7.

76 Ibid.

77 G. Torode, "Vietnam Set to Buy 6 Russian Submarines," *South China Morning Post*, Hong Kong, 28 April 2009.

78 C.A. Thayer, "Russian Subs in Vietnam," *USNI News*, 20 August 2012.

79 I. Timberlake, "Vietnam Aims to Counter China with Sub Deal: Analysts," *AFP*, 17 December 2009.

80 "Vietnamese Navy Orders DH-6 Twin-Otter 400s," *Defence Industry Daily*, 8 September 2013. Online. Available HTTP: <www.defenseindustrydaily.com/vietnamese-navy-orders-dhc-6-twin-otter-400s-06373> (accessed 20 September 2013).
81 R. Karniol, "Vietnam Bolstering Spratly Firepower," *Strait Times*, 10 May 2010.
82 "Russia Sells Second Batch of Gepard-Class Frigates to Vietnam," *Naval Today*, 8 December 2011. Online. Available HTTP: <http://navaltoday.com/2011/12/08/russia-sells-second-batch-of-gepard-class-frigates-to-vietnam> (accessed 21 September 2013).
83 "VN dam phan mua 4 tau chien cua Ha Lan," *BBC Tieng Viet*, 18 October 2011. Online. Available HTTP: <www.bbc.co.uk/vietnamese/vietnam/2011/10/111018_sigma_corvettes.shtml> (accessed 20 September 2013).
84 J. Grevatt, "Vietnam Signs Deal with Russia to Procure Su-30MK2s," *IHS Jane's Defence Industry*, 21 August 2013.
85 "Hien tai hoa quan doi khong phai la chay dua vu trang," *Vnexpress*, 8 December 2010. Online. Available HTTP: <http://vnexpress.net/tin-tuc/thoi-su/hien-dai-hoa-quan-doi-khong-phai-la-chay-dua-vu-trang-2152907.html> (accessed 23 September 2013).
86 Thayer, "Russian Subs in Vietnam."
87 D. Lague, "China Airs Ambition to Beef Up Naval Power," *International Herald Tribune*, 28 December 2006.
88 "Beijing Cashes in Prosperity in Massive Boost to Military Spending," *AFP*, 4 March 2007.
89 "An Underwater Threat," *Newsweek*, 10 May 2008.
90 "Chinese Nuclear Submarine Base," *Telegraph*, 1 May 2008.
91 C.A. Thayer, "The Structure of Vietnam-China Relations, 1991–2008," paper presented at the *3rd International Conference on Vietnamese Studies*, Hanoi, 4–7 December 2008, p.25.
92 "China Has Aircraft Carrier Hopes," *BBC*, 17 November 2008. Online. Available HTTP: <http://news.bbc.co.uk/2/hi/asia-pacific/7732679.stm> (accessed 30 September 2013).
93 "The Submarine Race in Asia," *New York Times*, 7 January 2014.
94 P. Parameswaran, "Indonesia to Buy New Submarines from Russia," *Diplomat*, 25 September 2015.
95 Thayer, "Russian Subs in Vietnam."
96 G. Torode, "Vietnam set to buy 6 Russian submarines," *South China Morning Post*, 28 April 2009.
97 J.R. Holmes, "Vietnam's Undersea Anti-Access Fleet," *Diplomat*, 1 November 2012. Online. Available HTTP: <http://thediplomat.com/2012/11/vietnams-undersea-anti-access-fleet> (accessed 1 November 2013).
98 L.N. Thong, "Muc tieu cua Tau ngam Viet Nam tren Bien Dong," *Dat Viet*, 19 December 2013. Online. Available HTTP: <http://baodatviet.vn/quoc-phong/quoc-phong-viet-nam/muc-tieu-cua-tau-ngam-viet-nam-tren-bien-dong-2362421/> (accessed 18 December 2013).

7 Internationalising the South China Sea issue, 2009–2011

In the mid-2000s, while the world hailed Beijing's message of "peaceful development," Hanoi increasingly felt resentful of what they called China's unlawful claim and assertive behaviour in the South China Sea. Nationalist elites in Vietnam believed that China deliberately used its military and economic might to thwart Vietnam's legitimate maritime rights. Even worse, Vietnam was basically left alone in front of China's realpolitik spearhead. As the appeal to socialist solidarity fell on China's deaf ears, the political elites gradually forged a consensus on more nationalist approach to the South China Sea dispute to refute China's claims and actions and mobilise domestic and international support to defend its case in the South China Sea. The year 2009 proved to be a turning point as the South China Sea started capturing international headlines after Chinese fishing and paramilitary ships' harassment of the US Navy ship, the USNS *Impeccable*, in March 2009. The incident was portrayed as the sign of increased geopolitical rivalry between rising China and the United States for primacy in the Asia-Pacific region. Hanoi noticeably seized such an opportunity to internationalise the South China Sea issue with hope that greater involvement of external powers and international scrutiny would force China to match its actions with its words.

Vietnam's formal claim to extended continental shelves, May 2009

Vietnam presented its legal case by tabling a submission, jointly with Malaysia, on the extended continental shelf in the southern coastline, to the Commission on the Limits of the Continental Shelf (CLCS) on 6 May 2009 and a partial report for its northern coastline on the next day.[1] The combination of these reports provided precise coordinates for the limits of Vietnam's EEZ and its extended continental shelf beyond 200 n.m. as measured from the baseline of its mainland coastline. Notably, no EEZ or continental shelf was delimited in Vietnam's submissions for the Spratly and Paracel features. It is another indication that Vietnam would view the South China Sea offshore islands as rocks that were not entitled to EEZs and continental shelves, or may have very limited weight in maritime delimitation. Otherwise, it should be included in the CLCS's work.[2] Vietnam's leading legal expert Nguyen Hong Thao opined that Vietnam, Malaysia and other ASEAN claimants seemed to agree that almost all disputed features are entitled to only a territorial sea.[3] The 2012 Law of the Sea of Vietnam made it clearer that the islands claimed by Vietnam fall under the purview of Article 121 of UNCLOS. The Vietnamese law specifies that insular formations that can sustain human habitation and have an economic life of their own are entitled to an EEZ or continental shelf of their own while rocks, which do not meet these criteria, are not.[4]

One Vietnamese official argued that the CLCS submission is a normal, legitimate means of the coastal states to assert its rights granted by UNCLOS.[5] It was said that its CLCS action was decided and prepared for almost a decade in advance to meet the deadline of 13 May 2009 set by the United Nations. Vietnam persistently conducted costly surveys to collect data, though China protested and dispatched ships to obstruct the work.[6] However, the Rules of Procedure of the CLCS provided that if there is a land or maritime dispute, "the Commission shall not consider and qualify a submission made by any of the states concerned in the dispute."[7] Undoubtedly, the Vietnamese must have anticipated China's protests that would disqualify their reports. In the context of China's quiet assertiveness against Vietnam's actions to explore and exploit resources within its EEZ, Vietnam's CLCS move could also be viewed as an initiative to clarify, and reassert, its maritime rights in terms of UNCLOS to gain the support of the international community. In this way, Vietnam's tenacious efforts might be seen as an attempt to defend the relevance and integrity of UNCLOS in defining maritime entitlements in the South China Sea region.

The submissions, together with other maritime boundary delimitation agreements that Vietnam signed with China, Indonesia, Malaysia and Thailand, represented consistent efforts on the part of Vietnam to align its maritime claims to the spirit and letter of UNCLOS. It was clear that Vietnam delineated the boundaries of its EEZ and extended the continental shelf in the central and southern coast in conformity with the rules established by UNCLOS. The only missing patch in the map of Vietnam's claim was the area beyond the Gulf of Tonkin and to the west of the Paracels. Currently, Vietnam and China are negotiating to delimit this area. Vietnam also redrew the map of its petroleum activities in a way more consistent with its adjusted claims. In the map, published by PetroVietnam in April 2011, all petroleum concession blocks are located within the continental shelves measured from the baseline of its mainland coast.

The joint submission by Vietnam and Malaysia and the partial submission by Vietnam forced China to clarify its position. Beijing sent two *notes verbales* to the CLCS on 7 May 2009. It was a surprise to legal experts that in these documents, besides disputing positions by Vietnam and Malaysia, China attached dash line maps to these *notes verbales* (see Figure 2.13). By this action China had for the first time admitted that the nine-dash line was somehow part of its claim in the South China Sea. It should be noted that the first cartographic, with eleven dashes, was produced by the Department of the Territories and Boundaries of the Ministry of Interior of the Republic of China in December 1946.[8] After defeating the Kuomintang, the Chinese communists continued to circulate the drawing without any formal clarifications. In 1953, two dashes in the Gulf of Tonkin were removed. China's first statement of interest in the South China Sea, the Declaration on Territorial Sea on 4 September 1958, made no mention to this broken line. The worst scenario for the Vietnamese was China claimed "historical rights"[9] in terms of the nine-dash claim. "Historical rights" was first officially mentioned in China's Act on Exclusive Economic Zone and Continental Shelf promulgated on 26 June 1998. Article 14 of the Act says China's claims to EEZs and continental shelves as specified in the legal document "shall not affect the 'historic rights' of the People's Republic of China."[10] One Vietnamese analyst clearly suspected that China's "historical rights" as mentioned in Article 14 would imply "other interests that China has claimed, such as the traditional rights of fishing in maritime zones of other countries, and the broken line claiming over 80 per cent of area of the South China Sea."[11] As a result, Hanoi lodged an objection to China's 1998 act, particularly refuting so-called historical interests that were beyond the bounds of UNCLOS.[12]

There had been no direct references to the nine-dash line in China's official documents before May 2009. However, the aforementioned *notes verbales* failed to clarify the nature of the nine-dash line and the status of the waters within. These documents state:

> China has indisputable sovereignty over the islands in the South China Sea and the *adjacent waters*, and enjoys sovereign rights and jurisdiction over the *relevant waters* as well as the seabed and subsoil thereof.[13]

Some legal analysts maintained that this statement contained many ambiguities that could not be consistently explained by UNCLOS. In other words, China's official publication of the nine-dash line map put it at odds with UNCLOS.[14] As Beijing surely knew about Hanoi's resolve to submit its claim to extended continental shelf before the deadline, China's nine-dash line ultimatum was a calculated move to inform its neighbours that UNCLOS is not the only basis for China's claim.[15] There were also different explanations for the nature of the nine-dash line, though none of them was official. Beijing obviously resisted any calls for clarification of the nature of the nine-dash line claim. In response to China's *notes verbales*, Vietnam stated that China's claim as manifested in the dash-line map is null and void, as it "has no legal, historical or factual basis."[16] China's nine-dash line claim was also challenged by Malaysia, the Philippines and Indonesia.

Tensions escalated among South China Sea claimants after the exchange of protests at the CLCS. As events unfolded, it was clear that China tried to translate the nine-dash line claim into de facto control of a large portion of the South China Sea.[17] A Vietnamese source confirmed that Chinese paramilitary vessels, mostly those of the Chinese Fisheries Administration and State Oceanographic Administration, increased the frequency of patrols and intensified the harassment and arrest of non-Chinese fishermen in the vast swathe of waters inside the nine-dash line since May 2009.[18] As noted in the previous chapter, a row over fishing between Vietnam and China had emerged since 2005 and tensions reached a high point in 2009. In this year, Chinese law enforcement forces detained thirty-three fishing boats and 433 fishermen of Quang Ngai Province for ransom.[19] These figures accounted for half of the arrests between 2005 and 2010.[20] On one single day, on 29 September 2009, China seized nineteen fishing vessels and 259 fishermen from Vietnam.[21] Though being arrested by other littoral states in the region as well, the Vietnamese fishermen felt especially aggrieved at China's ill-treatment of the arrestees. These fishermen reported that the Chinese captors not only confiscated all catches, but also damaged their boats, and demanded very high ransoms for their release.[22] According to Vietnamese media reports, between May 2008 and July 2010, at least six Vietnamese fishing trawlers were sunk by "unknown boats" (*tàu lạ*), which were suspected to be Chinese vessels.[23] It is possible that Vietnam's government-censored media used "unknown boats," as instructed, to avoid offending China.[24]

In May 2009, Beijing began to extend its unilateral fishing ban, which covers the northern part of the South China Sea (above the 12th parallel), from one month to three months between 15 May and 1 August. This duration concurred with the high fishing season for Vietnamese fishermen. As part of the plan, China deployed eight modern fishery administration vessels to "curb illegal fishing" in "the waters of China's exclusive economic zones, including the Nansha, Xisha and Zhongsha Islands."[25] The biggest Chinese fishery administration vessel, the Yuzheng 311, was also dispatched to the region. These vessels were mostly big, well-equipped, and capable craft, which were originally naval ships and were renovated for the purpose of fishery patrols.[26] Vietnamese fishermen complained that they were harassed and arrested by Chinese law enforcement forces even outside the area defined by the Chinese ban.[27] Since 2008, the China Marine Surveillance (CMS) force was tasked with regular patrols in the area that was deemed as "Chinese waters." It was reported that the CMS patrol reached as far as James Shoal, which is 50 n.m. off Sarawak on Borneo Island and 1,100 n.m. from the Chinese mainland. In April 2010, the CMS ship planted a sovereign marker on the shoal.[28] The Vietnamese sources also revealed that Chinese vessels often engaged in dangerous manoeuvring in circling around the Vietnamese ships with uncovered cannons and Chinese aircraft flying low to intimidate them.[29]

These South China Sea developments raised thorny questions about the rationale behind China's dramatic shift from charm offensive to assertiveness, its maritime strategy, and the nature of the nine-dash line claim. The lack of reliable data in China's decision-making gave rise to a number of hypotheses. Some scholars believed that China was confident about flexing its might in the South China Sea because it perceived that the power equation was tipping in its favour after the global financial crisis (2007–2008). Besides, a thirst for energy had driven China to take a more assertive stance in the South China Sea, which was widely believed in China to be its "Persian Gulf."[30] Chinese analysts often argued that China's assertiveness is of a passive nature as China mostly reacted to other smaller claimants' "provocations," particularly Vietnam's oil exploration activities, the Philippines' new baseline law, and Vietnam and Malaysia's CLCS submissions, or even the collusion of these countries with the United States.[31] Li Mingjiang believed that China was engaged in a non-confrontational assertiveness in the seas around China, which meant China would not initiate a fight, but if other claimants encroached on China's interest, it would respond forcefully.[32] In the same vein, You Ji held that Beijing was employing a "one-plus strategy." The idea was that if other claimants take one step against China's interest, China would take "one plus" steps to pre-empt other claimants' will to antagonise China.[33] The third major line of argument focused on China's domestic politics. It was argued that China did not have a coherent maritime strategy and a centralised body to govern all maritime agencies. As a result, these Chinese agencies, in a competition for resources, became more active in defending the country's interests in its southern maritime domain.[34]

Many observers blamed China's assertiveness for Vietnam and Malaysia's CLCS initiatives. From the Vietnamese perspective, China's assertive practices, such as patrols, harassment of non-Chinese fishermen, and interference with oil activities by other countries in the vast swathe of waters within the nine-dash line, predated the submission of the nine-dash line map to the CLCS. The difference was that after the war of words at the CLCS, China carried out the same sort of activity in a more overt and straightforward manner and with a higher level of frequency and rigor, resulting in many more encounters and incidents since 2009. It was clear that this policy dynamic was set off long before 2009 with China's efforts to build up the People's Liberation Army Navy (PLAN) Southern Fleet, China Fishery Administration, China Maritime Surveillance and other law enforcement agencies. In this light, the CLCS submissions provided the pretext for China to increase the intensity of its undertakings and expand its presence in the South China Sea. It was also argued that China was in a process of fundamentally changing to a more active and assertive geopolitical posture, no longer "biding its time and hiding its capabilities" as instructed by former Chinese leader Deng Xiaoping.[35] One Vietnamese analyst maintained that China became more confident to flex its muscles because it assumed that the US, as a declining power, was unwilling to intervene forcefully into regional affairs.[36] It should be recalled that during the Taiwan Strait crisis in 1995–1996, the Clinton administration responded strongly, sending two aircraft carrier battle groups to the region as a show of might to deter Chinese aggressive actions. This time Hanoi expected that Washington would have strong statements and actions against China's coercive measures.

China's unconcealed disregard of UNCLOS and aggressive posture pushed the Vietnamese leadership into two dilemmas. First, Vietnam had to stand firm before China's assertive actions but in a way that is least detrimental to its bilateral relations. Second, Hanoi felt the need to protect its fishermen and support them at sea to bolster the Vietnamese claim, but it had no capability to challenge Chinese civilian and military power at sea. The number of fishing incidents rose up partly because Vietnam, as well as other coastal states, defied China's unilateral ban. In spite of China's heavy-handedness, the Vietnam Fishery Association kept encouraging their fishermen to sail off for the purpose of "both doing business as usual and asserting Vietnam's sovereignty and jurisdiction."[37] When the fishing boats were captured, Hanoi issued protests through the statement of the MOFA spokespersons and diplomatic notes, and worked through bilateral channels with Chinese authorities to secure their release. As Hanoi became more anxious, the

Chinese Ambassador Ton Quoc Tuong (Sun Guoxiang) came to an interview with *Vietnamnet*, a popular online news outlet in Vietnam, to assuage the Vietnamese. Interestingly, he framed the strains as "a quarrel in the family," or "a problem between brothers" and advised the Vietnamese to wait for "the *ripe* time." Through this framing, Ton Quoc Tuong clearly discouraged Vietnam from seeking intervention from outsiders. He added,

> To resolve the disputes, it is better that two sides should be firstly based on the *common cause* (*dai cuc*), *general state of affairs* (*toan cuc*), and the *shared interests* of the two nations, and move forward with shelving disputes without affecting the normal and positive evolution of the two countries' relationship.[38]

He also applauded the Chinese leaders' proposal for "shelving disputes for joint development" as the only viable and realistic step pending final resolution in the South China Sea.[39]

The Vietnamese nationalist leaders obviously found it hard to swallow the Chinese metaphor of "a quarrel in the family" and to stay indifferent to China's vigorous expansion in the South China Sea. In their view, bilateralism alone did not help since the Chinese made use of it "to beat Vietnam under the blanket."[40] This resentful sentiment was privately echoed in various places. One Vietnamese military officer said, "We (Vietnam and China) take a lot more steps together now, but when we look at our footprints, we sometimes see it has been nothing but a crazy dance into a corner."[41] With regards to China-backed proposal of joint development, one Vietnamese analyst bluntly pronounced that it was the way China maximised the disputed zones and forced other claimants to accept China's sovereignty over the islands and its unreasonable nine-dash line claim.[42] Tran Truong Thuy, a research fellow at the Diplomatic Academy of Vietnam, summed up China's joint development concept by a saying: "what is mine is mine, what is yours is mine and we are willing to share."[43] Consequently, Hanoi became more active in seeking political support from other countries and in strengthening its defence capabilities. In addition, Vietnam tried to bring the South China Sea case to international public scrutiny as a way to delegitimise the Chinese claim and actions.

Facilitating South China Sea discussions in regional forums

Since early 2009, the South China Sea came under the spotlight of the international media as tensions involved the United States. It was reported that the US surveillance ship, the USNS *Impeccable*, was confronted by a group of five Chinese vessels, both military and law enforcement ships, in the area about 75 n.m. south of Hainan Island.[44] The *Impeccable* was undertaking the mission of collecting data about the Yulin base and Chinese submarines. The Chinese were clearly uncomfortable with the operation of the US surveillance ship near their critical naval base. In the Chinese view, intelligence data gathering within the EEZ of a coastal country was illegal. On the contrary, the US holds that it has a right to conduct military activities in the EEZ of other coastal states. US officials accused that the Chinese ships "aggressively manoeuvred around the *Impeccable* in "international waters."[45] The incident showed that the US and China had different views about the rights of foreign naval vessels in the EEZs of the coastal state. Interestingly, the location of the face-off was nearer to the coast of Vietnam than China.[46] Like China, Vietnam long expressed concerns about military activities of foreign warships within its EEZs. However, Vietnamese officials refrained from making official comments on the *Impeccable* incident. Instead, one Vietnamese analyst even argued publicly that Vietnam should not side with China, but should support international practices (implying military activities within the coastal state's EEZ) because the US was not a threat to Vietnam's territorial integrity and independence. He also argued that China would use the nine-dash line claim to intrude on Vietnam's EEZ anyway and it is likely that China would turn the waters within the nine-dash line into its exclusive military zone. In this vein, the presence of the US military ships in the South China Sea did not threaten Vietnam but helped to check the aggressive behaviour of PLA naval vessels and Chinese law enforcement vessels.[47] Right after the *Impeccable* incident, China deployed its biggest fisheries administration ship, Yuzheng 311, to the South China Sea on a mission to "protect fishing vessels around Nansha, Xisha and Zhongsha in China's southernmost maritime territories."[48]

In 2010, Vietnam took over as ASEAN chair from Thailand. After two years of engaging with the UNSC as a non-permanent member (2008–2009), Vietnam was more experienced and confident with multilateralism and was ready for the ASEAN chairmanship.[49] In August 2008, during the 41th anniversary of ASEAN, Vietnamese Prime Minister Nguyen Tan Dung asserted that Vietnam would play an active and responsible role in building the ASEAN community on the basis of the ASEAN Charter.[50] ASEAN had a "lost year" in 2009 with Thailand's chairmanship. In April 2009, the ASEAN Summit was disrupted by thousands of Red Shirt protesters who broke into the venue in Pattaya.[51] As noted earlier, the discussion on the guidelines to the DOC in this year effectively stalled and Thailand did little to help the process. Consequently, no progress was made in terms of implementing confidence-building measures as proposed in the DOC.[52] As the South China Sea was stirred up, in a press conference on 30 December 2009, Vietnamese Deputy Prime Minister cum Foreign Minister Pham Gia Khiem made it clear that maritime boundaries will be one of the priorities of Vietnam in 2010.[53]

The first half of 2010 witnessed China's continued projection of power into the South China Sea. A Vietnamese source made it known that during the first three months of 2010, thirty boats and 200 fishermen of Vietnam were assaulted and seized mostly by the Chinese authorities.[54] News about Chinese attacks on Vietnamese fishermen appeared more frequently in the Vietnamese media, rousing a broad-based criticism of China's maritime aggression.[55] At the same time, it was reported that Chinese fishing vessels, escorted by fishery administration ships, intruded more often, with a larger number, and deeper into Vietnam's territorial seas off Da Nang and Thua Thien Hue, and the Spratly and Paracel areas.[56] The expanded presence of Chinese fishing fleets and law enforcement vessels rang alarm bells in Hanoi about China's hegemonic behaviour in disregard of its commitment to "neighbourly friendship" and to the DOC.[57] In March 2010, China sent the Yuzheng 311 and Patrol Boat 202 for regular patrols and the protection of Chinese fishing vessels in the Spratly region. On 26 April, China announced the deployment of the Yuzheng 301 and 302 to replace the Yuzheng 311 and Patrol Boat 202.[58] On 29 April, China again announced a unilateral fishing ban, taking effect from 16 May to 1 August in the northern part of the South China Sea. The announcements were made on the eve of the visit of Vietnam's Prime Minister Nguyen Tan Dung to China to attend the Shanghai Expo where he met Chinese President Hu Jintao. About one week before, the Joint Working Group on the implementation of the DOC was convened in Hanoi. At the same time, Vietnam's Minister of Defence Phung Quang Thanh paid a visit to China for discussing military cooperation between the two countries. Vietnamese officials apparently made use of various bilateral talks to raise their concerns to the Chinese authorities.[59] However, Beijing was no longer sensitive or paid attention to Hanoi's anxieties.

On 23 April 2010, the *New York Times* reported that Chinese senior officials told their US counterparts in a private meeting that the South China Sea was now regarded as part of China's "core interests."[60] The Chinese usually applied the label of "core interest" to Taiwan and Tibet, implying there was no room for external intervention or negotiation. The article was translated into Vietnamese and published in *Vnexpress*, Vietnam's most popular online newspaper.[61] The Chinese assertion of "core interest" in the South China Sea allegedly appeared in the 2nd US-China Strategic and Economic Dialogue in Beijing on 24–25 May 2010.[62] These narratives sparked fear in Vietnam, as well as other regional countries, that China was developing a Monroe Doctrine in the South China Sea. In spite of inquiries and speculations, Beijing chose to keep silent, neither confirming nor denying the account. As a matter of fact, China's vigorous naval and maritime expansions spoke louder than words. The construction of the Yulin Naval Base in Sanya reinforced the PLAN's Southern Sea Fleet with greater undersea and surface capabilities, especially the deployment of Jin-class nuclear submarines and amphibious landing craft.[63] In April 2010, China launched a high-profile military drill with the involvement of warships from PLAN's North Sea, South China Sea, and South Sea fleets. In the eyes of military analysts, the drill was "unprecedented in its reach and scope" and an indication of Chinese acquisition of "higher level of operational flexibility in the simultaneous deployment of underwater, surface and air assets."[64] More often than before, Chinese strategists also expressed a strong intent to seek "active defence" and "far sea defence" beyond the first island chain.[65] Chinese warships were seen further in the Western Pacific, Indian Ocean, and Gulf of Aden either for drills or counter-piracy missions. Though these Chinese naval operations were not enough to pose a significant challenge to US dominance, they were a great source of concern to the middle and small powers in the region. China's naval build-up and doctrine of "active defence" were not seen as "defensive" in the Vietnamese eyes.

As the first to bear the brunt of China's growing power, Vietnam was alarmed about the fast pace of China's naval expansion. Notably, the Vietnamese were well aware of growing anti-Vietnam voices in the Chinese media, both in state-sponsored outlets and blogospheres by netizens.[66] Some Chinese extremist commentators even called for the use of force to subdue Vietnam and to scare other claimants and the US.[67] The worrisome point was that these opinions were permitted in China's strictly censured broadcasts. Inside Vietnam and among overseas Vietnamese communities, popular anger against China surged. Internet spaces were flooded with hostilities against China's behaviour and calls to "stand up for our sovereignty" and face the threats from across the northern borders. Under growing public pressure, the Vietnamese leadership appeared stronger and more determined to defend Vietnamese claims. On 1 April, State President of Vietnam Nguyen Minh Triet made a highly symbolic trip to Bach Long Vi to proclaim,

> Vietnam would not let any one infringe our territory, our sea and islands . . . We are not greedy to ask for what belongs to others while we will not give up an inch of our motherland.[68]

In an incident, Vietnamese fishing trawlers grouped together to challenge Chinese fishing craft and fishery administration vessels. When Chinese naval ships were called to the spot, all Vietnamese craft were gone. This spontaneous nature of the outbreak indicated that resentment among Vietnamese fishing community against Chinese repression ran deep and reached a dangerous level. The repeated incidents of assaults on Vietnamese fishing ships prompted a fierce debate in Vietnam on whether to arm fishermen as maritime self-defence militias in late 2009.[69] Despite being criticised as risky and dangerous, the idea was implemented tentatively with the establishment of two maritime militia platoons in Khanh Hoa in May 2012.[70] Clearly, this measure in no way challenged the domination of the Chinese maritime forces at sea.

The main thrust of Vietnam's hedging strategy in the South China Sea lay in its diplomatic bid to mobilise international support to disrupt China's resolve to exercise its power. To this end, Hanoi worked to expose legal weaknesses of China's claim and its bullying behaviour to international public juries and to seek multilateral measures to regulate claimants' behaviour. The ASEAN chairmanship offered Hanoi a golden opportunity to internationalise the South China Sea issue. The guidelines to implement the DOC and a COC were high on the agenda. On the eve of the ASEAN meetings, a Foreign Ministry official in Hanoi indicated that the upcoming ASEAN summits would give a push for an unambiguous and more legally binding code of conduct in the South China Sea.[71] However, the meeting of the Joint Working Group on 16 and 17 April 2010, which focused discussion on "new ways to promote the effectiveness of the DOC," did not yield any concrete results. The working-level group was clearly ineffective to deal with highly politicised and contentious DOC issues.[72] One Vietnamese analyst accused China of sticking to bilateralism because it advocated for consultations with relevant parties instead of ASEAN as a bloc.[73] There was a strong desire on the part of Hanoi to seek a more viable multilateral arrangement to inhibit China's adventurous overreach.

Much diplomatic manoeuvring must have occurred behind the scenes before a series of important ASEAN-led meetings in July 2010 in Hanoi. When it was played out in the meeting rooms, there appeared a stronger and concerted disapproval of China's recent behaviour in the South China Sea. The joint communiqué of the 43rd ASEAN Foreign Minister Meeting (AMM) in Hanoi in July 2010 stated:

> We (ASEAN Foreign Ministers) underscored the need to *intensify* efforts to ensure the effective implementation of the Declaration and looked forward to the eventual conclusion of a Regional Code of Conduct in the South China Sea (COC). In this connection, we welcomed the reconvening of the Meeting of the ASEAN – China Joint Working Group on the Implementation of the DOC in April, 2010 in Ha Noi and tasked our Senior Officials to work closely with their Chinese counterparts to reconvene the ASEAN – China Senior Officials' Meeting on the DOC *at the earliest opportunity*.[74]

In response to ASEAN's call for upgrading ASEAN-China dialogue on the DOC to senior official level, China resorted to delaying tactics again. At the ASEAN-China Foreign Ministers Meeting back-to-back AMM, Chinese Foreign Minister Yang Jiechi indicated that an ASEAN-China SOM on the DOC would be convened at an "appropriate time." Later, Yang confirmed that such a meeting would be held "when the conditions are ripe."[75] No explanations or clarifications were provided. Without a doubt, ASEAN alone had little leverage with China now.

The main act was played at the 17th meeting of ASEAN Regional Forum (ARF) behind the closed-door chamber of the National Convention in Hanoi. A Vietnamese source disclosed that thirteen foreign ministers, including six from ASEAN, openly spoke about the South China Sea issue and urged progress in the DOC and the COC.[76] The keynote of ARF-17 was the well-articulated remark by US Secretary of State Hillary Clinton who clearly addressed the broader audience and not just the ARF-17's participants in the room. After the meeting, she immediately reiterated her main messages to reporters. She stated,

> The United States, like every nation, has a *national interest* in freedom of navigation, open access to Asia's maritime commons, and respect for international law in the South China Sea . . . The United States supports a collaborative diplomatic process by all claimants by resolving the various territorial disputes *without coercion*. We oppose the use or threat of force by any claimant . . . While the United States does not take sides on the competing territorial disputes over land features in the South China Sea, we believe claimants should pursue their territorial claims and accompanying rights to maritime space in accordance with the UN convention on the law of the sea. Consistent with customary international law, legitimate claims to maritime space in the South China Sea should be derived *solely from legitimate claims to land features*."[77]

As revealed in the recent memoir of Hillary Clinton, this speech was carefully worded to express US disapproval of the Chinese position and actions in the South China Sea.[78] First, the reference to US national interest in the South China Sea was an explicit counter-argument to China's "core interest," implying that the US did not accept the Chinese "Monroe Doctrine" in the maritime domain. Second, the US clearly opposed any efforts to challenge the status quo by coercion. Third, by calling upon the claimants to derive their maritime claims solely from claims to land features, Clinton implicitly disqualified China's nine-dash line claim based on the doctrine of "historic waters." Last but not least, Clinton's vocal backing for ASEAN's basic principles and her push for furthering the DOC and forming a COC was a challenge to China's delaying tactic and its lip-service support of these initiatives. In short, Clinton's statement on the South China Sea largely pleased the ASEAN claimants while seriously angering Chinese representatives. Reportedly, Chinese Foreign Minister Yang Jiechi became angry at Clinton's initiative, which he called a pre-planned "attack on China." In response, he made a long and emotional remark, defending the appropriateness of bilateralism. He argued that internationalising or multilateralising the South China Sea issue would only "make the matter worse and the resolution more difficult."[79] Chinese media came up with a roar of rebukes against Clinton's intervention at the ARF, blaming her for driving a wedge between China and its ASEAN neighbours.

This debate over the South China Sea dispute was clearly an unprecedented development in the ARF. Before, ASEAN states were reluctant to raise the South China Sea issue at this forum as China repeatedly warned against any act of internationalising the issue. It should be noted that at the ASEAN-China Foreign Ministers Meeting prior to the historic ARF meeting, only the Philippine foreign minister brought up the South China Sea issue. Veteran Asia watcher Barry Wain revealed that US officials informed other ARF participants of Clinton's intention and asked them for support. China also knew the US's plan and worked behind the scenes to dissuade these ASEAN countries from joining the US.[80] If that was true, Chinese participants were perhaps shocked by the fact that six ASEAN countries, including four claimants (Brunei, Malaysia, the Philippines and Vietnam) and two non-claimants (Singapore and Indonesia), overtly disregarded China's demand. Yang also conveyed a subtle threat to Asian neighbours, stating, "China is a big country, bigger than any other countries here."[81] In the Vietnamese view, raising the South China Sea issue in regional forums and involving other powers would make it one of the central concerns in China's foreign relations, forcing China to back down from its unilateralism. It was expected that once the South China Sea issue becomes a priority of China's foreign policy, its decision-making would become much more centralised and competition among different agencies, which was deemed as one of the main reasons that China's renewed assertiveness since 2007 would come under greater control.[82] Consequently, for a quite a while, Hanoi repeatedly urged Washington to respond forcefully to China's strident assertiveness. At the ARF meeting, Vietnamese Foreign Minister Pham Gia Khiem kick-started the discussion and then gave the floor for other participants to speak on the South China Sea issue. The Vietnamese officials were satisfied with Clinton's remarks and what played out at the ARF arena.[83] China was largely isolated at the meeting.

Beijing's persistent heavy-handedness prompted a stronger interest on the part of Vietnam in hedging against more aggressive China in the future. To do so, Hanoi reached out to *other* powers, especially the US. As noted in Chapter 6, nationalist leaders, particularly the Prime Minister Nguyen Tan Dung and his deputy, Pham Gia Khiem, had a large amount of control over foreign and security policy. In the face of China's assertiveness, they increasingly viewed the US as the only player that could restrain Chinese military power. The presence of the US military in the region was in effect a check on Chinese expansionism. Besides, the United States had a broad network of alliances and partnerships in the region and any changes in its policy would have significant impacts on its allies and partners. Therefore, if Vietnam successfully got the US involved in managing Chinese behaviour in the South China Sea, its allies and partners would be likely to get on board.[84] Additionally, if the United States were involved, the South China Sea would always be under the spotlight of international media.

Clinton's speech at ARF-17 had a strong effect of drawing attention from international public, media, and academia on the South China Sea. Following this logic, Hanoi invested much of its diplomatic effort in engaging Washington strategically, downplaying differences in human rights and democracy. Since 2007, Vietnamese officials repeatedly asked their US counterparts to pay more attention to the East Asia and particularly to dissuade the US companies from dropping their projects in the waters offshore Vietnam. According to Carlyle A. Thayer, Vietnamese leaders gradually increased their engagement with Washington. In June 2008, Vietnam moved to lift its strategic dialogue with the US to the deputy minister level before doing the same with China. Generally, China was the first priority in Vietnam's foreign affairs hierarchy. The dialogue was clearly an important channel for Hanoi to express its concerns directly to Washington. In 2009, Vietnam declared that it would open commercial service facilities at Cam Ranh Bay to navies from any country. The US was the first and also the most frequent client to have its auxiliary ships (not warships) repaired at Cam Ranh Bay.

Security cooperation between Hanoi and Washington stepped up since both sides found their security interests converged in the context of China's growing assertiveness. As agreed during Prime Minister Nguyen Tan Dung's visit to the US in June 2008, the two sides inaugurated their first Political, Security and Defence Dialogue in Washington in October 2008. For its part, Washington was alarmed by the *Impeccable* incident in March 2009 when the US intelligence data gathering vessel was harassed by Chinese civilian ships. The Subcommittee on South China Sea and Pacific Affairs of the US Senate Committee on Foreign Relations held a hearing on territorial disputes and sovereignty issues in the East Asia in July 2009. At the hearing, Deputy Assistant Secretary of State Scot Marciel reaffirmed that the United States has "a vital interest in maintaining stability, freedom of navigation, and *the right to lawful commercial activity in East Asia's waterways*" (emphasis added). Marciel also pointedly protested against China's threats to American companies working with Vietnam to explore hydrocarbon deposits in Vietnam's EEZ.[85]

Deputy Assistant Secretary of Defence for South and Southeast Asia Robert Scher saw Chinese harassment of the *Impeccable* as "a clear violation of international norms of behaviour in ocean waters outside territorial seas."[86] At the ninth

Asia Security Summit (Shangri-La Dialogue) on 4–6 June 2010, US Secretary of Defense Robert Gates referred to the South China Sea as an "area of growing concern."[87] He stressed that "the sea is not only vital to those directly bordering it, but to all nations with economic and security interests in Asia."[88] Increased American attention on the South China Sea should be put in the context of its "pivot" to Asia-Pacific or the "rebalancing" by the Obama administration. According to Clinton, one of the major rationales behind the refocus on the Asia-Pacific was to manage the rise of China. People in Capitol Hill and the White House increasingly viewed China's rise as a danger to the alliance system built around the US leadership.[89] As a result, the US administration adopted a broad-based multi-pronged strategy to consolidate its leadership position in the Asia-Pacific: (1) revitalising its alliance system; (2) developing partnerships with emerging powers; (3) negotiating the Trans-Pacific Partnership as new regional economic base; (4) placing more emphasis on multilateralism, adhering to ASEAN Treaty of Amity and Cooperation (TAC); and (5) increasing its military presence, particularly deploying marines to Darwin, Australia, stationing US littoral combat ships in Singapore, and signing a troop rotation agreement with the Philippines (2014). The United States also planned to base 60 per cent of US naval assets in the Pacific by 2020.[90]

This convergence of interest resulted in an uptrend in US-Vietnam relations. Coinciding with ASEAN foreign minister meetings, Vietnam and the US held a joint celebration of the 15th anniversary of diplomatic relations in July and August 2010. On this occasion, Vietnam's deputy ambassador paid a visit to the aircraft carrier the USS *George H. W. Bush* in Norfolk, Virginia, while in the western Pacific the nuclear-powered USS *George Washington* parked off Vietnam's central coast to welcome on board a group of Vietnamese local government and military officers.[91] In August 2010, the two sides started non-combat joint exercises for four days when the guided missile destroyer the USS *John McCain* called at Da Nang's Tien Sa port. These activities included a search and rescue operation, damage control, maintenance and repair, and disaster training.[92] In this month, Hanoi and Washington also decided to set up an annual defence dialogue at the deputy defence minister level. Since a number of new mechanisms were put in place, senior defence and foreign affairs officers of both countries travelled more frequently to each another's capitals. Hanoi started sending its military officers to study at US military academies. Thanks to these programs, US ships also increased their presence in the area off the Vietnamese coast.[93] It should be also noted that Vietnam tried to persuade the US to lift its ban on sales of lethal weapons to Vietnam to reduce its reliance on Russian armaments.[94]

More substantively, with the support of Japan, Vietnam took advantage of its ASEAN chairmanship to lobby for admission of the US and Russia to the East Asia Summit (EAS) and ASEAN Defence Ministers' Meeting Plus (ADMM Plus). It should be noted that the US and Russia were sidelined in the ASEAN efforts to set up a regional high-level dialogue in the first half of the 2000s. In fact, the Bush Administration saw little value in the new grouping. However, as China expanded its military presence in the region, the Obama administration expressed greater interest in engaging with ASEAN. Clinton clearly valued both ASEAN and ARF "as important pieces of a strong, effective architecture for security and prosperity in Asia."[95] On the other side, Vietnam and other ASEAN countries saw the regional security architecture as unstable if the US were left outside. The developments in the South China Sea clearly touched a raw nerve in Southeast Asian nations about the prospect of China's violent rise. Indonesia, which used to see itself as neutral in the South China Sea dispute, was alarmed by the presence of Chinese vessels near its Natuna Islands. Reportedly, in June 2010, Indonesia patrol boats, in an attempt to arrest an illegal Chinese fishing boat, were threatened by China's Yuzheng 311.[96] The encounter prompted Jakarta to voice concerns at the ARF meeting in Hanoi and lodge a protest against China's nine-dash line claim on 8 July 2010, more than a year after Beijing first formalised this claim at the UN Commission on the Limits of the Continental Shelf.[97] ASEAN countries as well as Japan saw the benefits of keeping the US, Russia and other powers in the loop to balance China's growing power.

However, Vietnam's engagement of the US fell short of balancing against China. Hanoi did not want to join forces with the United States or to allow it to use its bases to deter China. It was mostly aimed at keeping the US in the region and involving the US in regional affairs, especially the South China Sea disputes. Hanoi was still in full control of its strategic and foreign policies, trying to borrow the influence of the US and other powers to check China's rising power. Vietnam kept its military cooperation with Washington highly symbolic and substantially modest. The naval exchange activities were non-combat in nature and all US ships to be serviced at Cam Ranh Bay were civilian, not warships. Hanoi had gone to great lengths to demonstrate to Beijing that it had no intention of siding with Washington against China strategically. After Vietnam-US naval activities in August, Vietnam's Deputy Minister of Defence Nguyen Chi Vinh went public to deny any collusion between US and Vietnam. He explained that these activities were purely to commemorate the 15th anniversary of establishment of diplomatic relations and the disputes in the South China Sea. Vinh also made an official visit to Beijing in late August 2010, where he restated Vietnam's "3 Nos" policy: no foreign alliances, no foreign bases in Vietnam and no relationship with another country against a third.[98] Vietnamese diplomats also echoed that view to reassure China about Vietnam's "closer relations" with the United States.[99]

After the exchange of accusations at ARF-17 in Hanoi, Chinese officialdom and media issued fierce protests against Vietnam for abusing its ASEAN chairmanship, and its alleged collusion with the United States and other countries to orchestrate the ambush on China. However, Hanoi refuted the Chinese account of strategic collusion between Hanoi and Washington to contain China. It argued that the South China Sea issue was raised at the ARF meeting because it was in essence a set of bilateral, multilateral and international disputes. Specifically, in the Vietnamese view, the South China Sea issue was composed of many problems, including bilateral dispute over the Paracels, multilateral dispute over the Spratlys and maritime boundaries, and issues of international importance such as freedom of navigation, maritime safety, human security, and regional peace and stability.[100] Vietnamese Foreign Ministry's spokesperson Nguyen Phuong Nga clarified Vietnam's position as follows:

> Issues that are related to other countries and parties like the *Spratly Islands* cannot be settled by Vietnam and China; they required the participation of other concerned parties. For issues that are not only related to countries that border the South China Sea such as maritime safety and security, they must be negotiated and settled by all countries that share this common interest.[101]

This argument gave Vietnam a reason to invite external powers in the category of South China Sea users to the discussions on managing the South China Sea disputes. In this vein, Vietnamese analysts framed China's assertive and unlawful actions as a danger to regional peace and stability, rather than purely bilateral matters between Vietnam and China. Consequently, the chorus at the ARF-17 meeting was simply a "coincidence of similar interests" among some ASEAN countries and external powers rather than coordinated actions.[102]

After ARF-17, both China and ASEAN showed signs of reconciliation. China gradually toned down its rhetoric and reduced its activities in the South China Sea to avoid the spiral of internationalisation. US officials reported that the Chinese seemingly kept away from the sensitive description of "core interest" when referring to the South China Sea. In a meeting with the press in late September 2010, the Chinese ambassador to the Philippines Liu Jianchao disclosed that China and ASEAN were conducting consultation on the draft code of conduct at the working level. Without going into details, he added that the parties were consulting each other on the outlines and the inclusion of sanctions against any violation of the code. Liu concluded, "Anything that is conductive to such a goal will be welcomed by the Chinese side. The most important thing for us is that everybody should move forward in the spirit of cooperation."[103] In the first ADMM Plus in Hanoi on 12 October 2010, China's Defence Minister Liang Guanglie did not comment directly on the South China Sea issue but called for "mutual trust." He assured the audience that "China's defence development is not aimed to challenge or threaten anyone, but to ensure its security and promote international and regional peace and stability" and "China pursues a defence policy that is defensive in nature."[104]

For its part, ASEAN might have feared the danger of pushing China too hard. In the run-up to the ASEAN-US Summit in Washington on 23 September 2010, the Chinese Foreign Ministry spokesperson warned against "any kind of reference that might be issued by the US and ASEAN over the South China Sea."[105] Reportedly, ASEAN tried to soften the draft joint statement compiled by the United States, by dropping a reference to the use or threat of force and the South China Sea.[106] As a result, the final statement of the 2nd US-ASEAN Summit came up with some common but vague language in the paragraph of regional peace and security:

> We reaffirmed the importance of regional peace and stability, maritime security, unimpeded commerce, and freedom of navigation in accordance with relevant universally agreed principles of international law, including the United Nations Conventions on the Law of the Sea (UNCLOS) and other international maritime law, and the peaceful settlement of disputes.[107]

One ASEAN diplomat explained that ASEAN did not want to create an impression that it was willing to do whatever the US said. "By deleting 'South China Sea' from the statement, we saved face of both China and the United States."[108] It seemed to be a consistent approach by ASEAN to avoid a war of words between China and the US. Therefore, on the eve of the First ADMM Plus, ASEAN defence ministers agreed among themselves to keep the South China Sea issue off the official agenda and the final statement. However, no restrictions were imposed on non-ASEAN ministers to speak about their concerns. As a result, the South China Sea was still raised at the first ADMM Plus by seven ministers, including the United States, Japan, South Korea and Australia. Interestingly, it was reported that Malaysia, Singapore and Vietnam also made reference to the South China Sea issue.[109] Vietnam's minister of defence took advantage of its chairmanship to conclude in the final statement of the meeting:

> The meeting noted that the member states are interested in maritime security cooperation and agreed that the collective efforts are required to address the challenges of piracy, human trafficking and disasters at sea. Some delegates touched upon traditional security challenges, such as disputes in the South China Sea [*sic*]. The meeting welcomed efforts by concerned parties to address the issue by peaceful means in conformity with the spirit of the Declaration on the Conduct of Parties in the South China Sea (DOC) of 2002 [*sic*] and recognized principles of international law, including the United Nations Convention on the Law of the Sea.[110]

Commenting on the outcome of the first ADMM Plus, Vietnam's Deputy Minister of Defence Nguyen Chi Vinh said, "I think there is good progress . . . so far. The South China Sea was not on the agenda, but ministers were still free to raise it in their speeches, and I think there is momentum there now."[111] As the Vietnamese expected, the US participants raised the South China Sea issue at the 18th and 19th ARF and subsequent EAS in 2011 and 2012. Clearly, the US has interest in keeping the South China Sea debate alive to prove its relevance to regional peace and security.

Bilateralism as a valve to defuse tensions and a pathway to move forward

In the second half of 2010, tensions were significantly reduced in the western part of the South China Sea as China lessened the intensity of its activities in the area. Chinese detainment of Vietnamese vessels and fishermen significantly decreased.[112] In September, China captured a Vietnamese fishing vessel and its crew. According to the Chinese, these fishermen were arrested on a charge of fishing with explosives and a fine of USD 10,500 was imposed. Vietnam lodged a protest to the Chinese embassy in Hanoi, demanding an immediate and unconditional release of the vessel and the crew. On the eve of the ADMM Plus in Hanoi, China suddenly discharged all of the Vietnamese fishermen unconditionally. One worrisome development for Vietnam was the PLAN's large-scale military exercise in the South China Sea in early November, which involved more than 100 surface ships, submarines and aircraft, and 1,800 marines. This was the China's fourth naval drill in the South China Sea in 2010.[113]

However, the Philippines and Japan came under pressure from China. In September 2010, a Chinese fishing trawler rammed into a Japanese Coast Guard vessel in the East China Sea. The Japanese Coast Guard then detained the captain of the trawler. China reacted angrily in a demand for the release of the captain and warned of "strong countermeasures."[114] Subsequently, Beijing suspended high-level exchanges with Japan and allowed anti-Japan protests in a couple of Chinese cities, and eventually banned rare earth exports to Japan. In March 2011, the Philippines reported that two Chinese vessels aggressively interfered with the operation of its seismic survey vessel near the Reed Bank, around 80 miles west of Palawan. It was also alleged that Chinese vessels intruded frequently into the Philippines' EEZ and unloaded materials to build structures near the Iroquois Reef and Amy Douglas Bank, which were claimed by the Philippines. The Philippines accused China of violating Article 5 of the DOC 2002 that prohibited the parties from "inhabiting on the presently uninhabited islands, reefs, shoals, cays, and other features."[115] Since then, consecutive maritime encounters between their forces further strained China's relations with Japan and the Philippines.

In 2011, Hanoi placed more emphasis on bilateralism than engagement in ASEAN-led multilateralism and with external powers. Vietnam was seen less active and assertive within ASEAN forums. Its defence relations with US and other powers were maintained at a low level. It was perhaps a result of some changes within Vietnamese leadership after the Eleventh National Congress of the Communist Party of Vietnam in January 2011. The new Secretary General, Nguyen Phu Trong, gave the first priority to mend Hanoi's relations with Beijing. Right after taking the office, Trong dispatched a special envoy, Hoang Binh Quan, to China to brief the Chinese leadership of the outcome of the Congress. Quan extended an invitation to Hu Jintao to visit Vietnam while Hu also invited Trong to Beijing. As a sign of conciliation and deference, Trong agreed to travel to Beijing first. During the first half of 2011, Vietnam also received a number of high-level ranking military officers and officials from Beijing to Hanoi. It was a reasonable assessment that Trong wished to have some achievements in the Vietnam-China bilateral negotiation on the maritime issues to mark his first trip to China in his capacity as party chief.

After some tranquil and amiable months, Vietnam faced a new row with China in the South China Sea. On 26 May 2011, two Chinese maritime surveillance ships manoeuvred to cut the exploration cable of the Vietnamese survey ship, *Binh Minh 02*, in the area just 120 km (80 n.m.) off the south-central coast of Vietnam and 600 km from China's Hainan Island.[116] Three days later, the Vietnamese Ministry of Foreign Affairs held a separate press conference to air footage of the incident and condemn China's actions. It should be noted that this was an escalated response in terms of publicity. For a decade, Vietnam mostly channelled its protests against China through official notes and statements of the spokespersons of the Ministry of Foreign Affairs.[117] At the conference, the Vietnamese officials called Chinese actions a violation of Vietnam's sovereignty and jurisdiction rights over its continental shelf and EEZ. Do Van Hau, Deputy General Director of PetroVietnam, told reporters that Chinese ships were well prepared to hinder and damage the operation of *Binh Minh 02*. The spokesperson for Vietnam's Foreign Ministry Nguyen Phuong Nga asserted that the Vietnamese naval forces will "do everything necessary" to protect peace and independence, sovereignty and territorial integrity of Vietnam.[118] On the other side, Chinese Foreign Ministry spokesperson Jiang Yu stated that Chinese ships were conducting "completely normal marine enforcement and surveillance activities in China's jurisdictional area."[119] A similar incident happened just two weeks later. On 9 June, a Chinese fishing trawler, escorted by two Chinese fishery administration vessels, got entangled with and broke the cable of another PetroVietnam survey vessel, *Viking II*, in the area (block 136–3) about 270 km (145 n.m.) off the southern coast of Vietnam and about 1,152 km (622 n.m.) from Hainan Island.[120] On this occasion, Vietnamese Foreign Ministry's spokesperson Nguyen Phuong Nga described Chinese actions as "premeditated and carefully calculated" and as intended to turn "the undisputed into an area under dispute in order to materialize China's nine-dotted line [*sic*] claim in the South China Sea."[121]

Under pressure from both inside and outside, the Vietnamese leaders appeared stronger and firmer in their determination to defend the country's sovereignty and territorial integrity. After the first cable-cutting incident, Vietnamese Minister of Defence Phung Quang Thanh brought the case to the Shangri-La Dialogue on 3–5 June 2011. Thanh viewed the incident as source of "considerable concern for the maintenance of peace and stability in the South China Sea" and demanded no repetition of similar actions.[122] His Chinese counterpart, Liang Guanglie, responded with a reaffirmation of China's commitment to "maintaining peace and stability in the South China Sea."[123] When the second cable cutting incident unfolded, Vietnamese Prime Minister Nguyen Tan Dung issued a remarkably strong testimonial. He declared, "We continue to strongly affirm and to manifest the strongest determination of all the Party, of all the people, and of all the army in protecting Vietnamese sovereignty in maritime zones of the country."[124] Two days before, State President Nguyen Minh Triet sailed to Co To Island in the Gulf of Tonkin where he restated Vietnam's resolve to protect the islands. He said, "We are ready to sacrifice everything to protect our homeland, our sea and island sovereignty."[125] On 9 June, a Manila-based Chinese diplomat announced that China would be conducting routine naval exercise in the Western Pacific and called on Vietnam and the Philippines to stop oil explorations in the South China Sea. In a response, Vietnam immediately announced a "routine" live-fire exercise on 13 June on Hon Ong Island off the central coast of Vietnam and banned all activities in the area during the period. Reportedly, the exercise lasted for nine hours and involved in coastal artillery and corvette-based missiles.[126]

Two cable-cutting incidents within one month prompted an unprecedented uproar of nationalism in Vietnamese communities inside and outside the country. Nationalistic commentaries in China's *Global Times*, a mouthpiece of the Chinese Communist Party (CCP), further fuelled xenophobic sentiments in Vietnam.[127] As a result, there was an unusual series of eleven consecutive anti-China gatherings on every Sunday since 5 June after information of alleged Chinese harassment of Vietnamese survey ships was published.[128] Clearly such a long series of anti-China rallies could not happen without toleration from the authorities. In 2007, such demonstrations were dispersed after two weekends. What was also obvious was that the Vietnamese authorities were also anxious about such mass gatherings and afraid that the situation would get out of control. Street demonstrators, intellectuals, retired officials, and dissidents demanded more transparency about the Communist Party and the government of Vietnam's foreign affairs, especially in their dealings with China. They also went further to table petitions to the ruling Communist Party of Vietnam and called for comprehensive reforms to increase the country's strength to counter Chinese threats. Undoubtedly, popular antipathy was both against the Vietnamese government's seemingly soft stance against China's aggressive assertiveness and against corruption domestically.[129]

Hanoi clearly attempted to "compartmentalise" South China Sea tensions, preventing them from spilling over to other fields or affecting overall relations with China. Amid the crisis, the Vietnamese navy continued its eleventh routine joint patrol with the Chinese navy in the Gulf of Tonkin on 19–20 June. Hanoi also kept on with high-level exchanges with Beijing as previously scheduled. On 25 June, as the war of words intensified, Hanoi took the initiative to send Deputy Foreign Minister Ho Xuan Son as a special envoy to Beijing to discuss the South China Sea issue with his Chinese counterpart, Zhang Zhijun. A joint press release was published after the meeting and indicated "the two sides laid stress on the need to *steer public opinion* along the correct direction, avoiding comments and deeds that harm the friendship and trust of the people of the two countries."[130] After that, the Vietnamese authorities gradually stifled nationalistic outbursts in the lead-up to such high-level talks. By the time Chinese State Councillor Dai Bingguo was about to visit Vietnam, Hanoi's security forces completely blocked all efforts to organise such demonstrations, through persuasion, intimidation and coercion. No rally happened by the end of August 2011. Apparently, nationalism is instrumental for Hanoi to exert additional pressures on China.

Hanoi rushed to dispatch Ho Xuan Son to Beijing to ease tensions largely because it wanted to minimise the effects of such incidents on the process of negotiating an agreement on principles for settlement of sea issues between the two countries. Hanoi expected that this agreement would be concluded during Trong's trip to Beijing at the end of 2011. What Hanoi gained from Son's travel to Beijing was China's commitment to accelerate negotiations on the agreement on basic principles guiding the settlement of the sea issues. The joint press release read,

> The two sides agreed to speed up the tempo of negotiations so as to early sign an agreement on basic principles guiding the settlement of Sea Issues between Vietnam and China, and boost the implementation of the Declaration on the Conduct of Parties in the South China Sea (DOC) and follow-up activities so that substantial progress will soon be achieved.[131]

It is clear that the agreement on principles was a prerequisite for negotiations on concrete controversial issues. China and Vietnam reached a consensus to start bilateral consultation on a set of fundamental guiding principles as a framework for resolving maritime differences in 2008. In 2010, despite friction, the two sides held five private meetings to discuss these principles.[132] Evidently, Hanoi managed to take advantage of the incidents to push China to pay more attention to the settlements of the disputes. At the end of August, Vietnam-China defence talks decided to set up a military hotline. In early September, Chinese State Councillor Dai Bingguo travelled to Hanoi to co-chair the fifth annual meeting of the Vietnam-China Steering Committee with Vietnamese Deputy Prime Minister Nguyen Thien Nhan. At the meeting, the two sides reached a consensus on accelerating "the efforts to speed up the negotiation and work out a mutually agreeable solution on the issue and pledge to work hard to sign an agreement as early as possible."[133] In October 2011, during his visit to China, Secretary General Nguyen Phu Trong witnessed the signing ceremony of the Vietnam-China Agreement on Basic Principles Guiding the Settlement of Sea-related Issues.[134] The Chinese were as usual content with ambiguity in the language of the agreement, which generally reaffirmed the two sides' commitment to seeking a long-lasting settlement of the disputes as well as examining opportunities for joint-development. Beijing would take it as evidence of progress through bilateralism. On the other side, the Vietnamese were satisfied with China's renewed commitment to negotiation and institutionalised bilateral dialogue on maritime issues. It was agreed that the two sides would meet twice a year to discuss the differences and set up a hot line to address emerging tensions.

In July 2011, China and ASEAN reportedly reached a breakthrough agreement on a set of guidelines for the implementation of the declaration of conduct (DOC).[135] It is possible that that breakthrough in Vietnam-China negotiations was reached during Ho Xuan Son's visit to Beijing in June.[136] The provision for an ASEAN caucus before meeting China was finally dropped. Vietnam eventually accepted vague language in the final text. Paragraph 2 of the agreement said: "The parties to the DOC will continue to promote dialogue and consultations in accordance with the spirit of the DOC."[137] In exchange for this visible victory, China had to accept the practice that ASEAN members would keep on their caucus prior the meeting with China.[138] This agreement was included in the official summary record of the meeting, not in the final text of the agreement. Such compromise allowed China to maintain face and avoid concrete obligations. China also needed a symbolic achievement to show the world that it could reach an agreement with ASEAN without interventions by external powers. In the meantime, ASEAN managed to continue its own practice and secure China's commitment to negotiating a COC. While some officials hailed the agreement as breakthrough, it did not have a significant effect on the state of affairs in the South China Sea.

Conclusion

As China was more determined to establish its mastery in the South China Sea, Hanoi moved to clarify and aligned its claims to UNCLOS, pushing Beijing to expose its nine-dash line claim. At the same time, Vietnam reached out to the world to denounce China's legally ambiguous claims and raised concerns about

China's coercive measures. Notably, Hanoi tried to use its ASEAN chairmanship in 2010 to facilitate discussion of the South China Sea issues in the key regional forums, particularly the ARF and ADMM Plus. Hanoi also made use of its chairmanship role to lobby for the admission of the US and Russia into the East Asia Summit and ADMM Plus to balance China's influence in this important mechanism. Whiling signalling their firm nationalist stance in the South China Sea, Vietnamese leadership was careful to avoid any spillover effects of the South China Sea tensions on other realms of bilateral cooperation and proactively reassured China of its policy of no military alliance. As the South China Sea came under international media spotlight, China gradually softened its stance and became more responsive to Vietnam's interest in resumption of bilateral talks on maritime issues and ASEAN's pursuit for the guidelines to implement the DOC.

Notes

1 Socialist Republic of Vietnam and Malaysia, "Joint Submission the Commission on the Limits of the Continental Shelf: Part I: Executive Summary," 6 May 2009. Online. Available HTTP: <www.un.org/Depts/los/clcs_new/submissions_files/submission_mysvnm_33_2009.htm> (accessed 30 July); Socialist Republic of Vietnam, "Submission to the Commission on the Limits of the Continental Shelf: Partial Submission in Respect of Vietnam's Extended Continental Shelf: North Area (VNM-N)," 7 May 2009. Online. Available HTTP: <www.un.org/depts/los/clcs_new/submissions_files/vnm37_09/vnm2009n_executivesummary.pdf> (accessed 31 July 2014).

2 R. Beckman, "South China Sea: Worsening Dispute or Growing Clarity in Claims?," *RSIS Commentaries*, 16 August 2010; R. Beckman, "The UN Convention on the Law of the Sea and the Maritime Disputes in the South China Sea," *American Journal of International Law* 107, no. 1, 2013, p.152.

3 N.H. Thao, "Vietnam's Position on the Sovereignty over the Paracels and the Spratlys: Its Maritime Claims," *Journal of East Asia International Law* 1, 2012, p.200.

4 Article 20 (2), The Law of the Sea of Vietnam, adopted on 21 June 2012.

5 Interview with an official of the Ministry of Foreign Affairs of Vietnam on 28 March 2014.

6 T.T. Thuy, "Recent Developments in the South China Sea: From Declaration to Code of Conduct," In: Tran Truong Thuy (ed.), *The South China Sea: Towards a Region of Peace, Security and Cooperation*, Hanoi: The Gioi Publisher, 2011, p.104.

7 Article 5, Annex I, Rules of Procedure of the Commission on the Limits of the Continental Shelf.

8 E. Franckx and M. Benatar, "Dots and Lines in the South China Sea: Insights from the Law of Map Evidence," *Asian Journal of International Law* 2, 2012, pp. 90–1.

9 In the Chinese documents, "historic rights" or "historic titles" can be called as "historical rights."

10 C.A. Thayer, "The United States and Chinese Assertiveness in the South China Sea," *Security Challenges* 6, no. 2, 2010, p.78; F. Dupuy and P.M. Dupuy, "A Legal Analysis of China's Historic Rights Claim in the South China Sea," *American Journal of International Law* 107, no. 1, 2013, p.129.

11 Quoted from Dupuy and Dupuy, "A Legal Analysis of China's Historic Rights Claim in the South China Sea," p.129.

12 "Dispute Regarding the Law on the Exclusive Economic Zone and the Continental Shelf of the People's Republic of China Which Was Passed on 26 June 1998," *UN Law of the Sea Bulletin* 38, 1998, p.55.

13 Permanent Mission of the People's Republic of China to the United Nations, "Note Verbale CML/18/2009," 7 May 2009. Online. Available HTTP: <www.un.org/depts/los/clcs_new/submissions_files/submission_vnm_37_2009.htm> (accessed 31 July 2014) (emphasis added) (see attached map). Permanent Mission of the People's Republic of China to the United Nations, "Note Verbale CML/17/2009," 7 May 2009. Online. Available HTTP: <www.un.org/depts/los/clcs_new/submissions_files/submission_mysvnm_33_2009.htm> (accessed 30 July 2014).

14 Beckman, "The UN Convention on the Law of the Sea and the Maritime Disputes in the South China Sea," pp. 152–3.

15 US Embassy in Beijing, "PRC: Cow's Tongue Claim Not Licked, Despite Objections from the Philippines and Vietnam," *Cable (Released by WikiLeaks)*, 5 March 2009. Online. Available HTTP: <https://search.wikileaks.org/plusd/cables/08HANOI1094_a.html> (accessed 13 December 2015).

16 Permanent Mission of the Socialist Republic of Vietnam, "Note Verbale No. 86/HC-2009," 8 May 2009. Online. Available HTTP: <www.un.org/depts/los/clcs_new/submissions_files/mysvnm33_09/vnm_chn_2009re_mys_vnm_e.pdf> (accessed 31 July 2014).

17 As the nine-dash line has no specific coordinates, it is impossible to know exactly how large the area within the dashed line is. According to the US Department of State, in its *Limits in the Sea* report in 2014, the dashed line covers 62 per cent of the South China Sea waters. See US Department of State, China: Maritime Claims in the South China Sea, *Limits in the Seas Report*, No. 143, 5 December 2014. In many articles, the figure is 80 per cent.

18 Interview with an official from Vietnam's Ministry of Foreign Affairs in Hanoi on 25 March 2014.

19 N. Nam, "Dung so Trung Quoc cam bien," *RFA Tieng Viet*, 29 May 2010.

20 T. Fravel, "Maritime Security in the South China Sea and the Competition over Maritime Rights," In: Patrick M. Cronin (ed.), *Cooperation from Strength: The United States, China and the South China Sea*, Washington, DC: Center for a New American Security, 2012, p.305.

21 L. V. Chuong, "Ke chuyen Hoang Sa (Ky 3)," *Tien Phong*, 15 May 2010.

22 P. Nga, "Vietnam Puts Paracel Row on Summit Agenda," *BBC*, 8 April 2010. Online. Available HTTP: <http://news.bbc.co.uk/2/mobile/asia-pacific/8609120.stm> (accessed 31 July 2014).

23 Sy Phuong, "Ngu dan kho vi lien tiep bi tau la dam," *Kien thuc*, 13 June 2010; Tri Nguyen, "Tau la tan cong ngu dan Viet Nam, 7 nguoi bi thuong," *Vnexpress*, 15 July 2009.

24 D. D. Dy, "Tau la cua ai?," *BBC Tieng Viet*, 30 May 2009; Duc Tam, "Tau la tan cong ngu dan Viet Nam la tau Trung Quoc," *RFI Tieng Viet*, 20 July 2009.

25 Z. Xin, "Reinforced Patrol Sails from Hainan," *China Daily*, 19 May 2009. Online. Available HTTP: <www.chinadaily.com.cn/china/2009–05/19/content_7790652.htm> (accessed 7 July 2014).

26 International Crisis Group, "Stirring Up the South China Sea (I)," *Asia Report No. 223*, 23 April 2012.

27 "Trung Quoc dua tau lon toi Hoang Sa," *BBC Tieng Viet*, 19 May 2009. Online. Available HTTP: <www.bbc.co.uk/vietnamese/vietnam/2009/05/090519_viet_china_sea_claim.shtml> (accessed 7 July 2014).

28 J. Zhang, "China's Growing Assertiveness in the South China Sea: A Strategic Shift?," *ANU National Security College Occasional Paper – The South China Sea and Australia's Regional Security Environment*, no. 5, 2013, p.22.

29 Interview with an official of Vietnam's Ministry of Foreign Affairs on 25 March 2014.

30 J. Zhang, "China's Growing Assertiveness in the South China Sea: A Strategic Shift?," p.20.

31 See T. Fravel, "China's Strategy in the South China Sea," *Contemporary Southeast Asia* 33, no. 2, 2011, pp. 292–319.

32 L. Mingjiang, "China's Non-Confrontational Assertiveness in the South China Sea," *East Asia Forum*, 14 June 2012.
33 Y. Ji, "Deciphering Beijing's Maritime Security Policy and Strategy in Managing Sovereignty Disputes in the China Seas," *RSIS Policy Brief*, October 2013.
34 See International Crisis Group, "Stirring Up the South China Sea (I)"; L. Jakobson, "China's Unpredictable Maritime Security Actors," *Report by Lowy Institute for International Security*, December 2014. Online. Available HTTP: <www.lowyinstitute.org/files/chinas-unpredictable-maritime-security-actors_3.pdf> (accessed 27 May 2015).
35 See D. T. Hai, "In Retrospect of China's Policy toward South China Sea Dispute since 2007," *International Studies Review (Diplomatic Academy of Vietnam)*, no. 24, June 2011.
36 Interview with an official of the Ministry of Foreign Affairs in Hanoi, 4 April 2014.
37 "Hoi Nghe ca phan doi Trung Quoc," *BBC Tieng Viet*, 15 December 2009.
38 T. Q. Tuong, "Cho dieu kien chin muoi de giai quyet tranh chap Bien Dong," *Vietnamnet*, 6 January 2010. Online. Available HTTP: <http://vnn.vietnamnet.vn/chinhtri/201001/Cho-dieu-kien-chin-muoi-giai-quyet-tranh-chap-bien-Dong-888092/> (accessed 11 June 2011) (emphasis added).
39 Ibid.
40 Interview with an official of the Ministry of Foreign Affairs of Vietnam in Hanoi, 7 March 2014.
41 Quoted from G. Torode, "The Closer to China, the Cooler It Becomes," *South China Morning Post*, 26 September 2009.
42 D. D. Huy, "'Gac tranh chap, cung khai thac' kieu Trung Quoc," *Tuan Viet Nam*, 21 January 2010. Online. Available HTTP: <http://tuanvietnam.vietnamnet.vn/2010–01–20-gac-tranh-chap-cung-khai-thac-kieu-trung-quoc> (accessed 3 August 2014).
43 R. C. Banlaoi, "Functional Cooperation and Joint Development," In: Wu Shicu and Nong Hong (eds.), *Recent Developments in the South China Sea Dispute: The Prospect of a Joint Development Regime*, Abingdon and New York: Routledge, 2014, p.229.
44 M. McDonald, "US Navy Provoked South China Sea Incident, China Says," *New York Times*, 10 March 2009.
45 T. Carpaccio, "Chinese Vessels Harass U.S. Navy Ship, Pentagon Says (Update 3)," *Bloomberg*, 9 March 2009.
46 G. Torode, "Right and Wrong Far from Clear in Open Sea," *South China Morning Post*, 14 March 2009.
47 N. T. Binh, "Cang thang Bien Dong va su lua chon cho Viet Nam," *Tuan Viet Nam*, 14 March 2013.
48 "China Patrols in South China Sea," *BBC*, 16 March 2009.
49 US Embassy in Hanoi, "Vietnam's 2010 ASEAN Chairmanship," *Cable (Released by WikiLeaks)*, 11 December 2009. Online. Available HTTP: <https://wikileaks.org/cable/2009/12/09HANOI925.html> (accessed 3 August 2014).
50 N. Hoang, "Vietnam se tiep tuc gop phan thiet thuc va quan trong vao su phat trien cua Hiep hoi cac quoc gia Dong Nam A-ASEAN," *Cong Thong tin Dien tu Chinh phu*, 7 August 2008.
51 "Thai Protests Disrupt ASEAN Summit," *Aljazeera*, 10 April 2009.
52 I. C. Storey, "The South China Sea: The Theatre for Emerging Strategic Competition," paper presented at the *Security Environment in the East Asian Seas*, Ocean Policy Research Foundation, Tokyo, 16–17 February 2011.
53 Trong Nghia, "Vietnam-Chu tich ASEAN 2010: Thach thuc lon nhat la ho so Bien Dong," *RFI Tieng Viet*, 1 January 2010.
54 Nga, "Vietnam Puts Paracel Row on Summit Agenda."
55 C.A. Thayer, "Recent Developments in the South China Sea: Grounds for Cautious Optimism," *RSIS Working Paper*, no. 220, 14 December 2010, p.25.
56 "Nhieu tau ca TQ vao lanh hai Viet Nam," *BBC Tieng Viet*, 6 February 2010.

57 Mac Lam, "Tau Trung Quoc lai tuan tra trong vung bien tranh chap voi Viet Nam," *RFA Tieng Viet*, 30 April 2010. Online. Available HTTP: <www.rfa.org/vietnamese/vietnam/chinh-tri/China-Ship-patrols-deep-inside-Vietnam-s-sovereignty-MLam-04302010204951.html> (accessed 6 August 2014).
58 "China Starts Regular Patrols of South China Sea," 26 April 2010. Online. Available HTTP: <http://english.gov.cn/2010–04/26/content_1592250.htm> (accessed 6 August 2014).
59 Lam, "Tau Trung Quoc lai tuan tra trong vung bien tranh chap voi Viet Nam."
60 E. Wong, "Chinese Military Seeks to Extend Its Naval Power," *New York Times*, 23 April 2010.
61 "Hai quan Trung Quoc tang suc manh," *Vnexpress*, 5 May 2010.
62 H.R. Clinton, "Interview with Greg Sheridan of The Australian," 8 October 2010. Online. Available HTTP: <http://m.state.gov/md150671.htm> (accessed 2 April 2015).
63 Thayer, "Recent Developments in the South China Sea," p.7.
64 M. Lelyyeld, "China Projects Power at Sea," *RFA*, 3 May 2010.
65 Wong, "Chinese Military Seeks to Extend Its Naval Power."
66 Interview with an official of Vietnam's Ministry of Foreign Affairs in Hanoi, 7 April 2014.
67 "Tranh chap Bien Dong ngay cang cang thang," *RFA Tieng Viet*, 16 May 2010; D.D. Dy, "Quoc te hoa," *BBC Tieng Viet*, 3 March 2010.
68 Hong Nga, "Bien Dong nong dan," *BBC Tieng Viet*, 4 April 2014.
69 Nam Nguyen, "Trang bi vu khi cho cac tau ca?," *RFA Tieng Viet*, 22 October 2009; V.M. Truc, "Dan quan tu ve bien, nen hay khong?," *Tuan Viet Nam*, 3 November 2009.
70 "Viet Nam thi diem lap dan quan bien," *BBC Tieng Viet*, 17 May 2012.
71 Nga, "Vietnam Puts Paracel Row on Summit Agenda."
72 Thayer, "Recent Developments in the South China Sea."
73 T.T. Thuy, "Recent Developments in the South China Sea: Implications for Regional Security and Cooperation," paper presented at the *Recent Developments in the South China Sea: Implications for Regional Security and Cooperation*, CSIS, Washington, DC, 30 June 2011.
74 "Enhanced Efforts towards the ASEAN Community: From Vision to Action," Joint Communiqué of the *43rd ASEAN Foreign Ministers Meeting*, Hanoi, 19–20 July 2010. Online. Available HTTP: <www.asean.org/communities/asean-political-security-community/item/joint-communique-of-the-43rd-asean-foreign-ministers-meeting-enhanced-efforts-towards-the-asean-community-from-vision-to-action-ha-noi-19–20-july-2010–3> (emphasis added).
75 "Chinese FM Refutes Fallacies on the South China Sea Issue," *China Daily*, 25 July 2010.
76 Six ASEAN countries were Vietnam, the Philippines, Malaysia, Brunei, Indonesia and Singapore. Other ARF participants speaking of the South China Sea issue were from the US, Japan, Australia, India, South Korea and the European Union.
77 Remark by US Secretary of State Hillary Rodham Clinton at the 17th ASEAN Regional Forum Meeting in Hanoi, 23 July 2010. Online. Available HTTP: <http://iipdigital.usembassy.gov/st/english/texttrans/2010/07/20100723164658su0.4912989.html#axzz3bIuS19us> (accessed 29 June 2014) (emphasis added).
78 H.R. Clinton, *Hard Choice*, E-book: Simon & Schuster, 2014, pp. 244–6.
79 "Chinese FM Refutes Fallacies on the South China Sea Issue."
80 B. Wain, "ASEAN Caught in a Tight Spot," *Strait Times*, 16 September 2010.
81 Quoted from Clinton, *Hard Choice*, p.304. It was also reported that Yang Jiechi said: "China is a big country and other countries are small countries, and that's just a fact" in J. Pomfret, "U.S. Takes a Tougher Tone with China," *Washington Post*, 20 July 2010.
82 Interviews with officials of the Ministry of Foreign Affairs in Hanoi, 7 April 2014.
83 G. Torode, "How the US Ambushed China in Its Backyard and What Happens Next," *South China Morning Post*, 25 July 2010.

84 Interview with officials of Vietnam's Ministry of Foreign Affairs in Hanoi, 25 March 2014.
85 Maritime Disputes and Sovereignty Issues in East Asia, Subcommittee on East Asia and Pacific Affairs, Committee on Foreign Relations, United States Senate, S. Hrg. 111–135, Washington, DC, 15 July 2009. Online. Available HTTP: <www.gpo.gov/fdsys/pkg/CHRG-111shrg53022/html/CHRG-111shrg53022.htm>.
86 Ibid.
87 R. M. Gates, "Strengthening Security Partnership in the Asia-Pacific," paper presented at the *9th IISS Asian Security Summit – Shangri-La Dialogue*, Singapore, 5 June 2010.
88 Ibid.
89 Clinton, *Hard Choice*, pp. 166–70.
90 See K. M. Campbell and B. Andrews, "Explaining the US 'Pivot' to Asia," *Americas*, no. 1, 2013.
91 C. A. Thayer, "Vietnam and the United States: Convergence But Not Congruence of Strategic Interests in the South China Sea," paper presented at the *4th Engaging with Vietnam Interdisciplinary Dialogue Conference*, Honolulu, 2012.
92 "U.S., China: Conflicting Interests in Southeast Asia," *Stratfor*, 12 August 2010.
93 J. Promfret, "China's Rise Prompts Vietnam to Strengthen Ties to Other Nations," *Washington Post*, 30 October 2010.
94 The ban was initiated in 1984. In 2007, the Bush Administration amended Traffic in Arms Regulations (ITAR) to allow the sale of non-lethal defence articles and defence services to Vietnam on a case-by-case basis.
95 Quoted from S. Simon, "US-Southeast Asia Relations: Growing Enmeshment in Regional Affairs," *Comparative Connections*, October 2010, p.4.
96 National Institute for Defense Studies, "China Security Report," Tokyo, 2011, pp. 18–19.
97 R. Beckman and T. Davenport, "CLCS Submissions and Claims in the South China Sea," paper presented at *The South China Sea: Cooperation for Regional Security and Development*, Ho Chi Minh City, 10–12 November 2010, pp. 23–4.
98 "Vietnam Reiterates '3 Nos' Defense Policy," *Vietnam News Agency*, 26 August 2010.
99 M. Liyao, "Vietnam Not Seeking Military Alliance," *China Daily*, 26 August 2010.
100 N. N. Duong, "Du am ARF and Quan he ASEAN-Trung Quoc tren Bien Dong," *Tuan Viet Nam*, 31 August 2010.
101 Quoted from G. Torode and M. Chan, "China Refuses to Yield on Paracels," *South China Morning Post*, 12 December 2010.
102 Duong, "Du am ARF and Quan he ASEAN-Trung Quoc tren Bien Dong."
103 "China, ASEAN Begin Discussion on Stronger Code of Conduct," *China Daily*, 30 September 2010.
104 T. Shanker, "The U.S. and China Soften Tone over Disputed Seas," *New York Times*, 12 October 2010.
105 Thayer, "Recent Developments in the South China Sea," pp. 16–17.
106 Ibid.
107 Joint Statement of the 2nd U.S.-ASEAN Leaders Meeting, New York, 24 September 2010.
108 Quoted from C. A. Thayer, "The United States, China and Southeast Asia," *Southeast Asian Affairs*, 2012, p.21.
109 Thayer, "Recent Developments in the South China Sea," pp. 16–17.
110 "First ADMM+ Chairman's Statement," *Vietnam News Agency*, Hanoi, in "First ADMM+ Chairman's Statement," *Vietnam News Agency*, 13 October 2010.
111 Quoted from G. Torode, "Vietnam Revives Guerrilla Tactics," *South China Morning Post*, 14 October 2010.
112 C. A. Thayer, "The Tyranny of Geography: Vietnamese Strategies to Constrain China in the South China Sea," paper presented at the *International Studies Association-52th Annual Convention*, Montreal, Canada, 16–19 March 2011.

113 M. Wines, "China States Naval Exercises," *New York Times*, 3 November 2010.
114 T. Branigan, "China Cuts Japan Contacts over Detained Trawler Captain," *Guardian*, 20 September 2010.
115 "PHL Asks China to Explain Ships near Reed Bank," *GMA News*, 1 June 2011.
116 "Vietnam Accuses China in Seas Dispute," *BBC*, 30 May 2011.
117 A. Watts, "Tensions Rise as Vietnam Accuses China of Sabotage," *Sydney Morning Herald*, 2 June 2011.
118 "Vietnam Demands China Stop Sovereignty Violation," *Thanh Nien*, 29 May 2011.
119 "China Reprimands Vietnam over Offshore Oil Exploration," *Reuters*, 28 May 2011.
120 "Chinese Ships Cause Disturbance in Vietnam's Waters Again," *Thanh Nien*, 10 June 2011.
121 Thuy Chung, "Chinese Boats Intrude Vietnam's Waters, Cut Cables Again," *Vietnamnet*, 2011.
122 Q. P. Thanh, "Responding to New Maritime Security Threats," paper presented at the *10th IISS Asian Security Summit, Shangri-La Dialogue*, Singapore, 5 June 2011.
123 L. Guanglie, "China International Security Cooperation," paper presented at the *10th IISS Asian Security Summit, Shangri-La Dialogue*, Singapore, 5 June 2011.
124 "Vietnam Reasserts Claim to Spratly and Paracel Islands," *Radio Australia*, 9 June 2011.
125 "Tuyen bo danh thep cua lanh dao Viet nam ve bao ve chu quyen," *Giao duc Viet Nam*, 9 June 2011.
126 C.A. Thayer, "China's New Wave of Aggressive Assertiveness in the South China Sea," *International Journal of China Studies* 2, no. 3, 2011, p.570.
127 Ibid., p.571.
128 "Vietnam Stops Anti-China Protest, Detains Many," *Reuters*, 21 August 2011.
129 D. Brown, "Vietnam Leaders Taken to Task on China," *Asia Times*, 26 June 2011.
130 "Vietnam-China Joint Press Release," *Vietnam News Agency*, 26 June 2011 (emphasis added).
131 Ibid.
132 Torode and Chan, "China Refuses to Yield on Paracels."
133 "Vietnam, China to Try to Hasten Talks on the Sea dispute," *Thanh Nien*, 8 September 2011.
134 "Nguyen tac giai quyet van de tren bien Viet-Trung," *TTXVN*, 12 October 2011.
135 C.A. Thayer, "ASEAN and China Consultations on a Code of Conduct in the South China Sea: Prospects and Obstacles," Paper presented to the *International Conference on Security and Cooperation in the South China Sea*, Russian Academy of Sciences, Moscow, 18 October 2013, p.4.
136 Fravel, "Maritime Security in the South China Sea and the Competition over Maritime Rights," pp. 44–5.
137 "South China Sea Guidelines Agreed," *Jakarta Post*, 21 July 2011.
138 See Fravel, "Maritime Security in the South China Sea and the Competition over Maritime Rights."

8 Navigating big power politics, 2011–2015

A stronger US presence and deeper involvement made the state of affairs in the South China Sea more complex and intractable. Though resuming bilateral talks with Vietnam on maritime issues, China continued to expand its presence in the South China Sea. Vietnam found itself trapped in a three-layer game in the South China Sea. At the core, the South China Sea problem represents a set of conflicts of interest among claimants on sovereignty over insular features and jurisdiction over different maritime zones. The second layer is the contest between China and ASEAN as a group in properly manage the existing disputes and the central role of ASEAN in handling regional affairs. As incidents unfolded, there was a widening divergence among ASEAN members on how to handle relations with China. The outermost layer is the contest between China and the United States for primacy in the Indo-Pacific region. Inside the country, the Vietnamese political elites faced stronger calls for legal actions and meaningful strategic relations with the United States to fend off revisionist China. It was now all the more difficult for Hanoi to defend its maritime interests without significant detriment to its relations with Beijing.

South China Sea's new normal: "hot peace" and increased US-China strategic rivalry

By the year 2012, the South China Sea was subject to increased tensions. Though Beijing showed signs of conciliation in terms of active participation in ASEAN-China negotiation on the guidelines to the implementation of the DOC and resumption of bilateral talks with Vietnam on delimitation of the area off the Gulf of Tonkin, Chinese law enforcement and fishing vessels, backed by the PLAN armada, continued to impose control over the South China Sea and suppressing any resistance of other claimants. The risk of armed clashes increased. Though there has been no exchange of fire, perilous manoeuvres, collisions and standoffs occurred more frequently between vessels from China and those of other claimants, thus stirring up nationalism in the related countries and increasing the likelihood of accidental overreaction and miscalculation. Tensions were not caused by accidents, but mostly by China's deliberate assertiveness and intimations. Vietnamese strategist Dang Dinh Quy described this situation as "hot peace," which implies no wars but daily standoffs and constant frictions.[1]

As time went by, it became clearer that China's maritime assertiveness was Beijing's newborn expansionist policy rather than some type of nationalism-driven "reactive assertiveness" or overdoing by unrestrained Chinese maritime agencies. China was determined to become a "true maritime power," and that goal was articulated in the 18th National Congress of the Chinese Communist Party in November 2012 and the 12th National People's Congress in March 2013.[2] The policy was set in motion in the period of Hu Jintao's "peaceful development" proclamation and manifested in the build-up of a large fishing fleet and a strong law enforcement squadron side by side with rapid naval modernisation in China. Beijing's maritime strategy had dual goals of sea control and sea denial. One the one hand, the Chinese used its overwhelming maritime power, including civilian, paramilitary, and naval forces, to suppress smaller claimants. On the other hand, they developed a range of deterrent capabilities to deny the control of the US navy over its near seas. As indicated in the standoffs in the *Impeccable* in 2009, the Scarborough Shoal in 2012, the Second Thomas Shoal, and in the Haiyang Shiyou 981 oil rig crisis in 2014, there was always a high level of communication and coordination among Chinese fishermen, law enforcement, and navy in the deployment of "cabbage strategy," a term coined by PLA General Zhang Zhaozhong to describe the formation of different layers of force to seize control over what China deemed disputed territories.[3]

The disputes in the South China Sea became even more complicated in the context of the United States' "pivot" to, or "rebalancing" in, the Asia-Pacific. As mentioned in Chapter 7, in July 2010, US Secretary of State Hillary Clinton surprised the Chinese audience by her statement at the ARF gathering in Hanoi that the US has national interest in the South China Sea. Subsequently, officials in Washington signalled greater activism and stronger accent on the Asia-Pacific regional diplomatically, militarily and economically. In September 2011, in her article *Asia's Pacific Century* to *Foreign Policy*, Clinton proclaimed the US policy of "pivot" from the Middle East to the Pacific in, declaring that the

> United States helped shape a region-wide effort to protect unfettered access to and passage through the South China Sea, and to uphold the key international rules for defining territorial claims in the South China Sea's waters.[4]

Later, US officials redefined their policy as "rebalancing" to avoid negative connotations associated with the word "pivot." During his visit to Australia in November 2011, President Obama confirmed the United States' greater engagement with the Asia-Pacific and revealed a plan to deploy US Marines and airplanes to Australia's Northern Territory on a rotational basis.[5] In June 2012, US Secretary of Defense unveiled a plan to redeploy 60 per cent of US naval assets to the Asia-Pacific region by 2020.[6] Diplomatically, the US officials took initiatives to strengthen its alliance system, develop new partnerships, and actively participate in multilateral forum. Economically, Washington strongly pushed for finalisation of the negotiation on the Trans-Pacific Partnership (TPP).[7]

The South China Sea had gradually become one of the fault lines of global politics. The Chinese were highly suspicious of Washington's forward presence, believing that the United States' rebalancing policy is designed to "contain" rising China.[8] Propagandists in Beijing usually labelled China as "a victim" of other countries' unilateral actions and blamed the US for instigating other claimants to meddle the South China Sea waters. However, it is more obvious from the strategic point of view that the PLA was trying to turn the South China Sea into a sanctuary for its strategic submarine force stationing in Hainan as well as a safe passage for them to the open sea.[9] This provided rationale behind China's activism in expanding military and civilian presence in this strategic body of water. On the part of the US, Washington was concerned about China's rapid naval expansions, which would pose a threat to its naval primacy in the region. Besides, it was also afraid that China will upset the legal maritime order underpinned by UNCLOS. As a result, it wanted to uphold the right to conduct surveillance and intelligence collection activities in China's EEZs under the guise of freedom of navigation. However, American officials were at pains to restate their neutral position over sovereignty dispute and disassociate their "rebalancing" with "containment."

The advent of new strategic landscape, featured by the US-China contest for primacy, has put all middle and small powers in the region, including Vietnam, in a strategic predicament. On the one hand, Vietnam is at the spearhead of China's naval and maritime expansions, which pose a more imminent danger to its foothold in the Spratlys and its jurisdiction over a large part of the EEZs off its shore. From the Vietnamese strategic point of view, the sea band beyond its long coastline is strategically and economically important to Vietnam. However, China's nine-dash line claim cut into 70 per cent of the EEZs that Vietnam claims under UNCLOS.[10] Vietnam has a strong interest in defending these areas but is short of capabilities to resist China's overwhelming naval and civilian forces. Vietnam's acquisition of six Kilo-class submarines is unlikely to change its power equation with China, which was operating 70 submarines.[11] Consequently, Hanoi was in a more pressing need for some source of counter-balancing power to deter aggressions from China. The United States, the only power that is militarily capable of checking China, is the promising option. Vietnam and the United States interests converged to the need of maintaining stability in the South China Sea as well as maintaining UNCLOS-based maritime order. The Obama administration's strategic refocus on Asia-Pacific has created opportunities for Hanoi to cultivate stronger security ties with Washington and seek its help to contain China's maritime ambition. However, from the Vietnamese point of view, the United States' interventions in the South China Sea affairs are not only for the purpose of maintaining stability and defending freedom of navigation in the South China Sea, but ultimately for the sake of containing rising China.[12] This state of affairs offers a favourable condition for Vietnam to transform its disputes with China to international issues to neutralise China's overwhelming power. However, it also entails risk of losing autonomy and getting deeply entangled into a "new Cold War" in Asia.[13]

Amid growing anxieties in the South China Sea region about China's rise, Vietnam exhibited a cool head with some degree of tolerance for strategic uncertainties. In spite of China's assertiveness and the United States' courtship, Vietnam has maintained its strategic autonomy, manifested in the reaffirmation of the "3 Nos" principle, namely no alliances, no foreign military bases in Vietnam, and no relations with one country against any third party, as part of its multi-component hedging strategy. Hanoi recognised "hot peace" characteristic of constant tensions and clashes with China as a "new normal" in the South China Sea, and there is no low-risk prospect for getting strategic help from outside. Officials in Hanoi were distrustful of balancing politics and repeatedly maintain that Vietnam would avoid being pulled into any big power's sphere of influence. They are equally concerned about the possibility that great powers like the United States and China would one day seek discreet bilateral covenants that are detrimental to Vietnam's interests.[14] It is clear that Vietnam did not want to turn itself into a pawn or a proxy in the chessboard of great powers. The subsequent sections in this chapter will describe how Hanoi showed resolve in the face of Beijing's expansionist attempts while avoiding escalations and open hostilities. In the same time, Vietnam tried to every way increase its relative value in strategic calculus of major powers and enhance bargaining power vis-à-vis China through self-strengthening and active international integration.

Vietnam's strategy of "cooperation and struggle" in managing its relations with China

The signing of the agreement on basic principles guiding settlement of maritime issues between Vietnam and China in 2011 did little to reduce the tensions in the South China Sea. The Chinese campaign of harassment and intimidation at sea continued, and the chain of actions and reactions persisted with escalating diplomatic spats. In April 2012, the Chinese forces reportedly seized two Vietnamese fishing boats together with twenty-one Vietnamese fishermen in the waters around the Paracels. In the same month, Chinese vessels engaged in a standoff with those from the Philippines in the Scarborough Shoal.[15] In May, Vietnam sent a note to protest that China issued passports embossed with the nine-dash line map.[16] It might be Chinese hope that Vietnam authorities' stamps on these passports could represent Vietnam's recognition of Chinese claims. Vietnam showed its disapproval by issuing visas on separate piece of papers rather than stamping on Chinese passports. The new Chinese passports later became a regional disgrace, when India, Vietnam, Taiwan and the Philippines all objected to such acts of manipulation by China.[17]

In June 2012, in a bid to affirm its claims, Vietnam's National Assembly passed the Law of the Sea of Vietnam, which reiterates Vietnam's sovereignty over the Paracels and Spratlys and its maritime rights given by UNCLOS 1982. The reading of this legal document unveiled that the Law of the Sea of Vietnam is essentially the codification of UNCLOS 1982 into Vietnam's national legislation. The adoption of such law had two meanings. First, it signified that Vietnam firmly bases its maritime claims on UNCLOS. Second, it was a show of determination to safeguard the country's rights in the face of China's assertiveness. It should be noted that the law was first proposed as early as 1998 but the debate and enacting of the bill had been repeatedly delayed due to disagreements among agencies over stipulations and deliberations to avoid disturbance to Hanoi's relations with Beijing.[18] By the adoption of the Law of the Sea of Vietnam amid rising tensions, Hanoi sent a clear message to Beijing that it would not back down in the face of Beijing's gunboat diplomacy.

China reacted furiously to Vietnam's defiant act. Right after the adoption of the Law of the Sea of Vietnam, the China Foreign Ministry summoned Vietnamese Ambassador in Beijing to make a loud protest, calling it "illegal, invalid and detrimental to peace and stability in the South China Sea."[19] In a well-prepared move, Beijing announced to upgrade the city Sansha, which was assigned to govern the Spratlys, the Paracels, and the Macclesfield Bank, from county level to prefecture level in terms of administration. This move represented Beijing's attempt to assert its claims through administrative and jurisdictional measures. A week later, state-owned China National Offshore Oil Corporation (CNOOC) offered tender for nine concession blocks off the central and southern coast of Vietnam, which were well within the EEZ and continental shelf that Vietnam claimed. It is clearly a political move on the part of Beijing, and no international companies were reported to heed CNOOC's bidding invitation.[20] Hanoi tried to denounce Chinese actions bilaterally and in ASEAN forums, but ASEAN failed to agree on any statement specifically naming China in its foreign ministerial meeting in July 2012. The rest of 2012 witnessed continuing unilateral and provocative acts on the part of China, which sparked concerns across the region. On 30 November 2012, Hainan authorities adopted new rules to allow Chinese police to board and seize foreign ships which "illegal enter" Chinese waters. Three days later, the Vietnamese authorities accused two Chinese trawlers of deliberately interfering and cutting the survey cable of Vietnamese exploratory ship *Binh Minh 02* in the area off the Gulf of Tonkin, 43 miles from Vietnam's Con Co Island but 75 miles from China's Hainan Island.[21]

The year 2013 witnessed a calmer atmosphere in the South China Sea for Vietnam. Incidents between Vietnamese fishermen and Chinese coast guards were somehow routinised, but no long-standing diplomatic tensions ensued. China showed a conciliatory gesture, agreeing to set up hotlines between navies and fishery agencies of the two countries.[22] However, anxiety and vigilance remained, prompting Hanoi to closely follow Chinese activities. A Vietnamese source revealed that Chinese forces conducted more than thirty naval exercises in the South China Sea in 2013.[23] Tensions between Hanoi and Beijing were somehow relieved perhaps because China turned its spearhead towards the Philippines after Manila brought China's nine-dash line claims and its "unlawful actions" to international arbitration in 2013, which will be discussed in a later section. China refused to participate in the court and tried in vain to persuade Manila to withdraw from the lawsuit. In the same year, China's expansions also rattled other littoral countries in Asia. In May, China angered Malaysia by staging a naval exercise in the area of the James Shoal. In November, China shocked Japan by declaring an Air Defence Identification Zone in the East China Sea, encompassing the airspace above the Senkaku/Diaoyu Islands. In early 2014, Chinese coast guard vessels imposed a blockade against the Philippines-controlled Second Thomas Shoal, and reportedly prevented the Philippines' ships from resupplying the Filipino troops stationed in a wrecked ship aground on the atoll.[24] It was now clear that China's maritime ambition spared no countries, even Malaysia, which had mostly been deferential to Beijing's positions.

Detente between Vietnam and China in the South China Sea proved to be short-lived. In May 2014, Beijing suddenly installed China-made giant oil rig Haiyang Shiyou 981 (HYSY 981), escorted by dozens of ships, in the area near the Paracels, but just 120 n.m. from the Vietnamese shore. The timing of deployment was a surprise to region observers because it took place on the heels of Chinese Prime Minister Li Keqiang's visit to Hanoi in November 2013 and right after President Obama finished his visit to four Asian countries in late April 2014.[25] Earnest Bower and Gregroy Poling speculated that China attempted to test the resolve of Vietnam, ASEAN countries and particularly the US. It should also be noted that Washington was then distracted by the Ukrainian political crisis and Russia's takeover of Crimea.[26] Dingding Chen argued that China action was prompted by oil and the belief that Vietnam, too much dependent on China economically, was helpless.[27] On the other hand, Do Thanh Hai believed the China-created oil rig crisis was just a diversion to draw international attention away from China's game-changing move of massive land reclamation in the Spratly area.[28] Without sufficient access to Chinese decision-making, China's calculations behind the deployment remained unknown. The only sure thing is that this action was not an initiative by the Hainan authority or any single agency. Such a large-scale and well-coordinated operation must have been given the green light from Beijing.

The Vietnamese regarded the deployment of the oil rig as a grave violation of the country's EEZ and continental shelf and sent its coast guard vessels to confront the cordon of Chinese ships. That led to a two-month dangerous square-off between Chinese and Vietnamese law enforcement vessels in this area and an intense diplomatic spat between Hanoi and Beijing.[29] It should be noted that China had deployed rigs in the maritime zones Vietnam claimed in 1997 and 2004. However, the HYSY 981 posed a greater security challenge to Hanoi in a number of ways. First, it stood out in the number of deployed ships and the level of physical violence. Chinese vessels, which are superior in terms of size, strength and equipment, reportedly rammed into and fired high-pressure water cannons on Vietnamese vessels. At least one Vietnamese ship was sunk and dozens were crippled. Second, the standoff generated a strong anti-China sentiment in Vietnam, which then erupted into large-scale demonstrations and deadly riots in a couple of localities in Vietnam. Hundreds of foreign factories, mistaken as Chinese ones, were devastated, and at least four Chinese nationals died.[30]

Hanoi managed the crisis with care. Vietnam showed its perseverance to resist China's intimidation, sending most of its coast guard vessels near the oil rig day and night to confront the overwhelming Chinese fleet. However, the VPA Navy kept its warships either onshore or away from the area to avoid escalation. Reportedly, Vietnamese officials at different levels had made around dozens of requests for talks, but their Chinese counterparts consistently rejected them.[31] Four hotlines between executives in Hanoi and Beijing apparently did not work well when they were most needed.[32] Vietnamese leaders then threatened to take legal actions against China and at the same time brought the issue to the domestic and international public, raising its objections through its partners, multilateral forums, and the international community. Observably, Hanoi conducted a public relations campaign to criticise China's gunboat diplomacy, projecting an image of China as a bully through a series of high-profile press conferences. International reporters were allowed on-board Vietnamese coast guard vessels to witness the aggressive manoeuvres of the Chinese boats. Vietnamese officials raised the South China Sea issue everywhere possible, in all bilateral meetings with their counterparts, in ASEAN meetings, and in the United Nations forum. Clearly, Vietnam's main front was not at sea, but in the diplomatic and public relations realm to inflict political costs on China. In the context of mounting international backlash, China withdrew the oil rig in mid-July 2014 before the deadline it announced previously. Interestingly, defiance is always followed by deference in Vietnam's management of the crisis. Though being angered at China's oil rig intrusion, Hanoi always kept open the bilateral door with Beijing during the intense standoff. After China's removal of the oil rig from the area, Vietnam took the first move to reconcile with China by sending the head of the Party Secretariat Le Hong Anh to improve the relations.[33]

Though being critical of the unilateral and heavy-handed approach in China's South China Sea policy, Hanoi has showed no sense of urgency in changing its China policy. The Vietnamese leaders repeatedly restated the twin objectives: to defend its sovereignty and legitimate maritime interests and to keep peace and preserve friendship with China.[34] Vietnamese Prime Minister Nguyen Tan Dung described Vietnam's China policy as "cooperation cum struggle."[35] Hanoi calibrated a mixture of defiance and deference to prove to Beijing that its coercions were not worthwhile. On the one hand, it has indicated a strong resolve to hold the line in front of perceived Chinese intrusions and, at the same time, rally international support to impose higher political costs on Beijing. On the other hand, Vietnam deliberately avoided tit-for-tat responses and insisted on bilateral talks to defuse tensions and look for ways forward. According to Vietnamese officials, the bilateral channel still serves as the primary conduit for two countries to seek longstanding resolution of the disputes, manage the incidents, and foster functional cooperation for the sake of confidence-building pending the final settlement.[36] Beyond the South China Sea, regular high-level meetings allow the two countries to communicate their strategic intents to avoid misperceptions and security dilemma.

In this regard, the Agreement on the Basic Principles Guiding the Settlement of the Sea-related Issues between Vietnam and China signed in October 2011 was significant in a way that it reopened the channel of regularised bilateral dialogue on management and resolution of existing disputes, which were effectively suspended since 2007. It was agreed that the heads of the two countries' negotiating teams would meet twice a year, or more if the circumstance necessitates, in order to review the results of the working groups. In the follow-up in February 2012, the two sides established two technical-level joint working groups, one to negotiate the delimitation of the area immediately beyond the Gulf of Tonkin and joint development in this area and the other to discuss maritime cooperation on the less-sensitive areas, including environmental protection, scientific research, search and rescue, disaster prevention and relief and so on. Between 2012 and 2015, Vietnam and China set up four more hotlines between their foreign ministries, fishery agencies, and defence ministries, apart from the hotline between their high-level leaders installed in 2009.[37] The establishment of the additional hotlines was generally indicative of intentions of both sides to manage incidents promptly and avoid escalations, though they may not work well on some circumstances.

As indicated in the agreement, Vietnam and China decided to move away from impasses on the Spratlys and Paracels to particularly focus on delimitation of the area beyond the Gulf of Tonkin and confidence-building cooperative activities. The two sides stressed the principle of gradualism and "easy-first, difficult-later."[38] Bilateral talks were structured the same way as the previous fruitful negotiations on the land border and the Gulf of Tonkin, starting with specialised working groups to narrow the scope of disagreement as much as possible from the technical point of view. Remaining issues were to be included into the agenda of the meetings at higher administrative and political levels. In addition to these mechanisms, defence leaders of Vietnam and China also meet each other annually, reaffirming the agreement that the militaries would not resort to force to resolve existing disputes.[39] The Joint Steering Committee on Bilateral Cooperation between Vietnam and China, chaired by their deputy prime ministers, is convened once a year to monitor all areas of cooperation. Above all, senior party leaders of both countries will also meet at least once a year to review and guide lower-level consultations. Interestingly, antagonism at sea has not alienated Hanoi from Beijing, but thickened problem-solving exchanges between them. No country in Southeast Asia had achieved such a sophisticated and broad-based channel of dialogue with China for managing and resolving maritime affairs and expanding cooperation.

The latest challenges for Vietnam were China's large-scale land reclamations and militarisation in the Spratlys. The project began in late 2013 and accelerated since mid-2014.[40] The satellite images compiled by the Asia Maritime Transparency Initiative at the Washington-based Center for Strategic and International Studies showed that China mobilised hundreds of dredgers to the Spratlys, working day and night to suck seabed sediment and pump it onto seven China-controlled reefs, namely Subi Reef, Fiery Cross Reef, Mischief Reef, Cuareton Reef, Gaven Reef, Hughes Reef and Johnson South Reef. The object was to create extensive above-water surfaces. China's island-building project startled all observers and sent shockwaves across the region because of the project's speed and scale. By August 2015, when China announced the completion of land reclamation, it was estimated that China built as much as 2,900 acres of new land, a pace and scope which surprised all observers.[41] In just a year and a half China reclaimed a landmass seventeen times larger than the total area reclaimed by all other claimants over four decades.[42] Reportedly, China had built three airstrips, a range of port facilities, radar systems, and logistic centres on the new islands. Most significantly, the airstrip on the Fiery Cross Reef, which has the longest runway in the Spratly area, could accommodate all types of military airplanes and fighters.

In the face of mounting apprehensions about Chinese militarisation of the Spratlys, officials in Beijing claimed that the new islands would be used for both civilian and defence purposes. There was a concern in Hanoi that China would claim EEZs and continental shelves for those man-made islands, which were originally submerged reefs and low-tide elevations.[43] However, Vietnamese strategists worried more about China's greater coercive and offensive capabilities in the South China Sea. Installations in the newly built islands would enable China to enhance power projection abilities as well as to support its fishing fleets and coast guards to exercise administrative control over the South China Sea. They warned about the possibilities that China would one day try to pose a blockade to the features controlled by other claimants.[44] They also speculated that Beijing would soon establish an Air Defence Identification Zone in the South China Sea as it did in the East China Sea.[45] From the legal point of view, Vietnamese analysts also raised concerns about the environmental and legal consequences of China's land reclamation. Though Hanoi loudly protested China's land reclamation and militarisation, there was not much it could do to stop it. This development indicated to Hanoi that economic interdependence and ideological similarity were unable hold China back, and management of Vietnam-China relations would become all the more difficult. Increased vulnerabilities to China's intense embattlement prompted Vietnam to shift more chips to the Western powers.

Vietnam backing the Philippines' legal proceedings but holding its legal option in reserve

On 22 January 2013, the Philippines requested to set up an arbitral tribunal under the Annex VII to the Law of the Sea Convention to address a range of issues related to the interpretation and application of the Convention in the South China Sea. In its Notification and Statement of Claim, the Philippines argues that China's nine-dash line claim is inconsistent with UNCLOS provisions and charges that China had "interfered the lawful exercise by the Philippines of its rights under the Convention, including within its own exclusive economic zone and continental shelves."[46] Clearly, Manila tried to avoid the issue of sovereignty over the features to focus on the issue of rights and obligations of the coastal states under UNCLOS. The Philippines' submission argues that none of China-controlled features in the Spratlys should be categorised as "islands" under Article 121 of UNCLOS. In its view, the Mischief Reef, McKennan Reef, Gaven Reef and Subi Reef, are low-tide elevations, while Johnson Reef, Cuarteron Reef and Fiery Cross Reef are rocks, and none of these features is entitled to EEZs and continental shelves.[47] Beijing protested the Philippines' legal initiation, insisted on bilateralism as only way to resolve the disputes, and applied pressures on Manila to force it to withdraw the lawsuit. As the Philippines persisted with its appeal and the tribunal was established, China refused to participate in the proceedings and issued a position paper, arguing that the tribunal has no jurisdiction on what it perceived as disputes over territorial sovereignty. In the Chinese view, the dispute over sovereignty over insular features should be resolved before maritime delimitation.[48]

Manila's legal action was directly prompted from the standoff in Scarborough Shoal in 2012 and its helplessness in front of China's determination to exclude the Filipino vessels from that area, just about 124 n.m. from the Philippines' Luzon but 550 n.m. from China's Hainan Island. The administration of President Benigno Aquino accused China of dishonouring a deal between them in mid-June 2012 to vacate the Scarborough Shoal. Manila asked Washington for help, but the Obama administration could not help it regain control of the Scarborough Shoal. Criticising China for violating the DOC, Philippine Foreign Minister Albert del Rosario attempted to forge a unified ASEAN reproach of China's actions during the ASEAN Foreign Ministers' Meeting (AMM) in Phnom Penh in July 2012. This endeavour was undercut by Cambodia, which was assuming the ASEAN chairmanship but played the role of China's proxy. As a result, for the first time in ASEAN history, this AMM meeting failed to issue a joint communiqué due to vast disagreement among its members over the South China Sea issue.[49] In 2011, Manila tried in vain to put forward its initiative of a Zone of Peace, Friendship, Freedom and Cooperation (ZoPFFC), calling all the claimants to clarify their claims, narrowing down the disputed area, demilitarise the features, and establish a joint development agency to manage undersea resources. Though obtaining support from Vietnam, Philippine diplomats were unsuccessful to gain approval from other ASEAN members for its initiative. So, it is a fair assessment that Manila's litigation was also a culmination of long-standing frustration in the Philippines about China's persistent assertiveness, US half-hearted support, and ASEAN disunity on the controversial issue involving China. In other words, Manila was effectively out of ammunition to stand up against China's overwhelming forces in the South China Sea.

Much to Beijing's displeasure, Hanoi implicitly supported the Philippines' legal proceeding, though it was not consulted beforehand. Deputy Chairman of Vietnam Foreign Ministry's National Border Committee said that countries have the right to settle the disputes in conformity with the UN Charter and international law.[50] No doubt, Vietnam and the Philippines share an interest in invalidating China's nine-dash line claim and strongly advocate a proper interpretation and application of UNCLOS 1982 in defining maritime zones and delimitation. They all were concerned about China's rapid militarisation and its "might-makes-right" approach in the South China Sea. As mentioned in Chapter 3, since the mid-1990s Vietnam was more open to settle the disputes over the Paracels and Spratlys in the International Court of Justice (ICJ), but the Chinese consistently rejected this option. As disputes over maritime zones emerged, Hanoi increasingly relied on UNCLOS to define and defend its maritime claims as a response to perceived China's expansive claims and assertive actions. After China signed the Crestone contract in 1992, Vietnam hired a Washington-based law firm to analyse the strength of its claim vis-à-vis that of China over the Tu Chinh and Thanh Long areas. In the context of China's increased assertiveness since 2007, Vietnamese analysts openly called for more serious consideration of the legal option, especially requests for advisory opinions on its maritime rights and obligations under UNCLOS. China's call for bidding for nine lots in Vietnam's EEZs in July 2012 prompted an internal debate in the Vietnamese officialdom on whether legal options would be helpful to denounce perceived illegal actions of China. No actions were taken at the last. In that stage, it seemed that Vietnamese legal experts were uncertain about how best to use third-party arbitration and how effective such options would be in constraining China. China's 2006 declaration to opt out of compulsory procedures with binding decisions under UNCLOS was seen as an obstacle.[51] Consequently, Hanoi had utilised international law primarily as a political tool rather than a pathway to resolve the disputes. By internationalising the South China Sea issue, Vietnamese diplomats sought every way to expose China's legally weak maritime claims and actions to international scrutiny with hope that China would back down.

The Philippines' legal proceeding opened up three legal pathways for Vietnam to address the South China Sea disputes. First, Vietnam could join the lawsuit initiated by the Philippines to challenge the legality of China's nine-dash line claim and its coercive actions in the South China Sea. Second, Hanoi could file a separate submission specifically tailored to challenge China's violations of Vietnam's rights to EEZs and continental shelves under UNCLOS. Third, it could take a wait and see approach while keeping minimal involvement in the Philippines' case to assert its claims and defend its rights and interests in case of necessity. After two years of consideration, on 5 December 2014, Hanoi decided to undertake the third option, lodging a Statement of Interest to ask the Permanent Court of Arbitration (PCA) between the Philippines and China in The Hague to take due regard of its opinions, rights and interests. Vietnam's Statement of Interest recognises the PCA's jurisdiction over the Philippine's case, restates Vietnam's claim to sovereignty over the Spratlys and Paracels, refutes China's nine-dash line claim, and reserves the right to seek to intervene appropriately if necessary.[52] Vietnam also went as far as to assert that none of the features mentioned in the Philippines' statement of claim "can enjoy their own exclusive economic zone and continental shelf, or generate maritime entitlements in excess of 12 nautical miles since they are low-tide elevations or 'rocks' under Article 121 (3) of the Convention."[53] Carlyle A. Thayer commented that, by such a statement, Vietnam basically made its legal case "through the back door." Interestingly, Vietnam filed its submission on the same day the US State Department released its *Limits in the Seas* report that questions the legal foundation of China's nine-dash line claim.[54]

After all, Vietnam still held its legal option in reserve. The Philippines' legal fire also created enormous pressures on the Vietnamese leadership from both inside or outside the country to take legal actions against China, either by joining the Philippines' case or initiating a separate lawsuit. The calls for legal option multiplied especially during the HYSY 981 crisis in mid-2014. Indeed, Vietnamese Prime Minister Nguyen Tan Dung openly threatened a legal case against China's oil rig intrusion and aggressive acts. A source close to Vietnam's politics revealed that the Politburo met and weighed a range of options, and the majority of Politburo members were in favour of international arbitration. Interestingly, not so long after the Politburo meeting, China pulled the oil rig and Vietnam held its legal fire after all.[55] According to Vietnamese specialists, though their opinions are similar in most aspects, Vietnam did not want to formally participate in the Philippines' proceeding as co-plaintiff, as the Philippines designed the case without notification to and consultation with Vietnam and other Southeast Asian claimants. Also, Vietnam does not want to be disadvantaged vis-à-vis China if the arbitration tribunal at the PCA has any ruling that ties its hands but not those of the Chinese.[56] By the end of 2015, the arbitration tribunal decided that it has jurisdiction over the case and the court entered the merit phase. That was regarded as initial triumph for the Philippines, as most Chinese arguments on jurisdiction and admissibility were rejected. Still, Vietnam remained cautious with any separate legal proceedings against China mostly because of possible disruption of the bilateral relations. After all, Vietnam was highly interconnected with China economically.

Yet, Vietnam was by no means ready to forgo the legal option. A senior Vietnamese official made it clear that Hanoi had prepared its South China Sea legal files for a long time and considered lawsuit a peaceful means to settle disputes. But Vietnamese leaders were always prudent about when and how legal actions should be taken.[57] So far, Vietnam has not been as desperate as the Philippines was when it lost control of the Scarborough Shoal to China. The Philippines had insufficient means to engage in a prolonged standoff with China in this area while its government was under great pressures from the population to challenge China's de facto control. As with the HYSY 981 crisis, Vietnam showed it had capabilities as well as determination to stand up against China's superior force. Also, it had greater room to manoeuvre in terms of soliciting support from ASEAN, Western partners, and the international community. Hanoi also indicated that it was willing to resort to the legal option if the Chinese would not back down. Still, the legal option was a high-risk one, with uncertain outcomes. After all, officials in Hanoi believe that the South China Sea wrangles are not merely legal disputes, but a set of complex, interrelated problems involving substantive strategic, political and economic consequences. It implies that in the Vietnamese view, arbitration alone would have limited effect on the resolution of the existing disputes.

International integration as pathway to exit China's orbit

The 11th National Congress of the Communist Party of Vietnam in January 2011 forged a consensus on the hedging policy. National interests were defined as the sole basis of Vietnam's foreign policy. Moreover, the Congress put forth the policy of pro-active international integration, signalling larger initiative and participation in multilateral political and economic arrangements. Also, Vietnam is committed to ASEAN's community building as a cornerstone of its foreign affairs. Last but not least, Vietnam vows to become a responsible member of the international community with willingness to abide with commonly accepted rules and norms, to make greater contributions to address global issues, and to dialogue with other countries on the issues of democracy and human rights.[58] These four guidelines were indicative of a stress on pragmatism over ideology over Vietnam's foreign policy.

In a bid to further these guidelines, in April 2013, the Central Committee adopted Resolution No.22-NQ/TW on integration (in short, Resolution 22), codifying "pro-active international integration" as a "major strategic orientation of the Party."

Resolution 22 was effectively an upgrade of Resolution 7 adopted by the Politburo in November 2001, which prescribed deeper economic integration into the international economic system. Resolution 22 prescribed that integration would not be limited to the economic sector, but would expand to other fields, particularly politics, security and defence, and culture. Economic integration (with advanced economies) was a priority while international cooperation in other fields must create favourable conditions for economic integration. Though the term "integration" implied inclusive connotation, it implies the door was now more open for expanding cooperation with Western powers in political and security realms. The resolution also stated that Vietnam would take a more active and positive stance in multilateral arrangements in order to "contribute to building just, democratic political and economic orders, prevent wars and conflicts, consolidate peace, and promote mutually beneficial cooperation."[59] This reflected Vietnam's desire to move from the back seat in multilateral institutions, from passive participation to a more active and leading role in order to shape international rules and norms.

Consequently, Vietnam exhibited a newfound extraordinary zeal for multilateralism. After being elected to the UNSC for the term 2008–2009, Vietnam continued to lobby for executive membership in the Human Rights Council for the term 2014–2016, the Economic and Social Council (ECOSCO) for the term 2016–2018, and the Board of Governors of the International Atomic Energy Agency (IAEA) for the term 2013–2015, the World Heritage Committee for the term 2013–2017, and the Executive Committee of UNESCO. Vietnam also prepared for its ASEAN chairmanship in 2020 and to run for UNSC again for the term 2020–2021.[60] At the same time, Vietnam is also committed to and has made considerable efforts towards the establishment of the ASEAN Economic Community (AEC). By the end of 2015, Vietnam and Singapore took the lead in implementing EAC measures, with 94.5 per cent completion.[61] In 2014, for the first time, Vietnam took part in United Nations Peacekeeping Operations (PKO), sending its first group of officers to Sudan. This marked a significant change in Vietnam's attitude towards PKO activities, which was viewed in the past by Hanoi as intervention into a country's domestic affairs and contrary to the principle of sovereignty and non-interference. The participation in PKO was now viewed as part of international integration in defence, which brings about international public goods and improves Vietnam's international prestige. Multilateralism has become a pillar of Vietnam's diplomacy, which may protect Vietnam from Chinese realpolitik in two ways. First, Vietnam had utilised these multilateral arrangements to raise its concerns about China's behaviour in the South China Sea if necessary. Second, these roles bolstered Vietnam's international stance, and helped it gain more friends and partners, which could provide political support in case it is needed.

Observably, Vietnam also accelerated its political and security engagement with the United States and other powers in the context of China's maritime assertiveness. In September 2011, Vietnam and the United States concluded a Memorandum of Understanding on defence cooperation, which lays out regular high-level defence dialogue and a range of cooperation on maritime security, search and rescue, experience exchange on peacekeeping operations, and humanitarian assistance and disaster relief. In June 2012, amid tensions between Vietnam and China about Vietnam's Law of the Sea and China's tender for nine blocks within the Vietnam-claimed EEZ, Hanoi invited US Defense Secretary Leon Panetta to take a highly symbolic visit to the Cam Ranh Bay. Reportedly, Defence Minister Phung Quang Thanh asked his US counterpart to remove the US ban on arms sales. In July 2013, Vietnam and the United States signed a declaration on the Vietnam-US Comprehensive Partnership, which encompassed a range of cooperation from maritime capacity building, economic engagement, climate change and environmental issues, education cooperation and promoting respect for human rights. In December 2013, US Secretary of State John Kerry unveiled a US plan to provide Vietnam with five patrol boats and a fund of USD 18 million to enhance the capacity of the Vietnamese Coast Guard.[62] In October 2014, Kerry announced that the US would now consider the sale of lethal weapons to Vietnam on a case-by-case basis to assist Vietnam in maritime domain awareness and maritime security capabilities.

In July 2015 came a major turning point, when Vietnam's Party Secretary General Nguyen Phu Trong made a historic visit to Washington. This was the first visit ever by a communist party chief to Washington, and President Barack Obama received him in the Oval Office in the capacity of a head of state. From the Vietnamese perspective, the White House's protocol represents the shift in the United States' position on Vietnam. Setting aside its criticism of the one-party regime, Washington now recognised the role of the Communist Party in Vietnam and Trong's role as Vietnam's head of state. In the same way, Trong's visit could be viewed as a transformation in Vietnam's domestic politics where pragmatism now dictates Vietnam's foreign policy. Even the most conservative figure in the party structure now recognises the importance of the United States to Vietnam's security and development.

The timing of Trong's visit indicated that China's HYSY 981 deployment and land reclamation in the Spratlys was the key stimulus for the shift. It should be noted that Washington extended an invitation to Trong as early as 2012 but the trip was not made until mid-2015.[63] There was some reluctance on the part of the party ideologues to accept the standing invitation. However, some signs of change came after the HYSY 981. Between July 2014 and July 2015, eight out of sixteen Politburo members made their way to Washington and at least six Cabinet-level US officials travelled the other way. In his visit to Beijing just two months before travelling to Washington, Trong failed to persuade Xi Jinping to stop China's ongoing island-building project in the Spratlys. Also, by mid-2015, the negotiation on the Trans-Pacific Partnership came to its final phase. If negotiators failed to reach a consensus by the end of 2015, there would have been no prospect for an agreement before 2017. Clearly, Trong's visit to Washington was not only rich in symbolic meaning but also important in substance, which signified that Vietnam was committed to integrate further into the US-led economic system through the Trans-Pacific Partnership. Hanoi also sent a stronger message to Beijing about its dissatisfaction. In November 2015, Vietnam welcomed Chinese President Xi Jinping in Hanoi while hosting a joint military activity with Japan in Cam Ranh

Bay.[64] The refusal to defer the Japanese warship's visit during the first visit of the Chinese president in a decade sent a subtle message to Beijing that Vietnamese deference should not be taken for granted.

Observers often depicted Vietnam's behaviour as a "balancing act," a "careful dance" and "tightrope walking" between the United States and China.[65] It is somehow true that Vietnam has tried to leverage its relations with the United States on China. It is equally tempting to believe that Vietnam is coming closer to the United States and to become its informal strategic ally. However, while Hanoi was trying to exit China's orbit, it did not fall into the embrace of other big powers. Hanoi deliberately deepened its hedging strategy, leveraging its enhanced relations with other powers to offset China's centripetal pull. It was manifest in a range of partnership with major powers and countries that Vietnam had developed over time. In 2012, Vietnam and Russia upgraded its strategic partnership to one more comprehensive. In 2013, Vietnam launched strategic partnerships with France and Italy, and three Southeast Asian nations, namely Indonesia, Thailand and Singapore. By the end of 2015, Vietnam established a comprehensive strategic cooperative partnership with China; a comprehensive strategic partnership with Russia; thirteen strategic partnerships with Japan, India, South Korea, the UK, Spain, Germany, Italy, Thailand, Indonesia, Singapore, France, Malaysia and the Philippines; and ten comprehensive partnerships with South Africa, Chile, Brazil, Venezuela, Australia, New Zealand, Argentina, Ukraine, the United States and Denmark.

As discussed in Chapter 5, partnerships with big powers and countries were part of Hanoi's hedging strategy to counterpoise China's influence and broaden its room for manoeuvre. Vietnam customised its relations with partners according to their strengths and Vietnam's security and development needs. For example, partnerships with China and Russia are comprehensive in all sectors. The UK is expected to be a good partner in the field of economy and education. France is a partner in energy, aviation and space technology.[66] However, there have been no clear and consistent criteria or a unified approach to rank partners as comprehensive or strategic or the like. Sometimes, it is dependent on circumstances, perceptions and preference of Vietnam as well as its partners. In the case of Australia, Vietnam proposed the brand of "strategic partnership" but Australia only accepted "comprehensive partnership." In the case of the United States, former Secretary of State Hillary Clinton put forth the proposal of strategic partnership, but Vietnam only accepted an upgrade to "comprehensive partnership."[67] Symbolically speaking, China enjoyed the superior status in the list of Vietnam's partners as the sole "comprehensive strategic cooperative partner." Russia ranked second as "comprehensive strategic partner" and was followed by thirteen "strategic partners" and ten "comprehensive partners" as mentioned earlier. Though the United States was situated at the lowest ladder of the hierarchy as a "comprehensive partner," it was obviously the most important hedge for Hanoi to reduce the risk from China. Consequently, Hanoi clearly wanted to moderate the pace of expansion in cooperation between Vietnam and the United States so that it could have room for further upgrade if China became more belligerent.

Rising economic nationalism

Since 2010, China's assertiveness also created an acute sense of economic insecurity in Hanoi. Amid tensions over the Japanese arrest of a captain of a Chinese fishing boat in the vicinity of the Senkaku Islands, China called for the release of the crew and exerted pressures on Tokyo by halting shipments of rare earth (an essential material to an array of manufactured products such as hybrid cars, wind turbines, and guided missiles) to Japan. This embargo was clearly imposed on Japan only, as shipments of rare earth minerals were still sent to Singapore, Hong Kong and other destinations.[68] During the Scarborough Shoal crisis in mid-2012, China also stopped buying bananas from the Philippines, claiming that "minibugs" were found in the shipments. This import restriction caused significant damage to the Philippines' banana farmers, which exported 30 per cent of their products to China.[69] Though China denied the relations of those incidents with territorial spats, it was indicative that Beijing was more than willing to use economic clout against its adversaries in territorial disputes.

China's inclination to use economic leverages sent out a wake-up call to Vietnam. As a direct outcome of its engagement policy, Vietnam has been increasingly connected to China economically. As mentioned previously, China has been the largest trading partner of Vietnam since 2004. However, Vietnam holds a damaging trade deficit with China, which increased dramatically from USD 200 million in 2001 to more than USD 20 billion in 2012, USD 28.9 billion in 2014, and USD 32.3 billion in 2015. With regard to the terms of trade, Vietnam was in a disadvantaged position, importing higher-value-added products such as consumer goods and machinery while exporting mostly minerals and commodities with low added values. It was critical that Vietnam increasingly relied on imports of semi-products and intermediate inputs for its manufacture of export goods. For example, about 50 per cent of the materials for Vietnam's garment and textile industries were imported from China.[70] China was also a key supplier of machinery and equipment for Vietnam's key electricity and mining projects. In the late 2000s, Vietnamese officials and economists believed that these dependencies were indispensable as Vietnam needed economic growth and such pattern of trade was normal as decided by the global production network.[71]

China's economic coercions on Japan and the Philippines made them change their minds. In December 2012, Deputy Foreign Minister Pham Quang Vinh warned China against using trade as a weapon to force other countries to change their approaches and back down from their territorial positions.[72] Hanoi was clearly worried that Vietnam would be the next target of China's economic manipulation and such reliance would tie its hands, as was the case of the legal option. Such a concern was reinforced by the HYSY 981 crisis in mid-2014. During this period, Chinese lenders suspended credit lines to engineering, procurement and construction contracts (EPC) in Vietnam.[73] The incident triggered unprecedented public discourse about the magnitude and implications of Vietnam's economic dependence on China. There were widespread concerns and a large number of calls for the government to address such situations and ultimately find ways to exit the Chinese orbit. At the same time, economic nationalism rose throughout cyberspace, with floods of complaints about China's toxic products as well as the quality and sluggishness of infrastructure projects built on Chinese loans. All these reinforced Vietnam's popular distrust of Chinese infrastructure initiatives such as the One Belt One Road (OBOR) and the Asian Infrastructure and Investment Bank (AIIB) first proposed by the Chinese government in October 2013. Vietnamese scholars questioned the hidden agenda of such initiatives, suspecting that such projects would further Chinese geostrategic ambitions.[74]

Though aware of this vulnerability, the Vietnamese government has not shunned China economically. Hanoi participated in the ASEAN-centred initiative on Regional Comprehensive Economic Partnership (RCEP) and also took part in China's infrastructural development initiatives. During the visit of party chief Nguyen Phu Trong to Beijing in April 2015, Vietnam and China agreed to establish a task force for infrastructure and financial cooperation.[75] It was clear that in a thirst for infrastructure development, Vietnam did not want to be left out from these China-led groupings and miss any source of finance at a time of global economic difficulty. However, Vietnam tried to lessen its dependence on China through diversification of its trade relations. After joining the World Trade Organization, Vietnam actively sought to develop a range of free trade agreements (FTAs) with the world's key economies. In addition to ASEAN-led FTAs, Vietnam has negotiated a range of FTAs with Japan, Chile, South Korea, Laos, the Eurasian Economic Union (Russia, Belarus, Kazakhstan and Armenia), the European Free Trade Association, or EFTR (Iceland, Liechtenstein, Norway and Switzerland), and the Trans-Pacific Partnership (Canada, Mexico, Peru, Chile, the United States, Australia, New Zealand, Singapore, Malaysia and Brunei). These negotiations were accelerated during the period 2012–2015. By the end of 2015, Vietnam concluded most of its major FTA negotiations except the RCEP. A short summary at this point showed that, for just a decade, Vietnam achieved FTA arrangements with fifty-five countries.[76] This figure was indicative of Vietnam's extraordinary efforts to strengthen its trade ties with the world's major economies.

Among these FTAs, the US-led Trans-Pacific Partnership was considered the most important to Vietnam. Generally, the TPP is considered as a critical element of the United States' rebalancing to the Asia-Pacific, and the primary vehicle for Washington to shape regional trade rules in the face of rising China. The TPP is far more than just a mere FTA that liberalises trade in goods and services, as its implementation will necessitate domestic economic and political reforms leading to a more competitive economic environment.[77] The most difficult changes for Vietnam (as well as China), as required by the TPP, are the removal of non-market preferential treatments of state-owned enterprises and the establishment of independent unions to protect the fundamental labour rights and to ensure collective bargaining. In addition, there are a range of TPP principles to ensure fair competition, protection of investors' rights, protection of copyrights and patent rights, and environmental sustainability. These institutional reforms clearly go against the main principles of the socialist regime's governance structure. Theoretically speaking, such reforms would weaken the economic and political control of the CPV.

Nonetheless, in the longer term, such reforms were necessary to strengthen the economy that had been ravaged by a large but inefficient state-owned enterprises (SOE) sector and rampant corruption. Vietnam was considered to be the largest benefactor of the TPP with greater access to advanced members' markets for its principal products such as aquatic and agricultural products, textiles and garments, shoes and leather, and electronic devices. TPP's "yarn forward" rules of origin regulation, which requires that only yarns made by TPP members may be sold on the TPP markets, may cause difficulties for Vietnam in the short run. To meet this requirement, Vietnamese producers have to look beyond cheap Chinese yarn to find suppliers in the TPP countries. However, in the longer term, the TPP will help Vietnam attract foreign direct investment and assist it with the development of domestic industries as well as the diversification of Vietnam's economy away from the current level of dependence on Chinese trade.[78] In other words, the TPP promises to advantage Vietnam at the expense of China and provide it with a range of alternatives beyond the China choice.

As mentioned earlier, by mid-2015, the Vietnamese leadership had to weigh benefits and risks and decide whether to walk away for the sake of the regime itself or join the TPP to make the country more prosperous and stronger. The trip by party chief Nguyen Phu Trong to Washington in July 2015 apparently cleared final obstacles to make Vietnam one of the founding members of the TPP. In early 2016, when the CPV was about to convene the 12th National Party Congress, its Central Committee discussed the result of the TPP negotiation and finally approved signing the TPP agreement.[79] This reflected a broad-based consensus among the Vietnamese leadership on integration into the US-led economic system. A new course has been set in motion. While Hanoi still maintains its strategic autonomy, economically it has already rebalanced to the West. The change was obviously prompted by the internal need to modernise the country and enable it to cope with increased threats and risks emanated from an assertive China.

Conclusion

Vietnam found it increasingly difficult to manage the South China Sea disputes and its relations with China. Despite some gestures of reconciliation in late 2011, Beijing continued to assert its claims and flex its muscle against other claimants. China appeared more determined to establish its mastery over the area through the occupation of the Scarborough Shoal, deployment of maritime assets to challenge other claimants' jurisdiction, and massive land reclamations in the Spratlys. Though being committed to peaceful resolution of the disputes and managing to put in place a range of mechanisms to discuss maritime issues with China, Hanoi found bilateralism unable to induce cooperation from China. China's stronger presence and forcefulness in asserting its claim drove Vietnam to strengthen its defence capabilities, further its partnerships with other powers, and proactively participate in multilateral forums to impose greater costs on

China's assertive actions. Hanoi deliberately avoided misperception in Beijing that Vietnam would collude with other powers against China. It was also reluctant to follow the Philippines to take legal option against China for fear that such action would alienate Beijing. Still, Vietnam was slowly but surely veering away from Beijing's orbit. Hanoi was worried that economic dependence on China would weaken its position in the South China Sea. As a result, Vietnam was more determined to reduce economic vulnerabilities through diversification and accept painful reforms to be a founding member of the US-led Trans-Pacific Partnership.

Notes

1 M.C. Tyler, "Vietnam's Hot Peace with China," *Australian Institute of International Affairs*, 2 June 2014. Online. Available HTTP: <www.internationalaffairs.org.au/australian_outlook/vietnams-hot-peace-with-china/> (accessed 19 January 2016).
2 S. Yoon, "Implications of Xi Jinping's 'True Maritime Power'," *Naval War College Review* 68, no. 3, 2015, p.41.
3 H. Kazianis, China's Expanding Cabbage Strategy, *Diplomat*, 29 October 2013.
4 H. Clinton, *American Pacific Century*, p.58.
5 P. Coorey, "Obama to Send Marines to Darwin," *Sydney Morning Herald*, Sydney, 17 November 2011.
6 J.E. Barnes, "U.S. Plans Naval Shift toward Asia," *Wall Street Journal*, 1 June 2012.
7 See R. Emmers, "The US Rebalance to Asia and the South China Sea Disputes," In: Leszek Buszynski and Christopher B. Roberts (eds.), *The South China Sea Maritime Dispute: Political, Legal and Regional Perspectives*, Milton Park: Routledge, 2015, pp. 150–63.
8 M. Yu, "Inside China: PLA Says War with U.S. Imminent," *Washington Times*, 27 June 2012.
9 L. Buszynski, "The South China Sea: Oil, Maritime Claims, and US-China Strategic Rivalry," *Washington Quarterly* 35, no. 2, 2012, 139–56.
10 P. Tran, "Vietnam Has Much at Stake in S. China Sea," *Defense News*, 28 March 2015.
11 C.A. Thayer, "Not Too Hot, Not Too Cold: A Vietnamese Perspective on China-U.S. Relations," paper presented at the *International Conference on China-US Relations in Global Perspective*, Wellington, New Zealand, 8–9 October 2015, p.10.
12 L.H. Hiep, "Viet Nam giua ba tang tranh chap Bien Dong," *Tuan Viet Nam*, 28 August 2012.
13 D. Trang and L. Kien, "Thuong tuong Nguyen Chi Vinh: VN khong phai la oc dao," *Tuoi Tre*, 1 January 2014.
14 G. Dyer, *The Contest of the Century: The New Era of Competition with China and How America Can Win*, New York: Alfred A. Knopf, 2014, pp. 102–9.
15 Tensions flared up as the Philippines' largest warship, the BPR *Gregorio del Pilar*, tried to arrest Chinese fishermen allegedly involved in illegal harvest of corals and clams in the area and was confronted by Chinese maritime surveillance vessels.
16 L. Thu, "Viet – Trung 2012: Song tu Bien Dong," *Vietnamnet*, 25 December 2012.
17 M. McDonald, "A New Map in Chinese Passports Stirs Anger across the Region," *New York Times*, 25 November 2012.
18 Interview with an official of the Ministry of Foreign Affairs of Vietnam, 28 March 2014.
19 "China Opposes Vietnamese Maritime Law over Sovereignty Claim," *Xinhua News*, 21 June 2012.
20 M. Brown, "Tension Mounts between Vietnam, China," *Voice of America*, 28 June 2012.
21 Thu, "Viet – Trung 2012."

22 "China, Vietnam Ink Agreement on Fishery Hotline," *Xinhua News*, 21 June 2013; "China, Vietnam Set Up Naval Hotline," *China Daily*, 7 June 2013.
23 "Bien Dong – nhin lai nam 2013 noi song," *Petro Times*, 1 January 2014.
24 Z. Keck, "Second Thomas Shoal Tensions Intensify," *Diplomat*, 13 April 2014.
25 A. C. Thayer, "China's Oil Rig Gambit: South China Sea Game-Changer?," *Diplomat*, 12 May 2014.
26 E. Z. Bower and G. B. Poling, "China-Vietnam Tensions High over Drilling Rig in Disputed Waters," *Centre for Strategic & International Studies (CSIS)*, 7 May 2014.
27 D. Chen, "China's Deployment of Oil Rig Is Not a Strategic Mistake," *Diplomat*, 20 May 2014.
28 D. T. Hai, "S. China Sea: The Beginning of Chinese Rule," *Today*, 12 June 2015.
29 B. Spegele and V. T. Khanh, "China Moves Oil Rig from Contested Waters," *Wall Street Journal*, 16 July 2014.
30 B. Spegele and V. T. Khanh, "China, Vietnam Try to Repair Ties after South China Sea Dispute," *Wall Street Journal*, 28 August 2014.
31 "Thao luan ve quan he Viet-Trung," *BBC Tieng Viet*, 5 November 2015.
32 "Duong day nong Viet-Trung 'khong hoat dong'?," *VOA – Dai Tieng Noi Hoa Ky*, 27 May 2014.
33 B. Spegele and V. T. Khanh, "China, Vietnam Try to Repair Ties after South China Sea Dispute."
34 V. Duy, "Phai luong truoc moi kha nang nham bao ve chu quyen dat nuoc," *Voice of Vietnam*, 2 July 2014.
35 "Viet-Trung 'vua hop tac, vua dau tranh'," *BBC Tieng Viet*, 19 November 2014. Online. Available HTTP: <www.bbc.com/vietnamese/vietnam/2014/11/141119_thu_tuong_vietnam_quoc_hoi> (accessed 20 January 2016).
36 Interview with Vietnam Ministry of Foreign Affairs officials, 25 March 2014.
37 H. Nhi, "Bo truong Quoc phong Viet – Trung dien dam," *Vietnamnet*, 31 December 2015; "Viet-Trung lap duong day nong ve hoat dong nghe ca," *Tuoi Tre*, 24 June 2013; "Khai truong duong day nong ngoai giao Viet-Trung," *Dan Tri*, 2 March 2012.
38 Thayer, "Not Too Hot, Not Too Cold," p.10.
39 B. Trung, "Quan doi Viet – Trung tuyet doi khong dung vu luc," *Vietnamnet*, 17 September 2012.
40 "China 'Must Stop' Land Reclamation in the South China Sea – Obama," *BBC*, 18 November 2015.
41 D. Alexander, "China's Land Reclamation in South China Sea Grows: Pentagon Report," *Reuters*, 21 August 2015.
42 Vietnam was estimated to reclaim around 80 acres, Malaysia 70 acres, Philippines 14 acres, and Taiwan 8 acres. See: R. O'Rourke, "Maritime Territorial and Exclusive Economic Zone (EEZ) Disputes Involving China: Issues for Congress," *Congressional Research Service Report*, 22 December 2015, p.28.
43 T. T. Thuy, "Construction in the South China Sea: A Comparative View," *Asia Maritime Transparency Initiative*, 18 February 2015.
44 Ibid.
45 Trang and Kien, "Thuong tuong Nguyen Chi Vinh."
46 "Notification and Statement of Claims," Department of Foreign Affairs, The Republic of the Philippines, 2013.
47 Ibid.
48 Ministry of Foreign Affairs of the People's Republic of China, Summary of the Position Paper of the Government of the People's Republic of China on the Matter of Jurisdiction in the South China Sea Arbitration Initiated by the Republic of the Philippines, retrieved at: www.fmprc.gov.cn/mfa_eng/zxxx_662805/t1217149.shtml.
49 For more insights into the juggle among ASEAN members behind the closed door, see B. Hayton, *The South China Sea: The Struggle for Power in Asia*, New Haven: Yale University Press, 2014, pp. 195–9.

50 T. Mai, "Phan ung cua Viet Nam ve viec Philippines khoi kien Trung Quoc," *Vnexpress*, 24 January 2013.

51 In 2006 the Chinese government lodged a declaration with UNCLOS saying that it "does not accept any of the procedures provided for in Section 2 of Part XV of the Convention with respect to all the categories of disputes referred to in paragraph 1 (a), (b), and (c) of Article 298 of the Convention."

52 "Award on Jurisdiction and Admissibility," In: Arbitral Tribunal Constituted under Annex XII to the 1982 United Nations Convention on the Law of the Sea (ed.), *PCA Case No 2013–19*, The Hague, 2015, p.20.

53 Ibid., p.73.

54 See Bureau of Intelligence and Research (US Department of State), "China: Maritime Claims in the South China Sea," *Limits in the Seas*, no. 143, 2014.

55 C.A. Thayer, "Vietnam, China and the Oil Rig Crisis: Who Blinked?," *Diplomat*, 4 August 2014.

56 Interview with legal experts of the Vietnam Ministry of Foreign Affairs, 28 March 2014.

57 C. Khanh, "Viet Nam da chuan bi ho so phap ly kien Trung Quoc," *Tien Phong*, 29 May 2014.

58 Vietnam Communist Party, "Political Report of the 10th Central Committee at the 11th National Party Congress," 2011.

59 Vietnam Communist Party, "Resolution No.22/NQ-TW on International Integration," 10 April 2013.

60 P. B. Minh, "Tam the moi cua doi ngoai da phuong Viet Nam," *Nhan Dan*, 10 December 2015.

61 "One Step Nearer to ASEAN Economic Community," *Vietnam News Agency*, 2015.

62 Thayer, "Not Too Hot, Not Too Cold."

63 "Hau truong chuyen tham My cua Tong Bi thu," *Vietnamnet*, 22 July 2015.

64 M. Petty, "Vietnam Talks Trust with China, Inviting Japanese Warship," *Reuters*, 6 November 2015.

65 See K. Kwok, "Balancing Act: Vietnam May Find Itself Hosting Barack Obama and Xi Jinping within Days of Each Other," *South China Morning Post*, 15 September 2015; D. Singh, "Vietnam's Adroit Balancing Act," *Strait Times*, 13 August 2015; P. Nguyen, "Vietnam's Careful Dance with the Superpowers," *East Asia Forum*, 21 January 2015; L. H. Hiep, "The Geo-Politics of Vietnam-US Rapprochement," *East Asia Forum*, 8 July 2015; H. L. Thu, "Vietnam's Precarious Strategic Balancing Act," *East Asia Forum*, 5 July 2014; T. T. Do, "Is Vietnam's Bamboo Diplomacy Threatened by Pandas?," *East Asia Forum*, 3 April 2014; D. C. McCornac, "Vietnam's Foreign Policy Tightrope," *East Asia Forum*, 12 October 2013.

66 L. Thu and H. Nhi, "Doi tac chien luoc va dau an doi ngoai 2013," *Vietnamnet*, 3 November 2012.

67 C.A. Thayer, "Why Vietnam's Foreign Policy Won't Change after Its Party Congress," *Diplomat*, 8 December 2015.

68 K. Bradsher, "Amid Tension, China Blocks Vital Exports to Japan," *New York Times*, 22 September 2010.

69 "The China-Philippines Banana War," *Asia Sentinel*, 6 June 2012.

70 "Nguyen phu lieu det may: 48% nhap tu Trung Quoc," *Tuoi Tre*, 3 April 2015.

71 T. V. Tho, "Viet Nam 40 nam qua va nhung nam toi: Can mot nen kinh te thi truong dinh huong phat trien," *Thoi Dai Moi* 33, July 2015.

72 "Vietnam Says China Must Avoid Trade Weapon in Maritime Spat," *Bloomberg*, 3 December 2012.

73 Gavin Bowring, "Vietnam Yields Cautionary Tale over Chinese Investment," *Financial Times (FT)*, 27 November 2014. Online. Available HTTP: <http://blogs.ft.com/beyond-brics/2014/11/27/vietnam-yields-cautionary-tale-over-chinese-investment/>

74 S. Denyer, "China's Assertiveness Pushes Vietnam toward an Old Foe, the United States," *Washington Post*, 28 December 2015.

75 T. Abe and A. Tomiyama, "China, Vietnam to Cooperate on New Trade Corridor," *Nikkei Asia Review*, 8 April 2015.
76 C. An, "Trien vong thuong mai Viet Nam 'sang' chua tung co voi 14 hiep dinh thuong mai tu do sap hoan tat," *Cafef*, 2 February 2016.
77 "The Pact Is a Win for Prosperity and Peace," *Nikkei Asian Review*, 8 October 2015.
78 "Possible Impacts of TPP on Vietnam," *Saigon Times*, 12 October 2015.
79 "Thong bao hoi nghi lan thu 14 Ban Chap hanh Trung Uong Dang khoa XI," *Nhan Dan*, 13 January 2016.

Conclusion

The South China Sea was one of the major security policy dilemmas for Hanoi in the post–Cold War period. After a decade of hostility with its powerful northern neighbour, the Vietnamese leadership realised that good relations with China best served Vietnam's national interest, constituting the prerequisite for shifting its focus on tackling domestic problems and fostering national development. In the meantime, they were under pressure to defend the islands in the South China Sea under the Vietnamese control and advance maritime interests in the South China Sea in a way to maintain the legitimacy of the ruling communist party at home. Therefore, though Vietnam did not match China in terms of military and economic power, Hanoi did not appease Beijing by abandoning remote islands for the sake of safeguarding basic territorial integrity. Also, since the Soviet Union collapsed, Vietnam had not attempted to develop a tacit military alliance with other powers against China.

Within these bounds, Hanoi's South China Sea policy oscillated between two competitive strategies, namely bandwagoning with and hedging against China. Bandwagoning, which was the strategy preferred by the conservative political elites, is the process of cultivating cordial political and security ties with China and coordinating foreign policy with China on the basis of shared ideology in return for China's protection and cooperation. On the other side of the spectrum, hedging, a strategy supported by the nationalist pragmatist leaders, represents a course of diversifying foreign relations, particularly putting more emphasis on multilateralism and bolstering Vietnam's relations with other major powers in order to discourage China's assertive actions. There is a strong case that the more assertive China became, the more Hanoi tilted towards a hedging strategy to defend its interests in the South China Sea.

As demonstrated in Chapter 1, Vietnam considered itself as legitimate owner of the Paracels and Spratlys (Hoang Sa and Truong Sa in Vietnamese). To support this argument, the Vietnamese published ample historical evidence that their ancestors regularly visited and exploited these offshore territories as early as the seventeenth century and that the Nguyen dynasty made an official claim to these insular features in 1816. In the Vietnamese view, successive state authorities, including feudal courts, colonial French authorities and the South Vietnamese government (1946–1975), and now unified Vietnam, effectively occupied these islets and continuously asserted the title. The Vietnamese refuted China's doctrine of first discovery and argued that Chinese states showed no interest in offshore territories beyond Hainan Island before the twentieth century. They also opposed China's use of force to take control of the Paracels and certain reefs in the Spratlys in 1974 and 1988 respectively. Vietnam's claim to the Spratlys also predates those of the Philippines and Malaysia, which came in the 1950s and 1980s respectively. Based on historical evidence and the principle of effective occupation, the Vietnamese believe that their claim is historically and legally superior to those of other claimants.

After reunification in 1975, Hanoi became increasingly interested in asserting maritime rights under international law, especially United Nations Conventions on the Law of the Sea. In 1977, Vietnam issued a statement claiming a range of maritime zones for its mainland and offshore islands. Just before the signature of UNCLOS 1982, Hanoi published a declaration delineating a straight baseline system along the Vietnamese southern and central coastline and defining the Gulf of Tonkin as "historic waters" over which Vietnam had sovereignty. Though Vietnam's legislation generally followed the spirit and script of UNCLOS 1982, its positions on the legal regime applied to Spratly and Paracel features, the waters in the Gulf of Tonkin and baseline systems were points of controversy. Vietnam's attempts to maximise its maritime jurisdiction was largely a result of a combination of different factors, most prominently deep-seated security concerns in the post-war period, prevalent distrust of international law among the then Vietnamese leaders, desire to control the resource-rich area and a response to radical interpretations of UNCLOS adopted by other countries in the region.

The end of the Cold War witnessed a transition from an assertive and confrontational approach to a more constructive and cooperative approach in Vietnam's handling of territorial disputes. As presented in Chapter 2, since 1975 the South China Sea has gradually emerged as one of the most important foreign policy and security problems for Vietnam. Upon taking control of the entire country, communist leaders in Hanoi became more assertive in defending sovereignty and exerting influence beyond their borders. That put Vietnam and its neighbours, China and ASEAN states, on a collision course for greater control of disputed areas as well as supremacy over Indochina. Vietnam's key solution to what it saw as China's "expansionist hegemony" was a comprehensive partnership, including a military alliance, with China's rival, the Soviet Union. With the extension of the Soviet Union's influence, Hanoi strongly asserted its sovereignty and regional influences, pursuing a competitive and confrontational strategy against China on all fronts.

Vietnam could not afford prolonged hostility with its neighbours and major world powers and finally chose to give up its influence over Cambodia for a better security situation at home. The burdens of the war in Cambodia, the square-off with China on all fronts, and the international embargo and blockade proved strategically, politically and economically devastating to the Vietnamese economy. However, it was not until the mid-1980s that adverse international transformations prompted Hanoi to reassess its security and foreign policy. To pursue a détente with China, the Soviet Union cut its economic and military support for Vietnam.

This state of affairs forced Vietnam to a defensive posture, where it sought to preserve the status quo rather than compete for regional influence. The naval skirmish with China in March 1988 marked a turning point, by exposing Vietnam's helpless maritime vulnerabilities and obliging it to moderate its international stance.

Increasing difficulties both at home and abroad cracked the consensus among the Vietnamese leaders on foreign affairs, particularly in terms of how to view and deal with China. The ideological conservative elites, particularly the party and military chiefs, preferred to bandwagon with China to seek China's protection and cooperation in resolving existing disputes. On the other hand, the pragmatist nationalist leaders advocated reaching out beyond the socialist group to find a solution to the Cambodia conflict and force China to moderate its position. The conservative leaders finally managed to bypass Foreign Minister Nguyen Co Thach, to accommodate Beijing in resolving the Cambodia issues to mend relations between Vietnam and China. They even proposed an ideology-based security alliance with China, but Beijing rejected this idea.

After normalising its relations with China and ASEAN countries, as indicated in Chapter 3, Vietnam actively engaged with its neighbours to seek a resolution of its outstanding territorial disputes. This effort was part of Hanoi's attempt to preserve peace and stability in its neighbourhood for the sake of economic development. Though China rejected the revival of an old-type alliance, conservative Vietnamese leaders continued to advocate multifaceted cooperation with China with the hope that it would facilitate peaceful settlements of the disputes. A thick network of bilateral mechanisms at various levels was established to bring this about. Vietnam and China set up three working groups to discuss "historical differences," which were code words for disputes over the land borders, maritime boundaries in the Gulf of Tonkin, and sovereignty over offshore islands. Both agreed to manage the disputes in a way that would not hinder their growing ties.

Despite these positive developments, China-related incidents in the South China Sea, such as its attempts to move into unoccupied reefs in the Spratlys, the deployment of oil rigs in disputed waters, and hydrocarbon explorations in the areas off Vietnam's southern coast, stirred up concern in Hanoi about China's expansionism. This provided pragmatist leaders with sound reasons to adopt a hedging strategy to expand their range of options. In this vein, Vietnam boosted its own military capabilities and reached out to other partners, especially the US and other Southeast Asian countries, with the hope of constraining China effectively. In July 1995, this multi-directional foreign policy resulted in Vietnam's membership in ASEAN, normalised relations with the United States, and the signing of a framework agreement with the European Union. Though the expansion of Vietnam's foreign affairs was also shaped by economic imperatives, the security and strategic concerns in the South China Sea figured significantly in all of Hanoi's calculations. Since 1992, Vietnam came to realise the importance of UNCLOS after China offered the US-based Crestone Company concessions to prospect for oil in the Tu Chinh area off the southern coast of Vietnam but far away from China's Hainan Island. This was the first instance that the disputes over the offshore islands such as the Paracels and Spratlys had an effect on maritime delimitation. The disagreement over the Tu

Chinh prompted Vietnam to review the legality of its claims and take UNCLOS seriously. In June 1994, Vietnam ratified UNCLOS and gradually aligned its claims to its spirit and text as a way to fend off China's excessive claims.

The period 1995–2002 saw Vietnam's dual-track engagement with China, bilaterally and multilaterally. On the one hand, Hanoi continued to put a premium on its regular bilateral party-to-party and state-to-state dialogues with China to facilitate negotiations on outstanding territorial disputes. These processes brought about the signature of the agreements on the land border and the maritime boundary in the Gulf of Tonkin in 1999 and 2000 respectively. The conclusion of these two significant agreements was the result of the convergence of several factors. On the part of China, Beijing wanted to fix the diplomatic row after the Mischief Reef occupation and promote an image of a benign China to the region. The agreements with Vietnam in resolving outstanding disputes and its participation in the ASEAN-led negotiation on a code of conduct in the South China Sea were part of China's "New Security Concept" to dispel the perceptions of China as a threat. As far as Vietnam was concerned, conservative Secretary General Le Kha Phieu invested much of his political capital to foster closer ideological relations with China. Phieu was blamed, even by other leading conservatives, for his personal efforts in reaching these deals with China and his allegedly unprincipled accommodation of China's demands. Surprisingly, these deals were generally perceived as satisfactory and necessary in the eyes of the leading pragmatist leaders, though minor disappointments were noted. However, Phieu was removed from the leadership because there were other allegations against him.

On the other hand, as demonstrated in Chapter 4, after some initial reservations, Vietnam played a more active role in ASEAN's efforts to craft a code of conduct in the South China Sea. The initiative began with the Philippines after the Mischief Reef incident as a way of utilising ASEAN to constrain China's creeping assertiveness. Vietnam joined ASEAN with limited experience of multilateralism. In early 1997, China deployed an oil rig in the disputed area. As bilateralism yielded no result, Vietnam appealed to other ASEAN members for support. China's backstep strengthened the belief in Hanoi that ASEAN mattered in the eyes of China. Besides, the Vietnamese gradually realised that if they took the back seat in the COC building process, they would have their claim to the Paracels excluded. As a result, Hanoi took a more active role to jointly prepare the COC draft for ASEAN discussions. From this point onward, ASEAN multilateralism towards a COC became a key component of Vietnam's policy to the South China Sea disputes.

Acute disagreements among the parties, including those over the scope of the application (or whether to include the Paracels), the set of activities that would be prohibited, and the binding effect of the code, threatened to bog down the entire process. Finally, with Malaysian mediation, all the parties agreed to a non-binding political statement, titled Declaration on Conduct of the Parties in the South China Sea, in 2002. The document, referred to as DOC, basically restated the pledge of all the parties to peaceful settlement and not to resort to the threat or use of force. It called for functional cooperation for confidence building, and further discussions on the COC.

Though Vietnam and the Philippines were not satisfied with the DOC, they had no interest in the collapse of ASEAN-China dialogues. Finally, they accepted the DOC as a confidence building measure and a stepping-stone towards the COC. However, with all its ambiguities, the DOC was essentially a powerless agreement, which contains a set of vague principles but no effective mechanisms to enforce them. In the aftermath, Vietnamese leaders continued to push for discussion over the implementation of the DOC and consultation on a binding COC. Nonetheless, the process was stalled because of an insurmountable deadlock in relation to the format of consultation. Vietnam preferred an ASEAN caucus before consultations with China while China insisted on its involvement from the beginning. As China appeared benign and cooperative, other ASEAN members had little incentive to oppose China. Even the Philippines jumped on China's bandwagon with the hope of reaping economic benefits from China's rise. In late 2004, China and the Philippines announced a joint seismic survey project in the Spratly area much to Vietnam's surprise. Though it strongly protested against this deal at first, Hanoi had no choice but to join it later. The deadlock of the DOC and COC processes and China's success in its joint seismic survey initiative indicated to Hanoi that China's growing influence in the Southeast Asian capitals could cripple ASEAN multilateralism.

Chapter 5 documented Vietnam's stronger engagement with other great powers since 2003 as a way to hedge against the rise of China. It should be noted that after the 9th Party Congress in 2001, ideologue Le Kha Phieu lost his job as the party chief to Nong Duc Manh, a politically moderate leader. The power base of the conservative sector weakened since retired conservative leaders such as Le Duc Anh and Do Muoi were no longer in the position to intervene in party politics. In this context, pragmatism gained ground in Vietnam's foreign policy. In the 8th Plenum of the 9th Central Committee, the Vietnamese leadership forged a consensus on the need to improve security and defence cooperation with the United States and other major powers. As the United States diverted its attention away from the region due to the war against terrorism, authoritative Vietnamese officials asked their US counterparts in private to watch China's growing influence over the region. They openly supported the American presence in the region and facilitated its involvement in the regional mechanisms. Vietnam also sought to establish regular security dialogue and cooperation under the framework of comprehensive and strategic partnerships with other powers, especially Japan and India. Vietnam's reaching out to other powers was part of a strategic hedge to negate China's influence and prevent it from dominating regional politics. However, the Vietnamese were prudent in calibrating their cooperation with other powers to the extent that it would not provoke China strategically.

At the same time, Vietnamese political elites were more determined to push for maritime development as a means to defend sovereignty and territorial integrity. In early 2007, the CPV Central Committee adopted an ambitious maritime strategic plan to develop a marine-based economy with special emphasis on hydrocarbon exploitation, the fishing industry, shipbuilding and shipping. That coincided with a new wave of China's assertiveness over the South China Sea. From 2002 to

2004, the South China Sea was relatively tranquil with few incidents that sparked tensions. Since 2005, disputes over fishing became heated with increased number of incidents and greater severity. Since 2007, China became more confident and determined to apply pressures on foreign oil firms and warned them off projects in Vietnam. Beijing's new game caused difficulties for Hanoi as foreign oil firms tended to withdraw from the Vietnamese projects because they did not want to risk their businesses in China. Furious at China's excessive claims and behind-the-scenes pressures, Hanoi looked to Washington for support. On many occasions, Vietnamese officials asked their US counterparts to back the US companies to continue lawful businesses and voice their concerns on China's bullying behaviour.

In 2008, it became clearer that Vietnam was beginning to boost its naval power. In early 2009, strategic analysts in the region were startled at Hanoi's decision to develop its underwater capabilities by purchasing six Kilo-class submarines from Russia. In the following years, Vietnam continued to add to its arsenal advanced aircraft and warships, high-precision missiles and high-calibre surveillance craft. Vietnamese defence officials publicly declared that these acquisitions were normal for defensive purposes. However, in the eyes of military specialists, Vietnam's hasty and costly naval modernisation at a time of economic difficulty was largely a response to China's naval expansions, especially its new strategic submarine base in Hainan and the growth of its blue-water navy.

Since 2009, the row in the South China Sea surfaced, as China no longer hid its ambitions and intensified its assertiveness at sea. China went public to threaten US companies not to explore in Vietnam's EEZ and it deployed naval vessels to intercept Vietnam's exploratory craft, and sent a number of paramilitary vessels to enforce its nine-dash line claim. These actions fuelled anti-China sentiment in Vietnam. From a sensitive issue that had been hardly discussed publicly, the South China Sea gradually attracted attention from the mass media and became a hot topic for public discourse. As ideology lost the ground, national interests gained strength as the basis for Vietnam's foreign policy in general and its approach towards the South China Sea in particular. In the face of China's assertiveness, Hanoi put more emphasis on forging national unity and an appeal to international public opinion to thwart China's overwhelming power. Domestically, the Vietnamese government initiated an unprecedented propaganda campaign to promote people's awareness of the country's maritime territories. Internationally, it supported efforts to publish Vietnam's historical and legal claims and to refute China's related arguments. In May 2009, Vietnam submitted its claim to an extended continental shelf to the United Nations to clarify its maritime claims and align them with UNCLOS. The reading of the submissions revealed that Vietnam was likely to treat the Paracel and Spratly Islands as rocks that were not entitled to their own EEZ and continental shelves. This move infuriated Beijing and forced it to attach a dash-line map to its note to the United Nations.

As outlined in Chapter 7, China's continued heavy-handedness prompted Vietnam to go further to internationalise the South China Sea dispute. Taking advantage of its ASEAN chairmanship, Vietnam brought the issue to the 17th ASEAN Regional Forum meeting in Hanoi in July 2010. At the meeting, US Secretary of State Hillary Clinton declared that the United States had a national interest in freedom of navigation, open access to Asia's maritime commons, and respect for international law in the South China Sea, much to Vietnam's approval but China's anger. Hanoi also worked to facilitate the United States and Russia's admission to the East Asia Summit to balance China's influence there and increased its engagement with Washington as a warning to China. Clearly, China's behaviour in the South China Sea was largely a stimulus for closer and warmer relations between Vietnam and the United States, as the two countries shared an interest in keeping China's maritime ambitions at bay. However, the ties between Hanoi and Washington were well short of a military alliance because Vietnam was not interested in challenging China militarily.

In 2011, the new Vietnamese leadership after the 11th National Party Congress were more interested in fixing relations with China and stabilising the South China Sea situation. The party ideologue General Secretary Nguyen Phu Trong signalled conciliatory gestures to China. Despite two incidents involving Chinese vessels cutting survey cables of the Vietnamese ships, Vietnamese authorities tried to calm domestic protests and sent an envoy to Beijing to discuss ways to defuse tensions. The two sides agreed to compartmentalise the disputes and accelerate the discussion on the basic principles to resolve the sea issues. Tensions gradually eased as Nguyen Phu Trong travelled to Beijing to sign the Agreement on Basic Principles Guiding the Settlement of Sea-Related Issues. The two sides also agreed to set up a hotline between the two defence ministries to better handle incidents at sea. This bilateralism also provided an impetus to complete the negotiations between ASEAN and China on the set of guidelines for implementation of the DOC.

Despite the signature of the Agreement on Basic Principles Guiding the Settlement of Sea-Related Issues, the South China Sea disputes continued to plague the relationship between Vietnam and China. In mid-2012, Vietnam adopted a domestic law of the sea, which was another step to honour UNCLOS and align its positions with the terms of the universal constitution of the ocean. China responded by offering a tender for nine blocks within the EEZ of the Vietnamese mainland to international oil firms. In May 2014, tensions flared up when in a surprising move, China deployed a giant oil rig escorted by hundreds of vessels of different types in the vicinity of the Paracels but well within the area that Vietnam claims its lawful EEZ and continental shelf. China also embarked on large-scale island building on at least six reefs in the Spratlys, turning them into artificial islands. These reclamation projects were clearly designed to strengthen China's foothold in the Spratlys and increase its power projection in the South China Sea. China's militarisation of the South China Sea effectively pushed Vietnam closer to the United States and other major powers.

As events unfolded, the disputes in the South China Sea were clearly not just about the ownership of valuable pieces of territory and resources, but about whether Vietnam, and other small claimants accept China's newfound ascendancy over East Asia. This problem is a continuation of what Vietnam had faced in the past, though in a less blunt way. These disputes have become more complicated as the South China Sea appears to be a theatre for China and US rivalry for regional dominance. Since 2009, the United States has stepped up its engagements in Asia-Pacific to defend its leadership that has come under challenge from the rapid rise of China. Under these circumstances, hedging prevailed over bandwagoning in Vietnam's foreign policy. Hanoi requested Washington to removal its arms embargo on Vietnam, trying to gain access to US military hardware in the maritime domain. Secretary General Nguyen Phu Trong finally accepted the United States' long-standing invitation to visit Washington as capacity of as head of state. At the same time, Vietnam observably continued to invest in naval modernisation and to deepen its partnership with major powers, including Japan, India, Australia and those in Europe, and would call on to their support if China behaves aggressively.

In a snapshot, over the last twenty-five years, Vietnam actively engaged in negotiations to settle territorial and maritime disputes with its neighbours because it generally needed a peaceful and stable regional environment for economic development. While a number of outstanding disputes had been settled, the disputes in the South China Sea proper, particularly the wrangles about the Paracels, the Spratlys and maritime boundaries, remained intractable. China's inclusive, expansive claims, absolutist view of sovereignty, increased military capabilities and assertive behaviour heightened concerns in the Southeast Asian capitals, including Hanoi. As a result, the bandwagoning strategy in terms of honouring socialist solidarity between Hanoi and Beijing, supported by the conservative faction among Vietnamese political elites, did not result in benign Chinese behaviour as expected. Hanoi gradually adopted a hedging strategy with various features, such as association with ASEAN, expanded political and defence cooperation with major powers, and appeal to international public opinions to name and shame China's bullying behaviour, together with promotion of national consciousness of maritime sovereignty and a defence build-up. Against this background, the pragmatist nationalist leaders in Hanoi clarified their maritime claims step by step to bring them in line with UNCLOS to seek protection from international law. However, Hanoi kept assuring Beijing of its strategic independence and carefully calibrated its strategic engagement with the United States so as not to provoke China into direct confrontation. All these measures were intended to sway China's aggressive agenda and force it to a more constructive approach in managing and resolving the disputes.

However, China's non-negotiable claim, rapid naval modernisation, and assertive posture made it increasingly difficult to Hanoi to preserve the status quo without detriment to its relations with Beijing. There are few prospects for effective management and long-standing settlement of the disputes in the foreseeable future. Relations between Vietnam and China peaked and have worsened due to greater disagreements over the South China Sea issue. Strategic distrust has been clearly growing because of China's persistent militarisation and disregard of Vietnam's interests. In the meantime, the rapport between Vietnam and the United States has economically, politically and strategically improved. Inside Vietnam, the political base of the conservative ideologues has weakened largely due to the economic and foreign policies they advocated have failed to make the country more prosperous and more secure. Consequently, ideology is fading and national interests-based pragmatism has increasingly dictated Vietnam's foreign policy. In the wider society, rising anti-China sentiment in Vietnam has eroded the foundation of Vietnam-China relations. In academic circles there is an unprecedented debate among the Vietnamese scholars about the possibility of Vietnam's strategic alignment with the United States to contain China. Taken together, these factors represent undercurrents that may trigger significant shifts in Vietnam's strategic policy in the future. It is premature to predict that Hanoi will depart from its current strategic independence or that the warmer relations between Hanoi and Washington could evolve into a military alliance against China. However, the seeds for strategic partnership between Vietnam and the United States have been sown and the grounds are being fertilised because China fails to change its behaviour in the South China Sea.

Bibliography

Abe, T., and Tomiyama, A., "China, Vietnam to Cooperate on New Trade Corridor," *Nikkei Asia Review*, 8 April 2015.

Abuza, Z., "The Lessons of Le Kha Phieu: Changing Rules in Vietnamese Politics," *Contemporary Southeast Asia* 24, no. 1, 2002, 121–45.

Abuza, Z., "Vietnam Buckles under Chinese Pressure," *Asia Times*, 29 July 2014. Online. Available HTTP: <www.atimes.com/atimes/Southeast_Asia/SEA-01–290714.html> (accessed 3 July 2015).

"Accord Seen Possible Off China, Vietnam," *Oil & Gas Journal*, 22 April 1996.

Acharya, A., "China's Charm Offensive in Southeast Asia," *International Herald Tribune*, 8 November 2003.

Acharya, A., "Seeking Security in the Dragon's Shadow: China and Southeast Asia in the Emerging Asian Order," *IDSS Working Papers*, March 2003.

Alexander, D., "China's Land Reclamation in South China Sea Grows: Pentagon Report," *Reuters*, 21 August 2015.

Amer, R., "Assessing Sino-Vietnamese Relations through Management of Contentious Issues," *Contemporary Southeast Asia* 26, no. 2, 2004, 320–45.

Amer, R., "The Sino-Vietnamese Approach to Managing Boundary Disputes," *IBRU Maritime Briefing* 3, no. 5, 2002.

Amer, R., "Sino-Vietnamese Relations: Past, Present and Future," In: A. Thayer and Ramses Amer Carlyle (Eds), *Vietnamese Foreign Policy in Transition*, Singapore: Institute of Southeast Asian Studies, 1999, 68–129.

Amer, R., and Nguyen, H.T., "The Management of Vietnam's Border Disputes: What Impact on Its Sovereignty and Regional Integration?," *Contemporary Southeast Asia* 27, no. 3, 2005, 429–52.

Amer, R., and Thao, N.H., Vietnam's Border Disputes: Assessing the Impact on Its Regional Integration, In: Stephanie Balme and Mark Sidel (Eds), *Vietnam's New Order: International Perspectives on the State and Reform in Vietnam*, New York: Palgrave Macmillan, 2007, 71–87.

An, C., "Trien Vong Thuong Mai Viet Nam 'Sang' Chua Tung Co Voi 14 Hiep Dinh Thuong Mai Tu Do Sap Hoan Tat," *Cafef*, 2 February 2016.

Anh Son, T.D. (Ed), *Hoang Sa, Truong Sa: Tu lieu va quan diem cua hoc gia quoc te (Paracels, Spratlys: Documentation and Opinions of International Scholars)*, Hanoi: Hoi Nha van Publisher, 2014.

"ASEAN Appreciates China's Position on Regional Nuclear Weapons Treaty," *Xinhua News*, 15 June 2003.

"ASEAN, China Sign Pact on Disputed Spratlys," *CNN*, 4 November 2002.

"ASEAN Endorses Establishment of ASEAN-China Joint Working Group on South China Sea," *Xinhua News*, 26 June 2005.

Award on Jurisdiction and Admissibility, In: Arbitral Tribunal Constituted under Annex XII to the 1982 United Nations Convention on the Law of the Sea (Ed), *PCA Case No 2013–19*, The Hague, 2015.

Ba, M. X., "Van de doi tac-doi tuong trong chien luoc bao ve To quoc (Issues of Object of Struggle and Object of Cooperation in National Defense Strategy)," *Tap chi Cong san*, 31 January 2015. Online. Available HTTP: <www.tapchicongsan.org.vn/Home/Nghien-cuu-Traodoi/2015/31758/Van-de-doi-tac-doi-tuong-trong-chien-luoc-bao-ve.aspx> (accessed 25 May 2015).

Balme, S., and Sidel, M. (Eds), *Vietnam's New Order: International Perspectives on the State and Reform in Vietnam*, New York: Palgrave Macmillan, 2007.

Banlaoi, R. C., Functional Cooperation and Joint Development, In: Wu Shicu and Nong Hong (Eds), *Recent Developments in the South China Sea Dispute: The Prospect of a Joint Development Regime*, Abingdon, Ox and New York: Routledge, 2014, 228–40.

"Bao Du Lich bi dinh ban (Du Lich Newspaper Suspended)," *BBC Tieng Viet*, 15 April 2009.

"Bao Trung Quoc: Viet Nam dang 'quoc te hoa' van de Bien Dong (Chinese Media: Vietnam Internationalising the South China Sea Issue)," *VOA Tieng Viet*, 2 March 2010.

Barnes, J. E., "U.S. Plans Naval Shift toward Asia," *Wall Street Journal*, 1 June 2012.

Bateman, W.S.G., and Emmers, R. (Eds), *Security and International Politics in the South China Sea: Towards a Cooperative Management Regime*, London and New York: Routledge, 2009.

Beckman, R., "South China Sea: Worsening Dispute or Growing Clarity in Claims?," *RSIS Commentaries*, 16 August 2010.

Beckman, R., "The UN Convention on the Law of the Sea and the Maritime Disputes in the South China Sea," *American Journal of International Law* 107, no. 1, 2013, 142–63.

Beckman, R., and Davenport, T., "CLCS Submissions and Claims in the South China Sea," paper presented at The South China Sea: Cooperation for Regional Security and Development, Ho Chi Minh City, 10–12 November 2010.

"Beijing Cashes in Prosperity in Massive Boost to Military Spending," *AFP*, 4 March 2007.

Bellaqua, J., "The China Factor in US-Vietnam Relations," *CNA Analysis & Solutions*, March 2012.

Betts, R. K., The Strategic Predicament, In: James William Morley and Masashi Nishihara (Eds), *Vietnam Joins the World*, Armonk, NY: M. E. Sharpe, 1997.

Bich Ngoc, "Quoc hoi hop kin ve Bien Dong: Hai long nhung . . . (National Assembly's Closed Door Hearing on the South China Sea: Pleased But . . .)," *Bao Dat Viet*, 6 June 2015. Online. Available HTTP: <http://baodatviet.vn/chinh-tri-xa-hoi/tinh-hinh-bien-dong-van-de-bien-dong/quoc-hoi-hop-kin-ve-bien-dong-hai-long-nhung-3271501/> (accessed 3 July 2015).

"Bien Dong – Nhin Lai Nam 2013 Noi Song," *Petro Times*, 1 January 2014.

"Bien va Dao Viet Nam (Vietnam's Seas and Islands)," *Cong tac Tu tuong Van hoa*, November 1993.

Binh, N. T., "Cang thang Bien Dong va su lua chon cho Viet Nam (South China Sea Tensions and Options for Vietnam)," *Tuan Viet Nam*, 14 March 2013.

Binh, P.T.T., "Thuc trang Phat trien Kinh te bien Viet Nam (Vietnam's Marine-Based Economy: An Overview)," *Dang Cong san Viet Nam*, 22 October 2009. Online. Available HTTP: <www.cpv.org.vn/cpv/Modules/News/NewsDetail.aspx?co_id=0&cn_id=366824> (accessed 20 January 2014).

Blagov, S., "US, Vietnam Scratch Each Other's Back," *Asia Times*, 21 July 2006.

Boczek, B.A., *International Law: A Dictionary*, Lanham, MD: Scarecrow Press, 2005.

Bo Ngoai giao, *Gioi thieu mot so Van de co ban cua Luat Bien o Viet Nam (Introduction to Basic Issues of the Law of the Sea in Vietnam)*, Hanoi: Chinh tri Quoc gia Publisher, 2004.

Bo Ngoai giao, *Su that ve Quan he Viet Nam-Trung Quoc trong 30 nam qua (Truths in Vietnam-China Relations over the Last 30 Years)*, Hanoi: Su That Publisher, 1979.

Bo Ngoai giao, *Van de Bien gioi giua Viet Nam va Trung Quoc (Border Issues between Vietnam and China)*, Hanoi: Su That Publisher, 1979.

Bonton, K., Domestic Sources of Vietnam's Foreign Policy, In: Carlyle A. Thayer and Ramses Amer (Eds), *Vietnamese Foreign Policy in Transition*, New York: St. Martin's Press, 1999, 170–201.

Bower, E., "The JMSU: A Tale of Bilateralism and Secrecy in the South China Sea," *CSIS Paper* 1, no. 23, 27 July 2010.

Bower, E.Z., and Poling, G.B., "China-Vietnam Tensions High over Drilling Rig in Disputed Waters," *Centre for Strategic & International Studies (CSIS)*, 7 May 2014.

"BP ngung Tham do o Truong Sa (BP Suspended Exploration in Spratlys)," *BBC Tieng Viet*, 14 June 2007. Online. Available HTTP: <www.bbc.co.uk/vietnamese/vietnam/story/2007/06/070614_bp_china.shtml> (accessed 13 August 2013).

Bradsher, K., "Amid Tension, China Blocks Vital Exports to Japan," *New York Times*, 22 September 2010.

Branigan, T., "China Cuts Japan Contacts over Detained Trawler Captain," *Guardian*, 20 September 2010.

Breckon, L., "China-Southeast Asian Relations: A New Strategic Partnership Is Declared," *CSIS Comparative Connections*, 1 Jan 2004. Online. Available HTTP: <http://csis.org/files/media/csis/pubs/0304qchina_seasia.pdf> (accessed 25 May 2015).

Brown, D., "Vietnam Leaders Taken to Task on China," *Asia Times*, 26 June 2011.

Brown, M., "Tension Mounts between Vietnam, China," *Voice of America*, 28 June 2012.

"Bully in the South China Sea," *Asian Wall Street Journal*, 17 March 2000.

Bureau of Intelligence and Research (US Department of State), "China: Maritime Claims in the South China Sea," *Limits in the Seas*, Washington, DC, 2014.

Bureau of Intelligence and Research (US Department of State), "Straight Baselines: VIETNAM," *Limits in the Seas*, Washington, DC, 1983.

Burghardt, R., "US-Vietnam: Discreet Friendship under China's Shadow," *YaleGlobal*, 22 November 2005. Online. Available HTTP: <http://yaleglobal.yale.edu/content/us-vietnam-discreet-friendship-under-china%E2%80%99s-shadow> (accessed 12 August 2013).

Buszynski, L., "ASEAN, the Declaration on Conduct, and the South China Sea," *Contemporary Southeast Asia* 25, no. 3, 2003, 343–62.

Buszynski, L., "ASEAN Security Dilemmas," *Survival* 34, no. 4, 1992, 90–107.Buszynski, L., "The South China Sea: Oil, Maritime Claims, and US-China Strategic Rivalry," *Washington Quarterly* 35, 2012, 139–56.

Buszynski, L., The Soviet Union and Vietnamese Withdrawal from Cambodia, In: Gary Klintworth (Ed), *Vietnam's Withdrawal from Cambodia: Regional Issues and Realignments*, Canberra: ANU Strategic and Defense Studies Center, 1990, 32–48.

Buszynski, L., and Roberts, C.B. (Eds), *The South China Sea Maritime Dispute: Political, Legal, and Regional Perspectives*, Milton Park: Routledge, 2015.

Buszynski, L., and Sazlan, I., "Maritime Claims and Energy Cooperation in the South China Sea," *Contemporary Southeast Asia* 29, no. 1, 2007, 143–71.

Caballero-Anthony, M., "Mechanism of Dispute Settlement: The ASEAN Experience," *Contemporary Southeast Asia* 20, no. 1, 1998, 38–66.
Campbell, K.M., and Andrews, B., "Explaining the US 'Pivot' to Asia," *Americas*, no. 1, 2013.
"Canada Warns of Rising Asian Conflict," *Spectator*, 26 July 1999.
Carlson, A., *Unifying China, Integrating with the World: Securing Chinese Sovereignty in Reform Era*, Singapore: NUS Press, 2008.
Carpaccio, T., "Chinese Vessels Harass U.S. Navy Ship, Pentagon Says (Update 3)," *Bloomberg*, 9 March 2009.
Carr, E.H., *Britain: A Study of Foreign Policy from the Versailles Treaty to the Outbreak of War*, London and New York: Longmans Green, 1939.
Carr, E.H., and Cox, M., *The Twenty Years' Crisis, 1919–1939: An Introduction to the Study of International Relations*, New York: Palgrave, 2001.
Chang, P.M., "A New Scramble for the South China Sea Islands," *Contemporary Southeast Asia* 12, no. 1, 1990, 20–39.
Chemillier-Gendreau, M., *Sovereignty over the Paracel and Spratly Islands*, The Hague and Boston: Kluwer Law International, 2000.
Chen, D., "China's Deployment of Oil Rig Is Not a Strategic Mistake," *Diplomat*, 20 May 2014.
Cheng, J.Y.S., "Sino-Vietnamese Relations in the Early Twenty-First Century," *Asian Survey* 51, no. 2, 2011, 379–405.
Cheng-Chwee, K., "The Essence of Hedging: Malaysia and Singapore's Response to a Rising China," *Contemporary Southeast Asia* 30, no. 2, 2008, 159–85.
Cheng-Chwee, K., "Rising Dragon, Crouching Tigers: Comparing the Foreign Policy Responses of Malaysia and Singapore toward a Re-Emerging China," *Biblio Asia* 3, no. 4, 2008.
"China to Accede to ASEAN Amity Treaty in June," *Kyodo News Service*, 29 April 2003.
"China Agrees to Talks with Southeast Asian Group on South China Sea Code," *BBC Monitoring Asia Pacific*, 25 November 1999.
"China, ASEAN Begin Discussion on Stronger Code of Conduct," *China Daily*, 30 September 2010.
"China, ASEAN See Closer Economic, Political Cooperation," *Xinhua News*, 19 August 2003.
"China, ASEAN Sign Joint Declaration, Forge Strategic Partnership," *Xinhua News*, 8 October 2003.
"China Backs Further Dialogue But Proves Wary about Change," *Bangkok Post*, 14 June 1996.
"China Has Aircraft Carrier Hopes," *BBC*, 17 November 2008. Online. Available HTTP: <http://news.bbc.co.uk/2/hi/asia-pacific/7732679.stm> (accessed 30 September 2013).
"China Is Accused of Fuelling Pacific Arms Race," *Telegraph*, 1 April 2007.
"China 'Must Stop' Land Reclamation in the South China Sea – Obama." *BBC*, 18 November 2015.
"China Opposes Vietnamese Maritime Law over Sovereignty Claim." *Xinhua News*, 21 June 2012.
"China Patrols in South China Sea," *BBC*, 16 March 2009.
"China-Philippines Banana War," *Asia Sentinel*, 6 June 2012.
"China Reprimands Vietnam over Offshore Oil Exploration," *Reuters*, 28 May 2011.
"China Starts Regular Patrols of South China Sea," 26 April 2010. Online. Available HTTP: <http://english.gov.cn/2010–04/26/content_1592250.htm> (accessed 6 August 2014).

"China and Vietnam to Hold Maritime Dispute Talks on April 9," *AFP*, 3 April 1997.
"China, Vietnam Ink Agreement on Fishery Hotline," *Xinhua News*, 21 June 2013.
"China, Vietnam Set Up Naval Hotline," *China Daily*, 7 June 2013.
"China Warns Exxon over Vietnam Deal," *Reuters*, 20 July 2008.
"China Willing to Discuss South China Sea Code," *Agence France-Presse*, 7 September 2012.
"China's Indisputable Sovereignty over the Xisha and Nansha Islands," Ministry of Foreign Affairs (People's Republic of China), Beijing, 1980.
"China's Top Legislator, Philippine House Speaker Holds Talks," *Xinhua News*, 31 August 2003.
"Chinese FM Refutes Fallacies on the South China Sea Issue," *China Daily*, 25 July 2010.
"Chinese Navy Fires at Vietnamese Fishing Ship, Injuring 5," *Kyodo*, 21 July 2007.
"Chinese Nuclear Submarine Base," *Telegraph*, 1 May 2008.
"Chinese Oil Drilling Sparks Vietnam's Ire," *Asian Wall Street Journal*, 25 March 1997.
"Chinese Ships Cause Disturbance in Vietnam's Waters again," *Thanh Nien*, 10 June 2011.
"Chinh phu bao cao tinh hinh Bien Dong truoc Quoc hoi (Government's Report on South China Sea Developments at National Assembly)," *Vnexpress*, 8 October 2014. Online. Available HTTP: <http://vnexpress.net/tin-tuc/thoi-su/chinh-phu-bao-cao-tinh-hinh-bien-dong-truoc-quoc-hoi-3090605.html> (accessed 8 November 2014).
"Chu quyen Bien dao vao De thi (Sovereignty over Seas and Islands Asked at Exams)," *BBC Tieng Viet*, 3 June 2012. Online. Available HTTP: <www.bbc.co.uk/vietnamese/vietnam/2012/06/120603_geography_graduation_question.shtml> (accessed 27 July 2014).
Chua, Y. T., and Tordesillas, E., "Six RP-Occupied Islands Covered in Controversial Spratlys Deals," *Vera Files*, 9 March 2008. Online. Available HTTP: <http://verafiles.org/six-rp-occupied-islands-covered-in-controversial-spratlys-deals/> (accessed 3 August 2013).
Chuong, L. V., "Ke chuyen Hoang Sa (Ky 3) (Paracel Stories, Third Episode)," *Tien Phong*, 15 May 2010.
Clayton, J., "Conflict in Spratlys Spurs Rift between Hanoi and Moscow," *Christian Science Monitor*, 14 June 1988.
Clinton, H. R., *Hard Choice*, E-book: Simon & Schuster, 2014.
Clinton, H. R., "Interview with Greg Sheridan of The Australian," 8 October 2010. Online. Available HTTP: <http://m.state.gov/md150671.htm> (accessed 2 April 2015).
Co, T. Q. *Hoi uc va Suy nghi (Memoir and Reflection)*, Hanoi, 2003.
Colson, D. A., "Sovereignty over Pulau Ligitan and Pulau Sipadan (Indonesia/Malaysia)," *American Journal of International Law* 97, no. 2, 2003, 398–406.
Coorey, P., "Obama to Send Marines to Darwin," *Sydney Morning Herald*, 17 November 2011.
"CQ-88: Vi sao Lien Xo lam ngo Trung Quoc xam luoc Truong Sa," *Bao Dat Viet*, 21 March 2016.
Crickton, J., "China Threatens Neighbours in South China Sea," *Global Geopolitics*, 24 October 2008.
Crispin, S. W., "Vietnam Muddles China's South China Sea Challenge," *Diplomat*, 13 June 2015. Online. Available HTTP: <http://thediplomat.com/2015/06/vietnam-muddles-chinas-south-china-sea-challenge/> (accessed 3 July 2015).
"Cuoc chien ngoai giao (Diplomatic Battle)," *BBC Vietnamese*, 12 February 2009. Online. Available HTTP: <www.bbc.co.uk/vietnamese/lg/vietnam/2009/02/090220_tranquangco_tc2.shtml> (accessed 13 February 2015).

Cuong, T. V., *Ngoai giao Viet Nam tu thuo dung nuoc den truoc Cach mang Thang Tam (Vietnamese Diplomacy from the Birth of the Nation until August Revolution)*, Hanoi: Hoc vien Quan he Quoc te, 2001.

Cyranoski, D., "Angry Words over East Asian Seas," *Nature* 478, no. 20, 2011.

"Dai Nam Thuc luc Chinh bien (Chronicle of Greater Vietnam: Main Chapter)," History Bureau (Nguyen Court), 1848.

"Dai Nam Thuc luc Tien bien (Chronicle of Greater Vietnam: Early Chapter)," History Bureau (Nguyen Court), 1844.

Dang Cong san Viet Nam, *Van kien Dai hoi Dai bieu Toan quoc lan thu VI (Documents of the 6th National Congress of the Communist Party of Vietnam)*, Hanoi: Su That Publisher, 1987.

Dang Cong san Viet Nam, *Van kien Dai hoi Dai bieu Toan quoc lan thu VIII (Documents of the 8th National Congress of the Communist Party of Vietnam)*, Hanoi: Chinh tri Quoc gia Publisher, 1996.

Dang Cong san Viet Nam, *Van kien Dai hoi Dai bieu Toan quoc thoi ky Doi Moi (Documents of the National Congresses of the Communist Party of Vietnam in the Doi Moi Period)*, Hanoi: Chinh tri Quoc gia Publisher, 2010.

Denyer, S., "China's Assertiveness Pushes Vietnam toward an Old Foe, the United States," *Washington Post*, 28 December 2015.

Dickie, M., and Tassel, T., "Manila Set to Propose Code of Conduct for Spratlys," *Financial Times*, 15 July 1999.

Dillion, D., and Tkacik, J.J.J., "China's Quest for Asia," *Policy Review* 134, December 2005/January 2006.

"Dispute Regarding the Law on the Exclusive Economic Zone and the Continental Shelf of the People's Republic of China Which Was Passed on 26 June 1998," *UN Law of the Sea Bulletin* 38, 1998.

Dixon, C., State, Party and Political Change in Vietnam, In: Duncan McCargo (Ed), *Rethinking Vietnam*, London and New York: RoutledgeCurzon, 2004, 15–26.

Doan Trang, "Cuoc chien khong can suc giua hoc gia VN va TQ (Asymmetric Battle between Vietnamese and Chinese Scholars)," *Tuan Viet Nam*, 11 March 2009.

Doan Trang, "Van de Truong Sa-Hoang Sa: Can mot no luc tong hop (Spratly and Paracel Issues: The Need for a Concerted Effort)," *Tuan Viet Nam*, 7 December 2008.

Do Ba, Toan Tap Thien Nam Tu chi Lo do thu (Handbook of the South' Road Map), *Hong Duc Ban Do (Reprinted in 1962)*, Saigon: Archaeologic Institute Library, 1686.

Dobson, W. J., "Now Vietnam Needs America to Ward off China," *Christian Science Monitor*, 17 April 1997.

Don, L. Q., *Phu Bien Tap luc* (Miscellany Records on the Pacification of the Frontiers), vol. 1 & vol. 2, 1776.

Dosch, J., "Managing Security in ASEAN-China Relations: Liberal Peace of Hegemonic Stability," *Asian Perspective* 31, no. 1, 2007, 27.

Dosch, J., "Vietnam in 2008: Foreign Policy Successes But Daunting Domestic Problems," *Southeast Asian Affairs*, 2009, 373–88.

Dosch, J., "Vietnam's ASEAN Membership Revisited: Golden Opportunity or Golden Cage?," *Contemporary Southeast Asia: A Journal of International and Strategic Affairs* 28, no. 2, 2006, 234–58.

Dosch, J., and Tuan, T. M., Recent Changes in Vietnam's Foreign Policy, In: Martin Gainsborough (Ed), *Vietnam: Rethinking the State*, London: Zed Books, 2010, 198–213.

Du, T., "Bien Dong va Chien luoc Dieu hau cua Trung Quoc (South China Sea and Chinese Hawkish Strategy)," *Tuan Viet Nam*, 6 December 2008. Online. Available HTTP: <www.viet-studies.info/kinhte/BienDong_DuTran_VNN.htm> (accessed 27 July 2014).

Duc Tam, "Tau la tan cong ngu dan Viet Nam la tau Trung Quoc (Unknown Vessels Attacking Vietnamese Fishermen Are Chinese)," *RFI Tieng Viet*, 20 July 2009.

Dung, N. T., "Building Strategic Trust for Peace, Cooperation, and Security in the Asia-Pacific Region," *Keynote Address to 2013 Shangri-La Dialogue*, 31 May 2013.

"Duong Day Nong Viet-Trung 'Khong Hoat Dong'?," *VOA – Dai Tieng Noi Hoa Ky*, 27 May 2014.

Duong, N. N., "Du am ARF and Quan he ASEAN-Trung Quoc tren Bien Dong (ARF Implications and ASEAN-China Relations about South China Sea)," *Tuan Viet Nam*, 31 August 2010.

Duong, N. N., *Vietnamese Foreign Policy since Doi Moi: The Dialectic of Power and Identity*, Canberra: School of Humanities and Social Sciences, University of New South Wales, 2010.

Dupuy, F., and Dupuy, P.-M., "A Legal Analysis of China's Historic Rights Claim in the South China Sea," *American Journal of International Law* 107, no. 1, 2013, 124–41.

Duy, V., "Phai Luong Truoc Moi Kha Nang Nham Bao Ve Chu Quyen Dat Nuoc," *Voice of Vietnam*, 2 July 2014.

Dy, D. D., "Quoc te hoa (Internationalisation)," *BBC Tieng Viet*, 3 March 2010.

Dy, D. D., "Tau la cua ai (Whose Unknown Vessels)?," *BBC Tieng Viet*, 30 May 2009.

Dyer, G., *The Contest of the Century: The New Era of Competition with China and How America Can Win*, New York: Alfred A. Knopf, 2014.

Dzurek, D. J., "The Spratly Islands Dispute: Who's On First?," *Maritime Briefing* 2, no. 1, 1996.

"East Asia Summit: In the Shadow of Sharp Divisions," *People's Daily*, 7 December 2005. Online. Available HTTP: <http://en.people.cn/200512/07/eng20051207_226350.html> (accessed 25 May 2015).

East, J., "Beijing Warns against Joint Military Games," *South China Morning Post*, 16 March 2000.

Elliot, D.W.P., *Changing Worlds: Vietnam's Transition from Cold War to Globalisation*, New York: Oxford University Press, 2012.

Emmers, R., The US Rebalance to Asia and the South China Sea Disputes, In: Leszek Buszynski and Christopher B. Roberts (Eds), *The South China Sea Maritime Dispute: Political, Legal and Regional Perspectives*, Milton Park: Routledge, 2015, 150–63.

England, V., "Spratlys Behaviour Code Hinges on China," *South China Morning Post*, 26 November 1999.

England, V., and Meixner, S., "China and ASEAN Reach Agreements on Sea Disputes," *South China Morning Post*, 2 November 2002.

Farrell, E. C., *The Socialist Republic of Vietnam and the Law of the Sea*, The Hague, Boston and New York: Martinus Nijhoff, 1997.

"First ADMM+ Chairman's Statement," *Vietnam News Agency*, 13 October 2010.

Fisher, R.D.J., "China's Naval Secrets," *Wall Street Journal*, 5 May 2008.

Flecker, M., "Archaeology Could Wreck China's Sea Claims," *Malay Mail Online*, 6 May 2015. Online. Available HTTP: <www.themalaymailonline.com/what-you-think/article/archaeology-could-wreck-chinas-sea-claims-michael-flecker> (accessed 18 May 2015).

Franckx, E., and Benatar, M., "Dots and Lines in the South China Sea: Insights from the Law of Map Evidence," *Asian Journal of International Law* 2, 2012, 98–118.

Fravel, T., "China's Strategy in the South China Sea," *Contemporary Southeast Asia* 33, no. 2, 2011, 292–319.

Fravel, T., Maritime Security in the South China Sea and the Competition over Maritime Rights, In: Patrick M. Cronin (Ed), *Cooperation from Strength: The United States, China and the South China Sea*, Washington, DC: Center for a New American Security, 2012, 31–51.

Frederick, Z. B., "Rapprochement between Vietnam and the United States," *Contemporary Southeast Asia* 32, no. 3, 2010, 317–42.

"Gac Ma-1988: Goi dung ten 'cuoc chien xam luoc cua Trung Quoc," *Bao Dat Viet*, 15 March 2016.

Gates, R. M., "Strengthening Security Partnership in the Asia-Pacific," paper presented at the 9th IISS Asian Security Summit – Shangri-La Dialogue, Singapore, 5 June 2010.

Ghosh, P., *International Relations*, New Delhi: PHI Learning Private Limited, 2013.

Goh, C. T., "Constructing a New East Asia," *Address at Asia Society Conference*, 9 June 2005.

Goh, E., "Great Powers and Hierarchical Order in Southeast Asia: Analyzing Regional Security Strategies," *International Security* 32, no. 3, 2007–2008, 45.

Goh, E., "Understanding 'hedging' in Asia-Pacific Security," *PacNet* 43, 2006.

Goldrick, J., and McCaffrie, J., *Navies in South-East Asia: A Comparative Study*, London and New York: Routledge, 2013.

Goodspeed, P., "China Resorts to Gunboat Diplomacy," *Toronto Star*, 20 September 1992.

Gouxing, J., "The Spratly Islands: China's Dispute with Vietnam," *Indochina Report* 24, no. Jul–Sep, 1990.

Grant, J., "China Rig Leaves Disputed Zone Oil Exploration Move Surprises Diplomats before Talks with Vietnam Next Week," *Financial Times*, 5 April 1997.

Grant, J., "US-Vietnam Military Ties," *Financial Times*, 22 March 1997.

Gred, T., "Beijing Agrees to Talks on Drilling," *South China Morning Post*, 1 April 1997.

Gred, T., "Deal to Escalate Row over Spratlys," *South China Morning Post*, 13 April 1996.

Grevatt, J., "Vietnam Signs Deal with Russia to Procure Su-30MK2s," *IHS Jane's Defence Industry*, 21 August 2013.

Guan, A. C., "The South China Sea Dispute Revisited," *Australian Journal of International Affairs* 54, no. 2, 2000, 201–15.

Guan, A. C., "Vietnam-China Relations since the End of the Cold War," *Asian Survey* 38, no. 12, 1998, 1122–41.

Guanglie, L., "China International Security Cooperation," paper presented at the 10th IISS Asian Security Summit, Shangri-La Dialogue, Singapore, 5 June 2011.

Hai, D. T., "In Retrospect of China's Policy toward South China Sea Dispute since 2007," *International Studies Review (Diplomatic Academy of Vietnam)*, no. 24, June 2011.

Hai, D. T., "S. China Sea: The Beginning of Chinese Rule," *Today*, 12 June 2015.

Hai, D. T., Vietnam's Evolving Claims, In: Buszynski Leszek and Christopher B. Roberts (Eds), *The South China Sea Maritime Dispute: Political, Legal and Regional Perspectives*, Abingdon and Oxon: Routledge, 2015, 83–110.

"Hai quan Trung Quoc tang suc manh (Chinese Navy Empowered)," *Vnexpress*, 5 May 2010.

Hamzah, B. A., "China Strategy," *Far Eastern Economic Review*, 13 August 1992, 22.

"Hanoi Reinforces Troops on Spratlys," *Kyodo*, 28 February 1995.

"Hanoi's Internal Divisions Hinder Its China Policy," *Strafor*, 2014. Online. Available HTTP: <www.stratfor.com/sample/analysis/hanois-internal-divisions-hinder-its-china-policy> (accessed 2 July 2015).

"Hau Truong Chuyen Tham My Cua Tong Bi Thu," *Vietnamnet*, 22 July 2015.

Hayton, B., *The South China Sea: The Struggle for Power in Asia*, New Haven: Yale University Press, 2014.

"Hien tai hoa quan doi khong phai la chay dua vu trang (Military Modernisation Is Not Arm Race)," *Vnexpress*, 8 December 2010. Online. Available HTTP: <http://vnexpress.net/

tin-tuc/thoi-su/hien-dai-hoa-quan-doi-khong-phai-la-chay-dua-vu-trang-2152907.html> (accessed 23 September 2013).

Hiep, L., "Vietnam's Hedging Strategy against China since Normalisation," *Contemporary Southeast Asia* 35, no. 3, 2013, 333–68.

Hiep, L., "Viet Nam bi 'lam phat' doi tac chien luoc," *BBC Tieng Viet*, 18 April 2013.

Hiep, L., "Viet Nam Giua Ba Tang Tranh Chap Bien Dong," *Tuan Viet Nam*, 28 August 2012.

Hoang, N., "Vietnam se tiep tuc gop phan thiet thuc va quan trong vao su phat trien cua Hiep hoi cac quoc gia Dong Nam A-ASEAN (Vietnam Continues to Contribute Substantially to ASEAN Development)," *Cong Thong tin Dien tu Chinh phu*, 7 August 2008.

"The Hoang Sa (Paracel) and Truong Sa (Spratly) Archipelagos and International Law," Ministry of Foreign Affairs (Socialist Republic of Vietnam), Hanoi, 1988.

"The Hoang Sa and Truong Sa Archipelagos: Vietnamese Territories," Ministry of Foreign Affairs (Socialist Republic of Vietnam), Hanoi, 1981.

Hoang, V. P., *Hai quan dao Hoang Sa va Truong Sa: Bo phan cua Lanh tho Viet Nam (Paracel and Spratly Archipelagos: Integral Part of Vietnam's Territory)*, Ha Noi: Quan Doi Nhan Dan, 1988.

Hoang, V. P., "May van de Phap ly trong Tuyen bo cua Chinh phu ta ve Duong Co So ven Luc dia Viet Nam (Legal Issues in Our Government's Declaration on Baselines for Vietnamese Mainland)," *Luat hoc* 1, no. 10, 1983.

"Hoi Nghe ca phan doi Trung Quoc (Fisheries Association Protesting against China)," *BBC Tieng Viet*, 15 December 2009.

"Hoi thao dau tien ve Chu quyen Bien Dong (First National Conference on Sovereignty in South China Sea)," *BBC Tieng Viet*, 18 March 2009. Online. Available HTTP: <www.bbc.co.uk/vietnamese/vietnam/2009/03/090318_biendong_conference.shtml> (accessed 6 March 2014).

Holley, D., "Vietnam Seen Preparing for War, China Warns Hanoi to Stop Invading Spratlys," *Los Angeles Times*, 6 April 1988.

Holmes, J. R., "Vietnam's Undersea Anti-Access Fleet," *Diplomat*, 1 November 2012. Online. Available HTTP: <http://thediplomat.com/2012/11/vietnams-undersea-anti-access-fleet> (accessed 1 November 2013).

Hong Chuyen, "Hiep dinh phan dinh Vinh Bac Bo quy dinh dieu gi (What Is in Agreement on Delimitation of the Gulf of Tonkin)?," *Infonet*, 8 April 2014. Online. Available HTTP: <http://infonet.vn/hiep-dinh-phan-dinh-vinh-bac-bo-quy-dinh-dieu-gi-post124151.info> (accessed 30 March 2015).

Hong Nga, "Bien Dong nong dan (South China Sea Heating Up)," *BBC Tieng Viet*, 4 April 2014.

Hoyts, M. A., Sino-Vietnamese Interests Collide in the South China Sea: A Case Study of the Disputed Paracel and Spratly Archipelago, MA Thesis, Asian Studies Dept., University of Hawaii 1994.

Hung, N. D., "Tap chi Nature se noi khong voi ban do luoi bo (Nature Says No to Cow-Tongue Map)," *Tuan Viet Nam*, 22 October 2011.

Huong Giang, "Giao duc nhan dan neu cao y thuc bao ve chu quyen, lanh tho quoc gia (Enhancing People's Awareness of National Sovereignty and Integrity)," *Thanh Nien*, 22 March 2009. Online. Available HTTP: <www.thanhnien.com.vn/news1/pages/200912/20090322005039.aspx> (accessed 31 July 2014).

Huy, D. D., "Gac tranh chap, cung khai thac" kieu Trung Quoc (Shelving Disputes, Jointly Developing in the Chinese Way), *Tuan Viet Nam*, 21 January 2010. Online. Available

HTTP: <http://tuanvietnam.vietnamnet.vn/2010–01–20-gac-tranh-chap-cung-khai-thac-kieu-trung-quoc> (accessed 3 August 2014).
Huy Duc, *Ben thang cuoc (The Winning Side)*, E-book: Osinbook, 2012.
International Crisis Group, "Stirring Up the South China Sea (I)," *Asia Report No. 223*, 23 April 2012.
International Crisis Group, "Stirring Up the South China Sea (II): Regional Responses," *Asia Report No. 229*, 24 July 2012.
Interviews with Vietnamese Officials in Hanoi in March and April 2014.
The Island of Palmas Case (or Miangas), United States v Netherlands, RIAA II 829, 1928.
Ivanovich, D., "The Risky Business of Petroleum Politics/U.S. Oil and Gas Firms Must often Weigh Instability in Some Areas with the Lure of Rich Reserves," *Houston Chronicle*, 28 July 1996.
Jakobson, L., "China's Unpredictable Maritime Security Actors," *Report by Lowy Institute for International Security*, December 2014. Online. Available HTTP: <www.lowyinstitute.org/files/chinas-unpredictable-maritime-security-actors_3.pdf> (accessed 27 May 2015).
Ji, Y., "Deciphering Beijing's Maritime Security Policy and Strategy in Managing Sovereignty Disputes in the China Seas," *RSIS Policy Brief*, October 2013.
"Joint Communiqué of the 36th ASEAN Ministerial Meeting Phnom Penh," 16–17 June 2003. Online. Available HTTP: <www.asean.org/communities/asean-political-security-community/item/joint-communique-of-the-36th-asean-ministerial-meeting-phnom-penh-16–17-june-2003> (accessed 19 May 2013).
"Joint Statement between the United States of America and the Socialist Republic of Vietnam," 25 June 2008. Online. Available HTTP: <http://vietnam.usembassy.gov/jointstatement_.html> (accessed 20 August 2013).
Kang, D.C., "Getting Asia Wrong: The Need for New Analytical Frameworks," *International Security* 27, no. 4, 2003, 57–85.
Karniol, R., "Vietnam Bolstering Spratly Firepower," *Strait Times*, 10 May 2010.
Keck, Z., "Second Thomas Shoal Tensions Intensify," *Diplomat*, 13 April 2014.
Keyuan, Z., "The Chinese Traditional Maritime Boundary Line in the South China Sea and Its Legal Consequences for the Resolution of the Dispute over the Spratly Islands," *International Journal of Marine and Coastal Law* 14, no. 1, 1999, 27–55.
"Khai Truong Duong Day Nong Ngoai Giao Viet-Trung," *Dan Tri*, 2 March 2012.
Khanh, C., "Viet Nam Da Chuan Bi Ho So Phap Ly Kien Trung Quoc," *Tien Phong*, 29 May 2014.
Khiet Hung, "Tien ra khai thac 'mat tien' bien (Tuoi Tre)," 1 June 2009. Online. Available HTTP: <http://tuoitre.vn/Chinh-tri-Xa-hoi/319257/tien-ra-khai-thac-mat-tien-bien.html–ad-image-0> (accessed 28 July 2014).
"Khong de Bien Dong anh huong quan he Viet-Trung," *Phap Luat Thanh Pho*, 24 October 2012.
"Khong de Bien Dong anh huong quan he Viet-Trung," *Vnexpress*, 8 September 2012.
Kiet, V.V., "Thu gui Bo Chinh tri (Letter to Politburo)," 9 August 1995. Online. Available HTTP: <www.diendan.org/tai-lieu/bao-cu/so-048/thu-vo-van-kiet-1995Hanoi> (accessed 29 June 2015).
Kim, J.C., "Politics of Regionalism in East Asia," *Asian Perspective* 34, no. 3, 2010, 113–36.
Kim, S.S., "China as a Regional Power," *Current History* 91, no. 566, 1992, 247–53.
Kivimäki, T., "The Unacknowledged Peace of East Asia," *Asia Insights* 2, 2009, 4.
Kivimäki, T. (Ed), *War or Peace in the South China Sea?*, Copenhagen, Denmark: NIAS Press, 2002.

Klintworth, G., The Outlook for Cambodia: The China Factor, In: Gary Klintworth (Ed), *Vietnam's Withdrawal from Cambodia: Regional Issues and Realignments*, Canberra: Strategic and Defense Studies Center, ANU, 1990.

Koh, D., "The Politics of a Divided Party and Parkinson's State in Vietnam," *Contemporary Southeast Asia* 23, no. 3, 2001, 533–51.

Lague, D., "China Airs Ambition to Beef Up Naval Power," *International Herald Tribune*, 28 December 2006.

Leahy, J., "Indonesia Seeks Clarification on Extension of Territorial Waters into Disputed Area," *South China Morning Post*, 22 July 1996.

Lee, K. C., "Vietnam Had No Regrets about Joining ASEAN," *Strait Times*, 10 September 1996.

Lee, L. T., *China and the South China Sea Dialogues*, Westport, CT: Praeger, 1999.

Legal Status of Eastern Greenland, Denmark v Norway, Series A./B., No.53, 1933.

Lelyyeld, M., "China Projects Power at Sea," *RFA*, 3 May 2010.

Lim, R., "The ASEAN Regional Forum: Building on Sand," *Contemporary Southeast Asia* 20, no. 2, 1998, 115–36.

Liow, J. C., Balancing, Bandwagoning, or Hedging? Strategic and Security Patterns in Malaysia's Relations with China: 1981–2002, In: Ho Khai Leong and Samuel C. Y. Ku (Eds), *China and Southeast Asia: Global Changes and Regional Challenges*, Singapore: Institute of Southeast Asia Studies, 2015, 281–307.

Liyao, M., "Vietnam Not Seeking Military Alliance," *China Daily*, 26 August 2010.

Lo, C., *China's Policy towards Territorial Disputes: The Case of South China Sea Islands*, New York: Routledge, 1989.

Loi, L. V., *Fifty Years of Vietnamese Diplomacy*, Hanoi: The Gioi Publisher, 2000.

Loi, L. V., *Ngoai giao Viet Nam (Vietnamese Diplomacy)*, Hanoi: Cong an Nhan dan, 2000.

Loi, L. V., *Nhung dieu can biet ve Dat, Bien, Troi Viet Nam (Land, Sea, and Sky of Vietnam)*, Hanoi: Tuoi Tre Publisher, 2007.

Loi, L. V., *The Sino-Vietnamese Differences on the Hoang Sa and Truong Sa Archipelagos*, Hanoi: World Publisher, 1995.

Loi, L. V., *Vietnam: Dat, Bien, Troi (Vietnam: Land, Sea, and Sky)*, Hanoi: Cong an Nhan dan Publisher, 1990.

London, J., "South China Sea Crisis Demands Vietnam's Leadership Breakthrough," *CogitAsia*, 19 May 2014. Online. Available HTTP: <http://cogitasia.com/south-china-sea-crisis-demands-vietnams-leadership-breakthrough/> (accessed 3 July 2015).

Long, N. V., *Hoang Sa-Truong Sa: Cac su kien, tu lieu lich su phap ly chinh (2000–2013) (Paracels and Spratlys: Event Log and Historical and Legal Documentation, 2000–2013)*, Ho Chi Minh City: Tre Publisher, 2014.

Long, N. V., *Hoang Sa-Truong Sa: Cac su kien, tu lieu lich su phap ly chinh (The ky XV-2000) (Paracels and Spratlys: Event Log and Historical and Legal Documentation, 15th Century – 2000)*, Ho Chi Minh City: Tre Publisher, 2013.

Luu, N., "Nhung viec lam di nguoc tinh huu nghi (Acts against friendship)," *Cong an Nhan dan*, 1 July 2009. Online. Available HTTP: <www.cand.com.vn/vi-VN/thoisu/2009/7/115633.cand> (accessed 9 July 2014).

Mac Lam, "Tau Trung Quoc lai tuan tra trong vung bien tranh chap voi Viet Nam (Chines Vessels' Intrusion to Vietnam's Seas)," *RFA Tieng Viet*, 30 April 2010. Online. Available HTTP: <www.rfa.org/vietnamese/vietnam/chinh-tri/China-Ship-patrols-deep-inside-Vietnam-s-sovereignty-MLam-04302010204951.html> (accessed 6 August 2014).

Mai, T., "Phan Ung Cua Viet Nam Ve Viec Philippines Khoi Kien Trung Quoc," *Vnexpress*, 24 January 2013.

Malik, M., "China and the East Asian Summit: More Discord Than Accord," *Asia-Pacific Centre for Security Studies*, February 2006. Online. Available HTTP: <http://apcss.org/Publications/APSSS/ChinaandEastAsiaSummit.pdf> (accessed 15 December 2015).

Manh, N. D., "Phat bieu của Dong chi Nong Duc Manh be mac Hoi nghi lan thu 4 Ban Chap hanh Trung uong Dang khoa X (Closing Remark of Comrade Nong Duc Anh at the 4th Session of the 9th Central Committee)," *Tap chi Cong san*, 25 January 2007. Online. Available HTTP: <http://dangcongsan.vn/cpv/Modules/News/NewsDetail.aspx?co_id=30397&cn_id=136235> (accessed 12 January 2014).

Manthorpe, J., "China Is Rolling Up Its Sleeves and Showing off," *Vancouver Sun*, 21 December 2007.

Maritime Disputes and Sovereignty Issues in East Asia, Subcommittee on East Asia and Pacific Affairs, Committee on Foreign Relations, United States Senate, S. Hrg. 111–135, Washington, DC, 15 July 2009. Online. Available HTTP: <www.gpo.gov/fdsys/pkg/CHRG-111shrg53022/html/CHRG-111shrg53022.htm%3E>.

Marr, D. G., "Sino-Vietnamese Relations," *Australian Journal of Chinese Affairs*, no. 6, 1981, 19.

McDonald, M., "A New Map in Chinese Passports Stirs Anger across the Region," *New York Times*, 25 November 2012.

McDonald, M., "US Navy Provoked South China Sea Incident, China Says," *New York Times*, 10 March 2009.

The Military Balance, 1990–1991, London: International Institute for Strategic Studies, 1990.

The Military Balance, 1995/96, London: International Institute for Strategic Studies, 1995.

Mingjiang, L., "China's Non-Confrontational Assertiveness in the South China Sea," *East Asia Forum*, 14 June 2012.

Minh, P. B., "Tam the Moi Cua Doi Ngoai Da Phuong Viet Nam," *Nhan Dan*, 10 December 2015.

Mitton, R., "China-Vietnam Ties Remain More Sour Than Sweet," *Asia Sentinel*, 14 November 2008.

Mitton, R., "Vietnam Blasts China's Plans for Paracels," *Strait Times*, 18 August 2007.

Mitton, R., "Vietnam, China Hold Crisis Talks over Territorial Spats," *Strait Times*, 28 July 2007.

Mitton, R., "Vietnam Sees Second Weekend of Anti-China Protests," *Strait Times*, 17 December 2007.

Morley, J. W., and Nishihara, M. (Eds), *Vietnam Joins the World*, Armonk, NY: M. E. Sharpe, 1997.

Nakashima, E., "Vietnam, U.S. to Improve Intelligence, Military Ties: Premier Discusses Goals before Visit," *Washington Post*, 17 June 2005.

Nam, N., "Dung so Trung Quoc cam bien (Don't be Afraid of Chinas' Sea Ban)," *RFA Tieng Viet*, 29 May 2010.

Nam Nguyen, "Trang bi vu khi cho cac tau ca (Arming Fishing Ships)?," *RFA Tieng Viet*, 22 October 2009.

Nambia, R., and Said, R., "Regional Code of Conduct Now Referred to Working Group," *New Straits Times*, 21 July 1999.

"Nanhai 215 Vessel Has Hauled Oil Drilling Platform KANTAN 3 of China to the Continental Shelf of Viet Nam," *Vietnam News Agency*, 19 November 2004.

National Institute for Defense Studies, "China Security Report," Tokyo, 2011.

"Nga giao ten lua phong thu cho Viet Nam (Russia Delivered Defensive Missiles to Vietnam)," *BBC Tieng Viet*, 19 October 2011. Online. Available HTTP: <www.bbc.co.uk/vietnamese/vietnam/2011/10/111019_russia_missiles.shtml> (accessed 20 September 2013).

Nga, P., "Vietnam Puts Paracel Row on Summit Agenda," *BBC*, 8 April 2010. Online. Available HTTP: <http://news.bbc.co.uk/2/mobile/asia-pacific/8609120.stm> (accessed 31 July 2014).

Ngoc Bach, "Nam 2020, Kinh te Bien dong gop khoang 53–55% GDP (By 2020, Marine-Based Economy Contributes 53–55 Per Cent of GDP)," *Bo Tai nguyen Moi truong*, 16 May 2011. Online. Available HTTP: <www.monre.gov.vn/v35/default.aspx?tabid=428&CateID=53&ID=101068&Code=0YDK101068> (accessed 12 December 2013).

Nguyen Dong, "8 ban do co chung minh Trung Quoc khong co Hoang Sa (8 Old Maps Proving China without)," *Vnexpress*, 29 July 2012. Online. Available HTTP: <http://vnexpress.net/gl/xa-hoi/2012/07/8-ban-do-co-chung-minh-trung-quoc-khong-co-hoang-sa> (accessed 3 August 2012).

Nguyen, P. P., "Oil Search Fuels Rising Tension in South China Sea," *Inter Press Service*, 21 March 1997.

"Nguyen tac giai quyet van de tren bien Viet-Trung (Principles Guiding Settlements of the Sea-Related Issues between Vietnam and China)," *TTXVN*, 12 October 2011.

Nha, N., Dau, N. D., Nghia, L. M., Thu, T.D.M., and Viet, V. Q., *Hoang Sa, Truong Sa la cua Viet Nam (Paracels and Spratlys Belonging to Vietnam)*, Ho Chi Minh: Youth Publisher, 2008.

Nhi, H., "Bo Truong Quoc Phong Viet – Trung Dien Dam," *Vietnamnet*, 31 December 2015.

"Nhieu tau ca TQ vao lanh hai Viet Nam (A Big Number of Chinese Fishing Ships Intruding Vietnam's Territorial Sea)," *BBC Tieng Viet*, 6 February 2010.

Ninh, V. V., "Tuong Viet Nam ke chuyen binh thuong hoa quan he voi Trung Quoc (Vietnamese General: Stories Behind Normalisation of Vietnam-China Relations)," *Vietnamnet*, 21 December 2011. Online. Available HTTP: <http://tuanvietnam.vietnamnet.vn/2011–12–20-tuong-viet-nam-ke-chuyen-binh-thuong-hoa-quan-he-voi-trung-quoc> (accessed 24 October 2012).

Norwegian Agency for Development Cooperation, "Study of the Vietnamese Shipbuilding/Maritime Sector," *Final Report*, June 2010.

"Notification and Statement of Claims," Department of Foreign Affairs, The Republic of the Philippines, 2013.

Odgaard, L., "Deterrence and Co-Operation in the South China Sea," *Contemporary Southeast Asia* 23, no. 2, 2001, 15.

Okabe, T., "Coping with China," In: James William Morley and Masashi Nishihara (Eds), *Vietnam Joins the World*, Armonk, NY: M. E. Sharpe, 1997.

"One Step Nearer to ASEAN Economic Community," *Vietnam News Agency*, 2015.

O'Rourke, R., "Maritime Territorial and Exclusive Economic Zone (EEZ) Disputes Involving China: Issues for Congress," *Congressional Research Service Report*, 22 December 2015.

Othman, Z., "Disputed Areas: ASEAN Calls for Self-Restraint," *Business Times*, 22 July 1996.

Parameswaran, P., "Indonesia to Buy New Submarines from Russia," *Diplomat*, 25 September 2015.

Path, K., "The Sino-Vietnamese Dispute over Territorial Claims, 1974–1978: Vietnamese Nationalism and Its Consequences," *International Journal of Asian Studies* 8, no. 2, 2011, 189–220.

Perlez, J., "U.S. Competes with China for Vietnam's Allegiance," *International Herald Tribune*, 19 June 2006.

Permanent Mission of the People's Republic of China to the United Nations, "Note Verbale CML/17/2009," 7 May 2009. Online. Available HTTP: <www.un.org/depts/los/clcs_new/submissions_files/submission_mysvnm_33_2009.htm> (accessed 30 July 2014).

Permanent Mission of the People's Republic of China to the United Nations, "Note Verbale CML/18/2009," 7 May 2009. Online. Available HTTP: <www.un.org/depts/los/clcs_new/submissions_files/submission_vnm_37_2009.htm> (accessed 31 July 2014).

Permanent Mission of the Socialist Republic of Vietnam, "Note Verbale No.86/HC-2009," 8 May 2009. Online. Available HTTP: <www.un.org/depts/los/clcs_new/submissions_files/mysvnm33_09/vnm_chn_2009re_mys_vnm_e.pdf> (accessed 31 July 2014).

Petty, M., "Vietnam Talks Trust with China, Inviting Japanese Warship," *Reuters*, 6 November 2015.

Phieu, L. M., and Huy, D. D., "Viet Nam truoc chu truong cua Trung Quoc doi voi Bien Dong (Vietnam and China's Policy toward South China Sea)," *Tuan Viet Nam*, 11 January 2009. Online. Available HTTP: <http://tuanvietnam.net/2009–01–11-viet-nam-truoc-chu-truong-cua-trung-quoc-doi-voi-bien-dong> (accessed 20 July 2014).

"PHL Asks China to Explain Ships Near Reed Bank," *GMA News*, 1 June 2011.

Phuong Loan, "Khong the giu chu quyen bang cam tinh (Feeling Cannot Help Defend Sovereignty)," *Vietnamnet*, 18 March 2009. Online. Available HTTP: <http://vnn.vietnamnet.vn/chinhtri/2009/03/836677/> (accessed 9 July 2014).

Politburo (CPV), "Resolution No.07-NQ/TW on International Economic Integration," *Hanoi*, 27 November 2001.

Pomfret, J., "U.S. Takes a Tougher Tone with China," *Washington Post*, 20 July 2010.

Porter, B., "Beijing Still Wants to See Spratly Code: Pragmatic Approach Urged in Developing Islands," *South China Morning Post*, 30 November 1999.

"Possible Impacts of TPP on Vietnam," *Saigon Times*, 12 October 2015.

Prescott, J.R.V., *Limits of National Claims in the South China Sea*, London: ASEAN Academic Press, 1999.

Prescott, J.R.V., Straight and Archipelagic Baselines, In: Gerald Blake (Ed), *Maritime Boundaries and Ocean Resources*, London: Croom Helm, 1987.

"Prime Minister Pham Van Dong's Letter to Chinese Premier Zhou Enlai," 14 September 1958. Online. Available HTTP: <www.rfa.org/vietnamese/ReadersOpinions/legali-of-p-v-dong-note-07162014052556.html> (accessed 18 May 2015).

Promfret, J., "China's Rise Prompts Vietnam to Strengthen Ties to Other Nations," *Washington Post*, 30 October 2010.

Quoc Phap, "Ban do 'duong luoi bo' tren Bien Dong: Duong yeu sach phi ly cua Trung Quoc (Cow-Tongue Map in the South China Sea: China's Illegal Claim)," *Thanh Nien*, 18 August 2009. Online. Available HTTP: <www.thanhnien.com.vn/news1/pages/200934/20090818003413.aspx> (accessed 9 July 2014).

Quoc Phap, "Truoc yeu sach 80% dien tich Bien Dong cua Trung Quoc: Khong chap nhan duong luoi bo (China's Claim to 80 Per Cent of South China Sea Unacceptable)," *Tuoi Tre*, 18 August 2009. Online. Available HTTP: <http://tuoitre.vn/Chinh-tri-Xa-hoi/332309/truoc-yeu-sach-80-dien-tich-bien-dong-cua-trung-quoc—khong-chap-nhan-duong-luoi-bo.html%3E> (accessed 9 July 2014).

Quynh, T.H., "Tiem nang Bien Viet Nam va nhung Dinh huong Chien luoc co ban de xay dung va phat trien (Maritime Potentials and Strategic Orientations for Development)," *Tap chi Cong san*, 25 July 2008. Online. Available HTTP: <http://dangcongsan.vn/cpv/Modules/News/NewsDetail.aspx?co_id=30463&cn_id=239397> (accessed 25 November).

Randall, L. S., "Bandwagoning for Profit: Bringing the Revisionist State Back In," *International Security* 19, no. 1, 1994, 72–107.

Randall, L. S., "Unanswered Threats: A Neoclassical Realist Theory of Underbalancing," *International Security* 29, no. 2, 2004, 159–201.

Rau, R., "Present and Future Maritime Security Issues in the Southeast Asian and South China Seas," *Contemporary Southeast Asia* 8, no. 1, 1986.

Raymer, S., "Oil Company Rush to Develop Vietnam," *Journal Record*, 22 March 1995.

Richardson, M., "Oil Rush Is Fuelling Fears on Spratlys," *International Herald Tribune*, 6 June 1994.

Richardson, M., "On Eve of Annual Talks, ASEAN Members Are Split over Spratly Dispute," *International Herald Tribune*, 23 July 1999.

"A Rig too Near," *Economist*, 29 March 1997.

Rodriguez, R. A., "Conduct Unbecoming in the South China Sea," *PacNet*, 21 May 2004. Online. Available HTTP: <http://csis.org/files/media/csis/pubs/pac0422a.pdf> (accessed 21 May).

Rosenberg, D., "China, Neighbors Progress in Fishery Agreements," *Asia Times*, 19 August 2005. Online. Available HTTP: <www.atimes.com/atimes/China/GH19Ad02.html> (accessed 17 February 2013).

Ross, R. S., "Balance of Power Politics and the Rise of China: Accommodation and Balancing in East Asia," *Security Studies* 15, no. 3, 2006, 355–95.

Roy, D., "China's Pitch for a Multipolar World," *Asia-Pacific Security Studies* 2, no. 1, 2003, 1–4.

Roy, D., "Southeast Asia and China: Balancing or Bandwagoning?," *Contemporary Southeast Asia* 27, no. 2, 2005, 305–23.

"Russia Sells Second Batch of Gepard-Class Frigates to Vietnam," *Naval Today*, 8 December 2011. Online. Available HTTP: <http://navaltoday.com/2011/12/08/russia-sells-second-batch-of-gepard-class-frigates-to-vietnam> (accessed 21 September 2013).

Samuels, M. S., *Contest for the South China Sea*, New York: Methuen, 1982.

Samuels, M. S., *Contest for the South China Sea*, London: Routledge, 2005.

SarDesai, D. R., *Vietnam: Past and Present*, Los Angeles: California Westview Press, 2005.

Schofield, C., Dangerous Ground: A Geopolitical Overview of the South China Sea, In: Sam Bateman and Ralf Emmer (Eds), *Security and International Politics in the South China Sea: Towards a Cooperative Management Regime*, London and New York: Routledge, 2009, 7–25.

Schuster, C. O., "Case Closed: The Gulf of Tonkin Incident," *History Net*, 7 August 2014. Online. Available HTTP: <www.historynet.com/case-closed-the-gulf-of-tonkin-incident.htm> (accessed 19 May 2015).

"Sea of Troubles," *Economist*, 25 May 1996.

Segal, G., "East Asia and the 'Constrainment' of China," *International Security* 20, no. 4, 1996, 28.

Severino, R. C., "ASEAN Beyond Forty: Towards Political and Economic Integration," *Contemporary Southeast Asia* 29, no. 3, 2007, 406–23.

Shanker, T., "The U.S. and China Soften Tone over Disputed Seas," *New York Times*, 12 October 2010.

Simon, S., "ASEAN and Multilateralism: The Long, Bumpy Road to Community," *Contemporary Southeast Asia* 30, no. 2, 2008, 264–83.

Simon, S., "US-Southeast Asia Relations: Growing Enmeshment in Regional Affairs," *Comparative Connections*, October 2010.

Simon, S., "Vietnam's Security: Between China and ASEAN," *Asian Affairs* 20, no. 4, 1994, 187–201.

Skehan, C., "Canberra Condemns ASEAN's Failure to Back Code," *Age*, 29 July 1999.

Snyder, C., "The Implication of Hydrocarbon Development in the South China Sea," *International Journal* 52, no. 1, 1996–1997, 142–58.

Socialist Republic of Vietnam, "Submission to the Commission on the Limits of the Continental Shelf: Partial Submission in Respect of Vietnam's Extended Continental Shelf: North Area (VNM-N)," 7 May 2009. Online. Available HTTP: <www.un.org/depts/los/

clcs_new/submissions_files/vnm37_09/vnm2009n_executivesummary.pdf> (accessed 31 July 2014).

Socialist Republic of Vietnam, and Malaysia, "Joint Submission the Commission on the Limits of the Continental Shelf: Part I: Executive Summary," 6 May 2009. Online. Available HTTP: <www.un.org/Depts/los/clcs_new/submissions_files/submission_mysvnm_33_2009.htm> (accessed 30 July).

Son, N.H., Vietnam: A Case Study in Naval Modernization, In: Geoffrey Till and Jane Chan (Eds), *Naval Modernization in South-East Asia: Nature, Causes and Consequences*, London and New York: Routledge, 2014, 121–34.

Song, Y.-h., "The South China Sea Declaration of Conduct of Parties and Its Implication: Taiwan's Perspective," *Maritime Studies*, March–April 2003.

"South China Sea Guidelines Agreed," *Jakarta Post*, 21 July 2011.

Spegele, B., and Khanh, V.T., "China Moves Oil Rig from Contested Waters." *Wall Street Journal*, 16 July 2014.

Spegele, B., and Khanh, V.T., "China, Vietnam Try to Repair Ties after South China Sea Dispute." *Wall Street Journal*, 28 August 2014.

"Spokesman Says Vietnam's Gas Pipeline Infringes on China's Sovereignty," *Xinhua News*, 10 April 2007.

"Spratly Plan Proposed," *Oil Daily*, 3 September 2003.

"Statement on the Territorial Sea, the Contiguous Zone, the Exclusive Economic Zone, and the Continental Shelf of Vietnam," National Assembly (Socialist Republic of Vietnam), Hanoi, 1977.

Stern, M.L., "U.S.-Vietnam Defense Relations: Deepening Ties, Adding Relevance," *Strategic Forum*, Institute for National Strategic Studies, National Defense University, No.245, September 2009.

Storey, I.C., "Conflict in the South China Sea: China's Relations with Vietnam and the Philippines (Part II)," *Asia-Pacific Journal: Japan Focus* 8, no. 9, 2008.

Storey, I.C., "Maritime Security in Southeast Asia: Two Cheers for Regional Cooperation," *Southeast Asian Affairs*, 2009, 36–58.

Storey, I.C., Recent Developments in the South China Sea: Cause for Concern, In: Tran Truong Thuy (Ed), *The South China Sea: Cooperation for Regional Security and Development*, Hanoi: Diplomatic Academy of Vietnam, 2010.

Storey, I.C., "The South China Sea: The Theatre for Emerging Strategic Competition," paper presented at the Security Environment in the East Asian Seas, Ocean Policy Research Foundation, Tokyo, 16–17 February 2011.

Storey, I.C., "Vietnam and the United States 2004–2005: Still Sensitive, But Moving Forward," *Asia-Pacific Center for Security Studies*, February 2005.

Storey, I.C., and Thayer, C.A., "Cam Ranh Bay: Past Imperfect, Future Conditional," *Contemporary Southeast Asia* 23, no. 3, 2001, 425–46.

Storey, I.J., "Creeping Assertiveness: China, the Philippines and the South China Sea Dispute," *Contemporary Southeast Asia* 21, no. 1, 1999, 95–118.

Storey, I.J., "Living with the Colossus: How Southeast Asian Countries Cope with China," *Parameters* 29, no. 4, 1999–2000.

"The Submarine Race in Asia," *New York Times*, 7 January 2014.

Sun, L., "Leaders of Vietnam, China Held Secret Talks," *Washington Post*, 19 September 1990.

Sutter, R., "South China Sea: Economic Issues," *CSIS Comparative Connections*, April 2009.

Sy Phuong, "Ngu dan kho vi lien tiep bi tau la dam (Misery of Fishermen Assaulted by Chinese Vessels)," *Kien thuc*, 13 June 2010.

"Thai Protests Disrupt ASEAN Summit," *Aljazeera*, 10 April 2009.

Thang, N. Q., *Hoang Sa, Truong Sa Lanh tho Viet Nam nhin tu Cong phap Quoc te (Paracels, Spratlys as Vietnam's Territories from Public International Law Points of View)*, Ha Noi: Tri Thuc Publisher, 2008.

Thanh Giang, "ASEAN Summit 9: ASEAN, China Sign Strategic Partnership Declaration," *Vietnam Business Forum*, 25 October 2003.

Thanh, Q. P., "Responding to New Maritime Security Threats," paper presented at the 10th IISS Asian Security Summit, Shangri-La Dialogue, Singapore, 5 June 2011.

Thanh, V. V., "Can khoi day y thuc giu gin bien dao cua cha ong (Raising People's Awareness of Ancestors' Seas and Islands)," *Tuoi Tre*, 23 March 2009. Online. Available HTTP: <http://tuoitre.vn/Chinh-tri-Xa-hoi/307537/can-khoi-day-y-thuc-giu-gin-bien-dao-cua-cha-ong.html – ad-image-1> (accessed 27 July 2014).

"Thao Luan Ve Quan He Viet-Trung," *BBC Tieng Viet*, 5 November 2015.

Thao, N. H., The Declaration on Conduct of Parties in the South China Sea: A Vietnamese Perspective, 2002–2007, In: Sam Bateman and Ralf Emmers (Eds), *Security and International Politics in the South China Sea: Toward a Cooperative Management Regime*, London and New York: Routledge, 2009, 207–21.

Thao, N. H., *Luat Quoc te va Chu quyen tren hai quan dao Hoang Sa va Truong Sa (International Law and Sovereignty over Paracel and Spratly Archipelagos)*, Hanoi: Cong an Nhan dan Publisher, 2009.

Thao, N. H., "The Settlement of Disputes in Bac Bo (Tonkin) Gulf," *Vietnam Law and Legal Forum* 7, no. 77, 2001.

Thao, N. H., "Viet-Trung va duong bien gioi phap ly, cong bang, huu nghi (Friendly and Just Border between Vietnam and China)," *Vietnamnet*, 2 January 2009. Online. Available HTTP: <http://vnn.vietnamnet.vn/chinhtri/2009/01/821775/> (accessed 17 January 2013).

Thao, N. H., "Vietnam and the Code of Conduct for the South China Sea," *Ocean Development and International Law* 32, no. 2, 2001, 105–30.

Thao, N. H., "Vietnam's First Maritime Boundary Agreement," *IBRU Boundary and Security Bulletin*, Fall 1997.

Thao, N. H., "Vietnam's Position on the Sovereignty over the Paracels and the Spratlys: Its Maritime Claims," *Journal of East Asia International Law* 1, 2012, 165–211.

Thao, N. H., and Amer, R., "Managing Vietnam's Maritime Boundary Disputes," *Ocean Development and International Law* 38, no. 3, 2007, 305–24.

Thayer, C. A., "China's New Wave of Aggressive Assertiveness in the South China Sea," *International Journal of China Studies* 2, no. 3, 2011, 555–83.

Thayer, C. A., "China's Oil Rig Gambit: South China Sea Game-Changer?," *Diplomat*, 12 May 2014.

Thayer, C. A., "Force Modernization: The Case of the Vietnam People's Army," *Contemporary Southeast Asia* 19, no. 1, 1997, 1–28.

Thayer, C. A., Military Politics in Contemporary Vietnam: Political Engagement, Corporate Interests and Professionalism, In: M. Mietzner (Ed), *Military Politics in Contemporary Southeast Asia*, London: Routledge, 2011, 65–86.

Thayer, C. A., "Not Too Hot, Not Too Cold: A Vietnamese Perspective on China-U.S. Relations." In *International Conference on China-US Relations in Global Perspective*. Wellington, New Zealand, 2015.

Thayer, C. A., "Political Legitimacy of Vietnam's One Party-State: Challenges and Responses," *Journal of Current Southeast Asian Affairs* 4, 2009, 47–70.

Thayer, C. A., "Political Legitimacy of Vietnam's One Party-State: Challenges and Response," *Journal of Current Southeast Asian Affairs* 28, no. 4, 2009, 47–70.

Thayer, C.A., "Recent Developments in the South China Sea: Grounds for Cautious Optimism," *RSIS Working Paper*, no. 220, 14 December 2010.

Thayer, C.A., "Russian Subs in Vietnam," *USNI News*, 20 August 2012.

Thayer, C.A., "Sino-Vietnamese Relations: The Interplay of Ideology and National Interest," *Asian Survey* 34, no. 6, 1994, 15.

Thayer, C.A., "The Structure of Vietnam-China Relations, 1991–2008," paper presented at the 3rd International Conference on Vietnamese Studies, Hanoi, 4–7 December 2008.

Thayer, C.A., "The Tyranny of Geography: Vietnamese Strategies to Constrain China in the South China Sea," *Contemporary Southeast Asia* 33, no. 3, 2011, 348–69.

Thayer, C.A., "The Tyranny of Geography: Vietnamese Strategies to Constrain China in the South China Sea," paper presented at the International Studies Association-52nd Annual Convention, Montreal, Canada, 16–19 March 2011.

Thayer, C.A., "The United States and Chinese Assertiveness in the South China Sea," *Security Challenges* 6, no. 2, 2010, 69–84.

Thayer, C.A., "The United States, China and Southeast Asia," *Southeast Asian Affairs*, 2012, 16–25.

Thayer, C.A., "Upholding State Sovereignty through Global Integration: Remaking of Vietnamese National Security Policy," paper presented at the Workshop on Vietnam, East Asia and Beyond, City University of Hong Kong, Hong Kong, 11–12 December 2008.

Thayer, C.A., "Vietnam and ASEAN: A First Anniversary Assessment," *Southeast Asian Affairs*, 1997, 364–74.

Thayer, C.A., "Vietnam, China and the Oil Rig Crisis: Who Blinked?," *Diplomat*, 4 August 2014.

Thayer, C.A., "Vietnam: Coping with China," *Southeast Asian Affairs*, 1994.

Thayer, C.A., *The Vietnam People's Army under Doi Moi*, Singapore: Institute of Southeast Asian Studies, 1994.

Thayer, C.A., "Vietnam on the Road to Global Integration: Forging Strategic Partnership through International Security Cooperation," paper presented at the Fourth International Vietnam Studies Conference, Vietnam Academy of Social Sciences and Vietnam National University, Hanoi, 26–28 November 2012.

Thayer, C.A., "Vietnam: The Tenth Party Congress and after," *Southeast Asian Affairs*, 2007, 379–97.

Thayer, C.A., "Vietnam and the United States: Convergence But Not Congruence of Strategic Interests in the South China Sea," paper presented at the 4th Engaging with Vietnam Interdisciplinary Dialogue Conference, Honolulu, 2012.Thayer, C.A., "Vietnam's People Army: Development and Modernisation," *Research Monograph*, 30 April 2009.

Thayer, C.A., "Vietnamese Diplomacy, 1975–2015: From Member of the Socialist Camp to Proactive International Integration," paper presented at the International Conference on Vietnam: 40 Years of Reunification, Development and Integration (1975–2015), Thu Dau Mot University, Binh Duong, 25 April 2015.

Thayer, C.A., Vietnamese Foreign Policy: Multilateralism and the Threat of Peaceful Evolution, In: Carlyle A. Thayer and Ramses Amer (Eds), *Vietnamese Foreign Policy in Transition*, Singapore: Institute of Southeast Studies, 1999, 1–24.

Thayer, C.A., Vietnamese Foreign Policy: Multilateralism and the Threat of Peaceful Evolution, In: Carlyle A. Thayer and Ramses Amer (Eds), *Vietnamese Foreign Policy in Transition*, New York: St. Martin's Press, 1999, ix, 294 p.

Thayer, C.A., Vietnamese Perspectives of the "China Threat," In: Herbert S. Yee and Ian C. Storey (Eds), *The China Threat: Perceptions, Myths and Reality*, New York: Routledge Curzon, 2002.

Thayer, C.A., and Amer, R. (Eds), *Vietnamese Foreign Policy in Transition*, New York: St. Martin's Press, 1999.

Thi Lam, "Massacre in the Gulf of Tonkin," *National Catholic Reporter* 41, no. 19, 11 March 2005.

Tho, T.V., "Viet Nam 40 Nam Qua Va Nhung Nam Toi: Can Mot Nen Kinh Te Thi Truong Dinh Huong Phat Trien," *Thoi Dai Moi* 33, July 2015.

"Thong Bao Hoi Nghi Lan Thu 14 Ban Chap Hanh Trung Uong Dang Khoa Xi," *Nhan Dan*, 13 January 2016.

Thong, L.N., "Muc tieu cua Tau ngam Viet Nam tren Bien Dong (Targets of Vietnamese Submarines in South China Sea)," *Dat Viet*, 19 December 2013. Online. Available HTTP: <http://baodatviet.vn/quoc-phong/quoc-phong-viet-nam/muc-tieu-cua-tau-ngam-viet-nam-tren-bien-dong-2362421/> (accessed 18 December 2013).

Thu, T.D.M., "Chu quyen tren hai quan dao Hoang Sa va Truong Sa (Sovereignty over Paracel and Spratly Archipelagos)," *Thoi Dai moi* 11, 2007.

Thuy, C., "Chinese Boats Intrude Vietnam's Waters, Cut Cables again," *Vietnamnet*, 2011.

Thuy, T.T., "Construction in the South China Sea: A Comparative View," *Asia Maritime Transparency Initiative*, 18 February 2015.

Thuy, T.T., "Nhung khuyen nghi sau Hoi thao Bien Dong (National Conference on South China Sea: Recommendations)," *Tuan Viet Nam*, 19 March 2009. Online. Available HTTP: <www.tuanvietnam.net/2009–03–19-nhung-khuyen-nghi-sau-hoi-thao-bien-dong> (accessed 9 July 2014).

Thuy, T.T., "Recent Development in the South China Sea: From Declaration to Code on Conduct," paper presented at The 2nd International Workshop, titled "The South China Sea: Cooperation for Regional Security and Development," Ho Chi Minh City, 11–12 November 2010.

Thuy, T.T., Recent Developments in the South China Sea: From Declaration to Code of Conduct, In: Tran Truong Thuy (Ed), *The South China Sea: Towards a Region of Peace, Security and Cooperation*, Hanoi: The Gioi Publisher, 2011, 101–17.

Thuy, T.T., "Recent Developments in the South China Sea: Implications for Regional Security and Cooperation," paper presented at the Recent Developments in the South China Sea: Implications for Regional Security and Cooperation, CSIS, Washington, DC, 30 June 2011.

Thuy, T.T., "South China Sea and the Disputes," paper presented at the Presentation at CSIS, April 2010.

Tich, D.T., *Dau khi Viet Nam (Vietnam's Oil and Gas)*, Ho Chi Minh City: Dai hoc Quoc gia TP Ho Chi Minh, 2001.

Timberlake, I., "Vietnam Aims to Counter China with Sub Deal: Analysts," *AFP*, 17 December 2009.

Tinh, T.X., "Van tai bien Viet Nam doi mat voi nhieu thach thuc (Vietnam's Shipping in Difficulties)," *Vietnam News Agency*, 18 December 2013. Online. Available HTTP: <www.vietnamplus.vn/van-tai-bien-viet-nam-doi-mat-voi-nhieu-thach-thuc/235851.vnp> (accessed 19 January 2014).

"To chuc 'Tuan le bien va hai dao Viet Nam' (Organisation of Vietnam's Seas and Islands Week)," *Tap chi Cong san*, 26 May 2009.

Toan, D.V., "Trien vong Kinh te bien Viet Nam (Prospect for Vietnam's Marine-Based Economy)," *Nhan Dan*, 22 April 2013.

Tomoda, S., Detaching from Cambodia, In: James William Morley and Masashi Nishihara (Eds), *Vietnam Joins the World*, Armonk, NY: M.E. Sharpe, 1997, 134–53.

Tønnesson, S., History of the Dispute, In: Timo Kivimäki (Ed), *War or Peace in the South China Sea?*, Copenhagen: NIAS Press, 2002, 6–23.

Tønnesson, S., "Sino-Vietnamese Rapprochement and the South China Sea Irritant," *Security Dialogue* 34, no. 1, 2003, 55–70.
Tønnesson, S., "The South China Sea in the Age of European Decline," *Modern Asian Studies* 40, no. 1, 2006, 1–57.
Torode, G., "The Closer to China, the Cooler It becomes," *South China Morning Post*, 26 September 2009.
Torode, G., "Diplomatic Balancing Act for Oil Exploration," *South China Morning Post*, 23 August 2008.
Torode, G., "Dispute at Sea Rocks the Boat in Vietnam," *South China Morning Post*, 15 December 2007.
Torode, G., "How the US Ambushed China in Its Backyard and What Happens Next," *South China Morning Post*, 25 July 2010.
Torode, G., "Right and Wrong Far from Clear in Open Sea," *South China Morning Post*, 14 March 2009.
Torode, G., "Vietnam Revives Guerrilla Tactics," *South China Morning Post*, 14 October 2010.
Torode, G., "Vietnam Set to Buy 6 Russian Submarines," *South China Morning Post*, 28 April 2009.
Torode, G., and Chan, M., "China Refuses to Yield on Paracels," *South China Morning Post*, 12 December 2010.
Townsend-Gault, I., "Preventive Diplomacy and Pro-Activity in the South China Sea," *Contemporary Southeast Asia* 20, no. 2, 1998, 171–90.
Tra Mi, "Dai su VN tai My tra loi phong van ve van de Bien gioi Lanh hai voi Trung Quoc (Interview with US Ambassador on Maritime Boundaries with China)," *RFA – Dai A Chau Tu Do*, 25 September 2008. Online. Available HTTP: <www.rfa.org/vietnamese/SpecialTopic/ChinaVietnamBorder/interview-with-VN-amb-in-the-US-on-Sino-Vietnamese-borders-issues-TMi-09252008115350.html> (accessed 12 March 2013).
Tran, P., "Vietnam Has Much at Stake in S. China Sea," *Defense News*, 28 March 2015.
Trang, D., and Kien, L., "Thuong Tuong Nguyen Chi Vinh: Vn Khong Phai La Oc Dao," *Tuoi Tre*, 1 January 2014.
"Tranh chap Bien Dong ngay cang cang thang (Increasing Tensions over South China Sea Disputes)," *RFA Tieng Viet*, 16 May 2010.
"The Treasure Island of Southeast Asia," *South China Morning Post*, 28 May 2004.
Tri Nguyen, "Tau la tan cong ngu dan Viet Nam, 7 nguoi bi thuong (Vietnamese Fishermen Attacked by Unknown Boats, 7 Injured)," *Vnexpress*, 15 July 2009.
Tri, N.M., and Koh, S.L.C., "The 7th Fleet Was Ordered to Move Away from the Disputed Area," *Diplomat*, 23 January 2014. Online. Available HTTP: <http://thediplomat.com/2014/01/lessons-from-the-battle-of-the-paracel-islands/> (accessed 17 March 2015).
Trong Nghia, "Ke hoach Tan cong Viet Nam la mot qua bong tham do (Vietnam Offensive Plan: Testing the Waters)?," *RFI Tieng Viet*, 16 September 2008.
Trong Nghia, "Vietnam-Chu tich ASEAN 2010: Thach thuc lon nhat la ho so Bien Dong (South China Sea: Most Challenging Issue for Vietnam's ASEAN Chairmanship in 2010)," *RFI Tieng Viet*, 1 January 2010.
Truc, T.C., "Khong the banh truong 80% dien tich Bien Dong (No Country Allowed to Claim 80 Per Cent of South China Sea)," *Tuan Viet Nam*, 13 June 2009. Online. Available HTTP: <www.tuanvietnam.net/khong-the-banh-truong-80-phan-tram-dien-tich-bien-dong> (accessed 9 July 2014).
Truc, V.M., "Dan quan tu ve bien, nen hay khong (Maritime Militias, Yes or No)?," *Tuan Viet Nam*, 3 November 2009.

Trung, B., "Quan doi Viet – Trung tuyet doi khong dung vu luc," *Vietnamnet*, 17 September 2012.

Trung, N., "Doi cho ngu phu tro ve nha (Longing for Fishermen Sailing Home)," *BBC Tieng Viet*, 23 October 2007.

Trung, N., "Loi ke cua ngu dan bi tau Trung Quoc ban (Fisherman Telling Story of Being Shot by Chinese Vessels)," *BBC Tieng Viet*, 23 October 2007.

Trung, N., "Phai chan dung nguy co tai dien kich ban Thanh Do 1990 (Stop the Revisit of Cheng Du Scenario)," 11 August 2012. Online. Available HTTP: <www.viet-studies.info/NguyenTrung/NguyenTrung_ChanDungThanhDo.htm> (accessed 26 October 2012).

Trung, N. C., "Thuc chat tu Dai hoi Dang IX tro ve truoc (tu thap ky 90 TK 20) la van de gi (What Are Key Issues in the Period Leading to the 9th National Congress (in the 1990s)?," 4 August 2009. Online. Available HTTP: <www.danluan.org/tin-tuc/20090804/thuc-chat-tu-dai-hoi-dang-ix-tro-ve-truoc-tu-thap-ky-90-tk20-la-van-de-gi> (accessed 15 March 2015).

"Trung Quoc dua tau lon toi Hoang Sa (China Sending Big Ships to Paracels)," *BBC Tieng Viet*, 19 May 2009. Online. Available HTTP: <www.bbc.co.uk/vietnamese/vietnam/2009/05/090519_viet_china_sea_claim.shtml> (accessed 7 July 2014).

"Trung Quoc ep Cong ty Dau lua cua My (China Pressuring US Oil Company)," *BBC Tieng Viet*, 20 July 2008. Online. Available HTTP: <www.bbc.co.uk/vietnamese/vietnam/story/2008/07/080720_exxonmobil_warning.shtml> (accessed 13 August 2013).

"Tu lieu lien quan den ban Kien nghi 2009—Ba la thu cua Dai tuong Vo Nguyen Giap gui den cac nha lanh dao ve van de khai thac bauxite o Tay Nguyen (2009 Recommendation: General Vo Nguyen Giap's 3 Letters to Leaders on Bauxite Development in Central Highland)," *Bauxite Viet Nam*, 6 March 2013. Online. Available HTTP: <http://boxitvn.blogspot.com.au/2013/03/tu-lieu-lien-quan-en-ban-kien-nghi-2009_6.html> (accessed 06 June 2014).

Tuan, H. A., "Vietnam's Membership in ASEAN: Economic, Political and Security Implications," *Contemporary Southeast Asia* 16, no. 3, 1994, 259–73.

Tucker, S. C., *Vietnam*, London: UCL Press, 1999.

Tung, N. V., "Vietnam's Security Challenges: Hanoi's New Approach to National Security and Implications to Defense and Foreign Policies," In: Eiichi Katahara (Ed), *Asia Pacific Countries' Security Outlook and Its Implications for the Defense Sector*, Tokyo: NIDS Joint Research Series No.5, 2010, 107–12.

"Tuong Giap gui thu nua ve bauxite (General Giap Sending another Letter on Bauxite)," *BBC Tieng Viet*, 27 May 2009. Online. Available HTTP: <www.bbc.co.uk/vietnamese/vietnam/2009/05/090527_vonguyengiap_bauxite.shtml> (accessed 6 June 2014).

Tuong, T. Q., "Cho dieu kien chin muoi de giai quyet tranh chap Bien Dong (Waiting for Ripe Time to Resolve South China Sea Disputes)," 6 January 2010. Online. Available HTTP: <http://vnn.vietnamnet.vn/chinhtri/201001/Cho-dieu-kien-chin-muoi-giai-quyet-tranh-chap-bien-Dong-888092/> (accessed 11 June 2011).

"Tuyen bo danh thep cua lanh dao Viet nam ve bao ve chu quyen (Strong Statements by Vietnamese Leaders on Sovereignty)," *Giao duc Viet Nam*, 9 June 2011.

Tyler, M. C., "Vietnam's Hot Peace with China," *Australian Institute of International Affairs*, 2014. Online. Available HTTP: <www.internationalaffairs.org.au/australian_outlook/vietnams-hot-peace-with-china/>.

"Uncharted Territory," *Nature*, 20 October 2011.

"An Underwater Threat," *Newsweek*, 10 May 2008.

UNEP, VIEP, and WWF, "Fisheries Subsidies, Supply Chain and Certification in Vietnam: Summary Report," September 2009. Online. Available HTTP: <www.unep.ch/etb/areas/

fisheries country projects/vietnam/Final Summary Report Vietnam.pdf> (accessed 12 August 2013).
"U.S., China: Conflicting Interests in Southeast Asia," *Stratfor*, 12 August 2010.
"US Deputy Secretary of State John D. Negroponte's Press Conference," 12 September 2008. Online. Available HTTP: <http://merln.ndu.edu/archivepdf/EAP/State/109503.pdf> (accessed 20 June 2013).
US Embassy in Beijing, "PRC: Cow's Tongue Claim Not Licked, Despite Objections from the Philippines and Vietnam," *Cable (Released by WikiLeaks)*, 5 March 2009. Online. Available HTTP: <https://search.wikileaks.org/plusd/cables/08HANOI1094_a.html> (accessed 13 December 2015).
US Embassy in Hanoi, "2008 Recap of the Sino-Vietnam South China Sea Territorial Dispute," *Cable (Released by WikiLeaks)*, 20 January 2009. Online. Available HTTP: <www.wikileaks.org/plusd/cables/09HANOI52_a.html> (accessed 20 July 2014).
US Embassy in Hanoi, "ASEAN-China Negotiations on South China Sea 'Guidelines' Stalled by Dispute over ASEAN's Negotiating Status," *Cable (Released by WikiLeaks)*, 17 April 2009. Online. Available HTTP: <https://search.wikileaks.org/plusd/cables/09HANOI362_a.html> (accessed 17 July 2014).
US Embassy in Hanoi, "ASEAN Partnership, Human Rights Dialogue, Embassy Compound Discussed with Assistant Foreign Minister," *Cable (Released by WikiLeaks)*, 27 October 2005. Online. Available HTTP: <http://wikileaks.org/cable/2005/10/05HANOI2857.html> (accessed 11 August 2013).
US Embassy in Hanoi, "Assistant Secretary Hill Visit to Vietnam," *Cable (Released by WikiLeaks)*, 7 March 2008. Online. Available HTTP: <http://wikileaks.org/cable/2008/03/08HANOI277.html> (accessed 15 August).
US Embassy in Hanoi, "BP Transfers Operatorship of South China Sea Blocks to Petro-Vietnam; Exploration Work Resumes," *Cable (Released by WikiLeaks)*, 16 May 2008. Online. Available HTTP: <http://wikileaks.org/cable/2008/05/08HANOI579.html> (accessed 15 August).
US Embassy in Hanoi, "Chinese Missteps in Vietnam Are a U.S. Opportunity," *Cable (Released by WikiLeaks)*, 28 January 2005. Online. Available HTTP: <http://wikileaks.org/cable/2005/01/05HANOI247.html> (accessed 12 August 2013).
US Embassy in Hanoi, "Congressman Chabot Meets with Foreign Ministry, National Assembly Representatives," *Cable (Released by WikiLeaks)*, 13 December 2004. Online. Available HTTP: <http://wikileaks.org/cable/2004/12/04HANOI3301.html> (accessed 11 August 2013).
US Embassy in Hanoi, "Conoco Philippines and BP Concerns about Projects in the South China Sea," *Cable (Released by WikiLeaks)*, 15 June 2007. Online. Available HTTP: <http://wikileaks.org/cable/2007/06/07HANOI1119.html> (accessed 13 August 2013).
US Embassy in Hanoi, "Covering the Spratlys: Silence Is Officially Golden," *Cable (Released by WikiLeaks)*, 5 February 2008. Online. Available HTTP: <https://search.wikileaks.org/plusd/cables/08HANOI133_a.html> (accessed 20 July 2014).
US Embassy in Hanoi, "Despite Popular Resentment, Vietnam's China Policy Marked by Pragmatism, Cautions, and Modest Gain" *Cable (Released by WikiLeaks)*, 23 September 2008. Online. Available HTTP: <https://search.wikileaks.org/plusd/cables/08HANOI1094_a.html> (accessed 13 December 2015).
US Embassy in Hanoi, "Final Thoughts from Hanoi," *Cable (Released by WikiLeaks)*, 4 September 2004. Online. Available HTTP: <http://wikileaks.org/cable/2004/09/04HANOI2438.html> (accessed 12 August 2013).

US Embassy in Hanoi, "Following Up on DPM Khoan Visit with VFM Bang," *Cable (Released by WikiLeaks)*, 29 December 2003. Online. Available HTTP: <www.wikileaks.org/plusd/cables/03HANOI3351_a.html> (accessed 3 December 2013).

US Embassy in Hanoi, "Foreign Ministry Summons Ambassador to Discuss Sino-Vietnam South China Sea Dispute," *Cable (Released by WikiLeaks)*, 11 September 2007. Online. Available HTTP: <http://wikileaks.org/cable/2007/09/07HANOI1623.html> (accessed 14 August 2013).

US Embassy in Hanoi, "MFA Goals for 2004 and Beyond," *Cable (Released by WikiLeaks)*, 11 February 2004. Online. Available HTTP: <http://wikileaks.org/cable/2004/02/04HANOI377.html> (accessed 19 August 2013).

US Embassy in Hanoi, "Newly-Appointed DPM Hai Nixes Gannon Project," *Cable (Released by WikiLeaks)*, 20 September 2007. Online. Available HTTP: <http://wikileaks.org/cable/2007/09/07HANOI1681.html> (accessed 15 August 2013).

US Embassy in Hanoi, "NSC Senior Director Michael Green Discusses China, Country of Particular Concern Designation, APEC, Prime Minister's Visit with Deputy Prime Minister Vu Khoan," *Cable (Released by WikiLeaks)*, 7 February 2005. Online. Available HTTP: <https://wikileaks.org/cable/2005/02/05HANOI315.html> (accessed 11 August 2013).

US Embassy in Hanoi, "PRC PM Wen's Visit to Hanoi: Trade Takes the Front Seat," *Cable (Released by WikiLeaks)*, 21 October 2004. Online. Available HTTP: <http://wikileaks.org/cable/2004/10/04HANOI2857.html> (accessed 12 August 2013).

US Embassy in Hanoi, "Scene-Setter for the Prime Minister's Visit," *Cable (Released by WikiLeaks)*, 13 June 2005. Online. Available HTTP: <http://wikileaks.org/cable/2005/06/05HANOI1394.html> (accessed 13 August 2013).

US Embassy in Hanoi, "Sino-Vietnam Territorial Dispute Entangles Multiple Multinational Energy Firms," *Cable (Released by WikiLeaks)*, 7 September 2007. Online. Available HTTP: <http://wikileaks.org/cable/2007/09/07HANOI1599.html> (accessed 14 August 2013).

US Embassy in Hanoi, "Some in GVN Apparently Unworried about Situation in South China Sea," *Cable (Released by WikiLeaks)*, 22 April 2008. Online. Available HTTP: <https://search.wikileaks.org/plusd/cables/08HANOI464_a.html> (accessed 22 July 2014).

US Embassy in Hanoi, "Uneventful, Unpublicized, But Not Unnoticed: 30th Anniversary of 1979 China-Vietnam Border War," *Cable (Released by WikiLeaks)*, 18 February 2009. Online. Available HTTP: <www.wikileaks.org/plusd/cables/09HANOI134_a.html> (accessed 20 July 2014).

US Embassy in Hanoi, "Vietnam MFA Disputes Details of Article on Clash with China over Spratlys," *Cable (Released by WikiLeaks)*, 20 July. Online. Available HTTP: <http://wikileaks.org/cable/2007/07/07HANOI1283.html> (accessed 14 August 2013).

US Embassy in Hanoi, "Vietnam Unenthusiastic about East Asia Summit," *Cable (Released by WikiLeaks)*, 6 January 2005. Online. Available HTTP: <http://wikileaks.org/cable/2005/01/05HANOI42.html> (accessed 13 August).

US Embassy in Hanoi, "Vietnam's 2010 ASEAN Chairmanship," *Cable (Released by WikiLeaks)*, 11 December 2009. Online. Available HTTP: <https://wikileaks.org/cable/2009/12/09HANOI925.html> (accessed 3 August 2014).

US Energy Information Administration, "Vietnam," *Country Analysis Brief*, 9 May 2012. Online. Available HTTP: <www.eia.gov/countries/cab.cfm?fips=VM> (accessed 15 August 2013).

Ut, L. V., "Google Maps can go bo 'duong luoi bo' (Google Maps Removing Cow-Tongue Line)," *Thanh Nien*, 16 October 2011.

Ut, L. V., "Thuyet phuc Science dang thu phan doi duong luoi bo the nao (How to Persuade Google to Remove Cow-Tongue Line)?," *Tia Sang*, 4 January 2012.

Valencia, M. J., "Asia, the Law of the Sea, and IR," *International Affairs* 73, no. 2, 1997.

Valencia, M. J., "South China Sea Beijing's Buffer?," *Washington Times*, 24 August 2001.

Valencia, M. J., Van Dyke, J. M., and Ludwig, N. A., *Sharing the Resources of the South China Sea*, Boston and Cambridge, MA: M. Nijhoff, 1997.

Valencia, M. J., Van Dyke, J. M., and Ludwig, N. A., *Sharing the Resources of the South China Sea*, Honolulu: University of Hawai'i Press, 1999.

Van Dyke, J. M., and Valencia, M. J., "How Valid Are the South China Sea Claims under the Law of the Sea Convention," *Southeast Asian Affairs*, 2000.

Vaughn, B., and Morrison, W. M., "China-Southeast Asia Relations: Trends, Issues, and Implications for the United States," *CRS Report for Congress*, 2006. Online. Available HTTP: <www.fas.org/sgp/crs/row/RL32688.pdf>.

Viet, H., "Tu Hoang Sa nghi ve tuong lai Bien Dong (Paracels and the Future of South China Sea)," *BBC Tieng Viet*, 13 January 2014. Online. Available HTTP: <www.bbc.co.uk/vietnamese/forum/2014/01/140113_biendong_hoangsa> (accessed 23 March 2015).

"Viet Nam phan hoi canh bao cua Trung Quoc (Vietnam's Response to Chinese Warnings)," *BBC Tieng Viet*, 12 April 2007. Online. Available HTTP: <www.bbc.co.uk/vietnamese/vietnam/story/2007/04/070412_vncnoilupdates.shtml> (accessed 15 August 2013).

"Viet Nam thi diem lap dan quan bien (Vietnam Piloting Maritime Militias)," *BBC Tieng Viet*, 17 May 2012.

"Viet-Trung Lap Duong Day Nong Ve Hoat Dong Nghe Ca," *Tuoi Tre*, 24 June 2013.

"Viet Trung 'tang cuong tin cay chinh tri'," *BBC Tieng Viet*, 5 November 2015.

"Viet-Trung 'Vua Hop Tac, Vua Dau Tranh'," *BBC Tieng Viet*, 2014. Online. Available HTTP: <www.bbc.com/vietnamese/vietnam/2014/11/141119_thu_tuong_vietnam_quoc_hoi>.

"Vietnam Accuses China in Seas Dispute," *BBC*, 30 May 2011.

"Vietnam Assembly Chairman Speaks on South China Sea Disputes," *BBC Monitoring Asia Pacific*, 21 September 1999.

"Vietnam Attracts Record Amount of Foreign Direct Investment," *Voice of America*, 1 November 2009.

"Vietnam 'coi trong' thong tin lanh hai (Vietnam Attaching Importance to Publicity on Maritime Issues)," *BBC Tieng Viet*, 23 March 2009.

"Vietnam Comments on China-Philippines Spratly Islands Oil Survey," *BBC Monitoring Asia Pacific*, 10 September 2004.

Vietnam Communist Party, "Political Report of the 10th Central Committee at the 11th National Party Congress," 2011.

Vietnam Communist Party, "Resolution No.22/Nq-Tw on International Integration," 10 April 2013.

"Vietnam Demands China Stop Sovereignty Violation," *Thanh Nien*, 29 May 2011.

Vietnam Directorate of Fisheries, "Stages in the Development of Vietnam Fisheries Sector," 12 July 2012. Online. Available HTTP: <www.fistenet.gov.vn/introduction/about-directorate-of-fisheries/history-of-fisheries-development> (accessed 14 September 2013).

"Vietnam Finds Success in Program Aimed at Building Oil and Gas Capacity," *Oil and Gas Journal*, 28 November 1994.

"Vietnam Invites Bids for 9 Oil/Gas Blocks, Boosts Investment," *Reuters*, 2 August 2011. Online. Available HTTP: <http://uk.reuters.com/article/2011/08/02/vietnam-energy-licensing-idUKL3E7J20A720110802> (accessed 14 August 2013).

"Vietnam lai bay to quan ngai (Vietnam Voicing Concerns, again)," *BBC Tieng Viet*, 29 November 2008.

"Vietnam Oil Output Sets Quarterly Record," *Asian Wall Street Journal*, 7 April 1995.

"Vietnam Plans Refineries," *Globe and Mail*, 21 June 1994.

"Vietnam PM Warns of Olympics Torch Relay Disruptions," *Reuters*, 20 April 2008.

"Vietnam Reasserts Claim to Spratly and Paracel Islands," *Radio Australia*, 9 June 2011.

"Vietnam Reiterates '3 Nos' Defense Policy," *Vietnam News Agency*, 26 August 2010.

"Vietnam Revises '95 Trade Deficit to a Record Level of 2.2 Billion," *Asian Wall Street Journal*, 17 January 1996.

"Vietnam Says China Must Avoid Trade Weapon in Maritime Spat," *Bloomberg*, 3 December 2012.

"Vietnam Says It Will Keep Reducing Size of Its Military," *Reuters*, 8 September 1992.

"Vietnam Seeks Closer Economic Ties with China's Western Region," *Xinhua News*, 21 July 2004.

"Vietnam Slams Chinese Move in the Spratlys," *Reuters*, 10 February 1995.

"Vietnam Stands for a Peaceful Settlement of the Dispute with China over the Truong Sa and Hoang Sa Archipelagos," *Vietnam Courier*, 1988.

"Vietnam Stops Anti-China Protest, Detains Many," *Reuters*, 21 August 2011.

"Vietnam-China Joint Press Release," *Vietnam News Agency*, 26 June 2011.

"VIETNAM/CHINA: Relations Firm Amidst Problems," *Oxford Analytica Daily Brief Service*, 21 December 2005.

"Vietnam-China Tonkin Gulf Fishing Agreement Opens Way for Cooperation," *BBC Monitoring Asia Pacific*, 2001.

"Vietnam, China to Try to Hasten Talks on the Sea Dispute," *Thanh Nien*, 8 September 2011.

"Vietnamese Citizens Protest National Geographic Mapping Error," *Thanh Nien News*, 2 March 2010. Online. Available HTTP: <www.thanhniennews.com/politics/vietnamese-citizens-protest-national-geographic-mapping-error-17482.html> (accessed 31 July 2014).

"Vietnamese Navy Orders DH-6 Twin-Otter 400s," *Defence Industry Daily*, 8 September 2013. Online. Available HTTP: <www.defenseindustrydaily.com/vietnamese-navy-orders-dhc-6-twin-otter-400s-06373> (accessed 20 September 2013).

"Vietnamese Premier Calls for Regional Pact on South China Sea," *BBC Monitoring Asia Pacific*, 7 October 2003.

"Vietnamese Premier Calls for South China Sea Code of Conduct," *BBC Monitoring Asia Pacific*, 29 November 1999.

"Vietnamese Prime Minister Calls for Further Cooperation with China," *Vietnam News Agency*, 13 January 2005.

"Vietnamese Shipbuilding," *Global Security*, June 2009. Online. Available HTTP: <www.globalsecurity.org/military/world/vietnam/shipbuilding.htm> (accessed 19 January 2014).

"Vietnamese Spokesman Comments on US Diplomats' Visit, Tour to Spratlys," *Voice of Vietnam*, 8 April 2004.

"VN dam phan mua 4 tau chien cua Ha Lan (Vietnam Negotiating a Deal for 4 Dutch Warships)," *BBC Tieng Viet*, 18 October 2011. Online. Available HTTP: <www.bbc.co.uk/vietnamese/vietnam/2011/10/111018_sigma_corvettes.shtml> (accessed 20 September 2013).

"VN day manh tuyen truyen bien dao (Vietnam Increasing Publication about Sea and Island Issues)," *BBC Tieng Viet*, 11 November 2009.

Vo, T. L., *Les archipels de Hoang Sa et de Truong Sa selon les anciens ouverages vietnamiens d'histoire et de geographie*, Saigon: Ministere de la Culture, 1974.

Vuving, A. L., "Changing Synthesis of Strategies: Vietnam's China Policy since 1990," paper presented at the Regenerations: New Leaders, New Visions in Southeast Asia, New Haven, 11–12 November 2005.
Vuving, A. L., "Strategy and Evolution of Vietnam's China Policy: A Changing Mixture of Pathways," *Asian Survey* 46, no. 6, 2006, 805–24.
Vuving, A. L., Turning Points in China-Vietnam Relations, In: Tang Shipping, Li Mingjiang and Acharya Amitav (Eds), *Living with China: Regional States and China through Crises and Turning Points*, New York: Palgrave Macmillan, 2009, 229–46.
Vuving, A. L., "Vietnam: A Tale of Four Players," *Southeast Asian Affairs*, 2010, 367–91.
Wain, B., "ASEAN Caught in a Tight Spot," *Strait Times*, 16 September 2010.
Wain, B., "China Snubs the Law of the Sea," *Asian Wall Street Journal*, 1 November 1996.
Wain, B., "A Code of Conduct in the South China Sea?," *Asian Wall Street Journal*, 10 March 2000.
Wain, B., "Loggerheads with Beijing," *Asian Wall Street Journal*, 6 October 2000.
Wain, B., "Maritime Manoeuvres: Lawyer Say Vietnam has a Strong Case," *Asian Wall Street Journal*, 20 July 1994.
Wain, B., "More Claims," *Far Eastern Economic Review*, 15 April 2004.
Wain, B., "Sea Battle: Vietnam Fires New Weapon in Oil Dispute: The Law," *Asian Wall Street Journal*, 16 June 1995.
Wain, B., "Taking Charge," *Far Eastern Economic Review* 165, no. 45, 2002.
Walt, S. M., *The Origins of Alliances*, Ithaca: Cornell University Press, 1987.
Waltz, K. N., *Theory of International Politics*, Reading, MA: Addison-Wesley Pub. Co., 1979.
Watts, A., "Tensions Rise as Vietnam Accuses China of Sabotage," *Sydney Morning Herald*, 2 June 2011.
Wheeler, C., "A Maritime Logic to Vietnamese History? Littoral Society in Hoi An's Trading World C.1550–1830," paper presented at the Seascapes, Littoral Cultures and Trans-Oceanic Exchanges, Library of Congress, Washington, DC, 12–15 February 2003.
"White Paper on the Hoang Sa (Paracel) and Truong Sa (Spratly) Islands," Ministry of Foreign Affairs (Republic of Vietnam), Saigon, 1975.
Williams, M. C., *Vietnam at the Crossroads*, New York: Council on Foreign Relations Press, 1992.
Wines, M., "China States Naval Exercises," *New York Times*, 3 November 2010.
Womack, B., *China and Vietnam: The Politics of Asymmetry*, Cambridge and New York: Cambridge University Press, 2006.
Womack, B., "Managing an Asymmetric Relationship in an Era of Economic Uncertainty," *Asian Politics and Policy* 2, no. 4, 2010, 583–600.
Wong, E., "Chinese Military Seeks to Extend Its Naval Power," *New York Times*, 23 April 2010.
Wu, S., and Nong, H. (Eds), *Recent Developments in the South China Sea Dispute: The Prospect of a Joint Development Regime*, Oxon and New York: Routledge, 2014.
Wu, S., and Zou, K. (Eds), *Maritime Security in the South China Sea: Regional Implications and International Cooperation*, Farnham: Ashgate, 2009.
Wurfel, D., Between China and ASEAN, In: A. Thayer Carlyle and Amer Ramses (Eds), *Vietnamese Foreign Policy in Transition*, Singapore: Institute of Southeast Asian Studies, 1999, 148–69.
Xian, L., "China Angered over Exxon Mobil Oil Agreement," *China Daily*, 23 July 2008.
Xin, Z., "Reinforced Patrol Sails from Hainan," *China Daily*, 19 May 2009. Online. Available HTTP: <www.chinadaily.com.cn/china/2009–05/19/content_7790652.htm> (accessed 7 July 2014).

Xu, B., "South China Sea Tensions," *Council on Foreign Relations*, 14 May 2014. Online. Available HTTP: <www.cfr.org/china/south-china-sea-tensions/p29790> (accessed 29 June 2015).

Yoon, S., "Implications of Xi Jinping's 'True Maritime Power'," *Naval War College Review* 68, 2015, 40–63.

Yu, M., "Inside China: Pla Says War with U.S. Imminent," *Washington Times*, 27 June 2012.

Zagoria, D., Joining ASEAN, In: James William Morley and Masashi Nishihara (Eds), *Vietnam Joins the World*, Armonk, NY: M. E. Sharpe, 1997, 154–72.

Zarembo, I., "Russia Floats Out Second Gepard Class Frigate for Vietnam," *RIA Novosti*, 16 March 2010. Online. Available HTTP: <http://en.ria.ru/military_news/20100316/158215375.html> (accessed 20 September 2013).

Zha, D., and Valencia, M. J., "Mischief Reef: Geopolitics and Implications," *Journal of Contemporary Asia* 31, no. 1, 2001, 86–103.

Zhang, J., "China's Growing Assertiveness in the South China Sea: A Strategic Shift?," *ANU National Security College Occasional Paper – The South China Sea and Australia's Regional Security Environment*, no. 5, 2013.

Index

For Product Safety Concerns and Information please contact our EU representative GPSR@taylorandfrancis.com
Taylor & Francis Verlag GmbH, Kaufingerstraße 24, 80331 München, Germany

www.ingramcontent.com/pod-product-compliance
Ingram Content Group UK Ltd.
Pitfield, Milton Keynes, MK11 3LW, UK
UKHW020012200926
475702UK00014B/1853

9780367186180